INNOVATIVE BUDDHIST WOMEN

Swimming Against the Stream

The Curzon Critical Studies in Buddhism Series is a comprehensive study of the Buddhist tradition. The series explores this complex and extensive tradition from a variety of perspectives, using a range of different methodologies.

The Series is diverse in its focus, including historical studies, textual translations and commentaries, sociological investigations, bibliographic studies, and considerations of religious practice as an expression of Buddhism's integral religiosity. It also presents materials on modern intellectual historical studies, including the role of Buddhist thought and scholarship in a contemporary, critical context and in the light of current social issues. The series is expansive and imaginative in scope, spanning more than two and a half millennia of Buddhist history. It is receptive to all research works that inform and advance our knowledge and understanding of the Buddhist tradition. The series maintains the highest standards of scholarship and promotes the application of innovative methodologies and research methods.

THE REFLEXIVE NATURE OF AWARENESS
A Tibetan Madhyamaka Defence
Paul Williams

BUDDHISM AND HUMAN RIGHTS
Edited by Damien Keown, Charles Prebish, Wayne Husted

ALTRUISM AND REALITY
Studies in the Philosophy of the Bodhicaryāvatāra
Paul Williams

WOMEN IN THE FOOTSTEPS OF THE BUDDHA
Kathryn R. Blackstone

THE RESONANCE OF EMPTINESS
A Buddhist Inspiration for Contemporary Psychotherapy
Gay Watson

IMAGING WISDOM
Seeing and Knowing in the Art of Indian Buddhism
Jacob N. Kinnard

AMERICAN BUDDHISM
Methods and Findings in Recent Scholarship
Edited by Duncan Ryuken Williams and Christopher Queen

PAIN AND ITS ENDING
The Four Noble Truths in the Theravāda Buddhist Canon
Carol S. Anderson

THE SOUND OF LIBERATING TRUTH
Buddhist-Christian Dialogues in Honor of Frederick J. Streng
Edited by Sallie B. King and Paul O. Ingram

BUDDHIST THEOLOGY
Critical Reflections by Contemporary Buddhist Scholars
Edited by Roger R. Jackson and John J. Makransky

EMPTINESS APPRAISED
A Critical Study of Nāgārjuna's Philosophy
David F. Burton

THE GLORIOUS DEEDS OF PŪRṆA
A Translation and Study of the *Pūrṇāvadāna*
Joel Tatelman

CONTEMPORARY BUDDHIST ETHICS
Edited by Damien Keown

INNOVATIVE BUDDHIST WOMEN

Swimming Against the Stream

Edited by

Karma Lekshe Tsomo

CURZON

First Published in 2000
by Curzon Press
Richmond, Surrey
http://www.curzonpress.co.uk

Typeset in Sabon by LaserScript Ltd, Mitcham, Surrey
Printed and bound in Great Britain by
TJ International, Padstow, Cornwall

British Library Cataloguing in Publication Data
A catalogue record of this book is available from the British Library

Library of Congress Cataloguing in Publication Data
A catalogue record for this book has been requested

ISBN 0–7007–1219–4 (Hbk)
ISBN 0–7007–1253–4 (Pbk)

Contents

Contributors viii
Glossary xiii

Introduction xvii

PART I THE WORLD OF BUDDHIST WOMEN

BUDDHIST WOMEN OF SOUTH ASIA

Chapter 1 Inaccuracies in Buddhist Women's History 5
Bhikkhunī Kusuma

Chapter 2 At the Cutting Edge: Theravāda Nuns in the Kathmandu Valley 13
Sarah LeVine

Chapter 3 Unity and Diversity Among Buddhist Nuns in Sri Lanka 30
Nirmala S. Salgado

Chapter 4 Factions and Fortitude: Buddhist Women in Bangladesh 42
Karma Lekshe Tsomo

BUDDHIST WOMEN OF SOUTHEAST ASIA

Chapter 5 Thammacarini Witthaya: The First Buddhist School for Girls in Thailand 61
Monica Lindberg Falk

Chapter 6 The Status and Values of the Santi Asoke *Sikkhamat* 72
Marja-Leena Heikkilä-Horn

Chapter 7 Rediscovering Cambodian Buddhist Women of the Past 84
Hema Goonatilake

Chapter 8 The Revival of the *Don Chee* Movement in Cambodia 91
Heike Löschmann

Chapter 9 Khmer Women: Buddhist Survivors 96
Nancy J. Barnes

Chapter 10 Dam Luu: An Eminent Vietnamese Buddhist Nun 104
Thich Minh Duc

BUDDHIST WOMEN OF EAST ASIA

Chapter 11 A Case of Ritual Zen: In Gratitude to Ānanda 123
Paula K. R. Arai

Chapter 12 Tiexiangsi: A Gelugpa Nunnery in Contemporary China 130
Ester Bianchi

Chapter 13 Birth, Death, and Resurrection of Shim Ch'ông: Mistress of the Spiritual Domain 142
Chan E. Park

Chapter 14 Lineage or Family Tree? The Implications for Gender 154
Miriam Levering

Chapter 15 Ordination, Legitimacy, and Sisterhood: The International Full Ordination Ceremony in Bodhgaya 168
Yuchen Li

BUDDHIST WOMEN IN THE HIMALAYAS

Chapter 16 Of Birds and Wings: Tibetan Nuns and their Encounters with Knowledge 201
Yolanda van Ede

Chapter 17 Yeshe's Tibetan Pilgrimage and the Founding of a Himalayan Nunnery 212
Kim Gutschow

Chapter 18 Born Buddhist is Not Enough 229
Tashi Zangmo

BUDDHIST WOMEN IN HAWAI'I

Chapter 19 Mary Foster: The First Hawaiian Buddhist 235
Patricia Lee Masters and Karma Lekshe Tsomo

Chapter 20 Bishop Jikyu Rose: A Tendai Ajari in Hawai'i 249
Joseph M. Gardewin

PART II WOMEN IN COMPASSIONATE SOCIAL ACTION

Chapter 21 Buddhism and the Media 265
Elizabeth J. Harris

Chapter 22 Diversity as Practice: Thinking about Race and "American" Buddhism 277
Lori Pierce

Chapter 23 Sexual Conduct and Misconduct: Buddhist Ethics in the West 285
Gabriele Küstermann

Chapter 24 Daylighting the Feminine in American Buddhism 294
Mushim Ikeda-Nash

Chapter 25 Buddhism, Human Rights, Women's Rights, and Democracy 302
Kassie Neou

Chapter 26 Engaged Buddhism: "Moving" and Recreating Women's Stories 312
Trina Nahm-Mijo

Chapter 27 Inner Transformation for World Peace 319
Tenzin Palmo

Epilogue Transforming Women's Position in Buddhism: Strategies 326

Bibliography 329
Index 336

Contributors

Paula K. R. Arai is currently Assistant Professor of Religious Studies and East Asian Studies at Vanderbilt University. She received her Ph.D. from Harvard University and is the author of *Women Living Zen: Japanese Buddhist Nuns.*

Nancy J. Barnes studied Buddhism, Asian languages and history in the United States, Germany, and Canada, and received her Ph.D. from the University of Toronto. She has taught at Wesleyan University, Trinity College, and the University of Hartford, and has published several articles on Mahāyāna Buddhism in China and India, and on women in Buddhism. Her current research interests are in two areas: women and Buddhist communities in ancient India, and religion and social change in modern Southeast Asia.

Ester Bianchi is a doctoral candidate in Indian and Oriental Asian Civilization at Ca' Foscari University of Venice. Her research focuses on Sino-Tibetan Buddhism and Chinese nuns, particularly the transmission of Tibetan religious traditions in China. She is the author of *The Iron Statue Monastery, Tiexiangsi: A Buddhist Nunnery of the Tibetan Tradition in Contemporary China* (in Italian, to be published in English).

Thich Minh Duc is a Vietnamese Buddhist monk who has taught at Plum Village and many Vietnamese temples in the United States. He is in the doctoral program in Human Science at Saybrook Graduate School and Research Center in San Francisco. He teaches Ethnic Studies at San Jose Community College and is a social worker at Youth and Family Services, San Mateo, California.

Monica Lindberg Falk is completing her doctorate in Social Anthropology at Göteborg University, Sweden. Her research focuses on the interconnectedness of gender, religion, and social change in Thailand. She conducted research among Thai Buddhist nuns during 1997–98 and is currently writing a series of articles on her findings.

Joseph M. Gardewin spent 27 years in the United States Air Force, retiring with the rank of Colonel in 1994. His interest in Buddhism developed during six tours of duty in Asia. He holds a master's degree in Political Science from the University of the Philippines with an emphasis on East Asia. Currently he teaches Asian Studies at Sacred Hearts Academy in Honolulu.

Hema Goonatilake received her Ph.D. from the School of Oriental and African Studies, University of London, in 1974. She was a senior faculty member at the University of Kelaniya, Sri Lanka, until 1989. Since then, she has served as a consultant to UNDP and UNIFEM, New York, and as the gender in development expert at UNDP, Cambodia. She was a founding member of Voice of Women, the first feminist group in Sri Lanka, and co-founder of the Center for Women's Research, Sri Lanka. Currently she is an advisor to the Buddhist Institute, Cambodia.

Kim Gutschow received her Ph.D. in Social Anthropology from Harvard University. She has published numerous articles on Buddhist nuns, celibacy and sexuality, irrigation and settlement, and Tibetan medicine. She was the anthropologist for a film on Zangskari children, called "Behind the Ice Wall." She is currently revising her dissertation, "An Economy of Merit: Women and Buddhist Monasticism in Zangskar, Northwest India," for publication.

Elizabeth Harris is Inter-Faith Officer for the Methodist Church in Britain. She has been a Research Fellow at Westminster College, Oxford, and from 1986–1993 lived in Sri Lanka where she earned her doctorate through the Postgraduate Insitute of Pāli and Buddhist Studies, University of Kelaniya. She wrote and presented the BBC radio series, "The Way of the Buddha."

Mushim Ikeda-Nash was originally trained in the Korean Zen lineage in Michigan and Toronto in the early 1980s. She has traveled widely to Buddhist centers in the United States, Canada, Mexico, and Korea. She writes a quarterly column on family practice for *Turning Wheel*, the journal of the Buddhist Peace Fellowship. She lives in Oakland, California, with her husband and ten-year-old son.

Marja-Leena Heikkilä-Horn has studied the Asoke group since 1991 and received her Ph.D. in 1996 based on this research. She has taught Southeast Asian history at several Finnish universities and has published an introductory text on Southeast Asian history in Finnish. She teaches Thai history at Stamford International College in Hua Hin, Thailand.

Gabriele Küstermann was born in Guatemala of German parents. She earns her livelihood in the green coffee trade in her family firm. In 1985, she met her teacher Geshe Thubten Ngawang of the Tibetisches Zentrum, Hamburg, and has completed a seven-year Buddhist studies program there. She has been a supporter of Sakyadhita: International Association of Buddhist women since its inception and serves as a member of its Executive Committee.

Bhikkhunī Kusuma received her Ph.D. from Buddhist and Pali University, Sri Lanka, for her research on Bhikkhunī Vinaya. In addition to her university teaching career in Sri Lanka, she has pursued research on Bhikkhunī Vinaya and Buddhist nuns in Sri Lanka and abroad. She was a founding member of Sakyadhita: International Association of Buddhist Women and head nun at the historic ordination of Sri Lankan *bhikkunīs* in Sarnath, India, in 1996.

Miriam Levering teaches Chinese Religion and Buddhism at the University of Tennessee at Knoxville. She edited *Rethinking Scripture*, a book on Sung Ch'an sermon forms and Tahui Tsung-kao's sermons on death, and has written a number of articles on women in Ch'an from the T'ang and Sung dynasties. Her most recent book, *The Zen of Women*, discusses the teachings of Sung dynasty Ch'an masters and the point at which women become fully recognized members of the Ch'an/Zen lineages.

Sarah LeVine is Research Associate in Human Development and Psychology, Harvard Graduate School of Education. She has carried out research on the socialization and enculturation of young children and the psychological development of women in Nigeria, Kenya, Mexico, and Nepal. Her books include *Mothers and Wives: Gusii Women of East Africa* and *Dolor Y Alegrea: Women and Social Change in Urban Mexico*. She is co-author of *Child Care and Culture: Lessons from Africa*.

Yuchen Li is a doctoral candidate in the Department of Asian Studies at Cornell University and an affiliate at the Modern History Institute, Academia Sinica, Taiwan. Her research interests include contemporary Taiwanese Buddhist nuns, the cult of Avalokiteśvara among the Bai people of China, and the relationship between community identity and gender. She is author of *Tadai da Biquiuni* (*Bhikṣuṇīs of the Tang Dynasty*) and *Cooking and Religious Practice*.

Heike Loeschmann completed her Ph.D. at Humboldt University, Berlin, in History and Ideologies of Southeast Asia. She has worked as a research fellow and tutor at Humboldt University and the Universities of Hamburg and Passau since 1991 and served as Executive Director of the Society for the Study of Khmer Culture in Germany and France. In 1993, she joined the Heinrich Böll Foundation, Germany, and served as project director and advisor to the Buddhist Institute, Phnom Penh, Cambodia. She is currently Head of the the Heinrich Böll Foundation's Asia Section.

Patricia Masters received a B.A. in Oriental Languages from UCLA, an M.A. in Buddhist Studies from UC Berkeley, and a Ph.D. in Political Science from the University of Hawai'i. She has been a fellow at the East-West Center's Institute of Culture and Communication, and has taught at the University of Hawai'i in the departments of Political Science and Public Health. She received a Fulbright Grant for her research on the Sarvodaya movement in Sri Lanka. She has been on the faculty of Antioch University's Buddhist Studies Program in Bodhgaya, India, since 1996 and is currently director of Antioch's Buddhist Studies Program in Kyoto, Japan.

Trina Nahm-Mijo is Professor of Psychology, Dance, and Women's Studies at Hawai'i Community College, where she has been teaching since 1978. She received her Ph.D. in Counseling Psychology from the University of California, Berkeley. Her dissertation: "The Spiritual and Physical Movement in Humans: An Inquiry into Human Growth Potential" examined mind-body integration as practiced in Eastern philosophy and explored dance as a psycho-therapeutic tool. She is a community activist who has started many programs involving education, human services, culture, and the arts.

Kassie Neou was born in the ancient Cambodian capital of Oudong. Trained as a teacher, he became head of TV and radio production for the Department of Education. When the Khmer Rouge took over Cambodia in 1975, he was sent to the rice fields. Suspected of speaking English, he was arrested and tortured. He escaped execution only by telling Aesop's fables and classic Khmer stories to his teenage guards. When Vietnam invaded Cambodia, he became a refugee, eventually arriving in the United States, where he worked to promote human rights and peace in Cambodia. In 1992, he returned to Cambodia with the United Nations peacekeeping mission and founded the Cambodian Institute of Human Rights in 1993. In 1998, he served as chief of operations for the Cambodian National Election Committee.

Tenzin Palmo was born and raised in England. In 1964, at the age of 18, she went to India to find a qualified teacher of Buddhism. Soon thereafter she received ordination as a novice nun and spent 18 years practicing in the remote Himalayan region of Lahaul. In 1973, she traveled to Hong Kong to receive the *bhikṣuṇī* ordination. Currently she is working to establish a monastery for the training of *togdenmas* (female yogic practitioners) near the community of Tashi Jong in northern India. Her story has been documented in *A Cave in the Snow.*

Chan E. Park teaches Korean language and literature at Ohio State University. She received her Ph.D. in East Asian Languages and Literatures from the University of Hawai'i for her research on *p'ansori*, a traditional Korean storytelling art in stylized singing. Through her writings and performance of *p'ansori*, she is helping to rekindle intellectual and public interest in traditional oral literature.

Lori Pierce received a B.A. from Lake Forest College, an M.T.S. from Harvard Divinity School, and completed her dissertation in American Studies at the University of Hawai'i at Manoa on Euroamerican Buddhists in the Japanese American Buddhist Church in the early 20th century. Her research and writing focus on the intersection of race, religion, and ethnicity in the United States and Hawai'i. She has been appointed the Owen Dunston Visiting Professor of History at Wabash College in Crawfordsville, Indiana.

Nirmala Salgado received her B.A. (Hons.) from the School of Oriental and African Studies, University of London, and her Ph.D. from Northwestern University. Originally from Sri Lanka, she is a mother and a professor in the Religion Department at Augustana College in Illinois. She has published several articles on *dasasilmātās*.

Karma Lekshe Tsomo teaches at Chaminade University in Honolulu. She is secretary of Sakyadhita: International Association of Buddhist Women and director of Jamyang Choling Institute, an education project for women in the Indian Himalayas. She holds master's degrees in Asian Studies and Religion from the University of Hawai'i and is a doctoral candidate in Philosophy. Her books include *Sakyadhita: Daughters of the Buddha*, *Buddhism Through American Women's Eyes*, *Sisters in Solitude: Two Traditions of Monastic Ethics for Women*, *Buddhist Women Across Cultures: Realizations*, and *Living and Dying in Buddhist Cultures*.

Tashi Zangmo was born in Wamrong Nangshing village in eastern Bhutan. After completing high school in Thimphu and serving in the Royal Government of Bhutan for four years, she earned a B.A. in Buddhist Philosophy at the Central Institute of Higher Tibetan Studies in Sarnath, India, in 1995, and another B.A. in Developmental Studies at Mount Holyoke College in 1999. She is co-translator of Nagārjuna's *Dharmasangraha*.

Glossary

ācārya (Pāli: *ācariya*) spiritual teacher; instructor; preceptor
anāgāmī (Pāli: *anāgāmin*) a non-returner, i.e., one who will achieve liberation without taking another human rebirth
anagārikā "homeless one;" a renunciant status that does not entail monastic ordination
ānāpāna mindfulness of breathing
ani (Tibetan) nun; paternal aunt
arhat (Pāli: *arahant*) one who has achieved liberation from cyclic existence
bhante term of address for Theravāda monks
bhikṣu (Pāli: *bhikkhu*) a fully ordained Buddhist monk
bhikṣuṇī (Pāli: *bhikkhunī*) a fully ordained Buddhist nun
bodhicitta the altruistic attitude of wishing to achieve Buddhahood for the sake of all sentient beings
bodhisattva a being dedicated to achieving enlightenment for the sake of sentient beings
brahmacāra (Pāli: *brahmacariya*) "the holy life;" celibacy
Buddha an awakened, enlightened one
Buddhahood the state of perfect enlightenment
Buddha nature the seed or potential to achieve perfect enlightenment
Buddhadharma the teachings the Buddha
ḍākinī enlightened energy in female form
Dalai Lama the spiritual and political leader of the Tibetan people
dāna the practice of generosity, one of the six perfections (*pāramitā*); offering food and so on to monastics
dasasilmātā ten-precept nun of Sri Lanka
Dharamsala Tibetan settlement in northern India; residence of H.H. Dalai Lama and the Tibetan Government-in-Exile
Dharma the path to liberation taught by the Buddha

Dharmagupta a school of Vinaya practiced in China, Korea, and Vietnam; the only Vinaya school with an extant *bhikṣuṇī* lineage

don chee a nun keeping eight, nine, or ten precepts in Cambodia

dukkaṭa an offense; a category of lesser transgressions for *bhikṣus* and *bhikṣuṇīs*

dukkha unsatisfactoriness; suffering

emptiness the true nature of phenomena

gurudharma (Pāli: *garudhamma*) eight special rules enjoined upon *bhikṣuṇīs*

gurumā term of address for nuns in Nepal

Heart of Wisdom Sūtra a popular Mahāyāna text on the nature of emptiness

jhānas stages of meditative concentration

jinfanyu a woman living in a monastic community in Taiwan who intends to enter the order

Jizō (Japanese) Kṣitigarbha Bodhisattva

karma the law of cause and effect

kaṭhina robe offering ceremony

kesaloma reflection on the repulsive nature of the body

khenpo (Tibetan) abbot

kleśa (Pāli: *kilesa*) afflictions; defilements

Kṣitigarbha the Earth Store Bodhisattva; in Japan, a protector of women and children

Kuan Yin (Chinese) Avalokiteśvara, bodhisattva of compassion

lama guru; a teacher or spiritual master in Tibet

Madhyamaka a system of philosophical tenets emphasizing emptiness as the "middle way" between eternalism and nihilism

mae chi a female renunciant in Thailand holding eight, nine, or ten precepts

Mahāprajāpatī (Pāli: Mahāpajāpati) Buddha Śākyamuni's aunt and stepmother

Mahāyāna "great vehicle," practiced predominantly in China, Japan, Korea, Mongolia, Tibet, and Vietnam

mānatta a disciplinary rite conducted before both Saṅghas in case of a serious offense

maṇḍala the abode of a tantric meditational deity or its visual representation

mantra Sanskrit sound syllables incorporated in religious practice

micchela a nun in Bangladesh

nirvāna (Pāli: *nibbāna*) liberation from cyclic existence

paṭivedha realization; penetration of the Dharma

pavāraṇā an inquiry held both Saṅghas after the rainy season retreat

prajñā (Pāli: *pañña*) wisdom

prātimokṣa (Pāli: *pāṭimokkha*) the rules of monastic discipline *pravrajyā* (Pāli: *pabbajjā*) "going forth," leaving the household life and becoming a renunciant

precepts guidelines for training in wholesome conduct

punya (Pāli: *puñña*) merit

Rinpoche "precious one;" Tibetan term of address for recognized reincarnate and other respected *lamas*

saddharma (Pāli: *saddhamma*) true teachings

sakadāgāmi (Pāli: *sakadāgāmin*) a "once-returner;" one who will take only one more human rebirth

Śākyadhitā "Daughters of the Buddha," the International Association of Buddhist Women

Śākyamuni (Pāli: Sakkamuni) the historical Buddha

samādhi meditative stabilization

śamatha calm abiding; tranquil concentration

saṃsāra cyclic existence; the process of birth and rebirth

Saṅgha the virtuous assembly; ultimately, realized "noble" beings; conventionally, the monastic order; in Western usage, Buddhist practitioners in general

saṅghadāna offering food and gifts to the monastic community

sāsana the Buddha's teachings

sentient being a being with consciousness or awareness; the beings of the six realms of existence (god, demi-god, human, animal, hungry ghost, hell being)

sikkhamat highest stage for nuns in the Santi Asoke movement in Thailand

śikṣā (Pāli: *sikkhā*) study, training, discipline

śikṣamāṇā (Pāli: *sikkhamānā*) probationary nun; a two-year training period for nuns preceding *bhikṣuṇī* ordination

śīla (Pāli: *sīla*) ethics; moral behavior

śīla-upādhya precept instructor

sotāpatti (Pāli: *sotāpanna*) one who has entered the stream (of the noble eightfold path)

śrāmaṇera (Pāli: *samaṇera*) a novice monk

śrāmaṇerikā (Pāli: *samaṇerī*) a novice nun

stūpa (Pāli: *thūpa*) a reliquary structure

sūtra (Pāli: *sutta*) Buddhist scripture; a discourse attributed to the Buddha

tantra specialized meditation texts and practices; deity yoga, the method of practice in the Vajrayāna school

thera "elder;" a *bhikṣu* with ten or more years' seniority

Theravāda "school of the elders," practiced predominantly in Burma, Cambodia, Laos, Sri Lanka, and Thailand

therī "elder;" a *bhikṣuṇī* with ten or more years' seniority

tila shin an eight- or ten-precept nun of Burma (Myanmar)

tonsure a rite of shaving the head in preparation for receiving monastic ordination

tulku a recognized reincarnate *lama* in Tibet
seiza formal Japanese sitting posture
upāsaka Buddhist layman with five precepts
upasampadā ordination as a *bhikṣu* or *bhikṣuṇī*; the rite of conferring the full precepts
upāsikā Buddhist laywoman with five precepts
uposatha Buddhist rite observed on full moon and new moon days
Vajrayāna secret mantra vehicle; tantric Buddhism
vihāra monastic dwelling
Vinaya monastic discipline
vipassanā insight; a contemporary school of meditation practice
Zen meditation; a Japanese Buddhist school

Introduction

More than five centuries before Christ, Śākyamuni Buddha affirmed women's spiritual potential. He mapped out a path to enlightenment that is accessible to all, householders and renunciants, regardless of class, ethnicity, age, or gender. The Buddha's methods of mental cultivation were open to everyone and offered women alternatives to conventional domestic roles. Yet, facing a host of obstacles that keep them marginalized and subservient, women in Buddhist cultures cannot help but question the discrepancy between Buddhism's egalitarian ideal and the practical limitations of their everyday lives.

Now that gender equity has become part of a new global ethic, enshrined in the Universal Declaration of Human Rights, it is time to explore how this principle can be applied to the world's religions. Increasingly global women's issues put Buddhism under a sometimes uncomfortable spotlight. Many Buddhists invoke the rhetoric of human beings' equal potential for enlightenment and assume that traditional structures are adequate to support women's practice, but they are not. The rhetoric of equality often masks the truth of women's subordination and lack of opportunities for education, training, and ordination. Without adequate structures to support women's practice, the ideal of spiritual equality remains an empty claim. These incongruities are the background and the rationale for a continuing inquiry into Buddhist women's history.

Creative Encounters

In *Innovative Buddhist Women*, the critical need for equal opportunities for education, ordination, and leadership for women in Buddhist cultures emerges as a common theme. From a variety of perspectives and disciplines, the authors examine Buddhist women's history anew. They document the lives of women who have wrought changes in traditional Buddhist structures, suggest how the tradition can be re-envisioned along egalitarian lines, and explore new, decentralized, gender-inclusive models of spiritual community.

Innovative Buddhist Women represents another phase of the creative encounter of authentically rooted Buddhist and feminist thought – one further step in the process of unpacking the implications of feminist ideas for Buddhism and of Buddhist ideas for feminism. From a feminist perspective, the Buddhist traditions need to evolve in ways that incorporate women's voices and actively transform political, social, and economic structures oppressive to women and children. From a Buddhist perspective, feminists can profit from Buddhist thinking on identity, emotion, wisdom, compassion, and psychological transformation.

The gender imbalance in Buddhist societies, gendered interpretations of Buddhist tenets, and inequitable authority structures in traditional Buddhist institutions all demand our attention. To identify effective ways of transforming outmoded attitudes and structures, it is essential to understand the ways in which Buddhist women have already been working to bring about change. Through their struggles and innovations, the women included here have played creative roles in the gender transformation of Buddhism. By swimming against the current of their times and their traditions, they have exemplified new directions and possibilities for Buddhist women around the world.

Enlightening Transformation: A Feminist Analysis of Buddhism

Innovative Buddhist Women tells the stories of remarkable Buddhist women, spanning culture and time, who have moved outside the mainstream. Some are unsung heroines, quietly meditating in forest huts. Others are acclaimed scholars, activists, artists, and teachers. Reading their stories, we begin to appreciate the extraordinary diversity of Buddhist women, united by their shared experiences as women and as Buddhist practitioners, despite differences of ethnicity, education, economics, and culture. From this diversity emerges a collective history and many common concerns.

Most articles included here were first presented as papers at 1998 conferences on Buddhist women organized by Śākyadhitā: International Association of Buddhist Women in Phnom Penh, Cambodia, and Claremont, California.[1] At these gatherings, scholars, practitioners, and scholar-practitioners, both lay and ordained, from a wide range of cultures and traditions, have explored women's history and potentialities in Buddhism. Kindled by women's burgeoning interest in Buddhism internationally, these gatherings have stimulated research and dialogue among Buddhist women. As women share their joys and frustrations, their knowledge and insights, they link and inform feminist scholarship and Buddhist practice in new, creative ways.

In the past 20 years, more than three dozen books on Buddhist women have appeared to enhance our understanding of Buddhist women's experiences. Some discuss women in early Buddhist history,[2] some document the lives of women in particular Buddhist cultures,[3] some speak specifically of Western women's experiences and concerns,[4] while others take a cross-cultural approach.[5] Integrating feminist perspectives and women's personal narratives, they illuminate women's diverse experiences in the Buddhist traditions.

Innovative Buddhist Women continues this conversation, placing Buddhist women's narratives and Western perspectives side by side. The articles here document the lives and ideas of courageous women who have challenged women's traditional roles in Buddhist cultures without any link to the women's movement in the West, as well as those directly influenced by feminist insights and platforms for change. Together they describe an emerging Buddhist feminist identity that spans national, ethnic, and ideological differences. Buddhist women's collective experience has global implications for development strategies, reproductive health policies, environmental dilemmas, and changing social values and structures.

Buddhist Women: Past and Present

Innovative Buddhist Women articulates fresh perspectives on Buddhist women's experience. Essays by Asian, Asian-American, and Western scholars and Buddhist practitioners document the lives of women who, individually or collectively, have set changes in motion within Buddhist societies. Through the voices of women themselves, these essays analyze pivotal issues of gender, ethnicity, authority, and spirituality that affect the lives of women in traditional Buddhist cultures and, increasingly, the West.

Part I surveys The World of Buddhist Women. Beginning with Buddhist women of South Asia, it gives glimpses of women's experiences from the time of the Buddha until today in India, Nepal, Sri Lanka, and Bangladesh. "Inaccuracies in Buddhist Women's History" sets the stage by evaluating the early roots of the controversy over full ordination for women. Through an examination of Pāli textual sources, Bhikkhunī Kusuma, herself a trailblazer in Buddhist scholarship and gender equality in Sri Lanka, investigates Mahāpajāpatī's launching of the order of nuns (*bhikkhunīs*), the eight special rules (*garudhammas*) imposed upon her, the alleged challenge to her ordination by her 500 female companions, Mahāpajāpatī's efforts to annul the first rule requiring nuns' obeisance to monks, and the unfulfilled prophecy of the Dhamma's decline due to the admission of women to the Saṅgha (the monastic order).

"At the Cutting Edge: Theravāda Nuns in the Kathmandu Valley" explores the construction of religious identity among female monastics in the Newar Theravāda Buddhist community. Through the stories of women such as Bhikkhunī Dhammavati, who runs away from home at the age of 13 to become a nun and eventually becomes a leader of the Theravāda movement and the quiet crusade for women's full ordination in Nepal, Sarah LeVine asks what motivates women to become nuns, what training they receive after ordination, and what transformations in outlook and identity occur as they live lives of renunciation in the modern world.

In "Unity and Diversity Among Buddhist Nuns in Sri Lanka," Nirmala Salgado asks similar questions about Theravāda nuns in Sri Lanka and discovers both similarities and differences. She investigates the choices open to women who choose the renunciant life, including the ambiguous status of *dasasilmātās* ("ten-precept mothers") and the recent movement to establish an order of fully ordained nuns (*bhikkhunīs*) in Sri Lanka, entailing changes in status, lifestyle, and expectations for women.

The experiences of Buddhist women in many cultures are virtually unknown to outsiders. In "Factions and Fortitude: Buddhist Women in Bangladesh," I discuss the lives and experiences of Buddhist women living in this predominantly Muslim country. Their experience naturally raises questions about the formation of cultural identity within the various Buddhist communities, Buddhism's influence on women's values and notions of gender, and also the options that Buddhist women, as members of Buddhist minority groups, have for coping with cultural endangerment, poverty, personal risk, and rapid social change.

The next section of Part I looks at Buddhist women in Southeast Asia. Two articles describe innovative movements in Thailand – one that has managed to stay within mainstream Buddhism and one that is decidedly outside. Monica Lindberg Falk leads off with her anthropological study of Thammacarini "Dhammajarinee Witthaya: The First Buddhist School for Girls in Thailand." She discusses the patriarchal nature of Thai culture and the monks' status as supreme moral agents. She notes the discrepancy between the position of the monks and the *mae chi* (nuns) in a country equally famous for its temples and its sex industry. Among the increasing number of nunneries that function independently of monks' temples, she focuses on the innovative education and training programs of Dhammajarinee Witthaya, designed to create realistic alternatives for young women in Thailand.

In "The Status and Values of the Santi Asoke *Sikkhamat*," Marja-Leena Heikkilä-Horn uses a sociological approach to examine the lives and attitudes of the controversial nuns (*sikkhamats*) of Santi Asoke. Comparing Santi Asoke to mainstream Thai Buddhism, she highlights the moral values attached to merit-making activities in Thai society. She argues that Santi Asoke challenges the mainstream on gender by ordaining women as *sikkhamats* and according them a status in the religious hierarchy that is very different from ordinary Thai nuns (*mae chi*).

Three articles discuss Cambodian Buddhist women. Hema Goonatilake takes a historical approach in "Rediscovering Cambodian Buddhist Women of the Past," discussing the achievements of eight significant personalities – queens and commoners – and the innovations they introduced in education, social welfare, dance, literature, and religion. In documenting their achievements, she offers a reinterpretation of women's role and potential in the Theravādin tradition as practiced in Cambodia.

Heike Löschmann brings the discussion of Cambodian women up to the present in her essay, "The Revival of the *Don Chee* Movement in Cambodia." She discusses the history of women in religious life in Cambodia, the elimination of *don chees* during the Pol Pot regime, and the commitment women have demonstrated in organizing the historic peace walks in their country. She describes the re-establishment of the *don chee* tradition as a movement toward gender justice, linking it with issues of cultural heritage, ethics, and development.

"Khmer Women: Buddhist Survivors" presents the lives of Cambodian women from another perspective. Nancy J. Barnes shares the stories of three Khmer women and shows how Buddhist values informed their psychological survival of war and shattering loss, as well as their adjustment to resettlement in the United States. She documents how these women, grounded in the Buddhist values they learned as children, have emerged as leaders in an immigrant society beset by mental health problems, physical disabilities, and generational conflicts.

It is sometimes assumed that Buddhist monks are necessarily hostile to nuns, when in fact they may be nuns' strongest allies. Thich Minh Duc's eulogy, "Dam Luu: An Eminent Vietnamese Buddhist Nun," is a case in point. In this personal account, a Vietnamese monk documents the pioneering efforts of a refugee nun who arrived in the United States with $20 in her pocket and managed to establish a flourishing temple and Buddhist institute for nuns by collecting and recycling refuse in San Jose, California. The community's tributes to this exceptional nun and the relics found after her death are evidence that enlightened qualities are beyond gender.

The next section, Buddhist Women in East Asia, begins with Paula Arai's "A Case of Ritual Zen: In Gratitude to Ānanda." Contrary to popular perceptions of Zen practice as limited to contemplation, Sōtō Zen monasteries incorporate a large body of ceremonial rituals in their practice. In one such ritual, the *Anan Kōshiki*, Sōtō nuns commemorate the kindness of the Buddha's attendant Ānanda, an early monk ally who was the principal advocate for women's admission to the Saṅgha. Dr. Arai notes that nuns often use ritual functions to express their emotional and political concerns. In this case, the nuns who pay homage to Ānanda, champion of women's rights, happen to be the very ones who won equality for nuns in Sōtō sect regulations.

In "Tiexiangsi: A Gelugpa Nunnery in Contemporary China," Ester Bianchi introduces a community of nuns that is exceptional in another way: Although their nunnery is located in China, their practice comes from

Tibet. She examines the community's eclectic approach, which blends Chinese and Tibetan influences in its liturgy, study program, meditation practice, ordination rituals, and lifestyle, and explains the significance that this eclectic approach has for Buddhism in China.

Chan E. Park considers another eclectic approach in "Birth, Death, and Resurrection of Shim Ch'ông: Mistress of the Spiritual Domain." The story of Shim Ch'ông, a Buddhist woman immortalized in folklore and *p'ansori* oral narrative for her filial piety, illustrates the Koreans' eclectic religious sensibility as expressed in the arts. A feminist analysis of both the story and the *p'ansori* art form that conveys it enrich our understanding of gender, society, and the arts in Korea.

The next two articles broach the pivotal question of lineage, hierarchy, and authority in Buddhism. Miriam Levering's article, "Lineage or Family Tree? The Implications for Gender," looks historically at the concept of Dharma transmission, how this tradition has ignored the accomplishments of women, and how it can be reconfigured to include them. In fact, this reconfiguring of tradition is already underway, particularly among Chinese nuns. As Chinese nuns begin to actively restructure Buddhist institutions, other traditions are beginning to realize that it will be hard for Buddhism to maintain its credibility as a liberating tradition if it fails to accord equal status to its own female clergy. The issue of full ordination has therefore become pivotal in the reenvisioning and restructuring of Buddhist traditions.

Yuchen Li describes Buddhist women's struggle for full ordination in "Ordination, Legitimacy, and Sisterhood: The International Ordination Ceremony in Bodhgaya." From several original angles, she documents recent initiatives to restore *bhikṣuṇī* ordination for women within the Theravādin and Tibetan traditions. Her extensive study explains the background of the full ordination controversy and the implications of access to ordination for Buddhist women internationally. Taking the historic 1998 ordination ceremony in Bodhgaya as a focus, she discusses the crucial role Taiwanese nuns play in disseminating Buddhism, the importance of full ordination for gaining equal access and authority, and the political and gender issues underlying the global restructuring of Buddhist institutions.

The next section, Buddhist Women in the Himalayas, begins with Yolanda van Ede's sociopolitical study, "Of Birds and Wings: Tibetan Nuns and their Encounters with Knowledge," presents the history of a Tibetan Buddhist nunnery in the eastern Nepal Himalayas and its encounter with globalizing forces of the modern world, in the form of Western Buddhist visitors to the region. It discusses the differences among Buddhist monastic communities arising from history, politics, ethnicity, economics, geography, and gender, and examines the power and gender dynamics of the unequal relations between groups and individuals as Buddhist and Western cultures meet.

Kim Gutschow's "Yeshe's Tibetan Pilgrimage and the Founding of a Himalayan Nunnery" describes the historic pilgrimage of a nun from Zangskar, Ladakh, who traveled to Tibet in 1940 to receive novice ordination in Lhasa. It documents how the pilgrimage gave Chomo Yeshe and her companions a new vision of monastic life and how their ordination gave them the status to instantiate that vision. Their pioneering efforts resulted in a women's monastic community on the cliff above their home village, where nuns continue to practice their ritual devotions to this very day.

An important question that arises in this anthology is: Who speaks for Buddhist women? Although 99% of Buddhist women live in Asia, it is often Western scholars who convey their stories to us. The contributions of these scholars are invaluable, yet in fashioning a gender compass that is culturally appropriate, it makes sense that we also listen to the authentic voices of Asian Buddhist women themselves. "Born Buddhist is Not Enough" is Tashi Zangmo's firsthand account of growing up in Bhutan. She describes her upbringing in a Buddhist family, her struggle to receive a Buddhist education in India, and the religious and psychological impact of Buddhist values on women in traditional cultures.

Creating a separate section for Buddhist women in Hawai'i illustrates women's right and prerogative to create their own categories. As illustrated by the 1893 overthrow of the Hawaiian monarchy, the imprisonment of Queen Lili'uokalani, and illegal annexation of the Hawaiian Islands by the United States, social and political systems have not always had women's best interests in mind. "The First Hawaiian Buddhist: The Life of Mary Foster" tells the story of Mary Elizabeth Mikahala Robinson Foster, a part-Hawaiian woman of royal ancestry, and how she came to embrace Theosophy and eventually Buddhism. It documents her meeting with the Sri Lankan Buddhist reformer Anagārikā Dharmapāla and her generous financial support for Buddhist projects which aroused the ire of her family. It also speculates on some possible reasons for her conversion: resistance to Christian cultural domination, response to immigrant Asian religious systems, and resonance between Buddhism and elements of Hawaiian spirituality.

Joseph M. Gardewin then tells the story of "Bishop Jikyu Rose: A Tendai Ajari in Hawai'i" and how this contemporary trailblazer toiled to build Koganji, a Tendai temple in Honolulu. In narrative style, it relates how a Japanese woman immigrated to Hawai'i from Japan, became a successful businesswoman, counselor, and healer, and was then inspired by devotion to Jizō Bodhisattva to create an eclectic religious practice and healing center in Honolulu's Mānoa Valley. It describes the core spiritual beliefs and practices of the temple's members and the innovations that Jikyu Rose has introduced.

Women in Compassionate Social Action

Part II of *Innovative Buddhist Women* looks at innovative Buddhist women in a different frame. Who are the women practicing Buddhism today and how are they practicing it differently? Women in Compassionate Social Action shows how women are breaking the mold in applying Buddhist ideals to issues of race, communications, sexual ethics, human rights, violence, and peace. First, Elizabeth J. Harris takes up the issue of "Buddhism and the Media." Noting the distorted representations of Buddhism that often appear in print and film, she argues that Buddhist women have a responsibility to become shapers rather than victims of the media. Moving between Pāli texts and contemporary societies in Asia and the West, she encourages women to present an image of Buddhism that is challenging and accurate, rather than simplistic and sensational. She explores alternative images, such as compassion in action, to counteract current stereotypes that spotlight sex and greed.

Next, in "Diversity as Practice: Thinking about Race and 'American' Buddhism," Lori Pierce considers racism as a structural and ideological question, and discusses its significance in the development of American Buddhist communities. She notes how the seemingly natural split between "American Buddhism" and "ethnic Buddhism" reflects the powerful racial ideologies involved in organizing institutional religious practices. Speaking from her own experience, the author argues that Americans are generally misinformed about the nature of race and racism in the U.S., as reflected in the domination of Euroamerican concerns, values, and practices in American Buddhism.

Gabriele Küstermann confronts another flashpoint in Western Buddhist circles in her essay, "Sexual Conduct and Misconduct: Buddhist Ethics in the West." She begins by explaining traditional Buddhist ethical theory and its application in the Western context. Then she considers the power dynamics between Asian teachers and Western students, and the social, cultural, and political factors that may result in misunderstandings and exploitation. Presenting a number of hypothetical situations for discussion, she alerts practitioners to potential problems and suggests appropriate responses.

Mushim Ikeda-Nash takes up the issue of power dynamics between teachers and students from a different perspective in, "Daylighting the Feminine in American Buddhism." Speaking from her vantage point as Zen practitioner and mother, she examines the key role women play in the movement toward greater grassroots participation and the empowerment of women within established Buddhist authority structures. Touching on such issues as parenting, friendship, cultural congruence, and the integration of Buddhist practice and everyday life, she examines the notion of a "feminine legacy" and its potential usefulness for realizing transformative compassion in American Buddhism.

Taking the issue of power to the political level, Kassie Neou's "Buddhism as a Tool for Human Rights, Women's Rights, and Democracy" examines the relationship between Buddhism and human rights in the context of Cambodian culture and the recent savage destruction by the Khmer Rouge. The author discusses Buddhist canonical teachings on human rights and nonviolence, and relates them to modern human rights efforts and political theory. He explains the implications these teachings have for women and how they are being utilized at the Cambodian Institute of Human Rights as a resource for teaching nonviolence to children and adults.

Next, Trina Nahm-Mijo explores the expression of Buddhist perspectives and values through the arts. Her essay, "Engaged Buddhism: 'Moving' and Recreating Women's Stories," presents cultural performance, especially storytelling and movement, as a means of Buddhist social action. She discusses the contemporary "engaged Buddhist" movement and its relevance for a growing body of performing artists who integrate social activism in their creative work. Based on her own performance work on racism, sexual slavery, and oppression in Tibet, she discusses the creative expression of Buddhist values and practices such as ethics, meditation, and wisdom, as a vehicle for meaningful and compassionate social change.

Recognizing meditation as the central performative aspect of Buddhism, this anthology concludes with Tenzin Palmo's interpretation of applied Buddhist practice: "Inner Transformation for World Peace." Drawing on over 30 years of meditation experience, mostly in a Himalayan cave, she explores the traditional tools of Buddhist practice that are available for effecting personal evolution and social change, and how women can apply these practical tools to create a culture of nonviolence in contemporary society. As complex as the world has become, it is perhaps appropriate to end with meditation, Buddhism's simplest and most effective technology for transforming the world.

★ ★ ★

Although it is impossible to acknowledge all the kind friends and mentors who have contributed to this volume, I wish to express my sincere appreciation to the authors and the innovative women and nuns who were the subject of their research and reflections. The authors' open-heartedness and cooperation in the seemingly endless process of revision was exemplary. Since their work was brought to light largely through the Śākyadhitā conferences in Cambodia and Claremont, I am deeply grateful to all those who helped organize, support, and document those memorable gatherings, including Hema Goonatilake, Heike Löschmann, Chan Sobunvy, Ranjani de Silva, Gabriele Küstermann, Emily Mariko, Frances Kissling, Lourdes Arguelles, Norma Pratt, Margaret Dornish, Karen Torjesen, Janice Tolman, Jacqueline Chase, Jill Schubert, the Heinrich Böll Foundation, and many others, too numerous to mention. For their tremendous kindness and expertise in the painstaking process of editing transcripts from so many different countries, languages, and computer programs, I extend my heartfelt thanks to Ellie Waters, John Powers, Ramdas Lamb, Caroline Sinavaiana, Adrienne Cochran, Patricia Masters, Darcy Jones, Lori Chu, and especially acknowledge the late Donnë Florence.

The different spellings that appear for non-English terms reflect an editorial decision to respect authors' preferences. For example, authors' use of either the Pinyin or Wade-Giles systems for transliterating Chinese have been retained and, especially, their use of either Pāli or Sanskrit (e.g., *bhikkhunī* or *bhikṣuṇī*). This editorial decision is complicated by the fact that some authors use both Pāli and Sanskrit, reflecting a mixture of terms and traditions in some countries, such as Nepal. The glossary at the beginning of the book will hopefully make these differences in terminology easier to negotiate.

Nuns in the Buddhist countries are known by many different terms – *dasasilmātā*, *bhikṣuṇī*, *sikkhamat*, *mae chi*, *don chee*, *tila shin*, *ani*, *jomo*, and so on – but I designate all celibate female Buddhist practitioners as nuns, without quotation marks. The question of terminology for Buddhist women renunciants is one that deserves a fuller treatment, since these terms of address often reveal implicit structural inequities and discriminatory attitudes. Suffice it to say here that there is power in language. On an elemental level, therefore, I feel that it is inappropriate to fence the term "nun" – as if to say "so-called nun" – when referring to women renunciants who lack access to higher levels of ordination. The quotation marks would imply that the vocation of these dedicated practitioners is something other than genuine or legitimate.

Although a case can be made for restricting the word *nun* to fully ordained nuns (*bhikṣuṇīs*) only, I would argue that there is no justification for such a distinction. Translating the term *bhikṣuṇī* as "fully ordained nun" is enough to differentiate between novices and fully ordained nuns, when that distinction is necessary. If male novices are commonly referred to as monks and accorded the status of Saṅgha members, then why not nuns? If we fail to recognize the renunciant status of women who are denied Saṅgha status by virtue of their gender, we diminish those nuns who persevere in their celibate religious practice despite being denied access to full ordination. In recognition of their commitment and courageous dedication, I therefore accord women renunciants the respect they deserve as nuns, whether or not they are socially recognized as such by their respective traditions and societies. This does not resolve the issue of language, of course, and we are compromised by using unsatisfactory terms – such as *ani* ("auntie") for nuns in the Tibetan tradition, or *dasasilmātā* ("ten-precept mothers") in Sri Lanka – which may have familial or sexist connotations, until we are able to fashion a more appropriate, respectful vocabulary for women religious specialists.

Finally, although it has become standard practice to refer to people journalistically by their surnames, I have opted to use personal names instead, since surnames are often not women's own. I have also dropped most honorary titles, since it is rare that women are fairly represented in the institutions that confer these titles. These editorial decisions are part of the ongoing task of creating a nurturing environment for women's independent, creative, and liberative scholarship and spiritual evolution.

Notes

1 Śākyadhitā ("Daughters of the Buddha"): International Association of Buddhist Women has organized international conferences on Buddhist women at Bodhgaya in 1987, Bangkok in 1991, Colombo in 1993, Ladakh in 1995, and Phnom Penh in 1998. The sixth international conference was held in Lumbini, Nepal, in February 2000. In North America, Śākyadhitā organized gatherings at Santa Barbara in 1990 and Claremont Graduate University in 1998. Previous publications on these events include *Sakyadhita: Daughters of the Buddha* (Ithaca, N.Y.: Snow Lion Publications, 1988), *Buddhism Through American Women's Eyes* (Ithaca, N.Y.: Snow Lion Publications, 1995), and *Buddhist Women Across Cultures: Realizations* (Albany, N.Y.: State University of New York Press, 1999), edited by Karma Lekshe Tsomo.

2 Kathryn R. Blackstone, *Women in the Footsteps of the Buddha: Struggle for Liberation in the Therīgāthā* (Richmond Surrey: Curzon Press, 1998); Bimala Churn Law, *Women in Buddhist Literature* (Varanasi: Indological Book House, 1981); Susan Murcott, *The First Buddhist Women: Translations and Commentaries on the Therigatha* (Berkeley: Parallax Press, 1991); Pānadure Vijirā Sīlmāthā, *The Enlightened Nuns of the Buddha Era* (Colombo: National Book Development Council of Sri Lanka, 1994); and Meena Talim, *Woman in Early Buddhist Literature* (Bombay: University of Bombay, 1972.

3 Tsultrim Allione, *Women of Wisdom* (London: Routledge & Kegan Paul, 1984); Shundo Aoyama, *Zen Seeds: Reflections of a Female Priest* (Tokyo: Kosei Publishing Co., 1990); Paula Arai, *Women Living Zen: Japanese Soto Buddhist Nuns* (New York: Oxford University Press, 1999); Tessa Bartholomeusz, *Women Under the Bō Tree* (Cambridge: Cambridge University Press, 1994); Pao Chang, *Biographies of Buddhist Nuns*, trans. Jung-hsi Li (Osaka: Tohokan, Inc., 1981); Lama Chonam and Sangye Khandro, trans., *The Lives and Liberation of Princess Mandarava: The Indian Consort of Padmasambhava* (Boston: Wisdom Publications, 1998); Anna Grimshaw, *Servants of the Buddha: Winter in a Himalayan Convent* (Cleveland: Pilgrim Press, 1994); Hanna Havnevik, *Tibetan Buddhist Nuns* (Oslo: Norwegian University Press, 1990); Marja-Leena Heikkilä-Horn, *Buddhism with Open Eyes: Belief and Practice of Santi Asoke* (Bangkok: Fah Apai Co., 1997); Chatsumarn Kabilsingh, *Thai Women in Buddhism* (Berkeley: Parallax Press, 1991); Chan Khong, *Learning True Love: How I Learned and Practiced Social Change in Vietnam* (Berkeley: Parallax Press, 1993); Shigeo Kikuchi, *Memoirs of a Buddhist Woman Missionary in Hawaii* (Honolulu: Buddhist Study Center Press, 1991); Jamyang Sakya and Julie Emery, *Princess in the Land of Snows: The Life of Jamyang Sakya in Tibet* (Boston: Shambhala, 1988); Miranda Shaw, *Passionate Enlightenment: Women in Tantric Buddhism* (Princeton: Princeton University Press, 1994); Kathryn A. Tsai, *Lives of the Nuns: Biographies of Chinese Buddhist Nuns from the Fourth to Sixth Centuries* (Honolulu: University of Hawaii Press, 1994); Tarthang Tulku (ed. Jane Wilhelms), *Mother of Knowledge: The Enlightenment of Ye-shes mTsho-rgyal* (Berkeley: Dharma Publishing, 1983); Joanne C. Watkins, *Spirited Women: Gender, Religion, and Cultural Identity in the Nepal Himalaya* (New York: Columbia University Press, 1996); and Janice

D. Willis, *Feminine Ground: Essays on Women and Tibet* (Ithaca, N.Y.: Snow Lion Publications, 1989).

4 Lenore Friedman and Susan Moon, *Being Bodies: Buddhist Women on the Paradox of Embodiment* (Boston: Shambhala, 1997); Rita Gross, *Buddhism After Patriarchy: A Feminist History, Analysis, and Reconstruction of Buddhism* (Albany, N.Y.: State University of New York Press, 1993); Sandy Boucher, *Opening the Lotus: A Woman's Guide to Buddhism* (New York: Ballantine Books, 1997) and *Turning the Wheel: American Women Creating the New Buddhism* (Boston: Beacon Press, 1993); June Campbell, *Traveller in Space: In Search of Female Identity in Tibetan Buddhism* (New York: George Braziller, 1996); Marianne Dresser, *Buddhist Women on the Edge: Contemporary Perspectives from the Western Frontier* (Berkeley: North Atlantic Books, 1996); Vicki Mackenzie, *Cave in the Snow: A Western Woman's Quest for Enlightenment* (London and New York: Bloomsbury Publishers, 1998); Maura O'Halloran, *Pure Heart, Enlightened Mind: The Zen Journal and Letters of Maura "Soshin" O'Halloran* (Boston: Charles E. Tuttle, 1994); Nan Shin, *Diary of a Zen Nun: Every Day Living* (New York: E. P. Dutton, 1988); Ellen S. Sidor, *A Gathering of Spirit: Women Teaching in American Buddhism* (Cumberland, R.I.: Primary Point Press, 1987); Joan Tollifson, *Bare Bones Meditation: Waking Up from the Story of My Life* (New York: Bell Tower, 1996); and Karma Lekshe Tsomo, *Buddhism Through American Women's Eyes* (Ithaca, N.Y.: Snow Lion Publications, 1995).

5 Martine Batchelor, *Walking on Lotus Flowers: Buddhist Women Living, Loving and Meditating* (London: Thorsons, 1996); José Ignacio Cabezón, *Buddhism, Sexuality, and Gender* (Albany, N.Y.: State University of New York Press, 1992); Thubten Chodron, *Blossoms of the Dharma: Living as a Buddhist Nun* (Berkeley: North Atlantic Books, 1999); Karma Lekshe Tsomo, *Buddhist Women Across Cultures: Realizations* (Albany, N.Y.: State University of New York Press, 1999), *Sakyadhita: Daughters of the Buddha* (Ithaca, N.Y.: Snow Lion Publications, 1988), and *Sisters in Solitude: Two Traditions of Buddhist Monastic Ethics for Women* (Albany, N.Y.: State University of New York Press, 1996); and Zen Lotus Society, *Women and Buddhism* (Toronto, 1986).

PART I

The World of Buddhist Women

BUDDHIST WOMEN OF SOUTH ASIA

CHAPTER ONE

Inaccuracies in Buddhist Women's History

Bhikkhunī Kusuma

The Buddha instituted a fourfold society consisting of *bhikkhus* (monks), *bhikkhunīs* (nuns), laymen, and laywomen. We can glean information about the very inception of the *bhikkhunī* lineage from authentic sources such as the Vinaya Piṭaka.[1] According to these texts and their commentaries, members of the Saṅgha were considered worthy of great admiration and respect, and spiritual progress was regarded as possible primarily for those "unburdened by the shackles of household life." The goal of *brahmacariya* ("the holy life," that is, celibacy) was upheld as good, divine, and holy. Today, as more and more educated women awaken to the responsibility of searching for solutions to social ills, choosing a life of renunciation may be even more worthy of respect than it was in the days of the Buddha.

In the Pāli canon, the Buddha laid down 311 rules of discipline for *bhikkhunīs*. These are the Pāṭimokkha rules which help ordained practitioners achieve mental tranquility, wisdom, and the goal of attaining *nibbāna* (liberation) in this very life. It is ironic that, although the Pāṭimokkha rules are carefully preserved in the Theravādin tradition, there are no *bhikkhunīs* in the Theravādin countries (Burma, Cambodia, Laos, Thailand, and Sri Lanka) to practice them. The *bhikkhunī* order was lost nearly 1,000 years ago in these countries and no attempt has been made even to study these rules for centuries.

Because of current efforts to revive the Buddhist order of nuns, the study of the lives and precepts of *bhikkhunīs* has become more important than ever before. On December 8, 1996, ten Sri Lankan women became ordained as *bhikkhunīs* in Sārnāth, India. This is the sacred site near Vārāṇasi, known as Isipatane in ancient times, where the Buddha delivered his first sermon. I was one of the ten *bhikkhunīs* ordained on that occasion. Along with others in the group, I am now studying and practicing the Vinaya rules, and continuing to study Pāli and the *suttas* intensively. In this article I discuss some obvious inaccuracies about *bhikkhunīs* recorded in the Buddhist canon, particularly in the text known as *Cullavagga*.

Cullavagga and the Samantapāsādikā Commentary

Both the *Cullavagga* and *Samantapāsādikā* texts refer to the ordination procedure of the first *bhikkhunī*, Mahāpajāpatī Gotamī, who was the aunt and stepmother of Buddha Sakkamuni (Sanskrit: Śākyamuni). The acceptance of eight special rules (*garudhammas*) constituted her ordination as a nun. In the Pāli, the eight *garudhammas* appear in the tenth *khandhaka* of the *Cullavagga*:

1 A *bhikkhunī* of even a 100 years standing should rise, greet respectfully, and bow down before a *bhikkhu* ordained even that day;
2 A *bhikkhunī* should not spend the rainy season retreat (*vassa*) in a place where there is no *bhikkhu*;
3 Every half month a *bhikkhunī* should ask the Bhikkhu Saṅgha to give the time for observing the *uposatha* and to send a *bhikkhu* to give an exhortation;
4 After the rainy season retreat, a *bhikkhunī* should conduct a *pavāraṇā* before both the Bhikkhu and Bhikkhunī Saṅghas with regard to three matters: what has been seen, what has been heard, and what has been suspected;
5 A *bhikkhunī* who has committed a serious offense should observe the *mānatta* discipline before both [Bhikkhu and Bhikkhunī] Saṅghas;
6 After a prospective *bhikkhunī* has been trained for two years in the six [*sikkhamānā*] rules, she should seek the *upasampadā* from both Saṅghas;
7 On no account is a *bhikhunī* to revile or abuse a *bhikkhu*;
8 *Bhikkhunīs* are forbidden to officially admonish *bhikkhus*, but the official admonishment of *bhikkhunīs* by *bhikkhus* is not forbidden.[2]

The Buddha is said to have proclaimed: "If you, Gotamī, undertake the acceptance of these eight *garudhammas*, that in itself will be your ordination." Mahāpajāpatī is said to have then accepted the *garudhammas* with great respect: "Just as a young woman fond of adornment of the body, having bathed, decks her head with lotus (*uppula*) flowers and jasmine (*vassika*) flowers, so do I accept the eight *garudhammas* as the condition for my ordination."[3]

Immediately after her ordination, after having spoken these words and having accepted the *garudhammas*, she questioned the Buddha about how the other Sakyan women should be ordained. The Buddha replied: "O monks, I allow *bhikkhunīs* to receive the *upasampadā* from *bhikkhus*." And so the monks ordained them. This makes it clear that it was only Mahāpajāpatī who accepted the *garudhammas* as the condition for her ordination, and not the other Sakyan women.

The *Cullavagga* records an interesting incident that occurred immediately after the ordination of the 500 Sakyan women by *bhikkhus*. These newly ordained nuns went before Mahāpajāpatī and said: "Lady, you are unordained. We have been ordained in accordance with the Buddha's instructions." This statement makes it clear that it was monks who ordained the Sakyan women, without the participation of nuns, and also that Mahāpajāpatī had not received ordination from monks. Obviously, Mahāpajāpatī and the 500 women were ordained in very different procedures. So Mahāpajāpatī became perplexed.

The question that arises here is why Mahāpajāpatī did not claim that she had already been ordained by accepting the *garudhammas*. She went before the venerable Ānanda once again and repeated to him the newly ordained nuns' claim that she was unordained. Ānanda then went to the Buddha and repeated the words to him. Thereupon, for the second time, the Buddha proclaimed: "Gotamī received the *upasampadā* when she accepted the *garudhammas*."

Many questions can be raised at this stage. First, why did the Sakyan women not know about Mahāpajāpatī's *garudhamma* ordination? Second, why did the women say: "Lady, you are unordained?" Third, why was Mahāpajāpatī in doubt about her *garudhamma* ordination? Fourth, why did only Mahāpajāpatī and not the others have to accept the *garudhammas*? Fifth, why did the Buddha proclaim the *garudhammas* to a laywoman? (Mahāpajāpati was not ordained at the time that he set forth these rules; this was before her ordination.) These and many other questions naturally arise in connection with this account of how the *garudhammas* were pronounced and Mahāpajāpatī's acceptance of them.

Obeisance to Elders of the Order

Another incident that occurred about the same time also raises questions. Immediately after her ordination, Mahāpajāpatī approached the Buddha through the venerable Ānanda and said: "I request one privilege from the Buddha. Is it possible to show respect for *bhikkhus* and *bhikkhunīs* by rising, greeting respectfully, and bowing down before them, according to seniority?" Because the first *garudhamma* reads, "A *bhikkhunī* of even a hundred years standing should rise, greet respectfully, and bow down before a *bhikkhu* ordained even that day," one naturally wonders why she asked such a question. If Mahāpajāpatī had already agreed to abide by this rule requiring nuns to pay obeisance to monks regardless of status, it does not make sense for her to ask the question, "Is it possible to respect *bhikkhus* and *bhikkhunīs* according to seniority?"

Ānanda is said to have taken her question to the Buddha, who replied, "This is not possible. This is not allowable. If even heterodox teachers do not allow such behavior toward women, how can I allow it?" Given the social climate of the day, the Buddha's response is understandable, yet the fact remains: only if Mahāpajāpatī were not obligated to observe the first *garudhamma* would it be reasonable for her to ask such a question.

A person reading the *Cullavagga* becomes confused when reading these statements, for according to the account, Mahāpajāpatī had already pledged to observe the first *garudhamma*. Why, then, would she ask whether it would be possible to show respect for *bhikkhus* and *bhikkhunīs* according to seniority?

The Buddha's response to her request as recorded in the *Cullavagga* only makes the issue more confusing. The Buddha purportedly says: "It is not proper for a *bhikkhu* to show respect to a laywoman by rising, greeting respectfully, and bowing down before her, and a *bhikkhu* who does so commits a *dukkaṭa* offense." According to this answer, it is an offense for a *bhikkhu* to show respect to a laywoman, but there is no mention of *bhikkhunīs*. It is clear that monks are not allowed to bow to laywomen, but whether or not a *bhikkhu* is allowed to pay respect to a *bhikkhunī* is not indicated. The reader cannot help but be perplexed. A careful reading of the text reveals that Mahāpajāpatī's question – whether it is possible for *bhikkhus* and *bhikkhunīs* to show respect according to seniority – remains unanswered. Yet it is not likely that the Buddha would evade such an important question.

Garudhamma and Vinaya Sikkhā[4]

The nature of the *garudhammas* and their status in relation to the Vinaya rules is also perplexing. There are a number of distinctions that set these two categories of rules apart. First, Vinaya rules are pronounced on *bhikkhus* and *bhikkhunīs*, but the *garudhammas* were pronounced on Mahāpajāpatī while she was still a laywoman, before her ordination. Second, the method of establishing Vinaya rules is also quite different from that of the *garudhammas*. For laying down a Vinaya rule, a member of the order must first commit an offense. The offense is then reported to the Buddha. The Buddha summons the congregation. The accused is brought before the assembly and is questioned about his or her misconduct. The accused pleads guilty. The Buddha then confirms that such behavior is improper for a monk or nun, explains what behavior is proper in such a circumstance, and admonishes those assembled to observe it. To avoid such misconduct in the future, a rule of discipline is laid down. The first offender is excused, or exonerated. If the rule later proves to be too severe or unworkable, the case is again brought before the Buddha and another rule is laid down to mitigate it. Some punishment or penalty is indicated. Conditions under which the rule does not apply are specified; for example, in the case of sickness, the first instance of the offense, insanity, and so on. The disciplinary rules of the monastic order were established in accordance with this procedure.

The *garudhammas* do not conform to any of these conditions. First, these rules were pronounced in reference to a person (Mahāpajāpatī) who was innocent of any misdeed. Since no offense was committed, no offense was reported. Second, the Buddha did not summon the congregation to lay down the *garudhammas*. Third, no punishment or penalty was instituted for breaking the *garudhammas*. Fourth, the *garudhammas* appear to apply to all *bhikkhunīs*, but in actuality there is no indication that they did. In fact, we find that many rules similar to the *garudhammas* were laid down later in accordance with the above procedure for establishing Vinaya rules. This leads one to question why Vinaya rules exactly like the *garudhammas* were introduced again at a later time. Either the *garudhammas* were not being strictly observed or the *garudhammas* were never intended to apply to all *bhikkhunīs*. Further evidence of the latter alternative is that these *garudhammas* are not found among the 311 rules of discipline included in the Bhikkhunī Pāṭimokkha and hence do not come up at the bimonthly recitation of the Pāṭimokkha.

In Sri Lanka, the *garudhammas* were not adhered to even in the third century B.C.E. Venerable Mahinda, the son of Emperor Aśoka of India, who brought Buddhism to Sri Lanka in the third century B.C.E., did not adhere to the *garudhammas* when he helped institute the Bhikkhunī Saṅgha there. The *Mahāvaṃsa*, an ancient Sri Lankan chronicle, describes how the first *bhikkhunī* Anulā and 1,000 other women were ordained.[5] In this account, it is clear that these women did not observe the two-year probationary period as *sikkhamānā*, which is one of the eight conditions stipulated in the *garudhammas*. All these women received ordination as *bhikkhunīs* upon the arrival of Saṅghamittā, Mahinda's sister. Because Saṅghamittā arrived six months after Anula's request for ordination, we know that their *bhikkhunī* ordination was not conducted after a two-year *sikkhamānā* training period, but just six months, at most, after their initial request. This is clear evidence that the *garudhammas* are not a Vinaya requirement, either as precept or as practice.

The Decline of the Sāsana

We find inaccuracies regarding women reported not only in the Vinaya texts, but also in the commentaries. The *Cullavagga* describes how the lifespan of the Buddha's dispensation would be reduced from 1,000 to 500 years due to the ordination of women. It records the following statement of the Buddha: "Ānanda, if only women did not leave the household and become ordained in the Tathāgata's *sāsana* (teachings), this pure, chaste, holy life of the dispensation would have lasted longer. However, Ānanda, now that women have left the household and been ordained, the lifespan of the *sāsana* will be reduced from 1,000 years to 500 years."

When we examine the commentary to the *Cullavagga*, however, we find a discrepancy. The commentator, Buddhaghosa, leads us to a new scenario: "Like a great reservoir when bounded by a dam would retain water, in the same way these *garudhammas* have been promulgated by the Buddha . . . so that through the going forth of women there will not be a decline to the dispensation. If the *garudhammas* had not been promulgated, the *saddharma* (true teachings) would have lasted only 500 years. Now, through the promulgation of the *garudhammas*, the *saddharma* will last another 500 years. Thus it will last 1,000 years." The commentary to the *Cullavagga* thus specifically contradicts the root text. While the *Cullavagga* reduces the lifespan from 1,000 years to 500, the commentary increases the lifespan from 500 years to 1,000. The reader becomes perplexed, wondering whether to believe the text or the commentary – or neither. Today the Buddha's teachings have been in existence for well over 2,500 years, which would seem to belie both predictions.

Buddhaghosa clearly does not agree with the view set forth in the *Cullavagga* and it is not difficult to understand why. Buddhaghosa wrote the commentary to the *Cullavagga* in the fourth century C.E., approximately ten centuries after the Buddha's passing. With his own eyes, he saw the *bhikkhunī* order that was then flourishing in Sri Lanka, long after the demise of the order predicted in the *Cullavagga*. Observing that the order had survived not only 500, but even 1,000, years after the Buddha's purported prediction, he was forced to revise the *Cullavagga*'s view in light of actual events.

I often ask scholars and monks what is meant by the statement that the dispensation would last only 500 years instead of 1,000. The typical response is: because the *arahant* (liberated) disciples lasted only 500 years. That leaves me with another quandary.

In his commentary, Buddhaghosa eventually increases the life of the *sāsana* to 5,000 years. During the first 1,000 years, he says, there will be *arahants* with the four analytical knowledges. The next 1,000 years there will be "bare insight" *arahants*. The next 1,000 years there will be *anāgāmin* (non-returners). The next 1,000 years there will be *sakadāgāmin* (once returners) and the next 1,000 years there will be *sotāpanna* (stream enterers). Adding these figures together, we find that the *paṭivedha* (realization or penetration of the Dhamma) will last for 5,000 years.

One begins to wonder whether the original statement that the *sāsana* would last only 500 years due to the ordination of women is really that of the All-Knowing Buddha. If it were, why did Buddhaghosa contradict the words of the Buddha? In many other instances the Buddha specifically mentioned that the causes for the decline of the dispensation are, for example, not keeping the Vinaya precepts, not practicing meditation, not attaining the *jhānas* (stages of meditation), not striving for sainthood, not practicing the seven factors of enlightenment, and so on. Nowhere except in the *Cullavagga* is there any indication that the decline of the Buddha's teachings would occur as a result of the institution of the *bhikkhunī* order. In my opinion, it is highly improbable that the Buddha would have instituted the *bhikkhunī* order had it meant the decline of the Dhamma.

Buddha's Initial Reluctance

When the Buddha first visited Kapilavastu, Mahāpajāpatī Gotamī became a *sotāpanna* after listening to the Mahādhammapāla Jātaka. Then she went before the Buddha and requested ordination: "Lord, it were well that women should obtain the going forth from home to homelessness in the Dhamma and discipline proclaimed by the Tathāgata." The Buddha is said to have answered: "Be careful, Gotamī, of women going forth from home to homelessness." The *Cullavagga* records that three times the Buddha refused her request to admit women to the order. It is significant that, in spite of this refusal, Mahāpajāpatī and her retinue donned the yellow robe and walked from Kapilavastu to Vaiśālī and requested ordination. Ānanda, seeing them, entreated the Buddha to permit the ordination, whereupon the Buddha acquiesced.

I think it is pertinent to point out here that these Sakyan women took a bold step in making this historic march in spite of the Buddha's reluctance. By their very honesty of purpose, they convinced the Buddha, as well as the tradition-bound Indian society of the fifth century B.C.E., that monastic freedom was as essential for women as for men. The Buddha, therefore, granted their request.

This incident is an eye-opener for us today. It proves beyond any doubt that if our intentions are pure, no amount of obstacles can hinder us. In all humility, I myself am a witness to this fact, for I am a Sri Lankan who dared to become a *bhikkhunī*.

But our battle is yet to be won. The newly ordained Theravādin *bhikkhunīs* are young in ordination and need advice, encouragement, and community support in all the tasks that lie ahead. We need to grow in numbers and to grow in the Dhamma and the discipline. To achieve our purpose, we need a united Bhikkhunī Saṅgha at the international level. In the Theravādin countries, we need to demonstrate that ours is a battle won after ten centuries. An important aspect of this process is revealing the many inaccuracies in Buddhist women's history, especially the history of Buddhist nuns.

Notes

1 The *Vinaya Piṭaka*, which describes the discipline required for *bhikkhus* and *bhikkhunīs*, has been carefully edited by Hermann Oldenberg (London: Pali Text Society, 1879–83, rpnt. London: Luzac & Co., 1964). It has been translated into English by I. B. Horner, *The Book of the Discipline*, Part I–IV (London: Routledge & Kegan Paul, Ltd., 1982); and by T. W. Rhys Davids and Hermann Oldenberg, *Vinaya Texts*, Part I–III (Delhi: Motilal Banarsidass, 1974).

2 A variant translation appears in Rhys Davids and Oldenberg, *Vinaya Texts*, Part III, p. 325.

3 Regarding the authenticity of these rules, Akira Hirakawa says, "According to the *Bhikkhunīkkhandaka* [sic], when the Buddha, in response to Mahāprajāpatī Gotamī's

request allowed women to become bhikkhunī, he also set forth the eight gurudharmas. However, their contents indicate that they were actually formulated later." *Monastic Discipline for the Buddhist Nuns* (Patna: Kashi Prasad Jayaswal Research Institute, 1982), p. 37.

4 Study, training, discipline (Sanskrit: *śikṣā*).

5 This number includes 500 women from the royal court and 500 other women.

CHAPTER TWO

At the Cutting Edge

Theravāda Nuns in the Kathmandu Valley

Sarah LeVine

In the late 1980s, in an audience with the Dalai Lama, Dhammavati Gurumā, a prominent member of the Nepalese nuns' order, asked His Holiness whether, in his opinion, women and men have equal spiritual potential and, if so, whether women can and should be ordained. On both counts he answered in the affirmative and urged her to seek ordination. A few months later she was visited in Kathmandu by Taiwanese nuns from Xilai Monastery in Los Angeles, a branch of Foguangshan Monastery in Taiwan. After observing and admiring the work that Dhammavati, her associates, and disciples were doing, the Taiwanese invited her and three other nuns to Xilai in 1988 to receive *upasampadā* according to Chinese rites. As one of those four nuns recently noted, "Of course, the Taiwanese are Mahāyāna and we are Theravāda, but we asked ourselves, 'What's the difference between the Mahāyāna and the way of Theravāda?' Well, we saw no difference. The Lord Buddha constructed both roads and both can take us to *nibbāna*." Without asking the senior Nepalese monks for permission which they knew would be withheld, they accepted the invitation and went to Los Angeles. There a quorum of nuns and monks ordained them according to the rites of the Dharmagupta lineage. The Dharmagupta lineage of monastic discipline had been brought in the fifth century from Sri Lanka to China. Unlike the Theravāda and the Mūlasarvāstivāda (Tibetan) lineages, it has survived in the Chinese, Korean, and Vietnamese traditions to this day.

Upon the nuns' return to Kathmandu, the senior monks refused to acknowledge their newly elevated status. In the monks' view, the lineage of *bhikkhunī* ordination had died out at least nine centuries ago and, once dead, could never be revived. If Nepalese nuns elected to be ordained by Chinese rites, that was their choice, but having done so, they were no longer Theravāda. In short, they should change their dress and adopt Chinese practices such as prostration and chanting in Mandarin. In the decade since their ordination, these nuns have met their monk critics regularly at community events, but have carefully avoided public confrontation. The nuns have not changed their dress or their practice and continue to regard themselves as Theravāda. When nuns are present at the Dhamma talks, the senior monks make a point of addressing them as "*anagārikā*" rather than "*bhikkhunī.*" The nuns have held their peace. Nevertheless, tensions have been mounting. In November 1997, a group of five nuns went to China to receive *upasampadā,* and in February 1998 a second group received *upasampadā* in an ordination ceremony organized by Foguangshan Monastery in Bodhgaya, India. To date there has been no public confrontation and there may never be. "That's not our Newar style," one nun explained. In private, however, certain senior monks have severely castigated those nuns who took *upasampadā.* The junior monks seem generally supportive, but most of their seniors remain categorically opposed, a position the nuns do not expect them to moderate. But time is on the nuns' side. Everything is impermanent: inevitably, the older generation will pass away and another more liberal one will take its place. More significantly, there are now 17 fully ordained Nepalese Theravāda nuns who, within a decade, will have been ordained long enough to give *upasampadā* ordination to new candidates themselves. "Until then," as one nun points out, "our novices will have to keep on traveling abroad for ordination. But why shouldn't they? That's what the Nepalese *bhikkhus* had to do until there were enough of them to give the *upasampadā* in Nepal."

In its modern form, Theravāda Buddhism has been an established presence in the Kathmandu Valley for less than 50 years. The Saṅgha, or monastic community, is composed of monks referred to as "*bhante*," nuns known as "*gurumā*," and devout laymen and laywomen (*upāsaka, upāsikā*). For the purpose of this discussion, I shall look first at those women who took ordination from the 1940s through the early 1980s, and second at those ordained in the last fifteen years. Why the 1980s watershed? Until the early 1980s, women were motivated to become nuns for three main reasons: in the case of young girls, either to avoid marriage, or, at a time when very few girls went to school, to acquire literacy skills in order to study the Buddhist scriptures; in the case of older women, to escape the marginality of marital breakdown or widowhood. Some women continue to join the order for these reasons. Today, however, virtually all middle and upper caste girls attend primary school and many have access to secondary and post-secondary education, so the desire for literacy is no longer a major motivating factor. As young Western-educated women move into the work force and become financially self-supporting, some experience less pressure to marry than young women did in the past. Thus, two of the three conditions that motivated women of an earlier generation to "go into homelessness" carry less weight with young women today. Rather, a new factor is operative: *vipassanā*, or "insight" meditation, whose objective is experiential understanding of impermanence.

Before the 1980s, a few monastics and laypeople were serious practitioners of various forms of meditation. Only after the introduction of *vipassanā* meditation from Burma did meditation become something that ordinary people could learn and benefit from. *Vipassanā*'s appeal was immediate and widespread. Women who wished to make it the central focus of their lives began to consider ordination in the belief that life in the nunnery offered optimal conditions for meditation practice.

Unlike Christian monastic orders, which place much emphasis on their recruits' having a "vocation," or spiritual calling, the Theravāda Buddhist order expects only that candidates have a sense of the inevitability of suffering in this world and, in consequence, a strong desire to "take refuge" in the Three Jewels: the Buddha, the Dhamma, and the Saṅgha. Even if at the outset the recruits' teachers and preceptors see minimal evidence of a spiritual calling, they are not dismayed; instead, they deem it their responsibility to instill the calling and then nurture its development. Although they do not expect virtuous conduct, concentration, or wisdom – the three pillars of the religious life – to be easily constructed, they are confident that over time adherence to monastic discipline, study of the Dhamma, and meditation will produce a mental disposition favorable to spiritual progress that will lead, if not to the attainment of *nibbāna*, at least to a better rebirth.[1]

This essay concerns the construction of religious identity by nuns in the Theravāda Buddhist community of the Kathmandu Valley of Nepal. I address two questions: first, what motivates women to become nuns, and second, what is the nature and impact of their training?

Female Renouncers in the Buddhist Tradition

Despite its doctrinal emphasis on soteriological inclusiveness, early Buddhism in India was marked by a profound ambivalence towards women. For the first five years, the Buddha did not admit women to his monastic order. Ultimately he did accept them, but to contain their alleged "hypersexuality, envy, greed and poor judgment,"[2] he imposed many more rules of conduct on nuns than on monks (311 as opposed to 227). Of primary importance are the eight special rules (*garudhamma*) which ensured female dependence on and subordination to monks.[3] While monks were authorized to give both levels of ordination to male novices, nuns could only give lower ordination (*pabbajjā*) to their female novices; full ordination (*upasampadā*) required a quorum of ten monks in addition to ten nuns. Such rules left nuns permanently relegated to a lower status.

Inscriptions indicate that nunneries were established in many parts of India until the third century C.E., but endowments were sharply reduced thereafter. The rise of Hindu devotionalism during that period may have been a factor in siphoning off lay support for nunneries. It is also possible that benefactors shifted their support to monks, whose scholarship and philosophical training prepared them for public roles in society. The nuns' lack of higher learning made them inferior recipients of *dāna* (gifts to monastics and monastic institutions) in the eyes of the laity, and therefore poorer "fields," or sources, of merit for donors.[4] In any event, lacking prestige and leadership, the Bhikkhunī Saṅgha vanished from India near the end of the first millennium. By the end of the 11th century, after the Coḷa invasions, it had vanished from Sri Lanka as well.

In the early 20th century in Sri Lanka, however, a handful of devout Buddhist laywomen renounced lay life under foreign leadership, using a rite of ordination of their own design. Since the Theravāda nuns' ordination lineage had died out many centuries before, these new renunciants called their ordination rite *pabbajjā*, or "going forth," rather than *upasampadā*, and termed themselves "*anagārikā*," or "homeless ones," rather than *bhikkhunī*, fully ordained nuns. Some years later, women in other Theravāda countries, including Nepal, followed their lead and also took the lower ordination. Except for a few individuals, Theravāda nuns did not press for full ordination until recently. The senior monks of their tradition strongly opposed such a move, for one thing. Besides, as Tessa Bartholemeuz has noted in reference to contemporary Sri Lanka, full ordination would have required the nuns to observe the full corpus of disciplinary rules, including the *garudhammas*, which would have subordinated them to monks.[5]

Thailand and Burma both received the Dhamma after the *bhikkhunī* ordination lineage died out. The great majority of nuns there seemed resigned to their ambiguous – and in the case of Thailand much inferior – status. In Nepal, however, a few nuns who had assumed leadership roles in the fledgling Theravāda community decided a decade or so ago to seek full *bhikkhunī* ordination. They argued that the definition of the word *bhikṣu* – "one who, fearing *saṃsāra*, goes out into the world and lives by alms" – applied to them as much to male monastics. They asserted that the Buddha, who regarded both sexes as equally capable of attaining enlightenment, therefore could not have been the source of the *garudhammas*. Rather, they reasoned, in the course of more than three centuries of oral transmission between the time when the Buddha promulgated the rules of conduct for nuns and the time they were written down, male prejudice had fundamentally altered and misrepresented the rules.

Theravāda Buddhism in the Kathmandu Valley

The Kathmandu Valley is one of the very few areas of the world where Hindus and Buddhists still practice their religions side by side as they did in medieval India. Hinduism and Buddhism have coexisted in the Valley for millennia.[6] The two religions have endowed Nepal's three main towns of Kathmandu, Patan, and Bhaktapur, as well as many smaller settlements, with an abundance of temples, monasteries, *stūpas*, and shrines. The indigenous Newar kings who dominated the Valley before their 1769 defeat by the Nepali-speaking Gorkhas always identified themselves as *śivamārgīs*, or Hindus.[7] Although the kings patronized and endowed Buddhist institutions, Hinduism, as the religion of the monarchy, enjoyed greater prestige. As a result, over the centuries Hindu religious practices and social institutions, including an elaborate caste system and many rites of passage, were adopted by the Buddhist population. Distinctions between the two traditions were further blurred when, in the middle ages, tantric practices became dominant in both. Buddhist monks, like Hindu priests, required consorts to participate in esoteric rites, and they abandoned monasticism. Taking the place of the Buddhist monks many centuries ago were two castes of householders, descendants of laicized forefathers: first, the family priest (*vajrācārya*) whose role was similar to that of the Hindu *brahmin* family priest (*purohit*), and second, the temple priest (*śākya* or *bare*) who was similar to the Hindu *pūjārī*.[8] These two castes continued to reside in, care for, and conduct rituals in the former temples and monastic courtyards surrounding them.[9]

In his 1877 introduction to a translation of the *Vaṃsāvalī* (the Nepalese chronicle), Daniel Wright noted that Mahāyāna Buddhism in its Vajrayāna, or tantric, form was the religion of the large majority of the Newar population. Thereafter, however, Buddhism declined in the face of the determination of the Rana family – oligarchs and de facto rulers of the kingdom from 1846 to 1951 – who imposed brahminical orthodoxy on the Newars. According to the 1991 census, Newars constitute 5.6 percent of the population of Nepal, half of whom – just over one million people – live in the Kathmandu Valley. Although a majority identify themselves as Hindus, often for the political and economic advantages that may accrue, many continue to worship the Buddha and bodhisattvas, celebrate Buddhist festivals, and worship at Buddhist temples and shrines, just as many Buddhists in Nepal celebrate Hindu festivals and worship at Hindu temples and shrines.[10]

In the 1920s, a desire for a "purer" form of Buddhism had motivated a handful of young Newar men to take ordination from Tibetan Mahāyāna monks.[11] Tibetan Buddhism had been a significant presence at the great *stūpas* of the Kathmandu Valley for over a thousand years and had always attracted some Newars to its monastic ranks. Despite close cultural and mercantile ties between Tibetans and Newars, however, Tibetan Buddhism never drew Newar adherents in significant numbers, perhaps because it is not sufficiently different from the indigenous Newar form of Buddhism to warrant making the shift. Language may have also been a factor for, although many Newar merchants speak colloquial Tibetan, the textual language presents a formidable challenge.

Theravāda Buddhism first appeared upon this uniquely syncretic religious scene in the 1930s. At that time, a handful of Newars began to regard their indigenous Vajrayāna religion as overly ritualistic and doctrinally stagnant. Judging their priests to be ignorant of the meaning of the Sanskrit texts they read, a group of Newars went abroad to seek better teachers and ordination. Not long after their ordination, they went on a pilgrimage to the Buddhist sacred sites of northern India. At Bodhgaya, where the Buddha attained enlightenment in the fifth century B.C.E., they met a Burmese Theravāda monk named Candramaṇi, a disciple of Anagārikā Dharmapāla, the pre-eminent Sinhalese Buddhist reformer. These monks were the first Newars to be exposed to Theravāda Buddhism in modern times.

The monks' meeting with Candramaṇi is also the first documented Nepalese encounter with the "modernist" Buddhist movement pioneered by Dharmapāla in Ceylon in the 1880s. In 1891, Dharmapāla founded the Maha Bodhi Society with the initial objective of reclaiming the Maha Bodhi Temple at Bodhgaya which, since the Muslim eradication of Buddhism in India in the late 12th century, had been in the hands of Hindu temple priests. By the 1920s the Maha Bodhi Society had evolved into the dominant Theravāda missionary organization and begun to teach a "rational" form of Buddhism in the Buddha's homeland.[12] This "rational" approach signified a Buddhism stripped of magical practices – a doctrine that did not conflict with modern scientific knowledge. The Burmese monk Candramaṇi's exegesis of the Dhamma so impressed the young Nepalese that they relinquished their previous vows and received Theravāda ordination.[13]

During the 1930s, other disenchanted Newar Buddhists – including three women – also went to India and were singularly impressed by the Theravāda monks they encountered. Some took ordination in India, while others went to study in Burma and Ceylon and took ordination there. When these Newars returned to Nepal in the late 1930s and early 1940s after studying abroad, their religious activities not only attracted lay support, they also drew the opposition of the autocratic government in Nepal at the time. The Ranas were persuaded by their priests and counsellors to prohibit all missionary activity by any religious group. They made an exception for Tibetan Buddhist monks, by now regarded as indigenous, but deemed Theravāda Buddhist monastics "subversive." The Theravādins thus found themselves classed with the Nepalese pro-democracy movement which at that time was working out of Delhi and Calcutta to overthrow the Ranas. Because their preaching activities were regarded as a threat to social cohesion in the "Hindu kingdom" of Nepal, they were arrested, imprisoned, or expelled as soon as they reentered the country. Not until 1946, after several unsuccessful attempts, did the small group of exiles win permission from the government to settle permanently in their homeland. After the Rana regime was overthrown in 1951, Theravāda Buddhists were finally allowed to proselytize freely, but even then they were allowed to make converts only among those who were Buddhist by birth.[14]

As heirs to the Buddhist modernist movement, Nepalese Theravāda monks and nuns emphasized the rational elements of Buddhism. Their purpose was to educate the laity in Dhamma and to purify Vajrayāna Buddhism of magical practices and caste distinctions adopted from Hinduism in medieval times. When it served their goals, however, they endorsed traditional Vajrayāna Buddhist practices. For example, they accepted the laity's prominent role in monastery affairs, the monastic initiation of young boys (*bare chuyegu*), the observance of Golan (a month during the monsoon season when priests traditionally gave daily teachings and the laity worshipped at shrines throughout Kathmandu Valley), and the singing of *bhajans* (devotional songs) – all practices unknown in other Theravāda countries. In the 50 years since they won the freedom to propagate their version of the Dhamma, Theravāda Buddhists have garnered strong support among the more progressive elements of the lay population. They have accomplished this through their energetic teaching, vernacular publications of religious texts, social and health programs, and more recently, *vipassanā* meditation courses and retreats. Although the laypeople may not have altogether abandoned Vajrayāna Buddhist practices, which in large measure define and structure their social relationships, many feel that their traditional religious structures are inadequate in the face of massive social and economic change.

From the 1950s onwards the small band of monastics led by the returned exiles grew slowly but steadily. In 1966 there were 44 Theravāda monks and 37 nuns;[15] in 1982, 60 monks and 65 nuns;[16] and in 1989, 59 monks, 72 male and female novices, and 70 nuns.[17] Until now, because Nepal lacks adequate educational facilities, young monastics have gone to other Theravāda countries to obtain advanced religious training. The fact that many of these young monks either stay in the country where they were trained or disrobe after completing their studies is a focus of great concern in the Nepalese Theravāda community. As of 1997, there were only 57 fully ordained monks in Nepal. There were 83 novices in training, about 50 of them abroad, but no certainty about how many would remain as monks once they completed their training. As the abbot of one of the major monasteries recently observed, "The order is hemorrhaging monks. I personally have sent fifteen novices abroad over the past ten years, and not one of them has returned to our monastery." In 1997, a seminary was established in Kathmandu where two dozen male and female novices between the ages of 10 and 16 presently receive both secular and religious education. The hope is that by keeping young monks and nuns in Nepal they will be sheltered from the seductive worldliness pervading more developed Theravāda countries. It is hoped that by the time these monastics go abroad for further training, they will be disciplined enough to resist whatever attractions they encounter. But Kathmandu is no longer as remote as it once was, and the lures of the world are much in evidence there, too. By the time these novices reach their 20s, many may also return to lay life.

The original group of missionary monks included a number of charismatic and revered teachers who seemed to thrive in adversity. But as the government's response shifted from antagonism to disinterest, the monks' spirit of purpose slowly evaporated. Today those charismatic leaders have all passed away, leaving the Nepalese Bhikkhu Saṅgha without a sense of direction. The senior monks, trained abroad in different countries and traditions, have repeatedly failed to provide effective leadership for the laity or a unified front for addressing major problems within the order itself. The younger monks, who came to maturity in easier times, are often viewed as uninspiring, unqualified, or lax in discipline. As one middle-aged layman remarked, "When I was young I venerated all monks, just by virtue of the fact that they wore the robe, but no longer. They should be going out to the villages, preaching to the people, but too many of them just stay in their monasteries and only come out when they're invited to eat in laypeople's houses, or to receive *dāna* (donations)."

By contrast, the number of nuns has continued to climb. In 1997 there were 80 nuns in Nepal and about 20 training abroad. The nuns' order might be half again as large if there were sufficient space to house all those who wish to join. Unlike monks, nuns very rarely disrobe. One reason may be that, unlike the Nepali-speaking majority (Parbatiyas), Newar women occasionally remain single, not due to a lack of attractive marriage proposal, but by choice. Thus Newar girls have an alternative to becoming a wife and mother. Still, by becoming a nun, an unmarried woman avoids being dependent on her father and brothers. Life as a nun – serving as a teacher, counselor, and ritual specialist – offers her a varied and stimulating life and, most likely, the affection and esteem of the laity. With admiration and envy, one young monk commented, "The people really love these *gurumā* [nuns]! Perhaps they find it easier to approach a woman about their problems, rather than a man."

For the great majority of nuns, "going into homelessness" involves a fundamental resocialization. As one nun put it, "When you shave your head, it's very difficult to go home again. It doesn't take long for a man to grow his hair, but for a woman it takes a very long time." Newar laymen must shave their heads upon the death and commemoration of a range of kin, so shaving the head is an ordinary event for males. But because the majority of Newar women have waistlength hair, shaving the head signals a vow of celibacy; psychologically, then, the event is a far more radical step for women than for men. After ordination a nun may continue to have daily contact with laypeople, but her shaved head, a visible symbol of her celibate status, sets her irrevocably apart from lay life. Although the order she joins may receive less financial support than the monks' and offer only cramped, decrepit quarters, it is has gained the esteem of the laity, due to its determined, effective leaders.[18]

The First Cohort

Almost all the first Nepalese nuns faced great opposition when they decided to become ordained. Widows might face less antagonism, but the families of young girls could rarely reconcile themselves to the idea of this lifelong commitment. Many girls were forced to run away from home to join the order. Then, because parental permission was required, they had to engage in lengthy negotiations with fathers who were often strongly opposed. Santi, a nun in her 50s, recalls:

> We were determined not to marry, but our fathers were equally determined that we should. Even later on, when they saw our shaven heads and our pink dresses, they couldn't accept that we were nuns. They kept on telling us, "Now take off that dress and put on a sari and come home!" But we knew what that meant. As soon as we got home, they'd get us married, and we wanted to be free to learn and to teach others about the Dhamma.

"I wanted to be free" is what almost all the older nuns declare – free from *dukkha*, in the form of agony in childbirth, subordination to mothers-in-law, quarrels between sisters-in-law in a joint family, fights with husbands over other women, and endless domestic drudgery. A nun named Sushila explains:

> On winter mornings, I'd stay in bed until eight o'clock, but my poor mother got up at three o'clock all the year round. When I was 12 years old a proposal came and my father decided to accept it. From his point of view, it was a good proposal, but from mine, it meant getting up at three o'clock every morning for the rest of my life!

So Sushila ran away. After 25 years in the order, she reports that whenever she meets her father, he still weeps to see her:

> When I left home he wasn't Theravāda. He was an old-fashioned traditionalist following Vajrayāna. Actually, he was very much opposed to our teaching. It took me ten years to convince him that Theravāda is good. Even so, he's still not reconciled to my being a nun and that I'm one for life. I'll never be coming home.

The group of monastics harassed by the Rana government in the 1930s and 1940s included some women. A few were expelled from Nepal and forced to spend time in exile. A nun named Dharmacarī spent time in a Burmese monastery before finally returning to Kathmandu to head a nunnery at Kimdol, near the great *stūpa* of Svayambhu. At that time no Nepalese nun had more than a smattering of religious training and, in a era when only two percent of the Nepalese population was literate (virtually all upper caste males), none had any secular education at all. The monks who brought Theravāda Buddhism to Nepal directed their ordinands' careers and, in this regard, they differentiated clearly between the potentials of monks and nuns. Young monks might get the opportunity to spend years studying in Burma, India, or Sri Lanka, but through the 1970s, few nuns got such a chance. Most nuns performed menial work in monasteries in the Kathmandu Valley. Although some learned to read certain simple religious texts, understanding the meaning was another matter. Most lived and died knowing very little about the Dhamma. As one nun recalls of her older companions, "They learned some Jātaka stories (about the Buddha's former lives) by heart, and to chant a little of this and that. But really they knew no more than simple laypeople." The nuns' primary function was to keep house for the monks. In the belief that their services earned them spiritual merit (*puñña*), they cooked and cleaned for the monks, washed their clothes, and performed other services that would have been inappropriate had they been fully ordained. With full ordination (*upasampadā*), they would also have to observe many additional rules and live apart from monks; as "homeless ones" (*anagārikās*), they could live nearby and work as servants.

The first nun to receive a religious education abroad was a girl from Patan named Ganesh Kumārī Śākya.[19] The Śākyas, hereditary priests of Newar Buddhist monasteries, are also called *śākyabhikṣus*, an echo of a distant past when their ancestors were monks. It was from among the Śākyas that the Nepalese Theravāda movement originally drew much of its support.[20] As goldsmiths and temple priests, the Śākyas plied their trades throughout Southeast Asia, especially Burma, where they served the Gorkha soldiers recruited into the British army in colonial times. In this way, certain Śākya families had considerable direct exposure to Theravāda Buddhism.

In 1947, when Ganesh Kumārī was 12 years old, her mother, a Theravāda convert, sent her to study Dhamma with a Burma-trained Nepalese monk. At that time there was a fledgling primary school for girls in Patan, but Ganesh Kumārī's father never considered sending his only daughter to school, or even his sons. Instead he hired a tutor to teach the children to read and write at home. At the local temple, Ganesh Kumārī studied scriptures and Pāli, and was rewarded with her teacher's praise. After one year, when the teacher left to study abroad, Ganesh Kumārī was aghast. She remembers thinking she had glimpsed *nibbāna*, but then it vanished. Then she learned that her father was negotiating a marriage for her and, even with her mother's help trying to slow down the proceedings, she knew the wedding could not be delayed indefinitely.

Soon a Burmese monk named Candramaṇi arrived to take the first teacher's place, and Ganesh Kumārī already knew enough Pāli to be able to communicate with him quite easily. But after a short time she learned that he, too, would be returning to Burma. When this monk saw Ganesh

Kumārī's despair, he offered to take her and two other female students with him, so that they could continue their studies in Burma. He had to leave Nepal right away because he was in the country illegally, but he promised to wait for them over the border in India. A few days after he left, while her mother distracted her father, Ganesh Kumārī slipped out of the house with a brother who intended to be ordained as a monk. Their father soon discovered their escape and had her brother intercepted at one of the check points that ringed the valley in those days, but Ganesh Kumārī and the other two girls managed to escape to India. The girls were soon reunited with their teacher Candramaṇi in Kushinagar, site of the Buddha's demise (*parinibbāna*). Under Candramaṇi's leadership, the town had become a center of Theravāda activity.

After some months the other two girls' father caught up with them and took them back to Nepal. Fearing that her father would catch up with her, too, Ganesh Kumārī and her teacher hastily set off for Burma. Many adventures awaited them, including a journey with a party of elephant traders on foot through the forests of Assam and Manipur, and a spell in a Burmese jail following her arrest at the Indian-Burmese border since she had no travel documents. Finally, Ganesh Kumārī, age 14, reached Rangoon. After negotiating her admission into Kemarama Nunnery in Moulmein and obtaining the sponsorship of a local family, she began her religious training. She remained in Burma for fifteen years, with only one short visit home. She heard nothing from her family for the first 18 months of her stay, but despite being so young and so far from home, she did not feel homesick. She remembers:

> I had a one-track mind. I'd come to Burma for one purpose only: to learn. I was burning to learn – anything, whatever they were prepared to teach me! To me, *dukkha* meant one thing above all else – being barred from studying the Dhamma.

In Burma she was much impressed by the independence of Burmese women:

> In Nepal, you hear the same stories all the time about the bitterness between the mother-in-law and the daughter-in-law. In Nepal daughters-in-law eat left-overs, they're treated like servants, but in Burma they do not have joint families. Young couples live separately from the parents. They have their own households.

The status of nuns was also higher in Burma than in Nepal. Novice nuns studied exclusively with other novice nuns, but their course of study was identical to that of novice monks. Nuns took the same examinations and were respected as scholars and teachers by the monks. Dhammavati, as Ganesh Kumārī became known after her ordination, was particularly impressed by the abbess of the nunnery in which she lived. She noted that this nun's counsel was sought by many eminent monks.

During the long years of her religious training, Dhammavati committed the Tripiṭaka to memory. She became convinced that women were equal to men and, by the same token, that nuns were equal to monks. But when she returned to Nepal in 1964, at the age of 28, this conviction was immediately challenged by senior members of the Nepalese Saṅgha. "It was like going from heaven to hell," she recalls. "Nepalese monks had a very bad case of the 'Asian disease' [regarding women as inferior to men]!" In Burma she had earned the Dharmācārya certificate, equivalent to a doctorate in Buddhist studies. She was the first Nepalese monastic to earn this certificate and it proved to be of vital importance in her struggles with the senior Nepalese monks in years to come. Although the monks might regard her as inferior on the basis of gender, they were forced to respect her on the basis of her qualifications.[21]

After she returned to Nepal, she assumed a leadership position in the nuns' order despite her youth. At that point the order consisted of a few dozen semi-literate women mostly living in monasteries, subordinate to monks. But Dhammavati had been educated in Burma, where monks and nuns lived separately and she was unwilling to live in close proximity to monks where she would be treated as inferior by monks with less training than she. At first her only alternative was to live in the home of a layperson. Each day she walked to a half-ruined temple where she opened a school for poor children. Her companion in this endeavor was Gunavati, a Burmese nun with the Dharmācārya certificate who had returned with her to Nepal. Together they decided to build a nunnery, adopting the Burmese model of creating a place for "virgins," nuns who had never been married. With an inheritance, Dhammavati bought a piece of property in the old section of Kathmandu. Collecting donations from relatives and sympathetic laypeople (many from women who secretly sold their gold bangles), she built a small structure in the courtyard of an ancient Buddhist *stūpa*. Rather than register the nunnery as the property of the Buddhist Saṅgha, as the senior monks instructed her to, she put it in her own name. And she named it Dharmakirti Vihar, to the enduring indignation of one senior monk who maintained that an *anagārikā* (not a nun) is not entitled to call her place a *vihāra*. Over the years, this monk repeatedly had her signboard torn down, but she patiently replaced it again each time.

In the early years, Dhammavati endured considerable hostility from the monks. They tried to prevent her from preaching in Kathmandu, on the grounds that as a woman she had no authority to transmit the Dhamma. Undaunted, Dhammavati continued to create a community of nuns and lay followers. Even if the monks refused her permission to teach in their monasteries, they could not prevent her from teaching on her own premises. Soon the laity were flocking to listen and learn. She and Gunavati invited a few young nuns to live with them in the nunnery, where they pieced together their own "modernist" Buddhist program. In addition to a rigorous religious curriculum for adults and children, they translated and published Pāli texts in Newari and Nepali, devised Theravāda alternatives to traditional Vajrayāna rites of passage, provided free health care in a clinic staffed by sympathetic medical personnel, published a monthly magazine, and led pilgrimage tours to the sacred Buddhist sites in India. With Dhammavati's encouragement and the financial support of her lay devotees, a number of disciples followed her example and built their own nunneries. Most were extremely simple structures – a group of small rooms around a courtyard with few amenities – but the resident nuns were largely free from the monks' control. Officially, the nuns were supposed to bring major problems to the attention of the Mahāsaṅgha, the Nepalese order in which nuns had little or no voice, but as one nun remarked, "We've made sure we haven't had any major problems!"

By the 1980s, Dhammavati and some of her male colleagues had produced many translations and explanations of Theravāda texts, but no one could claim that the standard of religious education in Nepal was equivalent to Thailand, Sri Lanka, or Burma. There were a few fine teachers in the valley, but they were all exceedingly busy. To study at an advanced level it was still necessary to travel abroad. Therefore, Dhammavati began to develop a network of nuns and laypeople in other Theravāda countries who would sponsor young Nepalese nuns to get religious training abroad.

The Second Cohort

A second cohort of nuns has become ordained since the early 1980s. A few nuns from better-off families live in their natal homes, usually in separate quarters where they can be independent of their kin, but most live in nunneries. Nuns who have never been married live separately from those who have been married, partly because the latter often maintain close attachments to children or, in the case of widows, to deceased husbands. "When they talk about love, which they often do, it's difficult for the rest of us," one Dharmakirti resident admits. "We can't help but feel envious, so that's why it's better to live separately." Today a few nuns still perform menial tasks for monks, but most among the younger generation are busy with their own programs.

In contrast to the first cohort of nuns, today's entrants have had considerable prior exposure to Theravāda Buddhism through the educational programs the order has been running for decades. Theravāda Buddhism in the Kathmandu Valley is no longer a missionary movement, but a fully institutionalized religion. Adolescent girls who do not want to get married and wish to become nuns no longer need to run away from home. Most come from devout Buddhist families and may have already been attending Dhamma classes on Saturdays for many years. In these classes they have had close contact with nuns as teachers and advisors, and may have taken temporary ordination at Dharmakirti Vihar or one of the other nunneries. Some have close relatives who are monks and nuns – grandfathers, grandmothers, brothers, sisters, or even parents – and are following a well-established family tradition.

Over the past decade several nunneries have begun to accept children when they are still quite young. A few are orphans, but most are from impoverished families who send their daughters to the nunnery to earn merit and in hopes that, as nuns, their daughters will have a better life. These little girls, some as young as eight, live in the nunnery and attend local government schools. Although young women from more affluent families may not be interested, in recent years monastic life has attracted a number of university graduates in their 20s and 30s. The trend toward higher educational standards is not limited to Nepal; primary education may have been sufficient for an earlier generation of Theravāda monastics, but today 12 to 14 years of secular education have become a prerequisite for advanced religious training in Burma, Thailand, and Sri Lanka.

Young girls who enter the order today invariably have had at least a few years of schooling. They assume they will be able to continue their secular education after they are ordained, to whatever level they wish. Although Dhammavati gave religious education first priority for many years, after traveling to the U.S., East and Southeast Asia, she has revised her views. She has come to believe that if Theravāda Buddhism is to survive and flourish in Nepal, it must shed the inflexible rule-ridden image to which the senior monks still cling. It must discard regulations that impede the efficient conduct of daily life and transform itself into a truly modern, international movement. She therefore stresses the need for education, secular as well as religious, and the need for learning foreign languages, including Chinese and English.

Meditation and Renunciation

The opportunity to practice meditation is another important factor in the decision to seek ordination. Dhammavati recalls that she rarely meditated when she was training in Burma in the 1950s. Meditation was optional and she was studying so hard, she had little time for it. Occasionally though, after her semester exams were over, she would stay in retreat to practice *kesaloma* meditation, reflecting on the repulsive nature of the body, its impermanence, and inevitable decay. In addition, from the abbess of her nunnery, she learned *ānāpāna* meditation – mindfulness of breathing. At that time *vipassanā* meditation was becoming very popular in Burma, but she had little exposure to it until she returned to Nepal. In 1981 Mahasi Sayadaw, a leading exponent, instructed some monks, nuns, and laymen during a visit to Kathmandu. The following year, U. S. N. Goenka, a teacher from an Indian-Burmese merchant family, made the first of many visits to Nepal to give *vipassanā* instruction. Coming from a Hindu background, he presented *vipassanā* as a technique that anyone could use, regardless of religious affiliation. Still, in Nepal he made the strongest impact among Theravāda Buddhists. The practice of *vipassanā* meditation identified them as progressive, modern Buddhists.

By the end of the 1980s, all the larger monasteries in the Kathmandu Valley were giving *vipassanā* instruction and two centers offered 10-day *vipassanā* retreats, one following Goenka and the other following U Pandita, a student of Mahasi Sayadaw. In both centers, nuns played important roles as teachers and board members. Although Goenka's first disciples were wealthy businesspeople, including some of Dharmakirti Vihar's most generous donors, people of more modest means also attended the retreats. Soon women of all ages and levels of society were learning *vipassanā* and finding that the practice empowered them. It helped them to control rage at oppressive mothers-in-law and alcoholic husbands, and to survive grief and loss.

Dissatisfied at not having enough time for meditation, some single women decided to become ordained. A nun named Subha confided, "I realized meditation was the most important thing for me, but my house wasn't conducive to practice. There was too much noise – my brother's children playing, the phone ringing – and there was always cooking and cleaning to be done." Previously an accountant in a government ministry, Subha was a devout Buddhist and a disciple of Dhammavati Gurumā since childhood. She never wanted to marry and had envisioned living with her parents indefinitely. "But people told me: after your father and mother die, you'll be alone, and who will take care of *you* when you're old?" Eventually she left government service and entered Dharmakirti Vihar, where she co-edits the monthly magazine. She is one of the few nuns who have not been abroad for religious training and has no desire to do so. For many years she studied in the classes that Dhammavati Gurumā offers to the laity. With a wry smile she says,

> That's enough for me. If I want to learn more, I can always read more books. But I didn't join the order to be able to study. I joined because I wanted to meditate. Before I came to live here, I imagined that I'd be spending hours in meditation every day. I didn't realize I'd be so busy! Still I have half an hour morning and evening, which is more than I had in my own house.

Youngsters may become serious meditators, too. In an increasingly technological society, where many Nepalese parents send their children to private schools and put great pressure on them to succeed, children find that meditation helps them concentrate. "Sometimes I want to play instead of doing my homework, but I've learned to push the thought out of my head," one twelve-year-old girl reports. She finds meditation soothing – one of the few uncompetitive aspects of her life. One hour sittings on Saturdays meet most children's needs, but others attend retreats expressly for children.

At these retreats, the "*yogis*" and "*yoginīs*" adhere to the same rigorous schedule as adults, for three to seven days rather than ten. A few of these children are so profoundly affected by the experience that they decide to ordain. One 14-year-old *gurumā* talks about meditation much as an addict might talk about drugs. The only child of a divorced mother, she experienced much economic hardship and emotional pain in her early life. She became a nun, she says, "to overcome *dukkha* and help other people overcome theirs."

New Possibilities

In recent years, the spread of Western education in the Kathmandu Valley has given Western-educated Newar women the chance to live fulfilling lives without "going into homelessness." For women who do not wish to marry, pursuing a career has become a socially acceptable option. Nepalese law dictates that women who are still unmarried at age 35 are eligible to inherit an equal share of their parents' property. Nevertheless, even at a time when the order of monks is facing a crisis in retaining members, the order of nuns continues to attract not only widows, orphans, and girls from poor families, but also university-educated women.

Nuns belonging to the first cohort of nuns in Nepal saw earning merit (*puñña*) as their goal, whereas today younger women aim at "wiping away the defilements (*kilesa*) and acquiring insight and wisdom (*paññā*)" – much more ambitious goals. Although the first Theravāda missionaries would be gratified to see the impact their movement has had in the Newar Buddhist community over the last 40 years, they might also be surprised to see that the laity's need for instruction, support, and solace is often being provided by nuns rather than monks.

Women find themselves "pulled" rather than "pushed" toward monasticism. The desire to "go forth" indicates that renunciation has become a viable alternative to marriage for many women. Even more important, however, is the highly visible example of a female Buddhist role model: the compassionate, humorous, and seemingly tireless Dhammavati Gurumā. The traditionally Vajrayāna Buddhist population takes the bodhisattva seeking to save all sentient beings as its ideal, rather than the *arahant* seeking personal salvation. To them, Dhammavati's selfless style of leadership may be more appealing than the style of the monks, whose simulation of the distant, disciplined Burmese model is more intimidating than inspiring. Both the conservative monks and the more progressive nuns accept Theravāda Buddhism as a uniquely efficacious path; both emphasize the rules of conduct which, if strictly observed, promote spiritual growth and, ultimately, liberation. Yet there is more than one Buddhist road to salvation, and by emphasizing the spirit of the precepts as much as the practice, Dhammavati and her disciples may ultimately have more success.

Notes

1 Edward Conze, *Buddhism: Its Essence and Development* (New Delhi: Munshiram Monharlal Publishing, 1994). Contemporary Nepalese Theravāda Buddhist monastics and laypeople commonly insist that *nibbāna* is attainable but believe that, in contrast to the Buddha's time when many people became *arahants*, things have degenerated to the point that today only one or two monks living in remote forest regions have attained *nibbāna*.

2 Quoted by Alan Sponberg from *Aṅgutara Nikāya* in "Attitudes Towards Women and the Feminine in Early Buddhism," in *Buddhism, Sexuality and Gender*, ed. José Ignacio Cabezón (Albany, N.Y.: State University of New York Press, 1992), pp. 3–36.

3 Elizabeth Nissan, "Recovering Practice: Buddhist Nuns in Sri Lanka," *South Asia Research* 4, no. 1 (1984): 32–75.

4 Nancy Auer Falk, "The Case of the Vanishing Nuns," in *Unspoken Worlds: Women's Religious Lives in Non-Western Cultures*, ed. Nancy Auer Falk and Rita M. Gross (San Francisco: Harper & Row, 1979), pp. 207–24.

5 Tessa Bartholomeusz, *Women Under the Bō Tree* (Cambridge: Cambridge University Press, 1995).

6 There is still no consensus among scholars as to which was the first form of high Indian religion to be introduced into the Kathmandu Valley. See Robert Levy, *Mesocosom* (Berkeley: University of California Press, 1990), p. 38.

7 In contradistinction to *buddhamāgīs*, or Buddhists.

8 The complex caste distinctions in Nepal are described in David N. Gellner, *Monk, Householder, and Tantric Priest: Newar Buddhism and its Hierarchy of Ritual* (Cambridge, U.K.: University of Cambridge, 1992), pp. 41–68.

9 David Gellner, "Buddhist Monks or Kinsmen of the Buddha? Reflections on the Titles Traditionally used by Śākyas in the Kathmandu Valley," *Kailash* 15, nos. 1–2 (1989): 5–20.

10 John Locke, *Karunamaya* (Kathmandu: Sahayogi Press, 1980), pp. 418–43.

11 Darasa Nevami, *An Autobiography of the Late Buddhist Yogi Mahapragyan* (Kathmandu, 1986).

12 Ria Kloppenborg, "Theravāda Buddhism in Nepal," *Kailash* 5 (1977): 301–21.

13 Heinz Bechert and J. U. Hartmann, "Observations on the Reform of Buddhism in Nepal," *Journal of the Nepal Research Center* 8 (1988): 1–28.

14 Kloppenborg, "Theravāda Buddhism in Nepal."

15 *The Buddhist* 37, no. 1 (1966): 26f.

16 Ramesh Chandra Tewari, "The Sociocultural Aspects of Theravāda Buddhism in Nepal," *Journal of the International Association of Buddhist Studies* 6, no. 2 (1983): 67–93.

17 Figures quoted by Gellner, *Monk, Householder and Tantric Priest*, p. 322.

18 In contrast to the rudderless, often fractious order of monks. Laura Kunreuther, "Newar Traditions in a Changing Culture," in *International Seminar on the Anthropology of Nepal: Peoples, Problems, and Processes*, ed. Michael Allen, (Kathmandu, 1994), pp. 338–48.

19 *Snehi Chora*, translated from Burmese into Newari by Jñanapūrṇika Bhante (Kathmandu, 1967).

20 In the late 1970s, 38.4% of Nepalese monks and 42.6% of Nepalese nuns were Śākyas. See Tewari, "The Sociocultural Aspects of Theravāda Buddhism in Nepal." Today, while the percentage of monks who are Śākyas has declined, the proportion of Śākya nuns has remained steady. Theravāda has also attracted less prominent, traditionally Buddhist groups such as the Urāys (merchant caste) and Jyāpus (farming caste).

21 As of this writing, three other Nepalese nuns have received the Dharmācārya certificate, but only one Nepalese monk.

CHAPTER THREE

Unity and Diversity Among Buddhist Nuns in Sri Lanka

Nirmala S. Salgado

In this article, I investigate the diversity among *dasasilmātās* ("ten-precept mothers," or nuns), with a view to assessing the options open to women who choose the renunciant life in Sri Lanka.[1] First, I explore the varieties of female ascetic experience found among *dasasilmātās*. Second, I document a recent attempt to organize and establish the *bhikkhunī* ordination among Theravāda Buddhist women from Sri Lanka. Third, I discuss the diversity of ordinations and religious practices found among female Buddhist renunciants in Sri Lanka today and investigate some unifying trends. The discussion is intended to demonstrate some of the pitfalls as well as the advantages that diversity presents.

Ten-Precept Mothers in Sri Lanka: Encounters with Diversity

Unlike Buddhist monks, potential female renunciants in Sri Lanka face few eligibility requirements. One consequence of this is that *silmātās* demonstrate vastly different levels of educational attainment as well as a variety of emphases in religious belief and practice. This has been perceived as a problem by government officials and concerned lay supporters, as well as some *silmātās*. In fact, in the mid-eighties, the Sri Lankan government began to make attempts to remedy the situation, using government and other funds to provide for a uniform education for the *silmātās* throughout the country, comparable to that of monks.[2] On a smaller scale, organizations such as Śākyadhitā and Sarvodaya have held separate training sessions for *silmātās* in and around Colombo.

The diversity in educational training and background has been perceived as problematic for at least two reasons. First, renunciants with a poor education are unable to win as much respect from laypeople as those who are well-versed in the Buddhist texts. Consequently, the *silmātās* seldom receive adequate donations (*dāna*) on which to live and are generally not recognized as community leaders. Additionally, *silmātās* with little or no education inadvertently lead members of the public to generally denigrate all *silmātās*. Often the *silmātās* are accused of abusing the symbolism of the saffron robes and their ascetic status in pursuit of lucre.[3] A second problem, which concerns government officials in particular, appears to arise from the diversity in background, educational attainment, and religious and social practice among the *silmātās*. Such diversity defies attempts to regulate the religious training of the *silmātās*. Moreover, it can result in *silmātās* of different hermitages criticizing one another's practice.

The diversity among *silmātās* is not without advantages. For example, the relative absence of uniform stipulations for women entering the renunciant life means that no woman is excluded from pursuing such a vocation. Most significantly, in a traditional society where women's main roles seem to be as wives and mothers, the alternative of being a religious "mother" remains accessible to all. Specifically, an aspiring *silmātā* need not come from an elite or educated background.[4] In fact, a woman from a less educated background might arguably enjoy an enhanced status through her chosen professional celibacy and poverty, whereas the reverse could be true for a Sri Lankan woman of more elite origins.

Diversity of Age and Location

It is generally estimated that there are about 3,000 *silmātās* in Sri Lanka today. According to government data (from the early 1980s) that was available at the time of this writing, out of 620 *silmātās* who responded to questionnaires, 110 were known to have passed "O" Level examinations.[5] The data also indicates that the largest number of *silmātās* ordained in a specific age group were ordained between the ages of 16 and 20 (130 out of a sample of 620),[6] and that out of 620, 323 indicated that they were unmarried at the time of their ordination.[7] While these figures do not account for all the *silmātās*, they give some sense of the diversity of educational backgrounds, ages, and previous marital status of the *silmātās* in Sri Lanka.

Typical hermitages of five to ten *silmātās* often reflect a wide range of ages among the nuns. Nuns originally from urban or rural backgrounds may be attached to hermitages that are either in or near urban centers or in more remote areas, regardless of their own origins. For this reason, it is difficult to determine whether a given *silmātā* can be classified as "urban" or "rural," since junior *silmātās* at a hermitage seldom stay at one hermitage for life. They often relocate, either in pursuit of a different type of religious training, for personal or health reasons, or possibly to establish their own hermitages later in life. In this context, *silmātās* benefit from having a variety of alternatives from which to choose, including the option of living under the tutelage of a head nun of their preference. Such alternatives, in turn, imply the freedom to choose between emphases in religious training (e.g., meditation or scholarship) and to relocate.

Diversity in Ordination: Ten-Precept Mothers and *Bhikkhunīs*

Dasasilmātās can be ordained in at least four different ways. First, there is ordination in the ten lay precepts (*gihi*) under the tutelage of a senior *silmātā*, the most common type of ten-precept ordination in Sri Lanka today. Second, *silmātās* may be ordained in the monastic ten precepts (*pävidi*), under the tutelage of a senior *silmātā*. This ordination is similar to the previous one in that it, too, involves a senior *silmātā* who essentially acts as a preceptor to the ordinand. However, this ordination, unlike the previous one, involves the affirmation of the ten precepts as one "rule," such that breaking any one precept incurs a violation of all ten. Technically, this ordination enjoys the highest religious status insofar as it symbolizes a stricter degree of renunciation. It is considered equivalent to the *sāmaṇera* or *sāmaṇerī* (novice) ordination. According to the estimate of one *silmātā* who has this type of ordination, no more than ten percent of *silmātās* in the country are ordained in this way. The first two types of ordination may also be conferred by both *bhikkhus* and *silmātās* together. Third, there is the ordination in the lay ten precepts under the tutelage of a Buddhist monk. This type of ordination, technically a "lay" ordination from the standpoint of the presiding monk, seems to be less common than the other two. It is essentially a lay ordination. A *silmātā* who undergoes this type of ordination would reaffirm it every two weeks by reciting the ten precepts after a monk, not unlike the manner of a layperson reciting the five precepts. Finally, some *silmātās* are self-ordained. Self-ordination is the least common of ordinations. I have encountered only two such cases since I began my field work in the mid-eighties.

Despite the technical differences in these types of ordination, laypeople characteristically do not discriminate among *silmātās* on the basis of ordination. In the eyes of most laypersons, one shaven-headed saffron-robed woman resembles another. In practice, however, the different types of ordination allow the *silmātās* different degrees of latitude in pursuing their vocations. Ultimately, at the present time it is probably the character of the individual *silmātā*, rather than the ritual of ordination, that determines her path and how she is received by the public. The female renunciant depends on alms donated by laypeople, and the manner of her ordination matters less than the fact of her asceticism. However, on the theoretical level, the ordination that sets the *silmātās* apart from the unordained laity is the monastic (*pävidi*) ordination alone. Laypeople often take the same ten lay (*gihi*) precepts as the *silmātās*, albeit on a temporary basis and without shaving their heads or donning the saffron robe. The importance of characterizing the ordination and status of the *silmātā* as lay (*gihi*) or renunciant (*pävidi*) has been a matter of debate in Sri Lanka for some time and has taken on a new dimension of meaning in the context of recent attempts to establish the higher or full ordination (*upasampadā*) for Theravādā Buddhist women in Sri Lanka.

The *silmātās* I interviewed in the mid-eighties were acutely aware that the laity discriminated between them and the fully ordained monks. The prospect of ever achieving full ordination seemed either irrelevant or unrealistic to the women I talked with at that time. The ensuing decade has witnessed significant developments both in the governmental and non-governmental support of the *silmātās*, as well as in the level of interest of the *silmātās* themselves. Today, the higher ordination (*upasampadā*) has become a realistic alternative. More *silmātās* than before seek the *upasampadā*, although some still remain skeptical and unsure as to how attaining the new status, *ipso facto*, might fulfill their daily needs, such as food and shelter. In the past decade, the *upasampadā* has been conferred on Theravāda Buddhist women from Sri Lanka on several occasions. These include the women ordained at Hsi-Lai Temple in Los Angeles in 1988 and 1997; those ordained in Sārnāth, India, in December 1996; and those ordained in Bodhgaya, India, in February 1998. Most recently, and for the first time ever, in March 1998, the *upasampadā* was conferred on Buddhist women from Sri Lanka, in Sri Lanka itself. While it may be premature to fully assess the impact of these ordinations at this time, it may be accurate to suggest that Buddhist monastics are pursuing a common agenda in introducing the *upasampadā* to Theravāda Buddhist women.

In August 1997, I visited a Sri Lankan forest hermitage where *silmātās* were undergoing training for the *upasampadā*. Rangiri Dambulla Arāṇya Senāsanaya, located near the village of Kalundäwa, was previously used as a meditation retreat. The *silmātās* here were among the women who received the *upasampadā* in Bodhgaya and Dambulla in 1998. The remainder of this essay will focus on my observations of this *bhikkhunī* training program.

Creating Unity: Initial Preparations for a Theravāda Bhikkhunī Sangha[8]

News of the ordination of ten Sri Lankan women in Sārnāth in December 1996 met with mixed reactions in Sri Lanka. Reflections on this ordination led concerned activists to reassess the establishment of *bhikkhunī* ordination within Sri Lanka. In February 1997, two months after the ordination ceremony in Sārnāth, India, *silmātās* from throughout the country,[9] supported by interested monks and laypeople, staged a meeting in Kurunegala, Sri Lanka. Among these supporters were: Inamaluwe Sumangala Himi, the head monk of the Rangiri Dambulla Rāja Mahā Vihāra; Raja Dharmapala, an ex-monk of the Dharmavedi organization; and *silmātās* who had been active in the government-sponsored *Samastha Lanka Silmātā Jātika Maṇḍalaya*, or "All Lanka Silmātā Organization." At the convocation they discussed the possibility of educating and preparing select *silmātās* for full ordination.

In March 1997, the Shrī Lanka Bhikkhunī Shāsanābhivriddhi Samvidānaya (The Sri Lanka Bhikkhunī Re-Awakening Organization, or SLBRO), a recently formed organization headed by Sumangala, Dharmapala, and leading *silmātās*, sent out letters to *silmātās* throughout the country. These letters outlined plans to provide an education for *silmātās* to better prepare them for taking the *upasampadā* and sought applicants for the proposed training program.[10] The selection committee formed to review the applications included the senior *silmātās*, Sumangala, and Dharmapala. From among the interviewees,[11] the committee selected 31 *silmātās*, 26 of whom eventually entered the training program and took up residence at the Senāsanaya in the forest. There were several criteria used in the selection process. First, *silmātās* had to be between 30 and 55 years of age. Second, they had to have been ordained for at least five years. Further, *silmātās* were expected to have a standard of general education that included at least eight Ordinary Level passes, and either three Advanced Level passes or qualifications in the government recognized *pracīna* examinations usually taken by monks. Finally, candidates had to show evidence of training in the Dhamma and meditation with respected teachers and were required to present two character certificates. Interviews of candidates, which were generally conducted for a minimum of 35 minutes, centered on assessing their knowledge of Theravāda Buddhist texts. On July 12, 1997, 26 trainees were given the *sāmaṇerī* ordination. Their training program began that month.

The buildings in the forest had originally been used by meditators associated with the Kanduboḍa Meditation Center near Colombo. However, the buildings had fallen into disrepair and were eventually appropriated by Inamaluwe Sumangala Himi. In 1997, Sumangala, a founding member of the SLBRO and keen supporter of the *bhikkhunī sāsana*, allowed the use of the buildings for training the *sāmaṇerīs*. The spacious training center included several individual *kuṭis* (huts) as well as a large hall with several small rooms, a *dāna shālāwa* or hall for taking meals, a building that serves as an administrative office, and another building that houses visiting laypeople who prepare and offer *dāna* (food as alms). At the time of my visit in August 1997, the *sāmaṇerīs* bathed in a nearby river. Tap water was available for other purposes, but there was no electricity. Classes for the *sāmaṇerīs* were held in a temporary one-room thatched construction, located close to a seated Buddha image.

The Training Program

The schedule below gives some sense of a typical weekday at the *sāmaṇerī* training program:

4:30 am Wake-up and wash
5:00 am Prayer and meditation

6:00 am	Routine duties (sweeping, cleaning)
7:30 am	Morning *dāna* (breakfast)
8:00 am	Break
9:00 am	Morning classes
11:00 am	Noon *dāna* (lunch)
11:30 am	Break (bathing, washing robes, homework)
2:30 pm	Afternoon classes
5:00 pm	Prayers, recitation of verses (*pirit*), meditation
7:00 pm	Free time for homework
10:00 pm	Bedtime

I attended a full day of classes during my visit to the training center in August 1997. A learned *bhikkhu* who visited the center each month to discuss the Pāli *suttas* with the *sāmaṇerīs* led the morning session. Sitting on a mat on the floor, on the same level as the *sāmaṇerīs*,[12] the monk conducted a discussion focusing on the exposition of the *Satipaṭṭhāna Sutta*. The *silmātās*, who did not possess copies of the text (because texts and copies of *suttas* are expensive), took dictation from the monk in both Pāli and Sinhala. The *bhikkhu*'s use of gender-inclusive language in his Sinhala explanation of the Pāli text prompted me to question him after class. He confirmed that even though the Pāli *sutta* only used the male form (*so*) in referring to the meditator, he considered it more appropriate to use both the male and female pronouns in the Sinhala. In particular, the *bhikkhu*, speaking from his personal experience, impressed upon the *sāmaṇerīs* the necessity of giving highest authority to the Buddha's teachings rather than to meditation instructors. Reminding them that no one taught Siddhārtha Gautama to attain enlightenment, he said that the *silmātās* themselves should not unquestioningly follow authority. In particular, he advised caution in accepting the authority structures of meditation centers, given that the meditation teacher was not necessarily an arahant.[13]

In the first afternoon session, the *bhikkhu* focused on the exposition of the *Vāseṭṭha Sutta* and led a discussion of the irrelevance of caste (*jāti*) in Buddhism. As at the earlier session, the *sāmaṇerīs* took dictation on the Pāli text and also wrote notes on the *bhikkhu*'s interpretation of it. Dharmapala conducted the second afternoon session, which centered on a reading of the *Bhikkhunī Khaṇḍaka* of the *Vinaya Piṭaka* (the Bhikkhunī Section of the *Book of Monastic Discipline*). This led to a critical analysis of the textual presentation of the *upasampadā* ritual of the *bhikkhunīs* during the time of the Buddha. A discussion concerning the procedures for the imminent ordination of the *sāmaṇerīs* ensued. At the end of the day I left the class session impressed not only by the depth of analysis of texts provided by the teachers, but also by the manner in which they had prompted open discussion on social issues pertaining to caste and gender, as well as the ease with which they related this information within the immediate context of the *sāmaṇerīs* who were preparing for full ordination. The last class held that day (which I did not attend) was an English language class, taught by a retired school teacher. The teachers training the *sāmaṇerīs* were all unpaid, supportive volunteers. It was not monetary concerns but rather dedication to the goals of the center that motivated them to assist the *sāmaṇerīs*.

The Curriculum and Arrangements for Alms

I was given a copy of the six-month curriculum that the *sāmaṇerīs* had just begun to implement. The curriculum included texts on the Dhamma (Buddhist teachings); meditation (perceived by the teachers as the cornerstone of Buddhist behavior); social issues pertaining to gender, caste, and class; and the disciplinary rules of nuns, including some comparisons with the Bhikkhu Vinaya. Specific topics included the *Bhikkhunī Pāṭimokka*, selections from the *Pirit Pota*, the *Cullavaggapāli*, selections from the *Dhammapada*, and training the *bhikkhunīs* for higher ordination. Additional texts included in the curriculum were the *Dhammacakkapavattana Sutta, Anattalakkhaṇa Sutta, Sāmaññaphala Sutta, Ariyapariyesanā Sutta, Alagaddūpama Sutta, Vāseṭṭha Sutta, Satipaṭṭhāna Sutta, Cakkavattisīhanāda Sutta*, and *Kūṭadanta Sutta*. A basic awareness of the history of the *sāsana* (the Buddha's teachings) included an overview of Buddhist philosophy and religious practice; the beginnings of Buddhism in India; the Buddhist councils and the spread of Buddhism under King Asoka; the beginnings of the *bhikkhunī sāsana*; the heritage of the *bhikkhunīs* and their service to the world; the establishment, spread, and decline of the *bhikkhunī sāsana* in Sri Lanka; the possibility of re-establishing the *bhikkhunī sāsana*; and the controversy pertaining to the eight special rules (*garudhammas*). One aspect of the history of Buddhism was the history of the first *dasasilmātās* in Sri Lanka and the life story of Sudharmachari Mäniyan, who is credited as initiating the ten-precept ordination in the country. Supplementary studies planned for the future include English and discussions on socially active ("engaged") Buddhism. Upon completion of the six-month training, the *sāmaṇerīs* were to undergo a written test and an assessment of their observance of disciplinary rules. The *upasampadā* was to be conferred on those who met the required standards.

The combination of *sāmaṇerīs* at the training center and those with their own associations and lay supporters from their home hermitages seemed to promise long-term advantages. Among the leading *sāmaṇerīs* of the SLBRO were women who had been active in the SMJM. They brought leadership and administrative skills with them, and were accepted as national leaders among *silmātās* in Sri Lanka. Additionally, individual *sāmaṇerīs* were careful to maintain their grassroots contacts and support. During the weekends the *sāmaṇerīs* would often visit their home hermitages and attend to matters that normally occupied them there. Several were head nuns of their own hermitages and were still responsible for their everyday functioning. Together the *sāmaṇerīs* represented a large, national constituency.

The daily alms for residents at the Senāsanaya were offered by lay donors who came from regions where the *sāmaṇerīs* have their hermitages. These lay donors, many of whom had traveled long distances, brought sufficient *dāna* for all the trainees, the teachers, and the *bhikkhus* at the center. They usually stayed overnight, then after cooking and serving *dāna* the following day, returned to their home villages. Apart from ensuring an adequate supply of provisions for those at the center, this arrangement also effectively encouraged the lay donors to support the *bhikkhunī* cause in Sri Lanka. It also provided a way of educating the lay donors (and indirectly their home villages) regarding the plans for the imminent *upasampadā* of *sāmaṇerīs*.

Plans for the Ordination

When I visited in August 1997, no specific date for the *upasampadā* had yet been set, although the aim was to carry out the ordination at the end of 1997 or early in 1998. I was shown the ritual boundary (*sīmā*) for the ordination ceremony; it was a vague circle of stones emerging from an area overgrown with grass and weeds. Monks, *sāmaṇerīs*, and laypeople I talked with believed the majority of Sri Lankan monks would sanction the higher ordination of women, but the *bhikkhus* who opposed the *bhikkhunī* ordination were more publicly vocal than those who supported it. Nevertheless, Inamaluwe Sumangala assured me that the *upasampadā* of the *bhikkhunīs* would have the support of all the *nikāyas*, and thus would avoid the sectarian divisions represented by the *nikāyas*.

Inamaluwe Sumangala has been a controversial figure since the mid-eighties, when he began to confer the *upasampadā* upon members of castes that had hitherto been excluded from ordination in the Asgiriya Chapter of the Siam Nikāya (sect).[14] Subsequently he established the Dambulla Chapter, without seeking the approval of the Mahānāyaka (Head Monk) of the Asgiriya Chapter. Although Sumangala has not breached any civil law, leading Asgiriya monks with whom I discussed this dispute in 1997 argued that he had committed a breach of Vinaya rules (monastic discipline) by independently conferring the *upasampadā* on *bhikkhus* in Dambulla. The monks from Asgiriya, together with other leading monks, have published letters to the editors of major newspapers protesting the conferring of the *upasampadā* on women.[15]

Sumangala explained that according to the Vinaya, a minimum of five *bhikkhus* needed to be present at the ordination of *bhikkhunīs*. He said that at least a hundred fully ordained *bhikkhus* from the three main *nikāyas* were expected to be present at the *upasampadā* ceremony that was being planned for the *sāmaṇerīs*. According to him, about ten (out of a total of

40) leading monks (Mahānāyakas) in the country had already pledged their support for the reestablishment of the *upasampadā* for women.

I asked Sumangala about the section of the rite where inquiries are made concerning the sexual identity of the ordinands. Senior *bhikkhunīs* are supposed to ask the following questions during the ordination ceremony: "You are not without sexual characteristics? You are not an hermaphrodite? Are you a human being? Are you a woman? Are you a free woman?"[16] These questions have been a major source of contention, because they indicate the necessity for a dual ordination, that is, an ordination conducted by both *bhikkhus* and *bhikkhunīs*. Sumangala responded that two senior *sāmaṇerīs* chosen from among the current trainees would take the place of *bhikkhunīs* for this purpose. The SLBRO legitimizes its case for *bhikkhus* alone conferring the *upasampadā* on women, without the presence of *bhikkhunīs* based on the authority of a Vinaya passage from the first ordination of Buddhist women which, according to Sumangala, includes the statement, "Monks, I allow nuns to be ordained by monks." This, he maintains, clearly gives *bhikkhus* the right to ordain women without the presence of participating *bhikkhunīs*.[17]

Benefits of the Ordination

Sumangala argued that a *bhikkhunī* ordination could not truly take root in Sri Lanka until an indigenous ordination had been performed there. He recalled a textual passage in which a similar statement was made by Bhikkhu Mahinda, King Aśoka's son, shortly before he ordained the first *bhikkhus* in Sri Lanka in the third century B.C.E.[18] According to Sumangala, the main benefit gained from the *upasampadā* for women would be their "necessary acceptance" (*avashya piligānīmak*) by society, which would then give them a "proper status" (*niyama tattvayak*). He believes that while the *silmātās* have to face many problems and that these cannot all be solved by the SLBRO, the granting of a "befitting status" (*nisi thäna*) to women in the *sāsana* would help resolve other problems. Leading *sāmaṇerīs* I interviewed at the training center corroborated this perspective.

Discussing the training program and the changes which the *upasampadā* might bring to Buddhist women, Dharmapala expressed an enthusiasm for cultivating among the trainees a socially "Engaged Buddhism,"[19] and "buddhism with a small b," rather than a Buddhism associated with party politics, or "Buddhism with a big B," as he described it. Dharmapala, who himself had been influenced by writers such as Thich Nhat Hanh, planned to introduce outside speakers who would explain this particular interpretation of Buddhism. His perspective was clearly reflected in the class sessions that he conducted, as well as in the overall six-month curriculum of the *sāmaṇerīs*. Yet his enthusiasm was tempered by concerns that, because of the newly gained recognition the *bhikkhunīs* had achieved, the lay donors might "spoil" them. In particular, he was anxious that some *bhikkhunīs* might abuse or flaunt their new status to attract material gain. He feared that the *bhikkhunīs* might become like some monks who enjoyed owning televisions and cars, possessions associated with wealth and status, and for which the monks are often criticized. To forestall such a possibility, Dharmapala spoke to me of a "Code of Conduct" that was being prepared. Among other things, this code stipulated that the *bhikkhunīs* would be barred from accepting a salaried job and would be expected to appeal to the SLBRO in cases of conflict, rather than directly to the law courts. A few months after my August 1997 visit, I learned that (for reasons that I have not yet been able to fully investigate) Dharmapala was no longer associated with the center. It is possible that the "Code of Conduct," a primary concern of his, was never finalized.

Although I was unaware of it when I visited the forest hermitage in 1997, ten *sāmaṇerīs* from the training center were among the women chosen for the dual ordination by Taiwanese *bhikkhus* and *bhikkhunīs* in Bodhgaya in February 1998.[20] Clearly, there had been a change of plans since my conversation with monastic and lay informants from the center the previous year. In March 1998, the recently ordained Sri Lankan *bhikkhunīs* participated in the *upasampadā* ceremony with other *sāmaṇerīs* from the center, in Sri Lanka itself.[21]

Although the two most recent ordinations in India have been conducted with the assistance of *bhikkhunīs* from different Mahāyāna countries, the organizers of these ordinations do not appear to compete or vie for status. The Sri Lankan women ordained in Sārnāth were ordained by Korean monastics, while those ordained fourteen months later in Bodhgaya were ordained by Taiwanese monastics. Both the Sārnāth and Bodhgaya ordinations were conducted in association with the Sri Lankan *bhikkhus* from the Maha Bodhi Society of India, working together with *bhikkhus* and *bhikkhunīs* from other countries. Hence, it might be accurate to assume that the various higher ordinations for Sri Lankan women, in fact, are evidence of unifying goals and cooperative efforts. It is noteworthy that the same Sri Lankan Buddhist monks have been involved in organizing the different *upasampadā* ceremonies.[22] These monks are connected with branches of the Maha Bodhi Society. In particular, Sumangala's decision to coordinate the Rangiri Dambulla ordination with the Bodhgaya ordination clearly indicates that at this point, cooperation, rather than divisiveness, has prevailed in the attempt to bring the *upasampadā* to Theravāda Buddhist women of Sri Lanka.

Conclusion

Recent attempts to confer full ordination on Theravāda women are evidence of common goals and unifying ideals. As yet it may be too early to assess the significance of these higher ordination ceremonies for female renunciants in Sri

Lanka as a whole. The focus on education and training women as *bhikkhunīs*, and the fact that *upasampadā* is now being made available to women, might indeed, as Sumangala suggests, give the ordained women a "necessary acceptance" and "befitting status" in society. What exactly this implies for the future of Buddhist women in Sri Lanka has yet to be determined. It is possible that the attempt at unifying women through *bhikkhunī* ordination could result in a trend towards Procrustean conformity which might compromise the freedom that the *silmātās* of diverse backgrounds have, until now, enjoyed. However, if the *silmātās* continue to co-exist with the emerging Theravāda *bhikkhunīs*, the number of alternatives from which potential female renunciants may choose will increase. An underlying question remains: in actuality, will the higher status that the Theravāda *bhikkhunīs* now seem to enjoy lead to more, or perhaps less, religious and social power for female renunciants? To what extent will implementing the higher ordination really make a difference? Perhaps the answer to these questions will be found in the willingness and ability of potential female renunciants as a whole to become *bhikkhunīs* rather than *silmātās*.

Notes

1 Part of the research for this paper dates back to my work in 1984, which was conducted under the auspices of the International Center for Ethnic Studies, Colombo. I am also grateful to a 1995 Augustana College Research Grant and for grants from the American Academy of Religion (1996) and the Augustana College Research Foundation (1997) that enabled me to conduct more recent research for this paper. I owe special thanks to Indira Salgado for helping organize my stay in Sri Lanka and Paul Westman for his comments on drafts of this paper.

2 For further information on this see N. Salgado, "Ways of Knowing and Transmitting Religious Knowledge: Case Studies of Theravāda Buddhist Nuns," *Journal of the International Association of Buddhist Studies* 19, no. 1 (1996).

3 This bias was evident to me when I began research on *silmātās* in the early 80s and I informed a university professor in Sri Lanka of my interests. She looked at me aghast and responded "Why do you want to study them? They are just beggars!"

4 Bartholomeusz argues that the earliest *silmātās* in Sri Lanka were drawn from the upper classes. See Tessa Bartholomeusz, *Women Under The Bō Tree* (Cambridge: Cambridge University Press, 1994), p. 107. While it is possible that today *silmātās* who found hermitages often come from privileged backgrounds, most junior *silmātās* whom I have interviewed come from humbler origins.

5 Reports of the Department of Buddhist Affairs in the Cultural Ministry (1982–1983), cited in K. L. M. B. Thamel, "A Study of the Dasa-Sil Māniyo (Consecrated Women) in the Buddhist Society of Sri Lanka" (M.A. thesis, University of the Philippines, 1983), p. 86. The figures indicate that 161 *silmātās* gave no indication of educational status.

6 Reports of the Department of Buddhist Affairs in the Cultural Ministry (1982–1983) cited in Thamel, p. 83. The figures show that 47 *silmātās* gave no indication of their age at the time of ordination.

7 Reports of the Department of Buddhist Affairs in the Cultural Ministry (1982–1983), cited in Thamel, p. 77. The figures show that 129 *silmātās* gave no indication of their marital status before ordination.

8 Informants include key *dasasilmātās* as well as monks and laypeople whom I interviewed in July and August 1997.

9 I have been unable to ascertain the precise number of *silmātās* present at this meeting. One of my informants said that there were about 200 *silmātās* present, but another perhaps more reliable source estimated that there were only about 80 *silmātās* present.

10 Letter from the SLBRO dated March 10, 1997.

11 There seems to be some discrepancy concerning the number of *silmātās* who were selected for interviews. One informant on the selection committee mentioned that there was a total of 80, but another informant on the same committee mentioned that there were only about 50.

12 This monk is unusual. Despite the senior status he enjoys by virtue of having received the higher ordination, unlike some, he did not object to sitting on the same, symbolically equal level as the *silmātās*.

13 The SLBRO seems to recognize the authority of the Dhamma as superior to any other teacher, as a matter of policy. An informational flyer concerning the organization that was prepared for laypeople in August 1997 states that the teacher of the organization is "no other than the Dhamma."

14 For an excellent analysis of a profile of this leading monk and his activities, see A. Abeyesekera, "Politics of Higher Ordination, Buddhist Monastic Identity and Leadership at the Dambulla Temple in Sri Lanka: The Case of Inamaluwe Sumangala," *Journal of the International Association of Buddhist Studies*, forthcoming.

15 I discussed the controversy concerning the Dambulla Chapter both with Sumangala and with leading monks from the Asgiriya Chapter. Both parties agreed that there was a "difference of opinion" concerning the right of Sumangala to establish a separate chapter, as well as the validity of a chapter thus established. This difference of opinion could lead to the Asgiriya Chapter's official rejection of the validity of the *bhikkhunī* ordination.

16 I.B. Horner, trans., *Book of the Discipline, Part 5,* Sacred Books of the Buddhists, Vol. XX (Oxford: Pali Text Society, 1992), p. 375.

17 Ibid. In the course of my conversations with them, other informants associated with the center also made reference to this passage.

18 For a further discussion of this passage, see E. W. Adikaram, *Early History of Buddhism in Ceylon* (Dehiwala: Buddhist Cultural Center, 1994), p. 56.

19 For a further discussion of Engaged Buddhism, see Christopher S. Queen and Sallie B. King, eds., *Engaged Buddhism: Buddhist Liberation Movements in Asia* (Albany, N.Y.: State University of New York Press, 1996).

20 Interview with Bhikkhunī Chueh Men, January 1, 1998.

21 See "Meheṇi sasanaya yali Sirilak pihita vū vagayi," *Dinamina* 12 (March 1998).

22 For example, Vipulasāra was associated with the ordinations at Sārnāth and Rangiri Dambulla, and Piyananda with the ordinations held in Los Angeles in 1988 and 1997, in Sārnāth in 1996, and the Rangiri Dambulla ordination in 1998. Also see Bartholomeusz, *Women Under the Bō Tree*, p. 187; "Unity is the Greatest Happiness," [Sri Lanka] *Daily News*, December, 19, 1996; and "Meheṇi sasanaya yali Sirilak pihita vū vagayi," *Dinamina*, March 12, 1998.

CHAPTER FOUR

Factions and Fortitude

Buddhist Women in Bangladesh

Karma Lekshe Tsomo

There has been little recent research on the history of Buddhism in Bengal and the area we now call Bangladesh; women there, in particular, have received little or no attention. I address this lack by introducing the Buddhist women of Bangladesh, presenting selected portraits of their lives, exploring the formation of their cultural identity as Buddhists and members of distinctive ethnic groups, and speculating on the future of women in Bangladesh. My research is based upon written sources, conversations and correspondence with members of the Bangladesh Buddhist Women's Association (Bangladesh Bouddha Mahila Samiti) since 1986, and observations gathered during a three-week stay in Bangladesh in 1998. This narrative examines the relationship between gender and religious identity among Bangladeshi Buddhist women, and their strategies for coping with cultural endangerment and rapid social change.

My travels in Bangladesh took me to homes and temples in cities, villages, and rural "tribal" areas. As a fellow Buddhist practitioner, I had the opportunity to closely observe the role that Buddhist beliefs and practices play in ordinary women's lives and also the variety of roles that Buddhist women play in society. As a *bhikkhunī* (fully ordained nun) in a country with few nuns and no lineage of full ordination for women, I had a unique opportunity not only to observe monastic practice of monks in Bangladesh, but also to assess the prospects for developing an order of nuns there in the future.

Based on my experiences in Buddhist cultures over the past 30 years, I approached my research with the assumption that an order of Buddhist nuns is beneficial for preserving Buddhist practice and cultural identity. I reasoned that capable leadership is essential to preserving traditional Buddhist cultures and, because monastic life provides an environment for intensive education and training, it is valuable for nurturing capable Buddhist leaders. Men in Buddhist cultures currently have many opportunities for religious education and training, but they also have many options in the worldly sphere, including secular education, business opportunities, international travel, and professional advancement. As a result, men who become monks do not always maintain a lifelong commitment to monastic life and do not always fully utilize their religious training. Women in Buddhist cultures typically do maintain their lifelong commitment to celibacy and monastic practice. When their leadership potential is tapped and they have opportunities for education and training, they can become effective teachers, translators, and organizers of Buddhist activities. It follows that investments in the monastic training of women are well-placed. Therefore an order of nuns is an asset to a group or country wishing to preserve Buddhist culture. I was interested to see whether this thesis would apply in the case of minority Buddhist cultures in Bangladesh.

Journey to Bangladesh

My first contact with Bangladeshi Buddhist women occurred when officers and members of the Bangladesh Buddhist Women's Association attended the first Śākyadhitā International Conference on Buddhist Women in Bodhgaya, India, in February 1987. Since those meetings, I have renewed acquaintance with these women at subsequent Śākyadhitā conferences and through correspondence. In 1987, they established a national branch of Śākyadhitā in Chittagong and since that time have contributed ideas and essays to Śākyadhitā publications. In hopes of learning more about their lives and practice I booked a ticket to Dhaka.

The three-week period between the fifth Śākyadhitā Conference in Cambodia and the International Full Ordination Ceremony in Bodhgaya in February 1998 was a perfect opportunity to undertake the trip. The day I left Bangkok, a group of Bangladeshi student monks at Wat Mahathat enthusiastically encouraged me to visit their country and stay at their home monastery, Dhammarajika Vihar, in Kamalapur, Dhaka. Over the years, the monastery has housed, educated, and trained thousands of Buddhist children and monks. Although the monastery has now fallen on difficult times, staying there gave me an opportunity to meet monks and students from not only the majority Barua community, and also from the Chakma, Marma, and other tribal communities.

Traveling out from Dhaka, I visited numerous homes, temples, and Buddhist archeological sites in and around Comilla, Tangail, Chittagong, Cox's Bazaar, and Bandarban. In addition to large temples such as Nobopandit Vihar and Bodha Vihar in Chittagong, I visited smaller temples in the villages, many staffed by active young monks. As an American *bhikkhunī* in Tibetan robes, I was something of an anomaly, but was nevertheless welcomed as a fellow Buddhist wherever I went. In my research, I was ably assisted by Bhikkhu Vivekananda, a Marma resident at Kamalapur Monastery and graduate student in social work at Dhaka University who was fluent in Marma, Bangla, Chakma, Rakkhaine (Burmese), English, and Japanese. Every day we met dozens of Buddhist women and men who spoke candidly about their lives, problems, and hopes for the future. It was a unique opportunity to learn more about their lives and hear stories of their cultural survival.

The Buddhist Heritage of Bangladesh

Between the fourth and eleventh centuries, Bangladesh was a powerful and thoroughly Buddhist land where thousands of monks in hundreds of monasteries studied the Dharma, taught, meditated, and gained realization.[1] Historical sites abound. In the north is Mahāsthan, one of several sites where, according to believers, the Buddha himself walked.[2] Other ruins of the Pāla Dynasty of Bengal (circa 750–1150 C.E.), such as Paharpur and Mainamati, dot the countryside, and only a tiny fraction of those that exist have been unearthed. The Mahāyāna teachings flourished throughout the land, producing such luminaries as Atiśa Dīpaṅkara Śrījñāna, the revered scholar-practitioner who initiated a revival of Buddhism in 11th-century Tibet. Reading the accounts of Chinese pilgrims[3] and observing the surviving ruins of ancient cities, it is easy to imagine the power and prosperity of these ancient kingdoms – part of a vast Buddhist cultural diaspora extending east from Magadha, where the Buddha achieved enlightenment. This Buddhist heritage is thought to have had a salutary effect on the people's national temperament; their non-martial nature was noted by the British as they attempted to fill the ranks of their armies.[4]

Many theories have been advanced to explain the inroads of Brahmanism and subsequent Muslim domination of Bangladesh. Aggressive conversion tactics, military conquest, proximity to ports where Muslim traders docked, promises of a blissful afterlife, and other theories have been advanced. Whatever the reasons, we know that for over 1200 years the people of Bengal were strongly influenced by Buddhist teachings and cultural norms. We also know that they strongly resisted the caste system and attempts to Sanskritize their language.[5] Although today Buddhists number less than one percent in a Muslim population of 120,000,000, there are more than 800 monks in 500 temples and *ārāmas* in the country. As a result of Arakanese influence, Buddhists in Bangladesh today follow the Theravāda tradition.

Buddhist Minorities in a Muslim Land

All Buddhist cultures in contemporary Bangladesh are cultures at risk. They are threatened not only by majority Muslim cultural domination and increasing Islamic fundamentalism, but also by secular influences, particularly consumer trends and the impact of Western culture via modern media. International sports, Hindi films, and Star TV (a tamer, South Asian version of MTV) beam daily into many homes among the country's 800,000 Buddhists. The images and values these programs convey do little to bolster Buddhist values or cultural identity. Women attempting to raise their children along traditional Buddhist lines are up against formidable competition.

The Buddhists of Bangladesh come from a broad range of ethnic and cultural backgrounds. The people distinguish themselves as belonging to either the Barua ("plains") Buddhist community or one of the tribal ("hilly") groups: Chakma, Marma, Tripura, Tongchengya, Mong, Cak, Kheang, Khumi, Murang, Moro, Lusai, Boam, Pangko, Banjogi, and so on. Although the origins of these diverse cultural identities are largely lost to us, historical records explain at least some of their background.

Physically, the Barua Buddhists resemble the peoples of the northern Indian plains from which their ancestors are said to have migrated. Most identify themselves as members of the Briji clan of the Licchavi people who immigrated from Vaiśālī, Magadha (now Bihār), as early as the time of the Buddha. According to their oral histories, these Briji migrants zigzagged along the paths in the hills of Assam, eventually settling in the plains around Chittagong with the help of local rulers.[6] The term "Barua," currently used as an ethnic designation as well as a surname by the majority,[7] is explained by the people themselves to derive from "bara," meaning "big, great," and "*ārya*," meaning "noble." Some believe that the title was applied to the migrants as they passed through Assam as a mark of respect, possibly associating them with the land of the Buddha's enlightenment. Barua Buddhists themselves are quite confident, even adamant, about this ancestral link with Magadha.

In appearance, Barua Buddhists are difficult to differentiate from the majority Muslim population in modern-day Bangladesh. Often the presence of women in their midst is the primary clue that they are Buddhists. Members of the Barua community have distinguished themselves in many fields: business, education, law, medicine, literature, and also on the battlefield, in the struggle for freedom from the British and more recently from Pakistan. Baruas are dominant in Buddhist activities in urban areas and have also dominated Bangladesh's Buddhist representation abroad, a point that has led to considerable controversy and resentment among other Buddhist groups.

Although both plains and hill tribe Buddhists belong to the Theravāda tradition, intermarriage is not considered desirable from either side. "We do not mix socially," is an oft-heard phrase. Although members of the hill tribes share certain characteristics and the cultural categories that distinguish them are not indelibly fixed, the sense of a shared identity among the hill tribes is a relatively recent phenomenon, developed primarily in response to attempts at domination from outside. Subtle ethnic tensions still exist among the groups, as they negotiate complex issues of cultural and economic survival in the face of massive in-migration, political disenfranchisement, social dislocation, and economic change. Buddhist women of all these groups, regardless of their ethnic identities, face similar challenges in their attempts to preserve traditional culture and promote Buddhist values among the youth. As their children become influenced by the popular media, it becomes increasingly difficult to interest them in visiting the temple rather than the sports field or cinema.

Prativa Mutsoody of Tangail

My first excursion outside Dhaka was to Tangail, a bustling town to the north. Soon after arriving at Dhammarajika Monastery, I traveled several hours by bus to Bharateswari Homes, a large girl's college in Tangail. There I met Ms. Prativa Mutsoody, a prominent Buddhist educator who taught at the Homes for decades and now serves as headmistress. After lunch, she told me her story.

In her youth, Prativa was a student leader at prestigious Dhaka University. When Mahatma Gandhi was assassinated, she and three close friends felt that, rather than tears and lamentation, the best way to express their grief was to follow the principles that the great being (*mahātma*) had taught. Therefore, the four young women made a lifelong pact to be vegetarians, abstain from taking an evening meal on Fridays, and devote themselves wholeheartedly to the benefit of society. Her friends eventually married and were not able to fulfill their aspirations, but Prativa has remained unmarried and vegetarian since 1949. She is highly respected, not only among the Buddhist community, but also by the members of other religious communities.

The personal shrine that Prativa keeps in her bedroom is neatly tended. In addition to pictures and a statue of Buddha Śākyamuni, she has arranged photographs of Sri Ramakrishna, Sri Aurobindo, and Swami Vivekananda. She finds this eclectic approach in keeping with the social and spiritual ideals of Mahatma Gandhi. She explained that on the full moon, new moon, and quarter moon days, she and Buddhist women living at the Homes gather to take the eight precepts.[8] The ritual serves to mark and maintain their spiritual companionship.

Prativa finds time for her religious devotions amid a busy professional schedule overseeing the educational development of 800 young women. The students in residence do not all come from Buddhist backgrounds; the majority are Muslim or Hindu. The Homes offers a secular curriculum of both primary and secondary education to both residents and day students, with classes in world religions and a choice of vegetarian or nonvegetarian meals. Bharateswari Homes is not a charity institution, but is financially self-supporting. The resident tuition of 7,000 takas per year makes Bharateswari Homes beyond the reach of ordinary families, but the school serves a valuable function in the community by providing girls and young women a solid academic curriculum, character education, and safety under Prativa's care. During our meeting at Prativa's home, an engineer from the Barua Buddhist community, a resident of Dhaka, arrived to confirm the admission of his nine-year-old daughter to the Homes. After he and his daughter paid their respects to Prativa in the traditional manner, bowing to the floor and touching both their hands to her feet, he expressed complete confidence that his daughter would be "100 percent safe" at the Homes. Similar declarations by officials of Agrasara Girl's College and Agrasara Orphanage, Buddhist institutions in Raozan ("Parents who admit their daughters here need have no fears for their safety"), implied that there are dangers to young women in other institutions.

Two teachers at Bharateswar Homes came to prepare lunch for my two monk companions and me before our meeting with Prativa. Because there were few Buddhists living in the area of Tangail, the opportunity to create merit by offering food to monastics was regarded as a joyous occasion. My companion *bhikkhus*, one Barua and one Marma, were seated on a raised platform in the place of honor (farthest from the door), while I was seated on a mat on the floor to the side. After the meal and the recitation of a short *sutta* by the monks, the women and children of the house and neighborhood gathered and, as often happened during my visit to Bangladesh, requested meditation instruction. After I gave them basic instructions on mindfulness of breathing (*ānāpānasati*), the women and children sat quietly in meditation for 20 minutes. It seemed as if they would have continued indefinitely had I not ended the meditation session.

Among the small crowd that gathered for meditation were two teachers from the Homes: Paisanu Marma, the daughter of a devout Marma Buddhist family, and Ananya Barua, an orphan who belonged to the "plains" Buddhist community. Although there had been no prior discussion of ordination, the two teachers suddenly declared, "Now we are convinced. We want to become nuns. Take us with you." Amused and somewhat taken aback, I asked how they had come to this decision. Ananya told me that, because she was an orphan, she was free to become a nun if she wished, without any hindrances from her family. Paisanu said that, because her family members are all devout Buddhists, she would not face any objections or obstacles in becoming a nun either. Referring to Paisanu, our host, Mr. M. K. Barua, engineer, commented, "She is very pious. She gives her entire salary to needy persons."

The two teachers discussed their aspirations to devote themselves wholeheartedly to Buddhist practice and regretted that there was nowhere they could go to become nuns. Since there is as yet no Buddhist studies program or training center available for women in Bangladesh, I suggested developing a daily study program of readings on Buddhism and short morning and evening meditation sessions each day. I expressed the hope that eventually Buddhist institutes for women could be developed both in India and Bangladesh. Everyone in the room agreed that if opportunities were available, many women would want to become nuns, and if pious, educated women like these two teachers became nuns, it would be an excellent beginning for a *bhikkhunī* order in Bangladesh.

Mira Barua of Ukhiya

The following week I traveled to Cox's Bazaar, a seaside resort at the southwest tip of Bangladesh, not far from the Burmese border. One day, after visiting Ramkot and other temples around Ramu, Bhikkhu Vivekananda and I arrived at Ananda Bhavan Vihar in the village of Ukhiya, about 45 minutes' drive from Cox's Bazaar. The simple temple, located on a small wooded hill, has several shrines, a bodhi tree, and a large reclining Buddha image that was brought from Thailand. Like many temples in Bangladesh, Ananda Bhavan Vihar also houses an orphanage, situated at the edge of the temple grounds, to care for some of the estimated one million children orphaned in the floods and other natural disasters that devastate the country annually. After wandering the grounds for a short time, we were ushered up a wooden staircase to a spacious room to meet the temple's abbot in the large wooden main hall of the temple. Demurely to the side stood a young woman named Mira Barua.

Mira Barua was born into a devoutly Buddhist family in Ukhiya and has been active in the life of the temple since childhood. Her family home is located amidst the gleaming paddy fields just five minutes away. Since she was a small girl, Mira has had a close relationship with Bhikkhu Rebato, the head monk of the temple, who is now 49. There are four *bhikkhus* and four *sāmaṇeras* at the temple, but no nuns. At 23, Mira is confident, capable, and an indispensable component of the temple's activities. As she served lunch to the resident monks and guests, the abbot described her approvingly as "very religious." After completing high school in Ukhiya, Mira pursued a degree in religious studies at Ukhiya College, taking classes in Pāli, Buddhism, and Islamic history. She now teaches Pāli, Buddhism, and Bengali at Ukhiya High School and to the 42 boys at the temple's orphanage school. When asked whether she would consider becoming a nun, her eyes sparkled with delight.

After lunch, we walked along the pathways through the rice fields to visit Mira's home. An altar with a Buddha image, simple offerings, and a string of prayer beads was clearly the focal point of the immaculate earthen home. As we entered the drawing room, her family members spread a mat on the floor and bowed to the monastics from a kneeling position, in Theravāda style. Except for a few posters of natural scenery sent by a brother working in Saudi Arabia, all the pictures decorating the room are religious in nature.

Her parents are faithful Buddhist practitioners, familiar with *vipassanā* meditation, and devoted to the *bhikkhus*, but when the question of Mira's future came up, they timidly admitted they would not agree to her becoming a nun. Although she would be living only five minutes away, it was hard for them to conceive of their daughter as a nun. Monks are revered in Bangladeshi Buddhist society, but nuns have no status and are virtually invisible.

Tribal Buddhist Nuns

At the time of my visit, the district of Bandarban technically was restricted territory due to ethnic tensions and the prospect of a peace accord, but there was no one at the check post, so we drove right through. A short drive through the gently rolling hills brought us to the township of Bandarban. On the right was a newly constructed cultural center, part of the government's efforts at restitution to the tribal people who have suffered years of attacks by settlers from the plains encroaching upon their lands. Just a few minutes further down the road, we arrived at a peaceful temple constructed of wood, with a large open Buddha hall in the center. After ascending the stairs and honoring the Buddha images in two small decorative shrines, we approached U Sumangala Mahathero,[9] the temple's abbot. As we paid our respects to him in a reception area arranged in one corner of the hall, we noticed a slight Marma nun watching us intently.

Ma Chan Daw Wadi was born in the village of Murongkyo in 1925 and grew up in Bandarban. When she was 29 years old, she received the ten precepts from U Sumangala, the abbot. Now 74, she has lived at the temple since then, serving the abbot and devoting her time to *vipassanā* meditation practice. She learned the technique of *vipassanā* from the abbot, who learned it during a stay in Burma (Myanmar). In the hut that Ma Chan Daw Wadi shares with another woman at the back of the temple, her possessions consist of a change of clothes, a mosquito net, and a few empty tins. The only valuable possession is a meditation text that rests on a makeshift table.[10] Her carefully shaved head and disciplined demeanor convey the intensity of her meditation practice. She has never traveled outside the area, nor cared to, but her eyes lit up as we spoke of Bodhgaya, sacred site of the Buddha's enlightenment.

Her companion Apuma has been staying at the temple for the last seven years. Apuma's father and brother are monks at the temple, and the abbot, U Sumangala, is her uncle. Apuma's husband suddenly left her about 30 years ago, and the suffering she experienced at that time convinced her of the truth of the Buddha's teachings. Now 60, she works in the temple and takes care of her father and uncle. She is deeply committed to meditation practice and plans to become a nun once her father has passed away.

At another temple nearby, I discovered three *micchela* (Burmese: *mae śila*, female precept-holders) from the culturally endangered Murong tribe. One is a 77-year-old nun who shaved her head and took precepts six years ago when a highly respected *sayādaw* (teacher) visited the temple. The other two women (64 and 52) received eight precepts and began living in the temple at the same time. One told me that she will shave her head as soon as her daughter grows up, and the other woman said she will also shave her head then. All three women are from Kaptai and said they get what food they need from the temple. Two of the women speak only their tribal language, but we were able to communicate through their companion, who speaks Marma.

The way these *micchela* live, work, and practice quietly in the temple, without Saṅgha status or privileges, is typical of the few nuns to be found in Bangladesh. Even without recognition from society, they feel fortunate to be able to stay in the temple, serve the monks, create merit, recite *suttas*, and meditate for the rest of their lives. Their simple needs are met by the monks they serve and, living in the temple, they are protected from the woes of worldly life. Although we have no records to prove it, nuns and female practitioners have probably practiced quietly and unnoticed like this for centuries.

Changes are afoot, however, that may open up new directions for Buddhist women in Bangladesh. The primary initiator of the innovations is U Paa Jotha Thero. Popularly known as Uchala Bhante, he is a young *bhikkhu* from the Marma royal family who was trained as an attorney. After becoming renowned as a judge, considered an outstanding accomplishment for a hill tribe member, he suddenly resigned his position, received ordination, and went to practice meditation in Burma for six years. Inspired by the large number of nuns (*tila shin*) he saw in Burma, he began organizing temporary ordinations for nuns after his return to Bandarban. In December 1994, he arranged an ordination for 62 monks and invited respected *mahātheros* from Burma to officiate.[11] The following year, he invited both monks and nuns to officiate, also giving girls and young women the opportunity to shave their heads, don the robes, receive nine precepts,[12] and temporarily experience monastic life as *micchela*.

Two ordinations have been held so far: 65 nuns were ordained in December 1995 and 68 were ordained in January 1997. The ordinations have attracted candidates from all over Bangladesh and from a variety of ethnic groups: Marma, Chakma, Barua, Tripura, Tongchengya, and Rakkhaine, in addition to three from Burma. Ordinarily a girl's mother or sister accompanies her to the ordination, helps cut her hair, and assists as she goes for alms. In some cases, like Tipu and Nobodita (two women I met at a wedding in Chittagong), both mother and daughter took precepts. Most of the nuns who participated in these two ordinations, like 14-year-old Au Mei Thowai, whom I met in Bandarban, disrobed after a month to continue their studies at school. However, seven of the newly ordained nuns, four Marma and three Barua, decided to remain as nuns and have gone to Burma to pursue studies in Pāli, Vinaya, and Abhidharma at temples in Rangoon (Yangon).

The ordinations organized by Uchala Bhante represent a bold new step and have had a powerful social impact on Buddhist society in Bangladesh. People told me that before these ordinations were held, the public was not aware that there was such a thing as *micchela*. Bhante had hoped to make the ordinations an annual event, but politics intervened. Now that a peace accord has been signed, hopefully putting an end to 15 years of hostilities in the hill tribe areas, he plans to continue the ordinations, establish a monastery for nuns, and build a Buddhist institute in Bandarban where both monks and nuns can get an education in Buddhist studies and temple management. On the topic of full ordination for women, he told me, "We have no problem with making the nuns *bhikkhunīs*. It is only a question of *who* will make them *bhikkhunīs*." After some initial resistance, he admitted that it may be possible to establish a *bhikkhunī* lineage in Bangladesh by inviting nuns from the Chinese tradition.

Bangladeshi Laywomen's Lives

One day, while staying at Agrasara Girls' College at Sudharsan Vihar in Raozan, about an hour from Chittagong, I visited the childhood home of the late Bhikkhu Viśuddhānanda, who was the founder of Dhammarajika Monastery in Dhaka. The family was widely respected because it had produced many monks. When Bhikkhu Viśuddhānanda's mother died, people told me, the ample courtyard of their traditional-style home was too small to contain all those who came to pay their respects. The reason for this fanfare, they explained, was that the woman had been the mother of a well-known *bhikkhu*. Her body was placed in the courtyard for several hours, during which time aggrieved friends and relations cried and expressed their sorrow. The body was then washed and covered with a single length of white cloth. After some time, the droves of people who crowded into the courtyard made it necessary to remove the body to the temple of Agrasara complex, five minutes away. There the body stayed for several days so that the villagers could come to pay their respects. At last it was cremated at a cremation ground a short distance from the village.

The photographs I viewed in the family's album showed crowds of hundreds of villagers surrounding the body as it lay in state in the courtyard of Agrasara Temple before the cremation. As is customary, a huge *saṅghadāna* (an offering of food and gifts to a gathering of *bhikkhus*, 60 in this case) was held on the seventh day after her passing, and again on the 15th and 30th, then monthly for six months, and annually thereafter. On these occasions, males in the family wear a white square of cloth pinned diagonally over the left shoulder and under the right arm "in tribute to their dead ancestors." Women in the family wear no special cloth, yet they are in charge of all the food preparation and cleanup. Offerings of fruits and vegetables, artistically carved and arranged, are placed on the altar. The men I spoke with volunteered that women are essential to men's ability to practice generosity (*dāna*), a central Buddhist virtue. Men, they say, are able to earn money, but they depend entirely on the women in their family to prepare and arrange offerings of food and provide hospitality to guests and the Saṅgha.[13] Significantly, although women ordinarily serve guests in the home, both ordained and lay, only men serve *bhikkhus* at a *saṅghadāna*. Men are therefore most visible in merit-making activities, even though behind the scenes it is women who make these activities possible.

Although it is rare at present, there is no restriction against women teaching Buddhism in Bangladesh. Priti Kana Barua, President of the Bangladesh Buddhist Women's Association, told me the story of her Aunt Babuillarma (lit., "Babul's mother"), a woman who became a well-known meditation teacher. Babuillarma grew up in Aburkhil, a large Buddhist village a half hour's drive from Chittagong, and studied meditation with a variety of teachers, including a monk at the old Jamitjuri Meditation Center. At the age of 55, she left family life and trained to become a teacher. Wearing a white sari, she gave meditation training to women and men at various meditation centers, conducting courses at least ten days long, until her death in 1997 at the age of 78.

Especially in contrast to the sequestering of women common among the Muslims, Buddhist women appear to enjoy a large measure of social equality and freedom of movement. Although there is no functioning order of nuns, several men told me, "Women are comparatively more religious than men in our country." One further informed me, "Mother Theresa, the most famous person in the world, is a woman." Indeed, women's presence in large numbers at Buddhist activities was very noticeable wherever I went in Bangladesh. Women take their children to the temples to listen to Dhamma talks, especially on Buddhist festival days. The most important days, celebrated in temples all over the country, are Buddha Purnima (Vesak), Ashwini Purnima (the conclusion of the monks' rains retreat), Kaṭhina Chibar Dāna (the ceremony of offering robes to monks), and Falguni Purnima (the ceremony of the "wish-fulfilling tree").[14] During Kaṭhina Chibar Dāna season, at the conclusion of the Saṅgha's rainy season retreat (*vassa*), robe-offering ceremonies are held at different temples on different days to give people more opportunities to accumulate merit. Women are lauded as the most conscientious donors. Many women observe precepts on new and full-moon days, and periodically invite monks to their homes for *dāna*. In addition to public devotional activities, many women told me that they meditate daily in their homes, chant *suttas*, tell Buddhist stories to their children, and attend meditation retreats whenever they get the chance. One day when I was asked to teach meditation in Aburkhil Village, over 150 women participated, many accompanied by their children.

The Gender Litmus Test

Although Bangladesh has very few nuns and no tradition of *bhikkhunīs*, wherever I went in Bangladesh I was accorded the same hospitality as a *bhikkhu*. Although this may not surprise the casual observer, such respectful treatment is not always the case for a nun, either in Asia or in the West. For a nun to be welcomed on a par with monks in a social situation is unusual and significant. The skill with which protocol was handled in a new and complex situation – coping with a foreign *bhikkhunī* – reflects the open-mindedness and flexibility of Bangladeshi Buddhists. The relative absence of gender discrimination was notable. Although *bhikkhunīs* do not exist in Bangladesh, many Buddhists bowed in the traditional manner without hesitation and with the same respect they would show to a *bhikkhu*. Some hesitated for a moment, but quickly computing *bhikkhunī* to be the feminine of *bhikkhu*, then paid their respects. Others, after running through the same computation, concluded it was inappropriate or unnecessary to bow to a nun. A few, visibly perplexed, quickly busied themselves with other duties to avoid having to deal with the unaccustomed situation. These different reactions suggest a complex admixture of factors affecting religious attitudes and behaviors. In addition to social constructions of gender, they were influenced by social status, age (older people generally being more devout), depth of Buddhist commitment, attitudes toward the ordained Saṅgha, personal patterns of observing traditional protocol, and, perhaps, uncertainty about foreigners' responses to traditional protocol, such as bowing.

One day I attended a huge *saṅghadāna* in the village of Raozan. More than 150 monks were served lunch in a huge tent decorated with colorful banners and streamers. Monks had been invited from towns and villages far and wide for the occasion, and the high-ranking monks were seated inside a building, chatting and catching up with the news, before the meal was served. Although I, being neither monk nor lay, did not fit neatly into any familiar category, the organizers were unfailingly polite and ultimately placed me with the monks. When it came time for lunch, I was seated next to the high-ranking monks I had come with and carefully served only vegetarian food.

After lunch, when the official program began, over a thousand people gathered under a huge awning for several hours of speeches. Somehow they had all been fed after the monks were served. Despite their demanding family responsibilities, women attended the function in far greater numbers than men, in a ratio of about four to one. I was seated on the stage in front amidst 150 monks, many of whom chewed betel nut concoctions, stretched their legs, and chatted during the proceedings. From this vantage point, I had an excellent opportunity to observe the behavior and reactions of the crowd. The speeches tended toward the polemic, with very little Dhamma content, repeatedly emphasizing the achievements of the Buddhist community and the need for even greater achievements. As time wore on, I could not fail to notice the exemplary behavior of the women; they sat quietly in neat rows, listening with full attention to the interminable windy speeches, while the men got up, sat down, talked, slept, smoked, and shuffled about. In my own windy speech, I remarked that the mindfulness and discipline the women displayed are vital qualities in Buddhist practice, and that women and men are equally responsible for creating and preserving Buddhist cultural identity. Women want to be active as teachers and leaders; all they lack is Buddhist education.

Buddhist Futures in Bangladesh

On the one hand, the lack of attention given to religious training for Buddhist women indicates a huge blind spot. On the other hand, Bangladeshi Buddhists are struggling for economic, social, and cultural survival with so very few resources available that it is a continual challenge even to support the monks. Buddhists in Bangladesh appreciate the freedom that their women enjoy in relation to Muslims and many take full advantage of whatever educational opportunities they have. The question of women's future prospects within Buddhism in Bangladesh therefore cannot be addressed without addressing the question of Bangladeshi Buddhism as a whole; that is, the health of half the religious body politic cannot be considered in isolation from the health of the whole. As an example, Buddhist studies programs at present are inadequate even for monks, much less for women. Of course it is possible to study Pāli and Buddhism at some government colleges and universities in Bangladesh.[15] But although women and men are equally free to take these classes, comprehensive Buddhist studies programs are not available, either to women or to men.

To ensure a healthy future for Buddhist women, Buddhism as a whole needs dedicated effort, vision, and support. Buddhists in Bangladesh are proud of their cultural heritage and keen to maintain it, particularly in the face of Muslim domination and a growing Islamic nationalism. Buddhist women and men already work conscientiously to sponsor Buddhist events, observe traditional marriage and funeral customs, celebrate all the Buddhist holy days, organize teachings and *vipassanā* meditation courses, reinforce Buddhist values in the family and community, maintain the temples, and support the monks' communities. They persevere in these efforts despite continual natural disasters, economic woes, extortion,[16] ethnic and religious discrimination,[17] the wooing of young Buddhist women by Muslim suitors, Christian and Muslim attempts at conversion,[18] communal and family dislocation associated with outmigration of Buddhist youths seeking opportunities abroad,[19] and myriad other social problems.

Nevertheless, I feel that the situation is potentially very positive for Buddhist women's development in Bangladesh for a number of reasons. First, in their beleaguered situation, Buddhists in Bangladesh clearly need to activate every conceivable resource to ensure their cultural survival. Second, women's capabilities are already recognized; Bangladeshi Buddhist men are proud of the accomplishments that Bangladeshi women have already demonstrated. Third, Buddhist women enjoy a large measure of social freedom. Unlike their Muslim sisters, they are not veiled. They have access to secondary and higher education, and enjoy considerable freedom in their choice of lifestyles. They have a strong voice in family decisions, including those related to their reproductive health. Although divorce is not common, there is no bar to divorce among Buddhists. Literacy is high, widow remarriage is permitted, and the incidence of domestic violence is relatively low. Buddhist women are free to frequent temples and to pursue Buddhist studies at the university level, if they so desire. All of these factors augur well for Buddhist women's future. If monastic facilities were available, many parents would no doubt allow their daughters to pursue a Buddhist vocation if they wished.

Considering all these factors, it is difficult to explain the absence of an effective order of nuns in Bangladesh. Yet in reconfiguring the gender landscape, this lack may be used to advantage. Without the precedent of an unrecognized order of nuns of ambiguous status, such as exists in other Theravāda countries, women in Bangladesh may be at liberty to create a viable, socially acknowledged order after their own vision. As an endangered minority facing cultural degradation and possible extinction, women in Bangladesh may have greater freedom to create an effective Bhikkhunī Saṅgha. In the face of this urgent cultural imperative, educated Bangladeshi Buddhists may be able to discard the gender baggage, cut through patriarchal tradition, and support women in their efforts to establish an erudite and active order of Buddhist nuns.

It is too early to determine exactly how the goal of creating a Bhikkhunī Saṅgha can be accomplished, but four elements are essential. First, women need access to Buddhist education. Systematic, comprehensive Buddhist studies programs to train women *and* men as translators, researchers, and educators are essential for the future of Buddhism in Bangladesh. Second, women need to cultivate allies among the established Buddhist hierarchy. A few highly placed *bhikkhus* have already traveled outside Bangladesh and witnessed the phenomenal achievements of *bhikkhunīs* active in Taiwan, Korea, and other countries. With encouragement, this exposure, combined with open-minded gender attitudes among Bangladeshi Buddhists as a whole, may convince these respected monks to become advocates of women's religious advancement. Third, Buddhist women from disparate ethnic groups need to consolidate their power and develop a sense of solidarity with other women. In their beleaguered situation, Buddhists in Bangladesh have no option but to overcome communal factionalism and rivalries. In this regard, a unified multi-ethnic coalition of women could be a powerful example. Fourth, most critical of all for the gender restructuring of Buddhist institutions in Bangladesh, is motivating Buddhist women themselves to work for women's advancement. With these four crucial factors in place, women could not only create a Bhikkhunī Saṅgha, they could also take leadership roles in restoring and revitalizing their cherished Buddhist heritage.

Notes

1 See James J. Novak, *Bangladesh: Reflections on the Water* (Bloomington, Ind.: Indiana University Press, 1993).

2 This is not an impossible theory considering Bengal's ease of access via the Ganges.

3 Fa Hsien visited in the fifth century; Hsuan Tsang, Tao-lin, Tcha-cheng and I-tsing in the seventh.

4 Novak, *Bangladesh: Reflections on the Water*, pp. 61–65.

5 Ibid., p. 141. Novak notes that the Bengalis put up fierce resistance during the Sena Dynasty despite great cruelties.

6 Priti Kana Barua, *Buddhism and Buddhists in Bangladesh* (unpublished monograph, 1997), p. 2.

7 Other surnames used among Barua Buddhists are Mutsuddi (alternatively spelled Mutsoody), Chowdhury (or Chawdhuri), Talukdar, Singh, and others. Ibid., p. 3. My Marma informants dismiss the author's inclusion of the Marma among Barua Buddhists and insist on being identified as a distinct ethnic group.

8 To abstain from killing, stealing, sexual conduct, false speech, ornaments and cosmetics, entertainments, luxurious seats and beds, and untimely food (i.e., any solid food after twelve o'clock noon).

9 The appellation "*thero*" indicates that a monk has been ordained for ten or more years (calculated by the rains' retreats); "*mahāthero*" indicates he has been ordained for twenty or more. The designations for nuns would be *therī* and *mahātherī*. These monastic landmarks are occasions for celebration.

10 For many years there was another nun, who had taken the precepts later in life. The two lived and practiced meditation at the temple together. When this nun became 80, she felt she was too old to stay in the temple, so she went to stay with her daughter.

11 Chief among them was U Kumara Sayadaw, an Āgama Pandita from Rangoon.

12 The nuns do not take the tenth precept against handling money, because they sometimes need to go to the bazaar to shop.

13 Despite financial limitations, hospitality is highly valued in Bangladesh. One gentleman told me with aplomb, "In Bangladesh, although rickshaws and baby taxis are proceeding recklessly, Buddhist people, including retired persons, are providing maximum guest-ification."

14 Falguni Purnima commemorates the Buddha's first visit home after achieving enlightenment, at which time his family accepted the new teachings and his son Rahula "accepted the yellow robe." Buddhists generally believe that the practice of generosity creates the

causes to enjoy high birth, wealth, beauty, fame, and happiness in future lives. In the rite of the "wish-fulfilling tree" (*kalpataru*, lit., "time tree"), Buddhists in Bangladesh offer money for wealth, paper for fame and knowledge, metal and string for talent and intelligence, and a plate of rice for happiness before a tree six to eight feet high. Afterwards the offerings are donated to the highest monk.

15 Notable Buddhist studies programs are available at Noapara College, Rangunia College, and Rangamati Government College, in addition to Chittagong University and Dhaka University.

16 Locally this is referred to as "terrorism." One friend confided, "You cannot even paint your own home without being asked to pay protection money." Foreign enterprises are understandably intimidated by this practice, which hampers foreign investment and slows economic development.

17 Evident in hiring, firing, admissions to educational institutions, scholarships, investment funding, training opportunities, and other spheres.

18 Informants report numerous alleged conversion attempts, for example, offers of Rs. 2,000 (a considerable sum) to male students at Dhammarajika Vihar by a particular priest. Although this priest has funded orphanages and hostels for needy Buddhist children, some look upon these efforts with suspicion, assuming his ultimate motivation is to convert poor Buddhist children to Christianity.

19 The quest for job opportunities in more developed countries does not always end happily. Undocumented workers may labor under appalling conditions, courting arrest and deportation. They are usually not paid a fair wage nor, after working abroad for many years, do they always settle easily back into Bangladeshi society.

BUDDHIST WOMEN OF SOUTHEAST ASIA

CHAPTER FIVE

Thammacarini Witthaya

The First Buddhist School for Girls in Thailand

Monica Lindberg Falk

In 1997–1998, I spent 15 months doing anthropological research on gender relations and Thai Buddhism.[1] My research focused on Buddhist nuns (*mae chi*) living at nunneries independent from monks' temples (*wat*) and was conducted primarily at Thammacarini Witthaya, a self-governing Buddhist nunnery in central Thailand. Autonomous nunneries are a rather recent phenomenon in Thailand; ordinarily communities of nuns are attached to monasteries for monks. I was interested in exploring whether living in autonomous communities had altered the category of *mae chi* and changed the situation of contemporary nuns. Meditation is often perceived to be more appropriate than education for nuns, so when I heard that Thammacarini Witthaya offered free secondary school for girls and *mae chi*, I became interested in learning more about the lives of nuns at this particular nunnery. I was introduced to the nuns by Mae chi Khunying Kanitha Wichiencharoen, an influential former lawyer and Buddhist nun who has dedicated her life to improving conditions for women, especially nuns. Mae chi Kanitha stresses the importance of education for women and is founding the first nuns' college in Thailand. Together with the Thai Nuns Institute, she is working to gain legal recognition for *mae chi* as Buddhist clerics, which would entitle them to receive free education and the other government benefits available to monks.

Buddhist Nuns in Thai Society

Theravāda Buddhism has been meaningful for Thai people since the first Thai kingdom in the Sukhothai period (1253–1350).[2] More than 90 percent of Thailand's 60 million people identify themselves as Buddhists. According to the dominant discourse of Buddhism, maleness is ranked above femaleness in both cosmology and in social praxis. In Thailand only men can be fully ordained. Although there have always been women who lived as renunciants and there are many notable women ascetics in Thai Buddhism, there has never been an order of fully ordained nuns.[3]

An order of nuns was founded by the Buddha in the sixth century B.C.E. In the third century B.C.E., the daughter of India's King Aśoka,

Saṅghamitta, went to Sri Lanka and founded an order of nuns that flourished until the 11th century, when it disappeared after the invasion of the Coḷas from south India. The Sri Lankan order survived in China, but the order of fully ordained nuns never spread to Thailand[4]. However, in all Theravāda countries, there are women who shave their heads and live as renunciants after having accepted eight or ten Buddhist precepts.[5] In Thailand these women are called *mae chi*.[6] The Thai Nuns' Institute favors the use of the Thai word *mae chi* for nuns, which distinguishes them from *upāsikās*, Buddhist laywomen.

In Buddhism, the sexual world of the layperson and the asexual world of the monk are separate domains with a sharp distinction between the ethical expectations enjoined upon celibate monks and ordinary laypeople. In Thailand only men are perceived as capable of crossing the boundary between the religious and the secular worlds. The significance of this transition is illustrated by the custom of a son's becoming a monk for a period of time, accruing merit for his parents.[7] A daughter customarily has no right to enter the religious realm, and therefore is in no position to transmit high-quality merit to her parents.[8]

Thai Buddhist cosmology is the primary force creating a social hierarchy in which monks are supreme moral agents.[9] Women in Thailand have no place in the Buddhist Saṅgha, which only embraces monks and male novices. Ideologically, Buddhism is open to everyone regardless of caste, class, race, or gender, and women and men are said to have the same spiritual potential. Yet when the monastic order for women was established, an additional eight rules were instituted for nuns, which ensures their secondary status.[10] Today there is no order of fully ordained nuns in Thailand and, although there are regional and individual differences in the way female ascetics are viewed, nuns are generally neglected and their status is low. Often their main responsibility is preparing food for the monks and themselves, and they do not have the same opportunities as monks to study and practice the Dhamma (Buddhist teachings).

Little is known about the history of *mae chi* in Thailand. There are indications that during the Sukhothai period there were women who followed the practice of being ordained during the rainy season. The first records of *mae chi* in Thailand are found in descriptions of the Ayutthaya kingdom (1350–1767). *Mae* means "mother" in Thai language. The origin of the "*chi*" is not clear, but it probably connotes the nuns' ascetic way of life.[11]

The present number of *mae chi* in Thailand is unknown, since *mae chi* are not necessarily entered on a temple's records. The *mae chi* who live at nunneries and private places are not counted at all. According to the Department of Religious Affairs annual report on monastery dwellers, there were more than 15,000 *mae chi* at temples in Thailand in 1996. In 1998 the

Thai Nuns' Institute, a national organization, recorded approximately 5,000 *mae chi* as their members. Some live at temples, others at nunneries. However, there is also an unknown number of nuns in Thailand who live at nunneries or private places without being members of the Thai Nuns' Institute.

When a woman leaves worldly affairs and enters monastic life as a *mae chi*, she usually takes the *mae chi* ordination from both *mae chi* and monks. Thai nuns are expected to follow the regulations stipulated by the Thai Nuns' Institute. *Mae chi* shave their heads and eyebrows, and wear a white robe consisting of a white blouse, a white long skirt (*phasin*), and a white cloth draped over the left shoulder. White can also be seen as a lay color; laywomen and men who observe the eight precepts on *wan phra* (Buddhist holy days) often wear white. White is the traditional color of mourning, and also the color expressing purity for participants in various rituals. White is also worn by males after their heads are shaved but before they receive the yellow robe from the Bhikkhu Saṅgha.

Thai Women's Access to Education

Educational level is a crucial factor in Thai women's lives. Many underprivileged girls in Thailand have no opportunity to continue their studies after completing primary school. Instead, they start working while very young in poorly paid jobs. More and more young Thai women seek employment in urban areas to help support their families. They have to cope with poor working conditions, are often treated harshly in factories, and many are recruited into the sex trade. The leaders of the Thammacarini School hope that educating these young girls may help prevent this.

A Thai woman's key duty is to her family, and her role is primarily defined within this context. The Theravāda world view assumes that women are more worldly than men and more attached to the realm of desire, which hinders their attainment of Buddhism's ultimate goal.[12] Women's lower prestige reflects their lack of access to "spiritual capital" in a political domain based on morality rather than cash.[13] Some scholars argue that this "materialistic" image of women legitimates prostitution as a realm where women can fulfil role expectations related to mundane concerns.[14] Some scholars therefore posit a correlation between the country's sex industry and absence of religious alternatives for women, such as an order of fully ordained nuns.[15]

Women in Thailand are expected to marry and bear children. If they remain single, they often live at home caring for their natal family. In urban areas today, it is not uncommon for well-educated women to choose a single life.[16] *Mae chi* also have the status of being single, but a woman cannot become a *mae chi* if she has obligations to support her family. If a woman has children, she must arrange for their care before she can be ordained as a nun. Common prejudices against *mae chi* depict them as women who have troubles and flee to the temple as a refuge. Women's motivations for becoming a *mae chi* are assumed to be negative: a "broken heart," illness, poverty, old age, or a disturbed mind as a result of bad *kamma*. Nuns are sometimes regarded simply as laypeople who follow eight precepts rather than five. Their legal status as *mae chi* is the same as that of pious laywomen (*upāsikā*), but I argue that their performance merits the status of ordained (*nak boat*).

Pioneering Mae chi

It is still rare in Thailand to find communities of nuns living independently from monks' temples, but the numbers of nunneries (*samnak chi*) are increasing every year. More than 20 years ago two Buddhist nuns – the late head nun, Khun mae[17] Sumon, and the present head nun, Khun mae Prathin – started the nunnery where one of Thailand's two *thammacarini* schools is located. A supporter offered them 40 acres of land in central Thailand, southwest of Bangkok, for the nunnery. The pioneering *mae chi* tell stories of the hard work required to drain the marshy land of water, plant trees, and erect buildings.

The financial resources for starting Thammacarini School came from many donors who agreed that impoverished girls and women needed more opportunities for education. Luang Pho Im, a Buddhist monk from Wat Somanas in Bangkok, helped to found Thammacarini School. He wanted to give girls and young women from poor families possibilities similar to those of underprivileged boys. Many boys from families without means can be ordained as *samaneen* (novices). *Samaneen* take the ten Buddhist precepts: the eight of the *mae chi* with one precept divided into two and an additional precept that prohibits touching money. Novices live at a temple and study at the temple school. Their duties include cooking, cleaning, and assisting the monks.

Khun mae Prathin Kwan-orn, head of the central Thailand nunnery, is also director of Thammacarini School. She was born in a province not far from the nunnery and the school. Khun mae Prathin and her younger brother were their family's only children. Their father was a construction worker, and their mother had a shop where she sold a variety of things. Khun mae Prathin was ordained some 35 years ago when she was 19. At that time it was not common for women to become nuns. It was especially unusual for a young, bright woman to live as a renunciant. Khun mae Prathin wanted to live a spiritual life and, she says, she wanted freedom. She did not believe that the lay life would meet her needs. She thought that there must be possibilities for women other than to be "locked up" in a marriage with the responsibilities of caring for a husband and children. Understanding their daughter's sincere wish to live an ordained life, her parents gave their permission. Thereafter, Khun mae was ordained at a temple of both monks and nuns. At this temple, monks and nuns had no contact with each other, and a large wall separated the nuns' dwellings from those of the monks. The nuns supervised themselves, and did not cook for the monks, as they do at many temples in Thailand.

Khun mae Prathin realized early the importance of education. She started her own secondary education while living at the nunnery where she was ordained. Later on she went to study Pāli in Bangkok. She completed her bachelor of arts and master of arts in India. It is still very rare for nuns to have the financial means to study. Khun mae Prathin was supported by some lay followers. When she returned to Thailand, Khun mae Prathin and her close friend Khun mae Sumon were invited to establish a nunnery on the donated 40 acres. These two nuns had studied together in India and Khun mae Sumon was one of the very few *mae chi* in Thailand who held a Ph.D. If they had not had the opportunity to start the nunnery, Khun mae Prathin says, she would probably have continued her studies.

The 20 years since they opened the nunnery have included a great deal of hard work. Khun mae Prathin had long pitied young women who had no chance to further their education. Khun mae Sumon and Khun mae Prathin made an early attempt to start a school for *mae chi*. At first there were 20 *mae chi* studying, but only two teachers. The work became too much, and the disappointed nuns had to close the school. However, they continued with the hard work of constructing buildings on the difficult marsh land. While they were building the *sala*, the main building at the nunnery, Khun mae Sumon became severely ill and passed away. Khun mae Prathin continued the work, with much help and support from the other *mae chi* at the nunnery.

Some years later the abbot Luang Pho Im, from Wat Somanas in Bangkok, suggested starting a secondary school at the nunnery. Khun mae Prathin was delighted to have a new chance to establish a school for girls and nuns in Thailand. This time conditions were better. They had buildings, better financial support, and more teachers. When Thammacarini School started in 1990, there were ten teachers, and today there are fifteen. The *mae chi* from the Bangkok temple, Wat Paknam Bhasicharoen, have been very important for Thammacarini School. When the school started, three *mae chi* from Wat Paknam went to work there. One of these was Mae chi Srisalab Upamai who was appointed the principal of the school.

Mae chi Srisalab was born in northeast Thailand, as were most of the school's students. When she was ordained as a nun, about 28 years ago, she was not interested in studying. Her main focus was the practice of meditation. However, she was ordained at Wat Paknam, a temple with the unusual policy of requiring every nun, except the very old *mae chi*, to study. Reluctantly she started the three grades of compulsory Buddhist studies. At the same time she studied lower and later upper secondary school work.

Unlike other temples in Thailand, the monks of Wat Paknam do not go on alms rounds in the morning, so the nuns must cook food for both monks and nuns at the temple. Mae chi Srisalab worked in the kitchen every day from early morning until noon, and in the afternoon she took classes. She recalls how tired she was during these years. The time for doing homework was very limited. She woke up before 4 a.m. for the morning chant. After that the morning was spent cooking. She went to classes in the afternoon, and the *mae chi* also had to attend afternoon chanting and meditation. There was no time for rest during the day, and Mae chi Srisalab usually went to bed late.

Mae chi Srisalab intended to do a period of intense meditation when she finished her Buddhist studies. However, some older nuns at Wat Paknam encouraged her to study Pāli. Although she was not really interested in further education, she fulfilled their wishes. While studying Pāli she also started to study for her bachelor of arts at the Open University, Ramkamhaeng. At the same time she was appointed to teach at Wat Paknam. After she had graduated from Ramkamhaeng University, she was chosen to be the principal of Thammacarini Witthaya. For three years she taught both at Wat Paknam in Bangkok and at Thammacarini School, which involved a considerable amount of time-consuming travel.

Mae chi Srisalab gradually developed a taste for studying. When she was more than 45 years old, she went to study for her master's degree in India. She spent three years in Poona and graduated in 1997. Upon her return from India she continued to teach and work at Thammacarini School. Mae chi Srisalab's way to education has not been as natural as Khun mae Prathin's, but today Mae chi Srisalab views studying as the key factor for helping girls and young women in Thailand.

Mae chi Yupin Duangchan is another nun from Wat Paknam who has been essential for Thammacarini Witthaya. She raises money for the school. Once a year, in late August, Mae chi Yupin helps the school organize a *phapha*, a fund-raising festival commonly held at Buddhist temples in Thailand. Thanks to her large network of supporters and her sincere dedication, the school has become known to people in Bangkok and other places who otherwise would not have come in contact with Thammacarini Witthaya. Every year at the *phapha*, people come in private cars and rented buses to visit the school and the nunnery. They give donations to the school, and the nuns treat their guests with plentiful delicious Thai food. The local monks are also invited, and there is a chanting ceremony performed by both monks and nuns.

Thammacarini Witthaya

When Thammacarini School started in 1990 there were 22 girls and 23 *mae chi* studying. Currently there are 60 students. Altogether there are 49 *thammacarini* (lay Dhamma students) and more than 50 *mae chi* living at the nunnery. More girls would like to attend the school, but to expand it further would require more facilities and funding. Most of the students live in dormitories with about 13 students to a room, while the *mae chi* sleep one or two to a room in separate quarters. The *thammacarini* do not shave their heads as the *mae chi* do. They wear the school uniform, a white blouse and a grey or blue skirt, every day except for *wan phra*, when they don white.

Both nuns and students must observe the eight Buddhist precepts. There are additional special rules for the *mae chi*, and the students observe 19 school rules. The different sets of rules are read out loud weekly in the *saalaa* (used as the preaching hall) by a *mae chi* and a senior student. The school rules concern daily practices and school standards. The rules include simple politeness, keeping personal dormitory space clean, class attendance, and respectful behavior.

Young girls who have finished six years of compulsory primary education (*prathom* 6, age 11 or 12) are welcome at Thammacarini School. This school is the only chance for most of them to continue their studies. The schoolgirls receive free room, board, and education, thanks to private donations. Since 1995, the Thai government has provided some support, but economic crises have decreased support drastically and delayed disbursements, adversely affecting the school's economic situation.

Initially Thammacarini School offered only three grades, equivalent to the first part of secondary education in Thailand. The curriculum later expanded to cover the final three grades of secondary education. The program covers three secular grades in two years. Everyone studies six basic subjects: English, Thai, mathematics, social studies, science, and Buddhism. Successful completion is required for further study in colleges or universities. Further, the girls learn vocational skills, such as typing, sewing, weaving, crochet, and flower making. Their studies in cooking and gardening provide a way for the school to cut costs as well as a way to teach these skills. The girls learn mostly by working with the *mae chi* at the nunnery's plantations and in the kitchen. The standard academic subjects are tested twice per year by the Non-Formal Education Department of the Ministry of Education. The students take all their tests outside the nunnery school, together with students from regular schools in the district.

The study of religious texts has traditionally been restricted to monks and male novices. The limited opportunity for *mae chi* to receive Buddhist education has accentuated women's lower status.[18] Nuns' and girls' lack of access to education was the motivation for starting Thammacarini School. The school gives both girls and *mae chi* Buddhist education as well as admission to a higher level of secular education, which raises the status of the *mae chi* and also give them new capabilities as nuns.

The Daily Schedule at the Nunnery

4:00	The nuns start the day with chanting and meditation.
5:15	The *thammacarini* start with physical exercise.
5:30	The alms round starts. Some of the *thammacarini* go with the nuns to help carry the alms.
7:00	Breakfast.
8:00	National anthem. Chanting.
9:00	The school day starts.
11:00	Lunch.
13:00	The school day continues.
16:00	Chanting and presentation of a Buddhist text.
17:00	Gardening, watering plants.
19:00	Meditation and chanting.

The nunnery is organized in teams that rotate duties such as cooking, cleaning, and other domestic chores. The students have lessons five days per week. On the day before *wan phra*, the *mae chi* and *thammacarini* usually work in the garden the whole day. On the day of *wan phra*, everyone at the nunnery formally recites the eight precepts. There are also extra sessions of chanting, meditation and Buddhist talks. In January every year, a 10-day retreat is organized. This special event provides an opportunity for the resident nuns and *thammacarini* to practice meditation more intensively, but laypeople are also welcome to take part. In keeping with an old Buddhist tradition, participants sleep outdoors under umbrellas with mosquito nets.

The students study at Thammacarini School for two to four years. In the school's eight years of existence more than 100 students have graduated. The students also receive a religious education, and about 100 *thammacarini* have completed the three grades of Dhamma studies (*tham suksa*). A few of the girls have decided to be ordained as nuns after completing school. *Mae chi* who want to pursue a university education can receive financial support from the nunnery and study at one of Thailand's open universities. However, most of the *thammacarini* students leave the nunnery for work and/or further studies at other places. Some 20 students have gone to college at their own expense after completing high school at Thammacarini Witthaya.

Changing Roles and Cultural Images

Giving is encouraged as the most meritorious and ethically valued activity for Thai laypeople as well as for monks in Thailand. The interaction between monastics and laity is vital for Thai society. Men who have committed themselves to the higher ideal by becoming monks are referred to as belonging to the religious realm (*lokottara*), in contrast to laypeople who belong to the mundane, secular realm (*lokiya*). The *lokottara* person is economically unproductive, and thus completely dependent on the productive members of the *lokiya* for material support. The assembly of monks provides a field of religious merit for ordinary people. There is a very firm boundary between the *lokottara* and *lokiya*, which is strictly maintained. The two worlds depend on each other, and this complementarity provides the basis for Thai Buddhism.

The *mae chi* are not legally part of the *lokottara*, and their daily activities have usually not included going on alms rounds. However, in areas with independent nunneries the laypeople's conception of the *mae chi* as merely pious laypeople has begun to change. At the nunnery where Thammacarini School is located, the nuns started alms rounds at the request of the laypeople who wanted to give *dāna* (donations of food and so on) to the nuns, just as they do to monks. At several nunneries in Thailand *mae chi* now collect alms in the early mornings. The monks' alms rounds are one of the most significant symbols of their belonging to the religious realm. To give alms to the ordained community ensures the giver a stock of spiritual merit. The monks' roles include officiating at ceremonies, teaching, and assisting the laity in various ways. As the nuns have gradually taken on responsibilities similar to monks, the life of nuns at this nunnery in central Thailand has become quite similar to the life of monks.

Expanding Opportunities for Women

Knowledge and education have long been important for Buddhist monks and nuns. In regional Buddhist traditions there have been ascetic women with deep knowledge of meditation but they have seldom had scholastic training. Nevertheless, these ascetic women are held in high esteem by Buddhist teachers and by the laity.[19] In modern state Buddhism, the secondary status of the *mae chi* has become more visible through the emphasis on female renunciants' lay status. However, their position as lay practitioners gives the *mae chi* freedom and makes it possible for nuns to build nunneries and run them independently. The existence of nuns as Buddhist leaders and heads of nunneries is a relatively new phenomenon in Thailand, but nunneries directed by nuns themselves have increased in number in recent decades.

Access to Buddhist as well as to secondary and higher education has long been an important issue for many *mae chi*. Nunneries with an interest in education can provide needed opportunities for *mae chi* and girls to study. In local communities with independent nunneries, the roles and cultural images of *mae chi* are changing. Some scholars predicted that involvement in social work would lower *mae chis*' status and more firmly attach them to the secular realm, but the opposite seems to have happened. The laypeople invite local nuns to collect alms food in the mornings like the monks do, and invite them to officiate at various ceremonies. The nuns are increasingly treated like members of the religious realm.

Preconceptions about Buddhist women's secondary role have started to change, but there is no homogeneity in attitudes toward *mae chi* in Thailand. Attitudes vary considerably among Thailand's five regions, and also between communities with and without independent nunneries. In many places nuns are still living in difficult circumstances, struggling with their ambiguous position and identity.

Nunneries and schools like Thammacarini Witthaya provide expanding opportunities for women. *Mae chi* are highly valued and respected in their new roles as educated nuns and teachers. However, the *mae chi* as a group do not aspire to take on the 311 precepts and become fully ordained nuns (*bhikkhunī*). They are content to be recognized for what they accomplish in their roles as *mae chi*. Through education and devout Buddhist practice, Thai Buddhist nuns are raising their status, but their position relative to Buddhist monks has not changed, even as they approach the boundary which separates the religious realm from the mundane.

Notes

1 This research was conducted with the permission of the National Research Council of Thailand and was supported by the Swedish Humanities Research Council, Swedish Council for Planning and Coordination of Research, and Vega Foundation.

2 Thai terms are romanized according to *Romanization Guide for Thai Script* (Bangkok: Royal Institute, 1968, rpnt. 1982). The spelling of personal names follows individual preferences.

3 K. Tiyavanich, *Forest Recollections: Wandering Monks in Twentieth-Century Thailand* (Honolulu: University of Hawai'i Press, 1997), p. 283.

4 Chatsumarn Kabilsingh, *Thai Women in Buddhism* (Berkeley: Parallax Press, 1981), pp. 30–31; and Hema Goonatilake, "Buddhist Nuns' Protests, Struggle, and the Reinterpretation of Orthodoxy in Sri Lanka," in *Mixed Blessings: Gender and Religious Fundamentalism Cross Culturally*, ed. Judy Brink and Joan Mencher (New York: Routledge, 1997), pp. 27–28.

5 In Buddhism laypeople take five precepts: to abstain from killing, stealing, sexual misconduct, lying, and intoxicants. The eight precepts are similar, but require abstinence from all sexual activity, plus three additional precepts: to refrain from meals after noon, cosmetics and entertainment, and sleeping on thick mattresses. The ten precepts are similar again, except that the seventh precept, refraining from cosmetics and entertainment, is made into two, and an additional precept, to abstain from using gold or silver (money), is added.

6 I use the word *mae chi* interchangeably with nun.

7 See Penny Van Esterik, ed., *Women of Southeast Asia* (Occasional Paper No. 9, DeKalb: Northern Illinois University, Center for Southeast Asian Studies, 1982); M. Ngaosyvathn, "Buddhism, Merit Making and Gender: The Competition for Salvation in Laos," *"Male" and "Female" in Developing Southeast Asia*, ed. W. J. Karim (Washington, D.C.: Berg Publishers, 1995); and Charles F. Keyes, "Mother or Mistress but Never a Monk: Buddhist

Notions of Female Gender in Rural Thailand," *American Ethnologist* 11, no. 2 (1984): 223–41.

8 A daughter's lifelong obligation to look after and, if necessary, support her natal family is seen as one explanation for why so many women from poor areas are engaged in sex labor today. See P. Phongpaichit, "Rural Women in Thailand: From Peasant Girls to Bangkok Maseuses," in *A Buddhist Vision For Renewing Society*, ed. Sulak Sivaraksa (Bangkok: Thai Inter-Religious Commission For Development, 1980); and S. Hantrakul, "Prostitution in Thailand," in *Development and Displacement: Women in Southeast Asia*, ed. G. Chandler, N. Sullivan, and J. Branson (Centre of Southeast Asian Studies, Monash University, Australia, 1988).

9 In official usage in Thailand, the term "*saṅgha*" refers to the order of Buddhist monks and novices. *Mae chi* are not regarded as part of the Saṅgha.

10 The eight special rules, or *garudhammas*, are: (1) A nun must always bow down before a monk, no matter how long she has been a nun; (2) A nun is not to spend the rainy season in a district where there is no monk; (3) Every half-moon the nuns must arrange for a monk to come and give teachings; (4) After the rains retreat the nuns are to hold an inquiry (*pavāraṇā*) before both Bhikkhu and Bhikkhunī Saṅghas; (5) A nun who is guilty of a serious offense must undergo the *mānatta* discipline before both Saṅghas; (6) After a novice has trained for two years in the six precepts, she should seek ordination from both Saṅghas; (7) A nun is not to revile or abuse a monk under any circumstances; and (8) Admonition of monks by nuns is forbidden; admonition of nuns by monks is not forbidden.

11 Kabilsingh, *Thai Women in Buddhism*, pp. 36–37.

12 A. Thomas Kirsch, "Buddhism, Sex-roles and Thai Society," *Women of Southeast Asia*, ed. Penny Van Esterik, p. 82.

13 A. Ong, "Center, Periphery, and Hierarchy: Gender in Southeast Asia," in *Gender and Anthropology: Critical Review for Research and Teaching*, ed. S. Morgen (Washington, D.C.: American Anthropological Association, 1989), pp. 294–312.

14 Khin Thitsa, *Providence and Prostitution: Image and Realiy for Women in Buddhist Thailand* (London: Change International Reports, Women and Society, 1980), p. 23.

15 For example, Kabilsingh cites Sulak Sivaraksa in *Thai Women in Buddhism*, p. 85.

16 W. J. Klausner, *Thai Culture in Transition* (Bangkok: The Siam Society, 1997), p. 71; P. Daorueng, "Sole Sisters," *Far Eastern Economic Review*, September 3, 1998, p. 98.

17 The term *khun mae* is an honorific title, usually used for the head nuns of a temple or nunnery.

18 Tiyavanich, *Forest Recollections*, p. 280; Kabilsingh, *Thai Women in Buddhism*, p. 41.

19 Tiyavanich, *Forest Recollections*, pp. 281–84.

CHAPTER SIX

The Status and Values of the Santi Asoke *Sikkhamat*

Marja-Leena Heikkilä-Horn

Santi Asoke, a Buddhist temple on the outskirts of Bangkok, is famous for its strict practices. Members of Santi Asoke eat only one vegetarian meal a day, walk barefoot, and have no Buddha statues in their temples. They emphasize recycling, natural agriculture, and anti-consumerism. Asoke temples are located in different parts of Thailand: Nakhon Pathom, Sisaket, Nakhon Ratchasima, Nakhon Sawan, Ubon Ratchathani, and Chiang Mai.

The group was founded by a Buddhist monk named Bodhiraksa who in 1975 officially resigned from the state monastic hierarchy, after criticizing behavior and beliefs in the established Saṅgha. The newly formed Asoke group encouraged members to teach actively in public parks, schools, and universities. They did so until 1989 when the leader, the monks, and the nuns were detained and accused of pretending to be Buddhists. The group was subsequently banned from preaching and a trial attempting to pronounce them illegal began. In December 1995, the monastics received a suspended sentence of two years.[1]

This article discusses the status and values of the Buddhist Santi Asoke nuns, known as *sikkhamats*. Included is a survey of the moral values of the *sikkhamats* related to merit-making (*tham bun*) and descriptions of how their values compare to those of mainstream Thai Buddhists. In addition, social values of the nuns are analyzed using answers from a questionnaire they completed about their lifestyle. Finally the article examines their hierarchical position and status within the Asoke group.

Santi Asoke Membership

In January 1995[2] the Asoke group consisted of 92 monks, 23 *sikkhamats*[3] (nuns), and four novices. This number fluctuates as some monks and *sikkhamats* disrobe, while others become ordained. However, the monks do not disrobe as frequently as in mainstream temples because, theoretically, the Asoke monks strive for a lifetime ordination. Even with this goal in mind, the intended lifetime ordination can be broken and the person can easily disrobe. Approximately ten *sikkhamats* have disrobed during the history of the Asoke group.[4]

There has been considerable mobility among the monks during the more than 25 years of Santi Asoke's existence. Dozens of monks have disrobed, some for health reasons, some for personal reasons, and others for breaking the Vinaya rules. Many have remained in close contact with the Asoke group, living in the vicinity of a center and practicing the Asoke lifestyle as laymen.

A similar mobility is evident among the *sikkhamats*, even though there are more restrictions and a longer waiting period for becoming a *sikkhamat*. Theoretically, it takes one year for a layman to become a monk, and two years for a laywoman to become a *sikkhamat*. In practice, however, since the number of *sikkhamats* is restricted to correspond to the number of monks, it takes several years to become a *sikkhamat*. The official ratio is four monks to one *sikkhamat*. In 1995, the population of the group adhered to this formula: 92 monks to 23 *sikkhamats*. Although reasons for this proportionate restriction have not been publicly stated, it seems clear that leaders of the group wish to ensure that the number of *sikkhamats* does not exceed the number of monks. If all the Asoke female lay followers were ordained, this would certainly be the case. Because the status and position of the *sikkhamats* is unique in the Thai Buddhist world (ordination is usually restricted to monks), allowing their numbers to increase might further infuriate mainstream monks who oppose Asoke's independent philosophy and practice of ordaining women.[5]

The Value of Merit-Making among *Sikkhamats*

To improve one's social and economic status in the next life, Thai Buddhists constantly strive to earn religious merit (*bun*), which affects future existences and, according to popular interpretation, the present life as well.[6] Merit-making is thus one of the main activities of the laypeople in Theravāda Buddhism, and ranking the merit-making activities can be used as a method to compare and analyze values in these countries. Despite the weaknesses and criticisms of this method,[7] it still provides one way to measure social values in the Theravāda Buddhist context. The method has been applied here in an attempt to evaluate the values of Asoke followers, monks and *sikkhamats* included, in comparison to the values of mainstream Buddhists in Thailand.[8]

In his study of a Thai Buddhist community, H. K. Kaufman distributed a questionnaire to 25 farmers in central Thailand.[9] When asked to rank the means of acquiring merit, the farmers ranked merit-making activities in the following order:

1 Becoming a monk
2 Contributing money to construct a temple

3 Having a son ordained as a monk
4 Making excursions to Buddhist shrines throughout Thailand
5 Contributing to the repair of a temple
6 Giving food to monks
7 Becoming a novice
8 Observing the five precepts daily[10]
9 Offering robes to monks at the *kaṭhina* ceremony[11]

Ten years later a similar ranking list was created by Stanley Tambiah after interviewing 79 "family heads" in a village in northeastern Thailand:

1 Completely financing the building of a temple
2 Becoming a monk or having a son become a monk
3 Contributing money to repair a temple or making *kaṭhina* offerings
4 Observing Buddhist holy days
5 Strictly observing the five precepts

To ascertain Asoke group's view of merit-making activities, I prepared a list of 15 activities and an "other" option. I asked members to choose the six most meritorious acts and to rank them in order of merit. The alternatives presented resembled those presented to mainstream followers by Kaufmann and Tambiah. To reflect the values of the Asoke group, the alternative of eating vegetarian food was added. Because the Asoke group includes many ordained women and female lay followers, the option of "becoming a *sikkhamat*" was included, balancing the male option of becoming a monk. Observing precepts was divided into two alternatives: observing eight precepts or five. Finally, the option of giving money to beggars was added, and the nature and extent of financial contributions were specified. The list of merit-making activities reads:

- Attending temple ceremonies every holy day
- Becoming a monk
- Becoming a *sikkhamat*
- Contributing money for the construction of a temple
- Contributing money for the construction of a hospital
- Contributing money for the construction of a school
- Contributing money to repair a temple
- Eating vegetarian food
- Having a son ordained as a monk
- Giving food daily to the monks
- Giving money to the beggars
- Giving 100 baht in a *kaṭhina* ceremony
- Giving 1,000 baht in a *kaṭhina* ceremony
- Strictly observing the 5 precepts
- Strictly observing the 8 precepts
- Other (explain)

Many individuals in the Asoke group felt conflicted about ranking the activities. Some persons did not respond at all, others ticked off all 16 alternatives as equally important, while some chose six alternatives as first priority and six as second priority, and so forth. Of the 16 *sikkhamats* responding to the questionnaire, three failed to respond properly to the question concerning the ranking of merit-making activities. The 13 *sikkhamats* who did respond properly formed a value pattern which decidedly differs from the general pattern in the Asoke group.

A majority of the monks and laypeople considered "becoming a monk" the highest form of merit-making. Of the 13 *sikkhamats*, only two selected "becoming a monk" as the best alternative for earning merit and these two chose "becoming a *sikkhamat*" as second most meritorious and "observing the five precepts" third. However, nine out of 13 *sikkhamats* (69 percent) chose the alternative of "becoming a *sikkhamat*" as the best way to earn merit, clearly demonstrating that they have developed a strong identity as *sikkhamats*. Five of these *sikkhamats* chose strict observance of the eight precepts as the second best alternative.

At this point the pattern disappears and responses become more diverse. For the third most meritorious activity, choices were fairly evenly divided among "eating vegetarian food," "observing the five precepts," and "observing the eight precepts." Choices for the fourth most meritorious activity included "observing the five precepts," "eating vegetarian food," and "observing the eight precepts." Among the alternatives mentioned under the "other" category were: spreading the Dhamma, serving the temple and society, helping needy people, and doing work that no one else is doing.

The patterns that emerged showed that the *sikkhamats* strongly emphasize the precepts. "Becoming a *sikkhamat*" is clearly the best alternative according to them, followed by "observing eight precepts" or "observing five precepts."

The Social Values of the *Sikkhamats*

Overall, responses from the *sikkhamats* clearly indicated the high value they place on observing precepts. When asked what first impressed them about the Asoke group, they mentioned the teachings of Bodhiraksa, the eating of vegetarian food, and the strict observance of the precepts. They also appreciated the group's diligence, simple lifestyle, friendliness, and its strictness in not accepting donations of money. When asked what aspects of mainstream Buddhist practice they took exception to, the *sikkhamats* were reluctant to offer a critique. The information I got centered on lifestyle: laxity in observing the precepts, handling of money, ownership of property, and so forth. The discussion below is based on members' responses to questions regarding their lifestyle and the reasons they chose to follow the Santi Asoke path.

When asked why is it good to eat vegetarian food, the *sikkhamats* emphasized the first precept – to refrain from taking life – more strongly than the monks. The practice of refraining from killing is seen not only as a means of avoiding demerit (*baap*), but also as a means of creating merit (*bun*).

In response to the question, "Why is it good to live a simple ascetic life?" the *sikkhamats* emphasized that living a simple life is less of a burden both for oneself and for society. One has more time to work for society and to help others. One mentioned that leading a simple life helps to control one's mind.

"Why is it good to eat only one meal a day?" elicited answers similar to the question on vegetarian food. In addition, the *sikkhamats* mentioned health issues, being less of a burden to those who prepare the food and to those who consume it. When asked "Why is it good to abstain from alcohol?" all respondents emphasized that alcohol is dangerous to health, wastes money, and causes many problems for human beings. From the Buddhist point of view, alcohol is not one of the four necessities – food, shelter, clothing, and medicine – mentioned in the Buddhist teachings, and it hinders one's concentration (*sati*). Some also mentioned that it can lead to association with bad company and the breaking of precepts.

In response to the question, "Why is it good to wake up so early?" the *sikkhamats* mentioned the fresh air, which is good for the health. Another advantage they mentioned is that it reduces laziness. When asked, "Why is it beneficial to wear simple (not fashionable) clothing? the *sikkhamats* responded that fashionable clothes are a waste of time and money. One said it is better to spend the time being "useful for society." Two others felt that fashionable clothes create passions, create demerit, and "deceive oneself and others." They felt that fashion demonstrates "greediness in your soul."

The Asoke group vigorously promotes a single lifestyle among their followers. Celibacy is, of course, required for monastics both at Santi Asoke and in mainstream Thai Buddhism. Only one of the 13 *sikkhamats* had previously been married, whereas 17 out of the 84 monks (20 percent) had been married. When asked, "Why is it beneficial to remain single and celibate?" the *sikkhamats* emphasized the freedom and independence to practice Dhamma and to work for society, not only one's family.

Two additional questions on the Asoke lifestyle elicited insight into the type of meditation promoted by the Asoke group. Responding to the question, "How do you meditate while working," the *sikkhamats* emphasized mindfulness – concentrating one's mind on the work – and the importance of analyzing one's mind. When asked about "the most important thing about the Asoke group for you," respondents mentioned the practice of Dhamma, spreading of Dhamma, the feeling of unity (*khwaam samakki*), the work for society, and the warm friendships among members of the group.

Translating Moral and Social Values into Practice

Among the values included here, the Asoke group emphasizes the precept to abstain from killing. For them, this should automatically translate to a vegetarian diet, since having animals killed for food clearly contradicts the first precept. Some members refuse milk products and eggs so as "not to bother the animals" by milking them or taking away their eggs.

Another important value emphasized by the group is anti-materialism. An ordained person should not possess anything except the minimum necessities: a knife for shaving, a sewing kit, an umbrella with a mosquito net, some clothes and eating utensils. The monks should not encourage the laypeople to possess property by blessing their private cars, shops, or lottery coupons.

The monks and *sikkhamats* in the Asoke group carry small booklets called property diaries (*banthk attaborikhaan*), in which they carefully note everything they have received from the laity, from toothbrushes to calendars and clothes. Only medicines are exempt. This booklet is then shown to the abbot of the center, preferably once a month. The value of each gift is mentioned, or at least estimated if the monastic feels it is inappropriate to question the donor.

The Asoke group emphasizes simplicity even in ceremonies and rituals. It focuses on the literary tradition of the Buddhist teachings and keeps rituals to a minimum. Members look askance at the elaborate rituals practiced by mainstream Buddhists. The rhythmic Pāli chanting, glittering statues of the Buddha, and other decorations are perceived as obscuring the essence of Buddhist doctrines. Belief in magic is discouraged. The group rejects the folk brahminical and magico-animistic practices that are prevalent in mainstream Buddhist monastic culture and that occupy a dominant role in the lives of ordinary, particularly rural, Thai people.[12] Rather than propitiating spirits (*phi*) and pondering their influence, anyone who is afraid of a ghost is encouraged to treat the spirit as a defilement (*kilet*) of the mind appearing in the form of a spirit (*phi*), and to confront it there. It is explained that because spirits do not exist in nature or in the outside world, but rather in the human mind, they cannot be conquered by magic rituals, but only by Buddhist practices aimed at reducing the defilements of the mind.

The Asoke group also vigorously emphasizes the third precept, to abstain from illicit sex. In Asoke ideology, sexual passion (*kama rakha*) is believed to be one of the basic defilements and all sexual activities seem to be classified as "illicit." Like mainstream monks and *mae chi*, the Asoke monks and *sikkhamats* are expected to live celibate lives. Lay followers are encouraged to follow the same practice and are encouraged to stay in the ascetic segregated dormitories where ten to twenty persons share a room. Even married couples are encouraged to abstain from sexual activities.[13]

The seventh precept encourages abstention from singing and dancing or even watching this kind of entertainment. This precept is sometimes held in abeyance at the Asoke centers, however, especially on national holidays when noisy festivities are arranged. The children and adults sing, play, dance, and act in small plays. The only restriction to this entertainment applies to those between the ages of 14 and 45; they are not allowed to dance because it might lead to sexual temptation.[14]

Santi Asoke constantly plays music over loudspeakers. The music is usually songs composed by Bodhiraksa with a Buddhist or moral message. Many songs from outside are accepted, however, after being screened by the monks to make sure they are inoffensive. At monthly children's parties, the children individually perform rock, pop, and folk songs, dance folk dances, and relate anecdotes in Thai or Lao.

Another break with the seventh precept is the practice of watching videos daily in all Asoke centers. After the monks have censored them, popular Thai and Chinese dramas recorded from Thai television circulate from center to center. From my observations, however, the censorship applies only to commercials; all the violence of the kungfu movies and the suggestive sex scenes in Thai dramas are openly shown. "The Sound of Music," "Little Buddha," and Charlie Chaplin films are regular favorites. The monks comment on the films as they are watching and others are expected to discuss the moral message of the films afterwards.

The seventh precept is also to refrain from wearing ornaments and jewelry. At Santi Asoke, one of the first signs that people have accepted the group's principles is when they remove their amulets, golden earrings, bracelets, and rings. Along with switching to a vegetarian diet, this could be interpreted as evidence of a "conversion experience," indicating their full acceptance of the Asoke lifestyle.[15]

Recruitment and Advancement in Asoke

To understand the social status of the *sikkhamats* in the Asoke group, it is important to examine the way in which members are recruited and advance within the group. In a questionnaire, I asked: (1) "How did you learn about the Asoke group?" (2) Where did you encounter the group for the first time?" and (3) "Where did you meet Bodhiraksa for the first time?"

Typically, *sikkhamats* discover Santi Asoke through reading books or by accompanying a friend on a visit to one of the centers, often during a national gathering. At one time, the monks and *sikkhamats* moved freely around, preaching and presenting slide shows, often at schools or teachers' colleges. In response to these activities, many teachers joined the group. These days people are often recruited through tapes. Most of the members recall the precise date of their first encounter with the group. *Sikkhamats* generally take more time than monks in deciding to follow the group, reject worldly life, and seek ordination.

Advancing toward Ordination

Laypeople wishing to become ordained in the Asoke sect usually follow a gradual prescribed pattern of advancement. First, they apply to become temporary guests (*akhantuka chon*) and stay in dormitories in the temple area. During their stay, they must follow a vegetarian diet and observe the eight precepts. Every seven days guests may prolong their stay by asking permission (*vikab*) from the senior monk or the person teaching that day. A temporary guest may leave after the seventh day, with no further obligations.

Nun
(*sikkhamat*)

Female
aspirant,
2nd stage
(*krak*)
18 months

Female
aspirant,
1st stage
(*pa*)
6 months

Temple
resident
18 months

Permanent
guest
6 months

Temporary
guest
3 months

A person must stay as a temporary guest for at least three months before applying to become a permanent guest (*akhantuka pracaam*). Guests in this category must also follow a vegetarian diet, keep the eight precepts, and extend their stay every seven days. After staying as a permanent guest for at least six months, a person can apply to become a temple resident (*aramik/a*). After staying as a temple resident for 18 months, a person may apply to become an aspirant (*pa*).

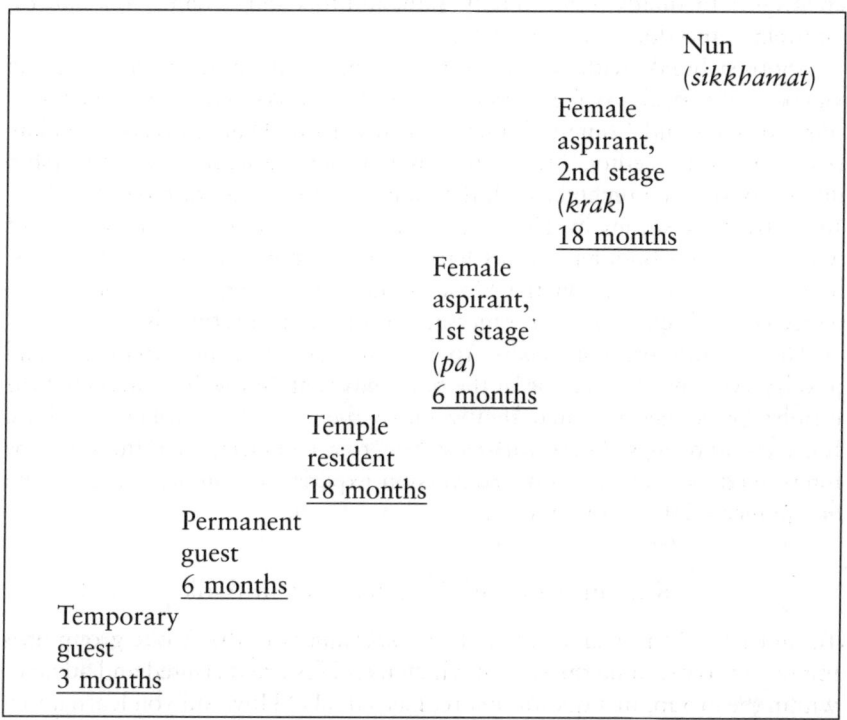

All aspirants are chosen from among the temple residents, and many wish to become ordained. Others do not wish to be ordained, especially women who, due to the restrictions on the number of *sikkhamats*, realize they have little chance of becoming ordained during their lifetimes. As a result, there is considerable mobility among temple residents. Many temple residents, as well as permanent and temporary guests, walk barefoot, eat only one meal a day, and wear deep blue peasant shirts (*mohom*) and trousers or sarongs.

The first serious step to ordination is to become a *pa*. After four months as a *pa*, a man advances to the next step; for a woman this takes six months. A male *pa* wears brown trousers, while a female wears a brown sarong. Both wear white shirts. Women may keep their hair long, but not longer than ten centimeters. The daily duties of the *pa* include assisting the monks and *sikkhamats*, washing clothes, cleaning public spaces and buildings, and helping in the kitchen, especially serving food to the monastics. Many aspirants also work in the schools.

The next step for a male aspirant is to become a *nak*. After four months he may become a novice (*samanutthet*). For female aspirants, the next step is to become a *krak*. A *krak* shaves her head and wears similar clothes as before, with the addition of a brown shawl (*sabai*) on her left shoulder for formal occasions. Technically, a *krak* can advance to become a *sikkhamat* after 18 months, but due to restrictions on the numbers of *sikkhamats* in relation to monks, many well-prepared *kraks* cannot become ordained. To become a *sikkhamat*, a woman must be less than 50 years old, but due to the long wait, many *kraks* pass the age limit before they are eligible for ordination.

Decisions concerning advancement are made by senior ordained members. The monks decide about advancement for male candidates, and *sikkhamats* decide on female candidates. They interview candidates on all levels, especially the *pa* and *krak*. After that, they bring their decisions to the monks, who do not pose any questions to the female candidates.[16]

There may be exceptions to these procedures. For example, the steps from *pa* to *nak*, or from *pa* to *krak*, do not follow automatically. A candidate may fail in the interviews or may hesitate to advance to the next position. Many aspirants resign their positions, but stay in the group as ordinary laypeople, sometimes continuing to live in the neighborhood of the temple, donating food to the monastics, and attending sermons.

The Status of *Sikkhamats* in Asoke

The hierarchical pattern of the Asoke closely follows the pattern of mainstream Buddhist monasteries and Thai society in general. The monks pay respect by prostrating (*kraap*) to the leader of the group, Bodhiraksa, who is also the most senior monk. Bodhiraksa himself pays respect only to the Triple Gem – the Buddha, Dhamma, and Saṅgha – along with the other monks during teachings. The *sikkhamats* pay respect by prostrating to Bodhiraksa, all the monks, and the eldest *sikkhamat*. Early on, this tradition distinguished the Asoke group from the mainstream, since the three bows are usually directed to the Triple Gem.[17] Even in the Asoke group, however, the three bows are often confused with paying respect to the Triple Gem.

Theoretically, novice monks have the same status as the *sikkhamats*, but in practice they are treated with more respect, in accordance with Thai tradition. The *sikkhamats* consequently bow to the novices. Aspirants are expected to pay respect to both the monks and the *sikkhamats*. Temple residents and permanent or temporary guests are all expected to pay respect to the *sikkhamats* as well as the monks. However, some male lay followers forget to pay respect to the *sikkhamats*. This behavior seems to be individual, rather than a general pattern.

Before the teachings, the laypeople pay respect by prostrating (*kraap*) to the leading monk, to whomever is teaching, to the group of monks and, finally, to the *sikkhamats*.[18] After the sermon, the laypeople are expected to bow three times again in the same order, to both monks and *sikkhamats*. When consulting the monastics, a layperson sits on the floor before the monk or *sikkhamat*, who sits either on a chair or on the floor of his or her hut (*kuti*). When talking to monks, a laywoman is expected to hold her hands in the greeting position (*wai*) all the time. The same is expected of a *sikkhamat* when talking to monks. These practices follow mainstream Buddhist traditions.

The senior-junior hierarchy among the monastics holds the same importance for the Asoke group as for mainstream practitioners. Monks pay respect to senior monks; instead of using given names, a junior monk refers to his senior as "*phante*," whereas the senior calls his junior "*awuso*," or by his name. The same format applies to the *sikkhamats*. During teachings and alms rounds, the monastics sit or walk in the order in which they were ordained.

During sermons, monks sit in the front on an elevated stage while the *sikkhamats* sit at the side on a somewhat lower stage. In Santi Asoke, the *sikkhamats* sit to the right of the monks while in Pathom Asoke they sit to the left, reflecting the flexibility in these arrangements. Female aspirants sit next to the *sikkhamats* on the floor, whereas male aspirants sit next to the monks on the floor. There is no traditional seating arrangement for laypeople; they sit scattered in no specific order. Although segregation of the sexes is preferred, in larger gatherings this preference sometimes disappears.

Administratively, at Santi Asoke three *sikkhamats* have been elected to represent the group in the outside world. They act as mediators between the monks and *sikkhamats*, and are responsible for the female aspirants as well as the female temple residents and permanent guests. These positions do not bestow higher status on the mediators. Higher status, both morally and in the hierarchy, is reserved for the oldest *sikkhamat* in Santi Asoke and the oldest *sikkhamat* in Pathom Asoke.

The *sikkhamats* hold conferences every half-month. An additional meeting is held once a month to discuss general problems of the group. This meeting is presided over by a monk. Meetings with the female aspirants are chaired alternately by the *sikkhamats* and the monks. *Sikkhamats* chair meetings of female temple residents and permanent guests, but never meetings of male aspirants or male temple residents.

Conclusion

Traditionally, women in Thai Buddhism hold positions subordinate to those of men. According to popular interpretation, a woman must be born as a man before she can aspire for enlightenment. The Asoke group challenges these assumptions by giving women the possibility of devoting their lives to religious practice. Thus far the group has ordained 23 women as nuns, albeit with the title of *sikkhamat*. The 23 *sikkhamats* in the group are highly respected by Asoke followers and, even if some lapses in paying respect do occur, the *sikkhamats* still hold social and hierarchical positions higher than mainstream *mae chi*. This elevated status reveals itself in responses to the questions above, where "becoming a *sikkhamat*" is selected as the second highest means of earning spiritual merit, a ranking favored not only by *sikkhamats*, but also by monks. This clearly demonstrates that, given the opportunity for ordination, Thai women can gain as much respect as most monks today. Furthermore, the fact that many *sikkhamats* chose "becoming a *sikkhamat*" as the highest merit-making activity indicates that their identity as nuns has now asserted itself strongly, even though their position defies traditional Thai Buddhist concepts.

Notes

1 More details of the trial can be found in Marja-Leena Heikkilä-Horn, *Buddhism with Open Eyes. Belief, and Practice of Santi Asoke* (Bangkok: Fah Apai, 1997). This book is based on my doctoral dissertation, "Santi Asoke Buddhism and Thai State Response" (Helsinki: Åbo Akademi University Press, 1996).

2 My statistics originate from January 1995 when I conducted fieldwork in Santi Asoke. By November 1997, there were over 100 monks and 24 *sikkhamats*.

3 The term *sikkhamat*, or *sikkha mata*, means "studying mother." Some laypeople call the nuns *mae nen*, which can be translated as "female novice."

4 Recently, Sikkhamat Thipdevi from Pathom Asoke disrobed. She had been in the group for 20 years and because of her high-society background and language skills, was well-known among researchers and journalists. She continues to dress in the manner of a *sikkhamat* with a long brown dress and shaved head. Another former *sikkhamat*, who disrobed about 18 years ago, remains in the neighborhood of the Santi Asoke center and visits the temple daily to talk with the *sikkhamats*, eat vegetarian food, and watch videos in the evening. Two other Santi Asoke *sikkhamats* disrobed for a time, lived outside the center, then rejoined the group and have been reordained.

5 For more about *mae chis*, see Chatsumarn Kabilsingh, *Thai Women in Buddhism* (Berkeley: Parallax Press, 1991), pp. 36–44.

6 For more about Thai concepts of merit, see Lucien M. Hanks, "Merit and Power in Thai Social Order," *American Anthropologist* 64, no. 6 (1962): 1247–61; Niels Mulder,

Monks, Merit and Motivation: An Exploratory Study of the Social Functions of Buddhism in Thailand in Processes of Guided Social Change (De Kalb, Il.: Center for Southeast Asian Studies, Northern Illinois University), 1969; and Ilana Friedrich, "Dissent through Holiness: The Case of the Radical Renouncer in Theravada Buddhist Countries," *Numen* 28, no. 2 (1981): 164–93.

7 See Jane Bunnag, *Buddhist Monk, Buddhist Layman: A Study of Urban Monastic Organization in Central Thailand* (Cambridge: Cambridge University Press, 1973), pp. 144–45; B. J. Terwiel, *Monks and Magic: An Analysis of Religious Ceremonies in Central Thailand* (Lund, Sweden: Scandinavian Institute of Asian Studies, Monograph Series No. 24), pp. 240–41; and Marja-Leena Heikkilä-Horn, "By Making Merit All is Gained: Buying Happiness, Power, and Wealth in Thai Buddhism," in *How Free are the Southeast Asian Markets*, ed. Nils H. Winter (Turku: Åbo Akademi University Press, 1994), pp. 149–74.

8 H. K. Kaufman, *A Community Study in Thailand* (New York: Bangkhuad, 1960); Stanley J. Tambiah, *Buddhism and the Spirit Cults in North East Thailand* (Cambridge, 1970).

9 Kaufman, *A Community Study in Thailand.*

10 The five precepts, usually taken by laypeople, are to refrain from killing, stealing, sexual misconduct, lying, and intoxicants.

11 Kaufman, ibid., pp. 183–84.

12 These practices are described in some detail in Thomas Kirsch, "Complexity in the Thai Religious System: An Interpretation," *Journal of Asian Studies* 36 (1977): 241–66; and Michael Ames, "Magic-Animism and Buddhism: A Structural Analysis of the Sinhalese Religious System," *Journal of Asian Studies* 23 (1964): 21–52.

13 For example, Major General Chamlong Srimaung has built separate huts for his wife in the centers where he has built houses (Pathom Asoke and outside Ratchathani Asoke). In this way, he and his wife do not share a bedroom, averting temptation and deflecting doubts from outsiders.

14 There can be exceptions even to this rule, as I observed during Mahapawarana in 1994 when some schoolgirls over the age of 14 danced folk dances.

15 For Stark and Bainbridge, a "conversion experience" was one characteristic of a sect member. Rodney Stark and William Sims Bainbridge, *The Future of Religion: Secularization, Revival and Cult Formation* (Berkeley: University of California Press, 1985), p. 21.

16 There is secrecy concerning these questions; I was not able to obtain any examples.

17 In Santi Asoke and Pathom Asoke, at the third bow the *sikkhamats* consciously turn toward the eldest *sikkhamat*, who then acknowledges the greeting by sitting straight.

18 The laypeople in Santi Asoke and in Pathom Asoke remember to turn toward the *sikkhamats* at the third bow. The same does not happen in the larger national gatherings.

CHAPTER SEVEN

Rediscovering Cambodian Buddhist Women of the Past

Hema Goonatilake

Very little is recorded about women who contributed to the evolving cultures of their countries. "History" largely recounts the activities and achievements of men. Women's roles remain understated or ignored. Often the stories of these women have been suppressed by the predominantly male historians who have interpreted history from a male perspective. Closer examination of documentation and anthropological sources reveals hidden layers of women's contributions and influences.

In Cambodia, from early historical times to the present, women occupied important roles not only in the conduct of family affairs, but also in the social and economic spheres. Women thus have contributed to the cultural evolution of their cultures. Yet, in Cambodia, as elsewhere, their stories are largely unrecorded or given little weight in historical documentation. This article unearths the histories of some of the women who made significant contributions to promote Buddhism in Cambodia from the earliest recorded period until recent times: six royal personages and two "commoners" who lived between the 12th and 19th centuries.

Jayarājadevī and Indradevī

According to Cambodian inscriptions and Chinese sources, Jayavarman VII was the greatest king in Cambodian history. By 1186 C.E., he ruled a large part of Southeast Asia, including Champa (part of present-day Vietnam), a portion of the Malay Peninsula, and the kingdom of Pagan (Burma). As reflected in religious monuments such as Bayon, Jayavarman VII was a Mahāyāna Buddhist who identified himself with the *bodhisattva* Avalokiteśvara. His son Tamalinda studied Buddhism with Burmese monks in Sri Lanka, went to Burma with them, and formed a Sinhala sect which later spread to Siam and Cambodia. Jayarājadevī was the first queen of Jayavarman VII (1181–1218 C.E.). Her older sister, Indradevī, became queen after her death.

The accomplishments of Jayarājadevī are known to us today largely through the Pimeanakas inscription in Angkor Thom, which was composed by Indradevī.[1] This inscription documents the achievements of both women, but is primarily a eulogy to Jayarājadevī. This rare inscription, which also provides important information on the life of the king, is the only source of information about these remarkable sisters. Though badly damaged, the inscription's 102 Sanskrit verses reveal Indradevī's literary skills reflected in her use of Sanskrit meters such as *indravajrā*, *upendravajrā*, *upajāti*, *vaṃśastha*, *vasantātilaka*, and *śloka*. It contains the following information.

> Although they came from a brahmin family, Jayarājadevī converted to Buddhism under the influence of her sister Indradevī. This fact reveals that Buddhism was attracting brahmins and members of the royal family at that time. Jayarājadevī's faith in the Buddha's teachings provided her sole source of comfort during a period of intense anguish while her husband was away in Champa.
>
> Jayarājadevī's older sister Indradevī initiated her into quietude and tranquility in the Buddha's teaching (*sugatasya santam*), away from the fire of torments.[2]

It appears that Jayarājadevī performed a ceremony by which she could see before her the image of her absent husband.

> She undertook a course of action with perfect adoration of the Buddha. She succeeded in this exercise. Her beloved one appeared in front of her eyes, even more beautiful than Bhīṣma. In her mind, suffering transformed into pleasure. As if answering her pleadings, her husband arrived back in the country just as a local deity manifested itself, through the merit of extreme devotion to her husband and her ceaseless imploring, by the force of her wish."[3]

As a mark of gratitude for her husband's safe return, Jayarājadevī increased her pious and charitable works.[4] She gave refuge to destitute girls abandoned by their mothers and had them ordained as nuns. The queen took these girls as her own daughters from a rich and prosperous village called Dharmakīrti, gave them clothes and gifts, and had them taught the prescribed rites. The queen also arranged for the nuns to act in a drama performance inspired by the Jātakas,[5] as an expression of her gratitude.[6]

This is the first reference to Buddhist nuns in the history of Cambodia and also the first reference to the dramatization of the Jātaka tales. Jayarājadevī's contribution to history thus includes her efforts to popularize Buddhist values among the people by dramatizing these well-loved stories. Today, many centuries later, Jātaka dramatization is still a favorite form of performing arts in Buddhist countries.

The inscription implies that Jayarājadevī made efforts to influence her husband, especially through the Jātaka performances, after his return from Champa. Through her literary proficiency, it appears that she encouraged him to emulate the *bodhisattva*. It can be therefore be surmised that she was responsible for her husband's subsequent transformation from a ruthless avenger of Cham brutality to an Aśoka-like king. The king's compassion toward the sufferings of his subjects echoes the words of King Aśoka.

> The bodily pain of his people became a pain of the soul for him [King Jayavarman VII], more painful to him than to the actual individuals, for it is the suffering of the State which makes kings suffer, and not their own pain.

King Jayavarman VII constructed 10 hospitals and 120 inns (*agnigṛiha*) and demonstrated compassion toward all living beings, including animals, apparently in emulation of Aśoka.

Jayarājadevī contributed magnificently to the principal temples of the kingdom[7] and erected many statues of her husband's parents, relations, and friends.[8]

After Jayarājadevī's death, Indradevī became queen.[9] Because of her great intelligence, the king named her head professor of three Buddhist colleges for women: Nagendratunga, the first college of "sacred sciences" (Buddhist doctrine), Tilokottara, and Narendrāśrama. In these colleges, she is said to have taught women, including the royalty, as brilliantly as Sarasvatī (goddess of wisdom) incarnate.[10] Even today Indradevī is considered the greatest woman scholar in Cambodian history. The inscription at Nagendratunga declares it to be the first college for women on earth.

Nang Keo-Keng-Ya of Lao

Information about Nang Keo-Keng-Ya is largely drawn from the *Chronicles of Lao*, *Niṭhan Khun Borom*,[11] *Phongsawadan*,[12] and the *History of Laos* by Mahā Śīla Viravong,[13] which has been compiled from different versions of Laotian chronicles.

Long ago, a Khmer monk by the name of Mahā Pasman found a Laotian prince named Fah-Ngum floating on a raft down the Mekong, rescued him from the current, brought him home, and educated him. When the prince was six years old, the monk brought him to the Khmer king Paramātha-kemarāja (Jayavarman Parameśvara) who ruled over the city of Angkor Thom. The Khmer king took Fah-Ngum into his household and raised him as his own son. When Fah-Ngum grew up, the king gave his own daughter Nang Keo-Keng-Ya in marriage to the prince in 1332 C.E.

The chronicles of this time record that Queen Keo-Keng-Ya looked after the affairs of the kingdom during the long periods when the king was away conquering different territories. The queen noticed that the people practiced the cult of spirits and performed animal sacrifices. Finding this distasteful, she insisted that if Buddhism were not introduced into the Lao kingdom, she would return to her father's kingdom to stay.[14]

In response to this ultimatum, King Fah-Ngum sent a mission to his father-in-law requesting that a delegation of Buddhist monks be sent to Lao to educate the people in Buddhist principles. The king responded by sending a delegation of 20 monks, including the king's own tutor Mahā Pasman, and three *mahātheras*: Mahādeva Lanka Cao, the elder brother; Pra Mahādeva Lanka, the younger brother; and Mahānandipanna Cao, who had come to Cambodia from Lanka.[15]

When the delegation arrived, they inspired great awe, and the place where the king and queen received them became an *ārāma* (monastery) for monks, later known as Wat Pasaman. The delegation brought with them a gold Buddha statue known as Phrabang, initially sent from Lanka as a gift to the Khmer, and a set of the Tripiṭaka.

The Lao chronicle gives prominence to the queen's role, not only in introducing Buddhism to Lao by insisting on the delegation of monks, but also in propagating the teachings. The chronicle clearly states that it was under the patronage of the queen that Mahā Pasman taught the Dhamma that then spread throughout the kingdom. A *vihāra* named after the queen, Vat Keo, was built, and the queen placed an emerald on the breast of the Buddha image there.[16]

The narrative concerning the death of the queen and its consequences throws further light on the authority she exercised in the kingdom and the influence she had on her husband:

> Queen Keo-Keng-Ya died in the year 1911 B.E. [Buddhist era, 1368 C.E.]. After she died, King Fa-Ngum showed signs of great disinterest in the administration of his once very well-organized kingdom.... The kingdom's affairs were handed over, without much attention on his part, to the mandarins of the palace who availed themselves of the opportunities to indulge in vice and acts of dishonesty. His subjects and some uncommitted mandarins were compelled, under these circumstances, to force his abdication and deported him to Mnong Nan in the year 1915 B.E. [1372 C.E.].[17]

In the legends of Khun Borom, an important place is given to the role played by the Queen Keo-Keng-Ya in the history of Laos – in the governing of the country as well as in the introduction of Buddhism. In many of the accounts written by modern historians, however, the only reference made to the queen is her marriage to Fah-Ngum. Very rarely does her name appear in any other chronicles.

Lady Penh

Not until the first half of the 15th century does one find the contribution of a woman who belonged to other than the royal class. Oral history relates that Lady Penh, a rich laywoman, built Wat Phnom ("Pagoda on the Hill"), which is an important pagoda in the city of Phnom Penh even today.

As the story goes, one day Lady Penh noticed an unusual *kokei* tree circling around in the Mekong river. On bringing it ashore, she discovered four statues of the Buddha and a statue of a deity tucked inside a crevice of the tree trunk. Intrigued, she fashioned an earthen mound behind her house and constructed a pagoda on top, in which she placed one of the Buddha statues and the statue of the deity. The deity came to be known as Neaktha Preah Chau, the focus of a spirit cult.

The other three Buddha statues were placed, it is said, in the three pagodas built a few years later during the reign of King Ponhea Yat (1434–1405). Wat Preah Pudghosa (Buddhaghoṣa) was located to the north of Wat Phnom, Wat Koh ("island") to the southeast, and Wat Lanka to the south, circumscribing the central position occupied by Wat Phnom.[18] According to oral tradition, these three pagodas illustrate the story of the fifth-century commentator Buddhaghoṣa, who traveled from India to the island of Lanka and wrote commentaries on the Tripiṭaka in Pāli based on the material available in the Sinhala language there at the time. During this time Phnom Penh, then called Catoumouk, became the capital of Cambodia. In the 19th century King Norodom moved the capital back from Udong[19] and renamed the city Phnom Penh, meaning "the hill of Lady Penh."

Queen Eng

The next reference to a woman's contribution to Buddhism appears in the 18th century. The wife of King Eng (1773–1796) actively participated in religious activities performed by the king during the last days of his life, as well as those performed by others after his death. At this time (1796), several new *vihāras* were erected to commemorate the king and transfer merit for his well-being in the afterlife. As requested by the king before he died, a new palace was built and a *vihāra* erected at the site of the old palace (Veang Chas). A statue of the Buddha was cast after the king's image, and Queen Eng had a special *vihāra* built to commemorate the king's soul.[20]

The queen continued to participate in religious activities during the reign of her son Chan, himself a patron of the Saṅgha. She sponsored the building of a monastery, Wat Thammakesar, and invited Preah Thamma Vipassanā Kong, King Eng's preceptor, from Siem Reap to ordain her son Snguon. This was a period of intense religious activity, largely initiated by the queen.

Queen Ang Duong

Queen Ang Duong, the wife of King Ang Duong (r. 1847–1860), is another royal personality who greatly promoted Buddhist activities. She fully supported her husband's patronage of Buddhism and, with a deep understanding of the Buddha's teachings, actively participated in all the religious activities the king performed. The king and queen woke up at five in the morning, washed rice and cooked it themselves, and offered it to the monks.[21]

After the king's death, Queen Ang Dong initiated many religious activities in the capital of Udong. When her son, King Norodom, moved to Phnom Penh, she did not join him, but remained in Udong to continue her Buddhist activities. She sponsored the building of two *vihāras*, one at Mount Preah Reachatroap and another at the old palace. She also had the *stūpa* on the mound repaired and subsequently enshrined the king's ashes in it. Her most significant religious act was to place the Buddha's ashes, brought from Lanka by a Cambodian *ācārya* named Ong, in the main *stūpa* of Wat Onnalom.

Princess Nuon

The first wife of King Norodom (1859–1904), Princess Nuon or Thamm, also made a contribution to Buddhism. She was a trainer in dance, but after the king died, she left the palace and lived as an ordinary person. In 1906, she built Wat Thann, also known as Nuon Muniram, and continued to support it.

Madam Sou Seth (Siddha)

Sou Seth (1881–1963) contributed to the popularization of Buddhism through her poetry. The youngest daughter of Madam Phlong and Mr. So, an official at the royal palace, Sou Seth learned Buddhism from her parents and, from a very early age, loved to listen to Dhamma discussions. Born with a talent for singing, she was trained by her mother to sing for royal dances.[22]

Sou Seth married a court official, but separated from him when her daughter was just three years old. She began to work as the supervisor of the royal dance troupe. Later, she served as the director of Mahori singers in the royal palace. She served as a senior trainer in singing in the royal palace during the reigns of Kings Sisowath, Monivong, and Norodom Sihanouk, and became known for introducing a new form of singing called *sakavadi*.

While serving in the palace, she wrote poetry, songs, and novels. *Bimbavilap* ("The Laments by Bimbadevī," wife of Prince Siddhārtha, who became the Buddha) remains one of the most popular Khmer poems ever written. Sou Seth wrote many other poems inspired by Buddhism, which were published as Dhamma books and distributed as Dhamma *dāna* (religious gifts).

In addition to her contribution as a composer of religious poetry, she built a dwelling for monks and an image house, and made frequent offerings to monks. After she retired from the royal palace, she became a ten-precept nun and lived in a small hut in Wat Batumvatai, the main monastery of Thammayuth Nikay.

Conclusion

Little attention has been paid by modern historians to the personalities discussed above, although three of the queens made significant contributions in their own right. Jayarājadevī's performance of the Jātaka stories in the 12th century marked the beginning of taking the Buddha's message to ordinary people. She also strongly supported the institution of Buddhist nuns, partially to give refuge to destitute girls. Indradevī's legacy stands as the best-known Buddhist scholar and teacher in ancient Cambodia. Nang Keo-Keng-Ya initiated the propagation of Lankan Buddhism to Laos, where it continues even today. The other women contributed by propagating Buddhism and building significant temples.

Although these women with powerful connections stand out in existing records, there were no doubt many other unsung nuns and laywomen who, in their quiet way, kept the spirit of Buddhism alive, especially through dark periods of history. Unfortunately, their stories have not been preserved.

Notes

1 See G. Coedes, *Inscriptions du Cambodge* (Paris: E. De Boccard, 1951) and R. C. Majumdar, *Inscriptions of Kambuja* (The Asiatic Society, Calcutta, 1953).
2 Verse 5.
3 Verses 60–65.
4 Verses 71–93.
5 Stories of the Buddha in former births.
6 Verses 79–80.
7 Verses 81–91.
8 Verses 92–93.
9 Verses 95.
10 Verses 98–99.
11 Translated in *Mission Pavie: Études Diverses* II (Paris, 1898), pp. 1–77.
12 Paul Le Boulanger, *Le Histoire du Laos Français* (Paris, 1930), pp. 41–51.
13 Maha Sila Viravong, *History of Laos* (New York: Joint Publications Research Service, 1959; Arno Reprint, Inc., 1964).
14 Ibid. (1959), p. 35.
15 This information is confirmed by an inscription at Wat Keo in Laos recorded at a later date (1602 C.E.).
16 See also *Mission Pavie*, vol. 2, pp. 32–34, 103–117.
17 *History of Laos* (1959), p. 38.
18 Pravatti-tikrong, *Roeung Preng Khmer* (Phnom Penh: Ministry of Education, Youth and Sport, 1997).
19 About 42 km. from Phnom Penh.
20 Yang Sam, *Buddhism in Cambodia 1795–1954*, M.A. thesis, Cornell University, 1990.
21 Eng Soth, *Aikasa Mahapurus Khmer* [Chronicles of Khmer Heroes] (Paris: Association Culturelle Pierres d'Angkor, 1985).
22 *Kampucha Suriya* (Phnom Penh: Buddhist Institute, 1970).

CHAPTER EIGHT

The Revival of the *Don Chee* Movement in Cambodia

Heike Löschmann

It was gratifying that the fifth Śākyadhitā International Conference on Buddhist Women was held in Phnom Penh, where many conflicts have threatened the peaceful intent of Buddhist practice. The effects of the strife in Cambodia were tempered by this gathering of Buddhist women who envision a more egalitarian, just, and peaceful world in which women have rights equal to men. Here I would like to present the side of Cambodia that continues to struggle for a more humane world, even in the face of difficulties. The Śākyadhitā conference helped to place Cambodian Buddhism within the efforts to reinstate and restore the fundamental respect for women's spiritual capacities that characterized the Buddha's own regard for women. The special agenda of the Daughters of the Buddha is rightly placed within a Cambodia searching for peace and social justice.

The Association of Nuns and Laywomen of Cambodia (ANLWC) was the host and main local facilitator of this conference. I was very pleased by this flowering of a connection between Śākyadhitā and the ANLWC. I was present and active in May 1995 when the Heinrich Böll Foundation sponsored the First National Conference of Cambodian Don Chees at Prek Ho Vipassana Center in Kandal Province. It was at that conference, outstripping the expectations of the organizers, that the ANLWC was founded. Those of us who had approached the 1995 conference of *don chees* with some trepidation, not sure how successful we would be in creating a framework for the development of Cambodian Buddhist women, have been delighted by the speed, facility, and commitment that have characterized the ANLWC's work from the very beginning. For its part, Śākyadhitā was among the first organizations to welcome the conference and the founding of the ANLWC, and, in August 1995, Śākyadhitā asked the ANLWC to host this event. So, less than two-and-a-half years after the effective beginning of an organized Cambodian Buddhist women's movement, we met in Cambodia for Śākyadhitā's Fifth Conference.

Support for the establishment of this Cambodian women's Buddhist organization confirms the larger agenda of the Heinrich Böll Foundation, which is committed to addressing issues of gender, racial, cultural, and

South-North problems while advocating social change and political education towards ecology, solidarity, democracy, and nonviolence. The foundation stands up for the liberation of women and men from economic, political, and cultural dependence, exploitation, and oppression. This includes unjust social structures, including patriarchal repression. Within Southeast Asia the foundation focuses especially on education and training programs to support cultural development and the strengthening of traditional knowledge and leadership. It hopes to integrate these aspects of society with appropriate modern capacities and knowledge to encourage sustainable development. These priorities have led the Heinrich Böll Foundation to support socially engaged Buddhist activities and projects in Thailand and Cambodia. In this context, it supports the development of women's religious organizations such as the Training Institute for Tibetan Nuns in Dharamsala and the work of the ANLWC. More recently, a training program was started in connection with the national branch of Śākyadhitā Sri Lanka to professionalize the skills of *dasasilmātās* and *bhikkhunīs* as leaders, counselors, and social workers.

The history of women in Cambodian Buddhism underlines the need for reestablishing traditional culture on a foundation of gender justice. Although records of Cambodian nuns exist, there is no proof of the existence of *bhikkhunīs* in Cambodia and the Saṅgha of fully ordained women in the Theravāda tradition faded out many centuries ago in Sri Lanka. Now women who enter religious life in Cambodia enter it as *don chees*. They take five, eight, or ten precepts and wear black and white, or white alone. Not being fully ordained, they receive little or no support from their communities or temples. A donation to a *don chee* is thought to garner no merit beyond what would accrue from donating to any beggar or poor person.

As far as is known, *don chees*, usually older women who have fulfilled their commitments to marriage and child-raising, have been a consistent feature of Cambodian life for a long time. Despite their continued presence, there is little evidence of support for their spiritual development and training.

Don chees, along with monks, were eliminated during the Pol Pot regime (1975–79). In 1979, however, the Vietnamese-backed government allowed the restoration of the monks' order, albeit under very controlled and stringent conditions. (For example, monks had to be over 50 years old, and there was no provision at all for Buddhist education). Apparently some women immediately entered the *wats*, resuming religious life to the best of their abilities as soon as it became possible. For the most part, they were relegated to taking care of the monks, cleaning and cooking, and their numbers were small. The only two references to *don chees* I have been able to find in the government records and decrees from 1979–89 are both negative. In 1982, the National Council of the National Front viewed them as a problem to be eliminated: "Apart from that we have to focus on another problem; it concerns the Achars and the *don chees*. In most of our *wats* we have at least twice as many of them as monks. We have to take appropriate action to decrease their numbers to solve the problem as soon as possible." (Signed October 1, 1982, by then General Secretary of the Council, Chea Sim.) The type of action they proposed can be inferred from the second reference, which appeared in the journal "Solidarity Under the Flag of the Front." There it instructs that old women seeking the shelter of the *wats* should be sent back home if any family exists to provide for them.

My own commitment to the development of *don chees* emerged out of my experience in Cambodia. I was originally sent to Cambodia by the Heinrich Böll Foundation in 1993 as a project advisor on cultural heritage and development issues. In addition to helping restore the Cambodian cultural and scholarly traditions by re-establishing the Buddhist Institute, the foundation endeavored to establish a development-oriented Buddhism which would assist the weak and poor to mobilize and help themselves. We believed that Buddhist ethics and morals could be restored by monks and *don chees* properly trained in Dhamma and monastic discipline through the sincere practice of the Buddhist teachings. They could serve society as teachers, counselors, and leaders. The aim of the 1995 conference was to assess the role, needs, and possibilities for Buddhist laywomen and *don chees* in resurrecting Cambodian Buddhism and developing Cambodian Buddhist activism. In response, Cambodian women formed the ANLWC and addressed the question of educating *don chees* as a first priority.

In actual practice, the situation of monks and *don chees* failed to meet expectations, and many complaints began to surface. Some claimed that people impersonated monks and *don chees*, and begged illegally in the markets. Others claimed that the scare resources for the renewal of Buddhism in Cambodia should be allotted to the monks and not "wasted" on old women.

Even in the face of these criticisms, Cambodian women in general and the *don chees* in particular are a very visible potential resource in the society. Women constitute 65 percent of Cambodians above the age of 40 and the vast majority of the elderly. Although no precise statistics exist, according to the best estimates some 10,000 Cambodian women are *don chees*. This number can be expected to increase as more women leave their reproductive years behind. At the moment the Association has 6,000 registered members. More and more younger women would opt for the monastic life if they had the opportunity.

Providing for these women in a way that facilitates their spiritual development and ensures a modicum of stability is not a trivial issue. One needs only to witness the commitment and dedication the contingent of *don chees* brings to Cambodia's annual Dhammayietra (peace walk) to see how powerful a potential force they can be for the transformation of Cambodian life and the development of peace and justice in the country. One of the Heinrich Böll Foundation's primary goals in Cambodia is to help establish a networking structure among the *don chees*, through the work of the ANLWC, to share resources, information, and wisdom, and to make Dhamma education more available to women. This work will expand as the number of *don chees* increases. Some of the inspiration for this initiative was the knowledge that gender imbalances (the disproportionate number of widows and single female heads of households) and aging encourage many women to make a commitment to the religious life.

As Don Chee Phich Narith, head of the ANLWC, demonstrates, Cambodian *don chees* have taken up the opportunity to develop their capacities with responsibility, alacrity, and commitment. The original conference in 1995 attracted some 100 Cambodian delegates in addition to participants from such other Theravāda countries as Thailand, Burma, and Sri Lanka. Since that time, liaison offices have been opened in 12 provinces, and a training center for Buddhist women has been established near Udong, some 40 kilometers from Phnom Penh. Dr. Hema Goonatilake assisted in designing training modules that include lessons in Dhamma and issues of globalization and development. Training materials have been published and disseminated. Don Chee Phich Narith has briefly outlined this development. In addition, Ms. Chan Sobunvy, Executive Director of ANLWC and Heinrich Böll Foundation Project Manager, played a dedicated role in this remarkable achievement. Efforts since the First National Conference of Cambodian *don chees* in 1995 have been fruitful and the accomplishments deeply heartening. Nevertheless, there is still a long way to go.

The enthusiastic development within the ANLWC and among the *don chees* has also been recognized and fully supported by the Saṅgharājas (patriarchs) of both Saṅghanāyakas (monastic orders). They also regard education and training programs for *don chees* as multiplying human resources in the form of teachers, social counselors, health workers, human and women's rights workers, and community leaders. Currently the support of the Heinrich Böll Foundation aims at equipping women with the professional skills required to play an active role in serving society, on a foundation of spiritual development.

The long-term agenda behind these developments is not difficult to see. The improvement of conditions for *don chees* will attract a greater number of younger, educated women to religious life and community service. These women, provided with real education and training, will not only become an important moral and spiritual force in Cambodia but, as in other Theravāda countries, may also become a reservoir of practitioners through whom a lineage of fully ordained nuns could be established. The *don chees* themselves do not see this as an immediate possibility, but rather one for the next generation, a generation that would receive adequate preparation for this responsibility. In the words of one *don chee*:

> Most of us are poorly educated. We have to study first, in order to be recognized as equal to monks in Cambodian society. We are not here to struggle for ordination as Buddhist nuns equal to men, as the *dasasilmātās* in Sri Lanka are doing. But we have to lay the groundwork for our daughters to be able one day to go and decide like our sons for or against the temple life. There is a long way to go, but we are taking some steps toward this vision for our future.

These developments among Cambodian Buddhist women and *don chees* are very exciting. In the long run, they will contribute to a change of gender relations in Cambodian society. Speaking both personally and on behalf of the Heinrich Böll Foundation, I feel honored to have helped facilitate the work that has begun and is continuing through the ANLWC. I hope that the Association can contribute to peace and prosperity in this war-ravaged country, building on a strong foundation of local traditions and wisdom.

CHAPTER NINE

Khmer Women

Buddhist Survivors[1]

Nancy J. Barnes

Almost 250,000 Cambodian[2] immigrants have settled in the United States during the past three decades.[3] Two waves of immigrants fled Cambodia during the American bombing and the civil war that ravaged their country in the early 1970s. A third group arrived in the early 1980s, survivors of the Khmer Rouge genocide of 1975–1979. Cambodians congregated, particularly in some of the larger cities on the east and west coasts of the United States, in Khmer communities. The largest of these are in Long Beach, California (south of Los Angeles), and Lowell, Massachusetts (north of Boston).

The majority of these refugees came from rural backgrounds. They had received little education in their homeland and arrived in America with few of the necessary skills for employment in their new country. Many had lost several family members during the Khmer Rouge genocide and arrived traumatized by these family losses and by their own experiences under that regime. Terrifying escapes across the border into Thailand and settlement in refugee camps to await emigration to Western countries capped their suffering.

With such histories, many Cambodian survivors have experienced difficulty adjusting to life in the United States, a culture very different from their own. Many suffer from chronic health problems, both physical and mental. Families are fractured by generational conflict, as children attend public schools and become Americanized. Parents either work multiple jobs to support their families, or remain at home, unable to understand the social system and unable to question it because of English language difficulties. In many families, parents and children literally do not understand each other – one generation speaks Khmer, the other English.

In Cambodian culture, the family is the center of each person's life. The parent-child relationship traditionally provided loving, close, and indissoluble bonds that became the pattern for other social interactions. Everything a child learned from her parents was grounded in Buddhist values. No one expected to have to endure life without a family. The love of parents, grandparents, siblings, and more distant relatives provided security and contentment – and in turn each child learned to return that love. Because these family units have been severely disrupted, this traditional structure no longer prevails. The current disarray of Khmer families in the United States is one of the greatest tragedies of the refugees' experience.

This bleak picture can easily overwhelm those who work with Khmer refugees. But this is not the whole story. There are also successful Cambodian families and individuals in America. Leaders have emerged from within the Khmer communities to help their compatriots heal and to restore the family and social cohesion that they remember from their own lives in Cambodia. Many of these new leaders are Khmer women.

Researchers disagree about the position of women in traditional Khmer society, and more inquiry is needed before a definitive portrait of women's roles and influence in pre-1970 Cambodia can emerge. Traditionally, Khmer society gave primacy to men. As heads of families and principal providers, fathers received the greatest respect. Women, mothers of families, also garnered esteem and frequently contributed to the family's income by running small trading businesses. Generally regarded as more competent than men at handling money, women traditionally managed the family's financial affairs as well. However, males were more highly valued within the society, and consequently boys were far more likely than girls to receive an education.[4]

Significant differences undoubtedly existed between customs in rural families and the ways girls from the urban middle class were raised. Especially after Cambodia won independence from France in 1953, new educational opportunities arose for girls. Public schooling became available to all children, but rural families were far less likely to send their daughters to school than urban middle-class families were.

Khmer women who have emerged as leaders of their communities in America often came from middle-class families and received a good education in Cambodia. However, the sense of self-respect and determination they now exhibit did not arise from public school education alone. It came from the nurturing structure of their families, and that nurturing was thoroughly grounded in Buddhist values. The stories of two women leaders show how traditional Khmer society has been able to produce outstanding women well prepared to help their fellow Cambodians in a new world.

Somaly Hay

Somaly is a dancer. Born in Phnom Penh into a prominent and well-to-do family, Somaly was sent with her older sister to the royal palace to study Khmer classical dance when she was only four years old. Most of her nine siblings had also been trained as dancers, but only Somaly persisted and developed a love of performing. She continued intensive study of classical dance at the palace until Prince Sihanouk's regime was ousted by a coup in

1970. After that she continued to train privately with her teachers from the palace. She also attended good schools, dividing her time between her studies and her passion, dance.

The Khmer Rouge took control of Cambodia in 1975, when Somaly was 16. Assigned to a work camp with other members of her family, Somaly watched most of her siblings and both of her parents die. Of her whole extended family, only five survived the killing fields. She believes that she herself survived only through divine intervention. In 1980 she escaped into Thailand, spending eleven months in a refugee camp where she worked as a health instructor among the other refugees. In 1981 she emigrated to the United States and settled in Connecticut, where she married and had two daughters.

Somaly travels all over the United States and Canada performing, lecturing, and teaching about Khmer culture and Khmer dance. She performs solo, as well as with her own troupe of dancers and a full orchestra of Khmer musicians. She trains young dancers, including her own daughters. One of Somaly's special joys is working with children. Many of her workshops are conducted for American students in schools, colleges, and universities, but she has also participated in community cultural programs for Cambodian-American adolescents at risk.

Somaly considers herself as much a teacher as a performer and believes her work with Cambodians is just as important as her work for Americans. She strives to contribute to the preservation of Khmer culture, which was nearly destroyed by the Khmer Rouge. Now that culture is in danger of slipping out of the grasp of young Cambodians in the Western world. For Khmer children, Somaly's teaching and her presence provide a link to their own heritage. In addition, spreading knowledge of Khmer culture through her art helps Somaly to open the minds of her American audiences toward their new neighbors from Asia.

Somaly has unflagging confidence in her own abilities. Her parents instilled this strength and confidence in her. Her mother in particular raised her children with strict behavioral guidelines relying on simple, basic values: do what is good, avoid what is bad. Fundamentally, that meant harm no one and no thing, and do not look down on other people, no matter what their position in society is. Somaly's mother was strong and certain of her own course in life. In contrast, by the time Somaly was born, her father was old and had retired. In his prime he had been as stern as her mother, but in his old age he enjoyed spoiling his daughter, and Somaly loved him for it. She adored her mother, who was her great moral guide and model, but her father was the joy of her life.

As a child, Somaly went to the pagoda every morning before school with rice for the monk her family supported. At the pagoda she learned how to be patient because she sometimes had to wait for the monk to finish his meditation before she could offer him the food. He and the other monks told the children simple, easy-to-understand stories to make them want to be good. Enthralled by his tales, Somaly spent hours listening to the monk both in the temple and when he came to her aunt's house every week to talk about the Buddha and his Dhamma. He continued to be her moral guide as she matured, intuiting her problems and gently guiding her through adolescent crises.

The monk, along with her parents, taught explicit lessons to Somaly, but she learned the most from observing their conduct in life situations. Her mother taught her an unforgettable lesson not long before her own death. In the Khmer Rouge work camp, everyone was starving, but Somaly's mother managed to find a few mangoes for the family to share. She told Somaly to give some to another man, who had always been unkind to them. When Somaly asked why he should receive a share, her mother replied, "Because he is dying and he should be able to feel satisfied before he dies."

Now Somaly tries to do good and to be kind always. She feels enormous respect and love for her parents, who taught her how to live, and for the monk, who was her guardian and solace. Respect for parents is automatic for most Cambodians of her generation because they grew up wrapped in a cloak of love and security that was enough to build a life on. But the culture that fostered respect and love, and bound parents and children to each other in the traditional Khmer family is being lost by Cambodians in America. Somaly strives to instill these values in her two very modern American daughters, but she finds it is the most difficult task she has ever undertaken.

Somaly is a survivor. She believes everyone has an internal source that helps them make it through troubled times. For her, this foundation is faith in the Buddhism she learned as a child from her parents' words, the monk's stories, and the good actions of them all. This is what gave her the strength of spirit to survive. It is not the doctrines of the *suttas* that sustain her; she does not know the scriptures well. She says she does not act like a "real" Buddhist anymore because she doesn't go to the pagoda (there are none near her home). Although she does not meditate the way she believes she should, she does sit quietly for an hour or more at least once a week before an altar she has set up in her home. She "prays," she says, and this restores her strength. Her parents and her monk are all dead now, but the foundation of faith in a way of living that they nurtured has given her the inner resources that make this young Khmer woman a leader among her people in a new world.

Theanvy Kuoch

Theanvy – or Vy as everyone calls her – grew up in a prosperous family in a town near Battambong in western Cambodia. Her parents had twelve children, but several died in infancy. The extended household also included a grandmother and several distant relatives. The tenth child, Vy grew up surrounded by nurturing parents and older siblings who constantly cared for one another and for her. As Vy's parents aged, her oldest sister began to assume the role of caretaker. Vy, too, learned the habit of caring for others as a youngster, tending to the needs of her ailing grandmother.

Vy's father, educated and successful in business, sent his son and some of his daughters to school, but it was on Vy that he fastened his hopes. A taskmaster, he demanded that she study hard and excel at school. She did not disappoint him. She went on to college and became a teacher in a private school. Her mother and two of her sisters remained illiterate.

Vy married and moved to Phnom Penh with her husband. But when the Khmer Rouge established their regime, she was sent to a work camp with her family. There she saw her brother and sisters, nieces, nephews, and mother die. Her father died soon after the Khmer Rouge were driven out by the Vietnamese. Her husband, son, and three of her sisters survived.

In 1979, while foraging for food, Vy was caught up in a skirmish on the border and swept across into Thailand. She spent almost two years in refugee camps before immigrating to the United States in 1981. It was eleven years before she finally was able to bring her son from Cambodia to her new home in Connecticut. She and her husband divorced.

During the many months she spent in refugee camps, Vy worked as a nurse, tending the physical wounds of mothers and children, and trying to ease their minds and spirits. The experience was a revelation to her, for she found that helping others heal also helped her to heal. In 1982, a year after she arrived in the United States, she began to study family therapy with a renowned therapist, eventually completing her master's degree. The same year she founded Khmer Health Advocates, the only health organization in southern New England that offers mental health care to Khmer refugees in their own language. In this work she has been aided by American health professionals, as well as Cambodian volunteers. Vy also heads the Refugee Health Program for the State of Connecticut. In that capacity, she serves not only refugees from her homeland, but also refugees and immigrants from other parts of the world.

Vy's plans for the future go beyond the original goals of Khmer Health Advocates. She and her co-workers in that organization have worked to heal the damaged minds and spirits of individual survivors of the Khmer Rouge genocide. Now Vy realizes that individuals cannot fully recover unless they are enfolded within a loving family and community, like most Cambodians knew in their homeland. Now her plans include recreating those caring, cooperative communities here in America. She seeks a few Khmer in each district to act as catalysts, reaching out to help their Khmer neighbors in small things and large, building networks of people in communities, thus ending the isolation so many refugees feel. Vy wants to help them help themselves re-establish the connections between generations and restore the dignity of old and young. This means reaching back into Khmer cultural roots that were centered in family and religion. Khmer Buddhist pagodas in the United States are too few and too scattered now. With a pagoda in every community, just as there was in every Khmer village, monks and nuns could provide the moral ground for the restoration of fulfilling lives to the Khmer people in America.

This is not a vision of Khmer society transported intact to a new country and preserved like a museum piece. Vy's plan also recognizes the need of immigrants to become part of the modern, complex American society around them. They must learn to help themselves and help each other to acquire needed language and job skills. Cambodians must regain their sense of self-worth. Vy believes that preserving the best of their own Khmer traditions, with family-centered Buddhist values, will help the Cambodian immigrants live with dignity as members of American society.

Now she hopes to find a few Cambodians willing to act as catalysts for the refugees in their communities. Then, calling on her own experience as a member of a caring family in Cambodia and as a professional family therapist in the United States, she will guide them as they learn to help their neighbors deal with their problems. Vy believes that if she thinks of defeat, or defines herself and other survivors only as victims, nothing can ever help them escape their situations.

Even as a child, Vy was a strong and confident person. The certainty of belonging to her family and feeling the love of her parents instilled an unshakable conviction of her own worth and her ability to act wisely. She also developed a profound sense of responsibility to others. She attributes her toughness to her stern and demanding father, while her nurturing compassion found its model in her gentle, loving mother. Even now, long after her parents' death, she turns to their photographs when she feels dejected, and the memory of them eases her mind.

Although Vy was not taught explicitly about Buddhism, she experienced it everywhere – it was ingrained in Cambodian culture. Yes, she was told to be generous and to help others, but mostly she absorbed Buddhist ways and Buddhist values from everyone she knew, especially her family and the monks at the pagoda. She did what she saw others doing. She came to believe that she had within herself all she needed to live a productive and fulfilling life.

Like other children, Vy was urged to go to the pagoda everyday to listen to the monks. Her parents would tell her, "Go to the monks. They have so much merit. They are gods." The monks, in turn, fostered respect for the parents, saying, "Your parents made you and took care of you. They are your gods. Love them and help them, and your own children will one day do the same for you." Monks and parents reinforced each other's messages of love, respect, caring, and responsibility. In Cambodia, Buddhism and the family were inseparable.

In America, the Venerable Mahaghosananda became Vy's spiritual guide. He is one of Cambodia's highest patriarchs and one of the few monks who survived the Khmer Rouge genocide. He is like a beloved grandfather to Vy, and she, in turn, cares for him like a granddaughter. His blessings boost her spirits, and she calls him the most wonderful person in the world. The Venerable Mahaghosananda also advised Vy when she wrote her master's thesis, for he recognized that family therapy as she practices it is a form of Buddhist practice. Her method incorporates compassionate action, emphasizing loyalties between generations as well as personal healing. As Mahaghosananda told her, it is a matter of giving with the whole heart and expecting nothing in return. It is Buddhism with a modern name. Venerable Mahaghosananda reminded Vy that to help others she must first learn to help herself. Then, helping others promotes further, deeper self-healing even though there is no expectation of reward.

Vy says that living through the Khmer Rouge years ultimately added to her strength of purpose, for it made her realize the fundamental value of life. The Khmer Rouge camps and the years among refugees in Thailand focused her desire to help others. She knows that she can never be at peace with herself unless she helps others. This sense of purpose, and Venerable Mahoghosananda's blessing, have restored her feeling of self-worth.

Conclusion

Not every story of Khmer women in the United States is as uplifting as Vy's or Somaly's. But many Khmer women have learned to be strong, of necessity. They have exceeded their own expectations of themselves and have made great strides in restoring health to their families and sanity to their communities. In America, many Khmer families are headed by women, because they lost their husbands to the Khmer Rouge in Cambodia, or to illness or alcohol here. These mothers make a strong daily impact on the communities in which they live.

Vy views her own life, and the lives of other Khmer women, as a logical continuation of the life patterns of countless generations of Cambodian mothers before them. In Cambodia fathers traditionally remained aloof from the intimacies of family life, focusing instead on providing the family's livelihood. There were exceptions, like Somaly's father, but for the most part the women provided the day-to-day nurturing. Mothers fostered in their children the willingness to communicate with others and to be open to others' needs and feelings. They taught their children the delicate art of give and take, and the value of being flexible. From the example of their mothers, children learned patience and forgiveness. Above all, mothers taught their children compassion, first toward members of their own families, then to the others in their communities.

Because of this primary responsibility of attending to the family's well-being, women have always been the principal healers in Khmer society. Mothers healed not only physical ailments, but also the suffering of mind and spirit. Mothers ministered to illnesses and nourished health in every aspect of their family's experience, for suffering, *dukkha*, is not just bodily illness or emotional discord, it is the condition of being in this world. Vy and Somaly and thousands of other Khmer women continue to do as their mothers did, and now they have become the mothers of all the survivors of the killing fields.

Vy believes that compassion is the heart of motherhood, as it is the heart of Buddhism. As her own mother lay dying of starvation in a Khmer Rouge work camp she forgave her son who had raged against her and cursed her. Vy observed her mother's compassion, not only for her own son, but also toward others who were in agony. She told Vy that she had nothing else left to give. Compassion was the only legacy she could leave to her children.

Vy, Somaly, and countless other Cambodian women now transmit that precious legacy to the next generation.

Notes

1 This paper is based on a series of interviews with Somaly Hay and Theanvy Kuoch, conducted in 1997. Additional background information in the introduction was derived from conversations with other Cambodian refugees and with Americans who work with them, and from published works including the following: Usha Welaratna, *Beyond the Killing Fields, Voices of Nine Cambodian Survivors in America* (Stanford University Press, 1993); and Jeremy Hein, *From Vietnam, Laos, and Cambodia, A Refugee Experience in the United States* (New York: Twayne Publishers, 1995).

2 In this essay, the terms "Khmer" and "Cambodian" are used interchangeably to refer to the people of Cambodia, their language, and their culture. "Khmer" is the term used by the people themselves, and "Cambodian" is the English equivalent.

3 The 1990 United States Census counted 147,000 Cambodians living in the United States. This number is believed by those familiar with Cambodian communities to be much too low. An estimated figure of more than 240,000 has been suggested.

4 For a summary of information on women in traditional Cambodian society and on education for boys and girls, see Nancy J. Smith-Hefner, "Education, Gender and Generational Conflict among Khmer Refugees," *Anthropology and Education Quarterly* 24, no. 2 (1993): 140–44.

CHAPTER TEN

Dam Luu

An Eminent Vietnamese Buddhist Nun

Thich Minh Duc

This is the story of Bhikṣuṇī Dam Luu, a Vietnamese nun who came to the United States in 1980 as a refugee with less than $20 and no knowledge of English. In less than two decades she made her presence known, both in the Vietnamese community and the community at large, in many positive ways. Her innovative work teaching Buddhism, training nuns, and nurturing the evolution of the Vietnamese tradition has had a strong impact on the development of Vietnamese Buddhism abroad.[1]

Buddhism in Vietnam

Buddhism was introduced to Vietnam in the early part of the first century C.E. from two directions: from India by Indian merchants and from China by people escaping war.[2] At the time, Vietnam (then called Giao Chau) was under Chinese domination and considered part of the Han kingdom. Since then Vietnamese Buddhism, blended with Confucian, Taoist, and indigenous beliefs, has become the foundation of Vietnamese culture and a central force in Vietnamese history. It was the force that unified the Vietnamese in their fight for independence from the Chinese in the eighth century and in their resistance to Chinese attempts at recolonization in the 13th and 14th centuries.[3] Buddhism served as the protector of traditional Vietnamese culture when the French invaded in the 18th century and attempted to Christianize the population.[4] In modern times, Buddhism served as the "national conscience" when Buddhists stood up and protested U.S. intervention during the Vietnam war.[5]

Throughout Vietnamese history, Buddhist men and women alike have contributed to preserving traditional culture, to transmitting Buddhist doctrines and values, to the struggle for independence from the French, and to the efforts for peace during the Vietnam war. Almost nothing has been recorded about Vietnamese Buddhist women's contributions, however. For example, the life of only one nun is included in *Thien Uyen Tap Anh* (*Eminent Figures in the Zen Garden*), a document compiled in the early 14th century C.E.[6]

Dam Luu was far from the only Buddhist woman or nun to have made remarkable contributions but, sadly, the accounts of the others have been lost. The women and men, nuns and monks who knew Dam Luu benefitted greatly from her presence and wisdom. Her story reminds us of the other Vietnamese Buddhist nuns whose stories we are missing.

Dam Luu in Vietnam

Dam Luu was born into a Buddhist family on August 4, 1932, in Ha Dong province, northern Vietnam. Her parents were very devoted to Buddhist practice. When Dam Luu was 2½ years old, her parents took her to nearby Cu Da Temple. When it was time to go home, the child cried and refused to go with her parents. Her parents did not want to leave her at the temple because she was so small, but she resisted so strongly, they had no choice. Dam Luu was left in the care of Bhikṣuṇī Dam Soan, the abbess of Cu Da Temple.

Dam Soan was one of the most respected members of the Vietnamese Buddhist community. A member of the Dong Do Buddhist order (a Zen school founded in Vietnam in the 14th century), she was widely recognized for her wisdom and devout practice. She was the abbess of several temples and director of Van Ho Buddhist Seminary, one of the first schools in north Vietnam where nuns could receive a formal Buddhist education. Dam Soan also taught Buddhism to the queen and royal family in Hue, then the capital of Vietnam. Working closely with Bhikṣu To Lien, a pioneer in the effort to rejuvenate Buddhism in Vietnam, Dam Soan gave special attention to the education of nuns.

Like the vast majority of women in Vietnam in the 1930s, Buddhist nuns at that time typically had few opportunities for formal education; most nuns were illiterate. Under the influence of Confucianism, Vietnamese society generally believed that women's social role should be limited to the home. Before marriage, young women were expected to obey their father; after marriage, their husband; and after their husband passed away, their son. Women were only allowed to learn skills related to housework: cooking, baking, sewing, and caretaking.

Under the guidance of Dam Soan, Dam Luu was ordained as a *śrāmaṇerikā* when she was 16 years old. With the continuing encouragement of her teacher, she traveled to different Buddhist centers in northern Vietnam to learn more about Buddhist doctrine and practice from other traditions. In 1951, when she was 19 years old, she was sent to Quan Su Temple in Hanoi to be ordained as a *bhikṣuṇī*. Even though she was underage, an exception was made because of her outstanding efforts in practice, broad knowledge of Buddhist principles, and sincerity in daily community life.

In 1952, when Dam Soan was invited to serve as the abbess of Duoc Su Temple in Saigon, she took Dam Luu with her as her attendant. With the support of the local monastic community, Dam Soan changed Duoc Su Temple into the first seminary for nuns in the south. The education Dam Soan offered was unusual. In addition to being taught traditional Buddhist scriptures, the nuns were given a Western education, even though Western education was not valued by most Vietnamese Buddhist monastics at the time.

In 1960, Dam Luu not only graduated from Duoc Su Seminary, but also passed the national examination for a high school diploma. At the end of 1961, she retired to Phuoc Hoa Temple, planning to focus on the study of the Mahāyāna Tripiṭaka. Her retreat was cut short in 1963 by President Ngo Dinh Diem's unjust treatment of the Buddhist community. She joined with other monastics to protest Diem's policies and demand religious freedom. As a result, she was jailed by Diem's government and only released after Diem was overthrown in a *coup d'état* later that year.

In 1964 the United Vietnamese Buddhist Church recognized the need to train monks and nuns in various secular fields, just as Dam Soan had foreseen in 1952. This was part of an effort to rejuvenate Buddhism both in Vietnam and abroad, and to meet the modern, and sometimes complex, needs of Vietnamese society. Certain Vietnamese monastics were selected to study abroad, in India, France, Japan, and Germany. They were provided with full scholarships by their schools and through the Vietnamese Unified Buddhist Church. Dam Huong, head of the Vietnamese order of nuns, approved Dam Luu's request to study social work and sent her to West Germany for five years. In an interview in 1986, Dam Luu explained: "I had seen so much suffering around us, right in front of our eyes. I wanted to do something practical to help eliminate some of the pain of the world. I love children and I wanted some knowledge of social work to help them effectively."

When Dam Luu returned to Vietnam in 1969, the war was becoming more intense. Thousands of refugees had left their homes and moved to the cities to avoid being bombed or caught in the fighting. The refugees included many children whose parents were either killed or unable to provide them with basic care. Out of compassion, the local monastic community decided to provide foster care for abandoned and parentless children. An orphanage named Lam Ty Ni was established based on the Western model and Dam Luu was appointed director. With the help of many volunteer nuns and monks, and various individuals and organizations, Dam Luu ran this orphanage until April 1975, when the communists took over the Saigon government.

Immediately after the takeover, Lam Ty Ni orphanage was dissolved by order of the new regime. The children under Dam Luu's care were sent to several locations. Some had no place to go, but Dam Luu was not allowed to speak with them. Secretly, she asked nearby temples to provide them with basic daily needs.[7]

In 1976 Dam Luu was pressured to make false accusations against a well-known monastic friend. Her own safety was repeatedly threatened, but she refused to go along with this government plot. Dam Luu secretly made arrangements through lay disciples for the children who were still with her to leave Vietnam. Soon after, she herself was able to escape.

Dam Luu's life in Vietnam was unusual in many respects: entering the nunnery at age 2½, being the first Vietnamese Buddhist nun to graduate from high school, receiving *bhikṣuṇī* ordination at 19, serving as attendant to Dam Soan (who established the first seminary for nuns in the south), and doing advanced studies abroad at a time when many nuns were illiterate. Indeed, Dam Luu became heir to an important tradition of educating nuns. Even though the war forced her to leave the orphanage, she risked her own welfare repeatedly to save the children and to save a colleague who was falsely accused, deriving strength from her profound conviction in the *bodhisattva*'s way of life.

Following the Buddha's teaching, "Refrain from evil, do what is good, benefit all sentient beings," Dam Luu was committed to the *bodhisattva* path.[8] Those who honor this path take upon themselves the task of rescuing all sentient beings and do whatever is needed to benefit them. Having taken the *bodhisattva* precepts, Dam Luu was involved in giving food, education, and related services to needy children, and risking her own safety to protect others.

Life as a Refugee

Dam Luu wanted to escape from Vietnam, but failed four times. Finally in 1978, disguised as a layperson, she boarded a small fishing boat and began a voyage to a new life. She was 46 years old. The boat was at sea for almost a week and lost its direction several times, but finally landed on an island in Malaysia. In a refugee camp in Kuchin, Malaysia, Dam Luu began life as a displaced person – a person with no country. She was surrounded by many desperate, emotionally drained, and angry refugees, anxious to blame others for their sufferings in Vietnam and in the camp.

Characteristically, Dam Luu decided not to look at others' faults or blame them, but instead used her time in the camp to reflect on the impermanence of life. One colleague, Minh Man, recalls her saying:

> I had actually started to meditate on impermanence seriously when I was on the boat leaving Vietnam. The boat was too crowded and there was not enough room for me lie down. I was pushed into a corner and from that corner I could observe what people did to each other. Surprisingly, I noticed that when the situation was bad and everybody was suffering, people fought with each other over tiny things. On the boat I reflected on the past lives of the Buddha related

in the *Jātakas*. The Buddha sacrificed everything for the benefit of other beings, including animals. He did not give much attention to himself. Without any attachment, he took care of others and never fought over the "little things" in life. As a prince, he had everything, but he abandoned all this because he believed it could not bring real happiness. These memories came back to mind and helped me restrain myself. I did not fight for a little room, a little water, or a little bit of food. I reminded myself that, as a Buddhist nun, I was not allowed to fight, argue, or be angry. Even though people in the boat did not know my real identity, I needed to live what I believed in.

Many people seemed to lose faith when confronted with misery in the camps. They did whatever seemed to benefit them, without thinking about what kind of karma they were creating. They acted as though there would be nothing after this life and therefore were not afraid of the negative karma they might accumulate in this short life. I observed and came to the conclusion that they were just nominal Buddhists who had neither learned nor practiced the doctrine. If they had learned the doctrine or practiced it seriously, they would not have done bad things to others and would not have changed their perspective on life in times of crisis. I decided to continue on the Buddhist path and try my best to do what the Buddha exemplified through his previous lives – to forget about myself and think of the welfare of others before my own.

Even under stress and deprivation, with her strong commitment to Buddhist practice, Dam Luu did whatever she could to honor the *bodhisattva* precepts. Not only did she refuse to participate in fighting against others for little conveniences in the camps, she also did whatever she could to make the lives of others less miserable. She told Minh Man:

During the time in the camps, I did not want to waste my time doing nothing and just waiting to resettle in another country. I decided to do something practical to help other refugees. With some money received from friends in Germany and the U.S., I provided the young people I met with extra food and clothing. Many of them were young and had never experienced traumatic events in their lives prior to their escape from Vietnam. They were lost, hungry for both food and love, and in need of someone to offer some guidance in dealing with their dim and unknown future.

I did whatever I could to eliminate their suffering. I cooked for them with whatever vegetables I found available. I was not a good cook, though, because I had not cooked for a long time; there was always somebody to cook for everybody at Lam Ty Ni Orphanage. Being a vegetarian I could not cook anything with meat for them, even

> though I knew that many of them used to eat meat. I realized that it was hard for them to be on a vegetarian diet.
>
> Once in a while, I gave them some money for personal use. They went to a restaurant run by an islander's family to have meals with meat. I was aware of what they did with the money I gave them, but I did not say anything. Many of them arrived at the camps with just shorts on their bodies. While waiting for the Red Cross to arrive and provide some relief, I used my money to buy them used clothes from local Malaysians. These clothes were not much, but were meaningful in a time of need.
>
> Many people thought that I was stupid, because I did not use the money my friends sent to take care of my own needs. When I heard this, I just laughed it off and did not respond. In my mind, however, I felt bad for the people who made that comment. They probably mistook wants for needs. At the time, I still had two sets of clothes and I did not need more. To me, those who did not have anything but one pair of shorts or pants were actually in greater need.

Dam Luu taught those around her the essence of Buddhism without telling them anything about Buddhist theology. She just lived what she believed in – practicing tolerance, relieving the sufferings of others, providing food and clothing to the hungry and cold, giving love and understanding to those without hope. Her life itself became a Dharma lesson, touching the hearts of people around her and often transforming their lives.

Hoa Vo, a refugee who lived at the same camp with Dam Luu, recalls:

> I arrived at the camp several months before her. There were about 500 refugees altogether in the camp. The camp was small and life was miserable because it was not receiving attention either from the United Nations High Commissioner for Refugees or the Malaysian Red Cross. Once a week, Red Cross staff came and gave us a weekly ration of canned food, but it did not last more than four days. There was no running water and we had a worse life than in Vietnam.
>
> I left Vietnam with a cousin; my parents entrusted me to his care. Unfortunately, after our arrival in the camp, we were not recognized as relatives and therefore not considered one household. Later, my cousin was accepted for resettlement in America, but I was not. After he left for the U.S., I was very depressed and lonely. I did not know what to do with my life. Whenever a new boat arrived, I would run from my tent to the shore to meet the new people. I always had some hope of meeting someone I knew. I wanted to find out what was happening in Vietnam, to get some news about my parents.
>
> One day when a boat came, I went out and saw a woman who stood patiently in the boat with two children, waiting while

everybody else in the boat rushed to land. I did not pay much attention to her at the time because I was busy asking others for information about Vietnam. Later I noticed that every day in the afternoon, that woman went, with a small book in her hands, to a place away from the tents where we all stayed. For a while, I thought she just wanted to find a quiet place to read her book. I was curious about her look of serenity among the chaos in the camps, where people always fought, argued, shouted, and screamed at each other. I thought that the book she read every day must be a very good one because she read it over and over every afternoon.

One day I ventured to stop the woman and ask if I could borrow the book she was reading. She looked at me and gently answered, "Of course, if you are interested you are welcome to read it. It is not a regular book, though. It is a prayer book that contains the Buddha's teachings. But let me ask you first: Why do you look so pale and wear only shorts and a worn-out shirt? Do you have enough to eat? Do you get anything else, like fresh vegetables, besides the canned foods provided by the Red Cross?"

When I told her that I did not have enough food, that I was tired of the canned stuff but had no choice because I did not know how to cook and I had nothing to cook with, she gently told me to drop by her tent the next day for some food. In talking with her, I totally forgot about the book. Instead I was excited about a home-cooked meal which I had not had for several months.

The following day, I came to her tent and found several other boys my age there. They were in the same situation that I was. We had lunch together in the open air and I thought it was the best meal of my life. It was nothing special, just boiled Chinese greens, white beans cooked with soy sauce, and steamed rice. The nicest thing was that we ate the meal as a family. I immediately came to look upon the group as my family, and asked if I could come back for a meal whenever I was out of food. She answered, "Of course, yes. You are welcome to come. Just let me know, so I will have enough rice for everybody."

I came back and many times she mended my shirt with a needle and thread given to her by an old woman in the same tent. Very often I thought of her as my mother. Later she bought me a new shirt when she received some money from her friends somewhere in America. I think it was $500. She gave each of us $20 for our personal use, gave some to other families with children, and kept $40 for herself and the two girls who were with her.

Two days after the first meal with the group, another boy told me that she was a Buddhist nun who went to a quiet place everyday to pray and meditate. Even though I went with my parents to the temple back home, I was not a real Buddhist. In my naive thinking at that time, religion was for older people and Buddhism was just another religion which emphasized the concept of compassion. I found out later through her that Buddhism deals with reality, not just the conceptual level. One evening I was lying on my mat among many others in my tent, trying to sleep, but I couldn't. I thought of her, of her cooking, of her mending my clothes, and I found myself crying. I realized that cooking and mending were really her acts of unselfish love. I have been a real Buddhist ever since.

Dam Luu's Life in America

In 1980, after staying at refugee camps for more than a year, Dam Luu finally arrived to start a new life in the United States. She was 48 years old and had less than $20 to her name. First she stayed at a temple in East Palo Alto, California, and took courses in English as a Second Language, but she always found time to help other refugees – taking them to medical clinics, grocery stores, and used clothing shops in a used Pinto given to her by a Vietnamese Buddhist. Being a woman in a strange land with a different culture, with no knowledge of English or financial resources, Dam Luu did not have much of a worldly base upon which to build. What she brought to America was a lifetime commitment to teach and practice Buddhism, her desire to serve others, her willingness to sacrifice and overcome obstacles, and her love for all sentient beings. With these qualities, at the request of some Vietnamese families, Dam Luu relocated to nearby San Jose in 1981 and established a temple.

The New Temple

Without much support from the small monastic community, Dam Luu started Duc Vien Temple on a modest scale. She rented a small house and used the living room as a Buddha hall. A multi-purpose tent was set up in the backyard to serve as a dining hall, lecture hall for Dharma talks, classroom for children to learn Vietnamese, and even a place for people to sleep over with their sleeping bags. Donations from Buddhists were not enough to cover the rent and expenses, so she sought a way to earn money without curtailing her religious activities. During the day Dam Luu served diligently at the small temple, and in the early morning and evenings, she collected cans at the public garbage dumps to redeem for cash. Later, with other older Buddhist women, she also collected newspapers. Penny by penny, she gathered resources for the temple. All the while, she continued to make herself available in whatever way she could to those in need, putting into action her strong conviction in the Vietnamese Buddhist credo:

compassion (for others), wisdom (to determine real needs and real sufferings), and involvement (acting courageously to help others eliminate suffering and obtain happiness). In a 1986 interview, she explained

> When people came and complained that they could not afford the rent, I always tried to match these people with a family that had an extra room to share. Others came to the temple out of loneliness and homesickness; I cooked for them, talked with them, listened, and encouraged them. I did my best to provide them with a substitute home environment in which people cared for each other. When people came and complained about the painful changes in their lives, I sat down and talked with them about their experiences, and helped them reflect on the impermanence of things in the world. I always tried to help them see the potential for growth inherent in their sufferings, no matter how painful they were. Very often I advised them to look at themselves first before blaming someone else for their problems. Causes and effects are very often intertwined, and it is hard to sort them out. I might not have been very helpful in resolving their emotional or psychological problems, but at least they knew that I cared and was willing to do my best to help.
>
> I did all these services without any supporting organization. I preferred to make decisions based on my determination of need. If I met someone who was in need, I wanted the freedom to make a decision right there and then. If I could not provide help myself, then I would ask someone else to aid me in providing help.

Through contacts with refugees who had arrived earlier, Dam Luu noticed that many younger Vietnamese spoke English to each other, not Vietnamese. They even spoke English to their grandparents, who did not understand them. Many young people had also absorbed aspects of American culture and behavior that were not harmonious with Vietnamese culture. If they did not speak Vietnamese, family conflicts often resulted. Many older Vietnamese complained that their grandchildren were assimilating too quickly into mainstream culture and losing their Vietnamese cultural roots.

Dam Luu addressed this problem in two ways. First, she advised the older Vietnamese to learn English so they could understand what was happening. Second, she began an innovative community-based program that thousands of Vietnamese organizations are now replicating: she opened a Vietnamese language school at the temple. Despite the grandparents' concern, the parents' response at first was not very enthusiastic. They complained of their busy schedules and the inconvenience of driving children back and forth; some even failed to see the need for their children to learn Vietnamese. With the help of volunteers, Dam Luu added something extra to attract more students – free lunch. The number of students increased rapidly. Vietnamese parents could leave their children at the temple on Sunday morning, go grocery shopping, and pick them up on the way back. Some parents even left their children at the temple all day, but that did not bother Dam Luu at all. The only problem was that Dam Luu and her volunteers had to cook dinner for the children. Dam Luu did not eat after lunch, and it was considered a violation of the Vinaya (monastic rules) for nuns or monks to cook on the temple grounds in the afternoon. When asked about this, Dam Luu laughed and alluded to the spirit of the rules:

> We need to understand the Vinaya with intelligence. The rule was established to prevent monks and nuns from developing an attachment to food and the care of their bodies. Furthermore, monks and nuns used to go out begging for food. If they had three meals a day and went out three times to beg, how much time would they have for meditation? Also, when we cook, hungry ghosts may suffer because they see the food but are unable to eat it. To prevent this suffering, we always perform a food offering ritual in the afternoon, chant scriptures, and pray for their liberation. My volunteers and I now cook in the afternoon, but in spirit it is not considered a violation of the monastic rules, because we do it out of compassion, for the sake of others.

Four years later, the temple had grown dramatically and was shifted to a new location in San Jose. The new temple was built in traditional Vietnamese style, with a large space allotted for classrooms to teach Vietnamese. The temple is still growing. In 17 years, Dam Luu had not only gone from a small rented house to a large traditional temple, but from a few volunteers to a large membership and staff of volunteers, many of them former students. The young students of Vietnamese had increased from four to 250. To this day, the students still get a free lunch on Sundays.

Dam Luu also began the first Vietnamese nunnery in America. In 1983, two years after she established Duc Vien Temple, several young women became novice nuns under Dam Luu's guidance. Soon Vietnamese nuns from across the U.S. came to her for Buddhist education. Over the years, the number of nuns grew to 20 and the nunnery became an established institution. Due to a lack of resources, no similar institution was available for monks in northern California, so Dam Luu allowed monks to join, too. With a teaching staff of four monastics, Dam Luu provided students with a basic yet comprehensive Buddhist studies curriculum. Those who also wished to pursue a secular education, including higher degrees, were supported financially by Dam Luu and her lay followers. Many graduates of this institute now teach Buddhism at temples in the U.S, Southeast Asia, and Europe. Some teach at Plum Village, the monastic community in France led by the well-known Vietnamese Zen master Thich Nhat Hanh.

With her unusually open-minded approach, Dam Luu created new options for Buddhist education and practice. She felt that the traditional Vietnamese curriculum focused too much on Chinese Mahāyāna texts and neglected the study of the Pāli canon and Theravāda meditation techniques. While Dam Luu herself was a Pure Land practitioner, she believed that all Buddhist practice methods could be helpful. Monks and nuns who attended her seminary were therefore taught theories and practices of many Buddhist traditions. With this non-sectarian attitude, Dam Luu financially supported students to study at a variety of centers and welcomed them back when they had finished. Some went to Burma to study *vipassanā* meditation and some to Plum Village to study mindfulness meditation with Thich Nhat Hanh. Dam Luu taught both the *śrāvaka* and *bodhisattva* precepts, emphasizing the *bodhisattva*'s spirit of engagement and dedication to transforming the suffering of sentient beings.

Innovations in Buddhist Education

Another of Dam Luu's initiatives was teaching Buddhism in the vernacular. In the refugee camps, Dam Luu noticed that many Vietnamese who claimed to be Buddhists did not behave in accordance with Buddhist principles. Faced with hardships and worldly temptations, their faith weakened and their behavior rapidly deteriorated. They forgot about compassion and wisdom and reacted just like anyone else. Dam Luu decided that the problem was partly a lack of knowledge of Buddhist principles, so in 1980 she experimented with something very new: teaching Buddhism in Vietnamese, instead of the traditional Sino-Vietnamese chanting that many Vietnamese could not understand. By making the Buddhist teachings more accessible to ordinary people, this innovation has had a significant impact on the development of Vietnamese Buddhism, both in the U.S. and abroad.

For more than a thousand years (from 111 B.C.E. to 938 C.E.) Vietnam was considered a Chinese province. The Vietnamese maintained their own ethnic identity under Chinese domination but were strongly influenced by Chinese language, customs, and culture. Chinese ideographs were the official Vietnamese writing system, used by successive dynasties in national examinations for government posts until 1918. Even today, most Vietnamese monastics still chant Buddhist scriptures written in Chinese characters. Eventually the Vietnamese language was romanized, but many words are still phonetic transcriptions of Chinese, which many Buddhists do not understand. Therefore many Vietnamese do not thoroughly understand what they are chanting, whether at the temple or at home.[9] They have great faith and devotion, but little knowledge of what the Buddha taught.

To make the scriptures more understandable to ordinary Buddhists, Dam Luu boldly countered tradition by creating her own Vietnamese prayer book. She selected scriptures of practical value in daily life to use for services at her temple. Her innovation was greeted with enthusiasm by the younger, American-born generation of Vietnamese and much criticism from the older generation. Some accused her of abandoning the authentic tradition, and some threatened to discontinue financial support for the temple, but these accusations and threats did not prevent Dam Luu from following her convictions. As Dam Luu explained to the layman Nghia Tran in 1983:

> Somebody has to start a new way in this new environment. When the Buddha was alive, chanting scriptures was unheard of. After the Buddha passed away, monks and nuns began to recite what he had taught. The whole thing about scriptural chanting is to bring back to life what the Buddha taught. Years ago the Vietnamese used Chinese and many of them understood Sino-Vietnamese. Nowadays not many Vietnamese understand Sino-Vietnamese, so there is no reason to chant in that language.
>
> Furthermore, the Buddha taught us two principles in the practice of Buddhism. First, whatever we do must be in accordance with the teaching of the Dharma. Second, we must present the teachings in accordance with social conditions and the tastes of the population at that time. I do not see anything wrong with chanting scriptures in Vietnamese. Although you may have some problems with the musical tones at first, believe me, you will understand the teachings better.

Dam Luu's idea of chanting Buddhist scriptures in Vietnamese has now gained wide support at many temples in the United States.

Still, Dam Luu felt that chanting the scriptures in Vietnamese was not enough. Just two weeks after her temple opened, she also began giving weekly lectures on Buddhism in Vietnamese. Her intent was to provide lay Buddhists with practical methods for applying Buddhist principles in their busy daily lives in the United States. This was a major departure from Vietnamese Buddhist tradition. Normally, lay Buddhists prayed and chanted at the temple under the guidance of monastics, but lectures on Buddhism were offered only about three times a year during major celebrations. Only at Dam Luu's temple did lectures become a weekly event, with free cassettes available to those who could not attend. From 1995 on, lectures were translated into English, too, for the benefit of the younger generation. Visiting scholars and practitioners from different traditions were invited to lecture at the temple, and free books on Buddhism, in both English and Vietnamese, were provided through private donations and temple subsidies. Today Duc Vien Temple is one of the major distributors of free Vietnamese Buddhist publications.

Dam Luu eventually began teaching at other temples, too. As a specialist in Vinaya and Pure Land, she was invited to lecture at temples in Canada, Europe, and India. She was selected to preside over international ordination ceremonies organized by Thich Nhat Hanh at Plum Village, ordaining new monastics from Spain, South Africa, Australia, and other countries. Sister Chan Khong, a longtime associate of Thich Nhat Hanh and a senior nun who studied with Dam Luu at Plum Village, paid her this tribute:

> All of us, your monastic children, are trying to learn your life of non-attachment. You walk over money, but monetary dust cannot settle [on your feet]. You step on fame, but fame does not have even a tiny effect on your character. You stand firm and fearless against threats from strong *māras* [destructive forces]. You have built one of the greatest temples, but the grandeur of the temple has not changed the way you look at life or the way you treat others. Many people love you, but you have no personal attachment whatsoever, because you see reality. You are great mountains, immense rivers, and vast oceans. You are a bright dew drop and a beautiful silent flower that adorns the path of innumerable Buddhas.[10]

Dam Luu's Personal Qualities

Although Dam Luu headed a large monastic community of nuns, she lived the simple lifestyle of an ascetic. She took only one meal a day and never owned more than three sets of clothes. When someone gave her a gift, she would accept it, but typically gave it away as soon as the giver left. Although she became well-known for her selfless service among Buddhists in Vietnam and abroad, she took care to avoid fame. In fact, she felt that it was more difficult to deal with praise and fame than with slander, disdain, or blame. In 1996, she told her disciples:

> It very easy to become attached to favorable news, and it only makes our ego bigger. If people praise us for doing something good for others and we become attached to praise, we tend to look for similar praise later when serving others. When that happens, we are no longer doing good out of compassion, for the benefit of others, but for the sake of our own ego. Our actions become full of unwholesome seeds that prevent us from being free. Freedom, in my Buddhist practice, means not being influenced by unwholesome mental defilements such as greed, anger, false views, doubt in our own ability, pride, arrogance, torpor, and stinginess. To be fully liberated, we have been taught to practice the six perfections.[11] If we are attached to what people give us, such as fame, and have problems letting it go, then where is the perfection of giving? If people only praise us and nobody slanders, criticizes, or insults us, how can we fully practice the perfection of patience? If our minds are disturbed by slander and insults, or inflated by praise, where is the perfection of meditation?

Dam Luu took these practices very seriously in her work and daily activities. She never wished to be equal with others, but instead considered herself inferior. To nuns and monks her own age, she referred to herself as "your daughter" (*con*). To younger nuns and even laypeople, she addressed herself as "your servant" (*toi*). In response to her, many monks referred to themselves as "your son" (*con*). Dam Luu always replied, "I dare not." Titles never bothered her; she treated people the same no matter whether they addressed her as "master" (*thay*), "elder nun" (*su ba*), "nun sister" (*su co*), "nun teacher" (*ni su*), or even "wicked nun" (*ba vai*), as protesters did in their demonstrations against her in 1994 and 1998.

These demonstrations, during which Dam Luu faced an angry, outspoken group of Vietnamese political extremists, provide an unusual opportunity to observe Dam Luu's compassion, courage, and strong determination to do what she thought was right. In 1994, one of the most respected living Vietnamese Zen masters, Thich Thanh Tu, visited the San Jose area. Acting according to the monastic rules and her own wisdom, Dam Luu invited this well-known master to give a lecture at her temple. Her invitation angered a group of anti-communist extremists in the San Jose Vietnamese community. Members of this group argued that since Vietnam was a communist country and communists did not trust religious people, the visiting Zen master and his associates must be communists disguised as religious persons. In their view, anybody who was allowed to leave Vietnam, including Venerable Thich Thanh Tu, must be a communist, so they organized protests in front of Duc Vien Temple that lasted for days. They broadcast propaganda over the public media that slandered both Dam Luu and the master. They pressured, harassed, and even threatened Dam Luu, in hopes that she would cancel the invitation. Undisturbed by the protests, widely circulated accusations, and mudslinging aimed at her and her temple, Dam Luu refused to cancel the lecture and went forward with her plans. Many members of the community were concerned for her safety, but Dam Luu did not seem at all disturbed. In 1994, she told me:

> As Buddhists, we must have the courage to do what we believe is right, in accordance with the Vinaya and for the benefit of the many. With fifty years of meditation practice, Thich Thanh Tu has many spiritual insights. I believe that our Buddhist community will learn much from his teachings. Therefore we should go ahead with our plans. I take full responsibility for this. I am not afraid of any threats or pressure from outside. All that concerns me is whether I can leave this world with a smile, knowing I tried my best to do all I could to benefit others. I do not want to leave this world with the regret that, out of fear for my own safety, I did not do what was right.

On the day of Thich Thanh Tu's lecture, thousands of people flocked to the temple to listen to the monk, among them many non-Buddhists. By the end of his first talk in the morning, 538 people had signed up to "take refuge," the first step in becoming a Buddhist. Only about 30 people showed up to protest outside the temple gate, not thousands as the organizers had hoped. It rained very hard that day and the weather was cold. Dam Luu asked that the temple gate be opened, to offer the protesters shelter from the rain and allow them to protest under the temple's roof. The nun who was asked to open the gate was reluctant, feeling that the protestors did not deserve this consideration and fearing it would create a greater disturbance. Dam Luu explained her perspective to Bhikṣuṇī Nhu Nguyen in 1996:

> The protesters deserved care and respect. No matter how bad their deeds may be, they still have Buddha nature. They still have the seeds of enlightenment, love, and understanding in their mindstream. They may be protesting out of ignorance or because they were given biased information. In any case, they should not be blamed for what they are doing. The real troublemakers are greed, anger, and ignorance – not human beings.

Thus, remarkably, the temple gate was opened for the protesters to come inside. Hot tea and lunch were provided to everyone present that day, including the protesters. Some had lunch and tea with the community they had earlier opposed. Three days later, two protesters returned to the temple to apologize for their actions based on anger and misinformation.

Dam Luu and Duc Vien Temple made the news again in 1998 under similar circumstances. This time Thich Tri Dung, a 93-year-old monk from Vietnam, during a visit to the U.S., visited Duc Vien Temple and stayed overnight. Using the same arguments as before, some anti-communist groups protested Dam Luu's decision to host this old monk by demonstrating noisily in front of the temple gate. One night they even entered the nuns' living quarters to harass Dam Luu and her disciples. Every day for almost two weeks, even after the monk had left, the noisy protests continued. Angry protesters again called Dam Luu rude names and harassed people who came to the temple. One of Dam Luu's colleagues called a meeting to discuss how to deal with this alarming and annoying behavior. An attorney suggested that the temple take out a restraining order, and sue a radio station and a magazine for libel for repeatedly calling Dam Luu "a wicked Communist who disguises herself as a Buddhist nun." At that time, Dam Luu was undergoing chemotherapy for cancer, but when she returned and was briefed, she responded:

> Monks and nuns have many rules to live with, according to the Vinaya, but most important are the promises that they make at their ordination: (1) From now until the end of my life, when people hurt me, I vow not to do or say anything to hurt them in return; (2) From now until the end of my life, when people slander, blame, or insult me, I vow not to

> do anything to gain revenge; and (3) From now until the end of my life, when people are angry at me, I vow not to return their anger with anger. I sincerely thank you for your efforts to help, but I really think we should not take any of these measures. What we need to do is maintain our inner peace and pray for those who do not have it.

The group sat silently for some time. In they end, they did nothing to fight back. Two days after the meeting, the entire monastic community of northern California issued a statement supporting Dam Luu's position. The demonstrators did not return to protest again.

★ ★ ★

Dam Luu arrived in the United States with nothing but compassion, wisdom, and the courageous commitment to start a new life. She shared the teachings and served others without discrimination: nuns, monks, laypeople, and the protesters outside the temple gate. Since 1981, she has contributed significantly to the development of Buddhism internationally. The temple she built is regarded as one of the best examples of Vietnamese traditional architecture outside Vietnam. The monastic community she founded has produced many fine teachers and abbesses for temples throughout the country. Dam Luu's initiatives in educating monastics and the laity, creating a vernacular liturgy, serving humanity without discrimination, and following a non-sectarian Buddhist approach are now being emulated at temples in the U.S. and abroad. In 1998, Thich Nhat Hanh told members of the monastic community at Plum Village:

> You are so fortunate. You have been around her so much and learned from her so often. She lived in a temple since childhood, faced great obstacles and pain, and conquered them all to become a highly accomplished nun. Her *bodhicitta* never wavered.[12] From the time she became a nun, every day she respected and appreciated the robes she received: "How beautiful they are, the robes of a nun! They are the robes of the fields of merit. I bow my head to receive them. I vow to take them with me, life after life." Her vows, courage, and spirit have always been strong. ... She displayed fearless courage in many situations and did not bend under pressure from any quarter. She always did what was correct and caring, and refused to do what was wrong or cruel. Many times, I have bowed to her virtue of fearlessness.[13]

After several years of living with cancer and diabetes, Dam Luu passed away at her temple on March 26, 1999, surrounded by many nuns and monks who had gathered from centers throughout the world. After Dam Luu's body had been cremated for five hours at 2000 degrees, a remarkable discovery was made: she had left the world many multicolored relics, or *śarīra*. Originally this term was used for parts of the Buddha's body, such as hair or fingernails. After the Buddha passed away and his body was cremated, the term was applied to the bones and teeth that remained. In Buddhist cultures, relics are found only among the remains of those who attained a very high level of spiritual realization. According to the *Suvarṇaprabhāsa Sūtra*, these colorful relics are the result of a life of continuous practice of morality (*śīla*), concentration (*samādhi*), and wisdom (*prajñā*). In Dam Luu's case, pieces of bone turned distinctive colors: red, green, yellow, black, pink, blue, and ivory. Her bone marrow crystallized into blue, pink, and yellow pearl-shaped drops. Such an occurrence is extremely rare and is considered to be evidence of her very high level of spiritual achievement in Buddhist practice.

Notes

1 Sources for this paper include Dam Luu's personal notes, my conversations with her on many occasions over the last 20 years, telephone interviews with people who knew her, and tapes of Dam Luu's lectures. I would like to thank Minh Man, Dieu Minh, Nhu Nguyen, Nghia Tran, and Hoa Vo for sharing their knowledge of Dam Luu's life. Special thanks to Karma Lekshe Tsomo and Ruth Richards for encouraging me in this research and for their patient, careful, and compassionate efforts in editing several drafts of this article.

2 Lang Nguyen, *Viet Nam Phat Giao Su Luan* [Discussions on Vietnamese Buddhism] (Paris: La Boi, 1973); and That Le Manh, *Mau Tu* [Mou Tzu] (Saigon: Van Hanh University, 1974).

3 Le Van Sieu, *Viet Nam Van Minh Su Cuong* [A History of Vietnamese Civilization] (Saigon: The Ministry of Education, 1972).

4 Thich Nhat Hanh, *Vietnam: Lotus in a Sea of Fire* (New York: Hill and Wang, 1966).

5 Huu Chung Nguyen, email to author from Toronto, March 17, 1999.

6 Cuong Tu Nguyen, *Zen in Medieval Vietnam, A Study and Translation of the Thien Uyen Tap Anh* (Honolulu: University of Hawai'i Press, 1997). The situation in Chinese Buddhism is similar; the Chinese canon contains only one small book – the *Pi Chiu Ni Chuan* [Stories of Eminent Buddhist Nuns] – that records the lives of nuns. It mentions nuns who lived from the fourth to sixth centuries, but only a few of them, and briefly.

7 Interview with Dieu Minh, 1998.

8 Tri Tinh Thich, *Bo Tat Gioi Bon* [The *Bodhisattva* Precepts] (Saigon: Sen Vang Publisher, 1964), p. 21.

9 Thich Nhat Hanh, *Tuong Lai Thien Hoc Viet Nam* [The Future of Vietnamese Zen Buddhism] (Paris: La Boi Publisher, 1982).

10 Letter to Dam Luu on the occasion of her birthday, August 1998. Translation mine. Note that "non-attachment" here does not connote a lack of caring or concern, but rather a pervasive love and compassion for all beings without exception, unmarred by self-interest or clinging.

11 Generosity, morality, patience, joyful effort, concentration, and wisdom.

12 *Bodhicitta* is the altruistic intention to liberate all living beings from suffering.

13 Thich Nhat Hanh, "*Nhu giot suong mong manh* [As a dew drop]," audio cassette of a talk given August 4, 1998. Translation mine.

BUDDHIST WOMEN OF EAST ASIA

CHAPTER ELEVEN

A Case of Ritual Zen

In Gratitude to Ānanda

Paula K. R. Arai

Japanese Buddhist history is filled with women's courageous acts and personal victories – from the first ordained Buddhist in the sixth century, to the innovators of the Heian Period (794–1185), to the inclusive spirit of the Kamakura Period (1186–1333), to the perspicacity and determination of nuns in the Tokugawa Period (1600–1867), to the leaders in educational and institutional reforms in the 20th century. In particular, documents during the last century confirm that Sōtō Zen nuns were undaunted by the male-dominated sect administration. They directed the course of their lives with the understanding that Dōgen (1200–1253), the recognized founder of Sōtō Zen Buddhism in Japan, supported women. Through the mode of ceremonial ritual, nuns have found a powerful way to express their emotional and political concerns. One particular ritual – the *Anan Kōshiki* – functions to legitimize and empower the nuns, yet is cloaked in the non-contentious gesture of gratitude.

Numerous questions surface when one considers the ritual dimension of Zen. For example, why are activities found in daily life – like walking, eating, and face-washing – ritualized in a Sōtō Zen monastery? What is the relationship between doing *zazen* and offering incense, flowers, and tea to a figure of Dōgen? How do Sōtō Zen Buddhists reconcile the teaching that "practice is enlightenment" (*shushō ittō*) with the fact that monastics receive payment to chant *sūtras* on behalf of a person who died 49 years ago? The quest for understanding leads in various directions: to temples and monasteries both small and large, rural and urban; to documents dating back many centuries; theoretical and concrete studies of custom, culture, and human proclivity; inquiries into political, social, and economic ramifications; the analysis of doctrine as well as the rejection of doctrine.

Through an examination of an exclusive nuns' ritual, the *Anan Kōshiki*, I seek a more informed insight into the nature of Zen rituals and the role they play in the development of community. An interesting note about the Zen community in general is that this *kōshiki*, performed only by nuns, is not included in the *Zoku Sōtōshū Zensho*, a text that purportedly includes all major texts, regulations, and rituals of the Sōtō Zen sect. Nonetheless, the

Anan Kōshiki is one of many in a genre of ritual ceremony called *kōshiki*. Such ceremonies are performed on special occasions. They are designed for praising and offering gratitude to important Buddhist figures, such as Śākyamuni, Bodhidharma, Jizō Bosatsu (Kṣitagarbha Bodhisattva), and the *rakan* (*arhats*).[1] The core impetus of this variety of ritual is to express indebtedness to these figures for one's own practice. Hence, this genre of ritual is especially interesting to explore in light of the generalization that Zen has been cast into the "self-power" dichotomy found in the analysis of Buddhist orientations.

The *Anan Kōshiki* ceremony is performed by Sōtō nuns to symbolically thank Ānanda for what they maintain was his act of wisdom in entreating Śākyamuni to allow women to enter the path of the renunciants. The minimal historical information available gives us some clues to the influences and circumstances that inspired this ritual. The first mention of this ceremony is found in Fa Hsien's notes on having seen nuns in India perform a ceremony to Ānanda. More research is required to trace the history of this ritual. My research begins with the Japanese development of the ritual in the form of a *kōshiki*, a type of ceremony that was produced primarily in the Heian and Kamakura periods. For example, Genshin (942–1017) wrote a number of *kōshiki*, including the *Eikan ōjōkōshiki*. Myōe Shōnin (1173–1289) wrote *kōshiki*, which can be found in his *Shiza Kōshiki*.[2] The *Anan Kōshiki* is one of them. In Kōzan-ji's Sūtra Pavilion (*kyōzō*), there are three texts: *Anan sonja kōshiki*, *Anan sonja santan*, and *Anada sonja kōshiki*. The *Anan sonja kōshiki* was probably copied during the middle of the Edo period.[3] The *Kōzanji Engi* mentions that on April 21, 1224, at Hiraoka Zenmyō-ji (a nuns' temple)[4] a *kuyō* (ceremony) was held to open the eyes of sixteen *rakan* (*arhat*) and *Anan sonja* statues. A nun, Kaikō, had founded this temple after her aristocratic husband, Nakamikado Chūnagon Muneyukikyō, died in the Shōkyū battle. Her articulated intention was to pray for her husband. Kaikō was the disciple of Myōe. Many widows who had suffered losses in this war gathered at her temple. It is likely that the *Anan Kōshiki* was compiled for the nuns at this temple and they performed the ritual there.[5]

Kankō-ni of Owari no kuni, present-day Nagoya, copied the *Anan Kōshiki* text from Kōzan-ji in July of 1829. She requested permission from the head of Kōzan-ji to use the ritual text, and then she recreated the ceremony. The *saimon* (or body of the ritual text) was written by Kōsen, the 28th generation successor of a Nagoya temple named Manshō-ji. A wood block carving was made and the ritual text was made available to nuns in the region.[6] With the advantage of historical perspective, we can see that the revitalization of this nuns' ritual occurred on the eve of nuns' launching into a public and institutionalized effort to bring egalitarian practices to bear on Sōtō regulations. Not only was the timing in sequence, but the actors were directly related. Kankō-ni was Mizuno Jōrin's teacher, and

Mizuno Jōrin was the main founder of what is now Aichi Senmon Nisōdō in Nagoya, Japan.

This relationship of events and people strongly suggests that performing a ritual that acknowledges the legitimacy and wonder of being Buddhist monastic women helped cultivate a community of women who were not dissuaded by the male-dominated institutional attempt to treat nuns as though they were inferior to monks. In an historical analysis of Sōtō Zen nuns, the revitalization of the *Anan Kōshiki* can be seen as an act that started the wave that led to Sōtō nuns' fighting for and, by the 1960s, winning equal regulations in the institutional records of the Sōtō Sect administration. The power of *Anan Kōshiki* lies in its affirmation of nuns. Doing the ritual makes nuns feel validated, confident, and joyful about being nuns. "Isn't it great to be a nun?!" The validation for their life lies in the mouths of the Buddha and one of his closest disciples. The ritual ends with a declaration that all women can attain enlightenment. From this vantage point, the erroneous ways of the male-dominated institution are considerable, yet surmountable. Through the empowerment received from the performance of the *Anan Kōshiki*, the nuns are authorized to demand that Buddhist truth be practiced over narrow-mindedness.

Kōshiki is a type of ritual ceremony in Zen that is opposite from the iconoclastic impulse common in popular western representations of Zen. *Kōshiki* are ritualized communal reifications of individuals. They are ritualized practices of gratitude. The act of jointly praising and offering gratitude to Ānanda makes the nuns a distinct group. First, it reminds the nuns that they are women in a 2,500-year-long line of women committed to fully living their lives according to the Buddha's teachings. This also identifies local monastic women to the laity in attendance. Meanwhile, the ritual teaches people, both lay and monastic, what being an exemplary Buddhist entails. In this way, the *Anan Kōshiki* contributes to establishing the meaning and content of being a Zen Buddhist. The profound influence of *bonbai* (esoteric chanting) and the dramatic method of carrying the *bonbai* text illustrate the connection Zen has with esoteric Buddhism, perhaps the Ōhara Tendai sect, so we see Zen not "alone" or "pure." The values that are manifested and inculcated in the ceremony include respect, gratitude, remembrance, compassion, giving merit to others, that words are powerful – not "beyond words and letters" – and that monastic life is quite normal. Through this ritual, and numerous other activities, the Sōtō nuns practice body-to-body transmission, not just mind-to-mind transmission. In short, the ritual explicitly tells us that women's bodies are free from the five limitations normally imputed to them[7] and that women are capable of attaining enlightenment. Even a cursory examination of the *Anan Kōshiki* reveals that the power of Zen is not in "self," but in community.

The entire *kōshiki* is still performed at Aichi Senmon Nisōdō today, although it is only performed once every six to eight years. A ceremony called the *Anantan* is done at the end of the *kōshiki*. This ceremony is much shorter in length and is performed on the seventh day of the month at the nuns' monastery.

Structure of the *Anan Kōshiki* Ritual

The *Anan Kōshiki* ritual begins with the ringing of bells, a resounding call to begin the ritual in gratitude to Ānanda. The altar in the worship hall is elaborately prepared with an image of Ānanda, and offerings of candles, flowers, and incense are made. The laity in attendance sit to the sides, leaving the space directly in front of the altar open for the nuns to perform the various sections of the ritual. The nuns wear their formal ceremony robes, with the abbess dressed in silk brocade robes, reserved for extremely important rituals.

Sangege: This section opens the ceremony. A *gātha* (verse) is chanted three times while three nuns walk around the worship hall. The first nun in the procession carries an incense burner, the second nun sprinkles pure water with a pine branch, and the third nun scatters lotus blossom petals.

Shichisan: Next, the Four Wisdoms (*catvārijñānāni*) are chanted in Sanskrit by all the nuns:

> *Oṃ vajrasattvasaṃgrahād vajraratnam anuttaram vajra dharmagā-vanaiḥvajra karmakaro bhava.*[8]

Nyōhachizu: In this part of the ceremony, two nuns play cymbals. The non-melodic pattern helps to focus on the ritual. It functions like an offering of sound.

Offerings: The traditional offerings of incense, tea, rice, cakes, prostrations, and bows are made to Ānanda. The head celebrant, or *shikishi*, leads this part of the ceremony. Each motion is performed with great respect and reverence, helping inculcate the attitude of gratitude.

Saimon: During this section a nun eloquently explains the purpose of the ceremony. In contrast to the esoteric chanting and classical language used in other portions of the ritual, at this point the *saimon* clarifies the meaning of the ceremony in everyday language. This underscores the sincerity, rather than mere formality, of this ritual act to praise and thank Śākyamuni and Ānanda for their compassion for women.

Bombai: This Sanskrit chanting heightens the power of the ritual. It is a ritual element borrowed from the esoteric Buddhist sect, Tendai. The notation for this chant indicates pitches like points on a compass. It is not a readily recognizable script, which increases this chant's sense of mystery and power. It subtly demonstrates the nuns' ability to chant something entirely unintelligible to the average lay audience participant. This helps to establish the nuns' status in the community.

The chant recited is: *nyorai myō shiki shinze*, "The wondrous form, body, and world of the Thus Come One (*tathāgata*)." The emphasis in the chant is on the word "myō," which means wondrous. The abbess, Aoyama Sensei, explains that this may be a *gātha* written by Mahāprajāpatī (*Shogan no Fujin*) after seeing the enlightened Buddha, expressing her joy and wonder upon seeing him in his enlightened state. Even if this is historically inaccurate, it makes sense in reference to this ritual. It indicates that these nuns recognize the relationship between the Buddha and Mahāprajāpatī as one of respect.

Sanbonshaku: This tripartite element of the ceremony borrows a ritual element developed during the T'ang dynasty. It is a reference to the *Prajñāparamitā* in 25,000 lines. Three nuns chant in front of the altar. One scatters lotus petals while another intermittently shakes the *shakujo*, or staff with rings.

Shikimon: During this section, the many qualities of Ānanda are praised. First, he is praised as one who practiced hard and renounced the world. Next, the nuns articulate their gratitude and indebtedness to him for enabling them to become renunciants. They recount how Ānanda asked Śākyamuni three times for women to be allowed to join the Saṅgha. The nuns chant, "*Nyonin tokudo no daishi*," meaning "Great teacher of women's ordination." In the third part of this section they praise various aspects of Ānanda. First, they praise Ānanda's countenance, presence, and appearance. They then praise him for his dedication in serving as *jisha*, or attendant, of Śākyamuni for 25 years. Next, they praise him for the merit of having heard many scriptures or teachings from the Buddha. Finally, they praise him for his magnanimous heart, likening his compassion to the size of the universe.

At this point the liturgy expresses profound gratitude to Śākyamuni for heeding Ānanda's plea: "Please somehow recognize your mother."[9] The ritual acknowledges that when the Buddha heard this, he accepted the request. It then stresses that when the women heard his acquiescence, they became ecstatic. Together the nuns then say, "We [at the ceremony] give praise, express gratitude, prostrate, and chant exaltations to Śākyamuni." As is typical of all Buddhist rituals, the merit accrued during the ritual is then shared with all living beings.

The highlight of the ritual occurs when the lead chanter, the *ino*, chants loud and clear, "We sentient beings all together realize the Buddhist way. Now all women, like Queen Vaidehī, transform their bodies with five limitations and attain rebirth in heaven."

The *Anantan* Ritual

The *Anantan* ritual is much shorter and less elaborate. The structure of the ritual is similar to the *Anan Kōshiki*. It is performed regularly on the evening of the seventh day of each month, much more frequently than the *Anan Kōshiki*.

The head chanter begins by chanting the refrain: "*Namu daihi Anan son* (Praise to the great compassion of Ānanda)." She then begins chanting the ten praises to Ānanda. All in attendance chant the refrain after each of the ten praises for:

1 Both Śākyamuni's enlightenment and birth;
2 The bliss of all in the five heavens;[10]
3 Those in the three realms who are near Buddha;
4 The frequent chorus of the supreme subtlety of the Dharma;[11]
5 Women's ordination and the eight rules;
6 Recording the peerless teachings of Vulture's Peak;
7 Compiling the scriptures in one lifetime;
8 Receiving beautiful gold brocade and hanging it on pillars;
9 Causing light of three kinds of gods to appear;
10 Entering the eternal stream of *nirvāna*.

The ritual ends with, "Praise to the great compassion of Ānanda."

Following the *Anantan* ceremony, a ceremony for the benefit of the ancestors of all those present is performed. Most likely, this is one reason people attend the ceremony, intending to gain merit for their departed ancestors.

After all the ceremonies end, Aoyama Sensei stresses that it is due to the kindness of Ānanda that we now have the Buddhist scriptures based on the Buddha's teachings. Having been Śākyamuni's attendant for 25 years, he is remembered as the one who recited the Buddha's teachings at the First Council after the Buddha's passing, where they were recorded for posterity. Aoyama Sensei does not reiterate the issue of nuns' ordination at this point.

This ritual reminds the laity that the nuns are to be respected, because they represent a lineage that stretches directly back to Śākyamuni Buddha. The nuns do not need to educate the laity on this point nor convince them that they deserve respect; the ritual automatically establishes their legitimation and worth. If there were ever any doubt, performing this ritual also affirms for the nuns themselves that they are indeed in a venerable line and are not inferior. A compelling sense of empowerment is generated among the nuns during the ritual.

I do not have concrete proof that performing this ritual resulted in the nuns' struggle for equality in the sect regulations, but I do not think it was mere coincidence that the very same nuns who won their equality are those who revived this ritual of gratitude. Furthermore, evidence I gathered in surveys and interviews of these Sōtō Zen nuns demonstrates that gratitude is central to their attitudes and their responses to circumstances. They have gained numerous opportunities and effectiveness, overpowering male-dominated sect institutions with their practice and turning events into opportunities to be grateful. Their gratitude became a powerful tool, enabling them to transform their circumstances of inequality into equality.

Notes

1 Others include: *Hōon Kōshiki*, *Dentō Kōshiki*, *Nehan Kōshiki*, *Yakushiji Kōshiki*, *Hokke Kōshiki*, *Daihannya Kōshiki*, *Shari Kōshiki*, *Aizen Kōshiki*, and *Fudō Kōshiki*.

2 Ebie Gimyo, "Anan Kōshiki," *Sōtō-shū Jissen Sōsho*, vol. 8, ed. Sōtō-shū Jissen Sōsho Hensan Iinkai (Kiyomizu-shi, Shizouka Prefecture: Daizōsha, 1985), p. 291.

3 Ibid.

4 No longer standing.

5 *Sōtō-shū Jissen Sōsho*, p. 292.

6 Ibid., p. 293.

7 The *Lotus Sūtra* mentions that men and women have five obstacles to Buddhist practice. The five obstacles for women are that they cannot become: (1) a Cakravartin king (Tenrin-ō), (2) King of Brahma Heaven (Bonten-ō), (3) Śakra god Indra (Taishakuten), (4) Mārā, or (5) a Buddha.

8 T. 8664. T refers to Junjirō Takakusu, *Taishō shinshū daizōkyō* (Tōkyō: Daizōkyō Gakujutsu Yōgo Kenkyūkai, 1923–32).

9 *Anan Kōshiki*, reprint of ritual manual (Kyoto: Kaibashoin, 1986).

10 Beings experience bliss simply by gazing at Ānanda.

11 Ānanda was like a tape recorder, able to recite all the teachings he had heard, which is why we now have the texts.

CHAPTER TWELVE

Tiexiangsi

A Gelugpa Nunnery in Contemporary China

Ester Bianchi

Tiexiangsi ("Iron Statue Monastery") is located in Chengdu, Sichuan Province, in Southwest China. It is the only nunnery in China (Han territory) following the Gelugpa (*dGe lugs pa*) tradition, founded in Tibet in the 14th century by the monk-scholar Tsongkhapa. The Gelugpa tradition is associated with the Dalai Lama and the Panchen Lama, and has been the most influential school in Tibet since the 17th century.

In China, the Gelugpa tradition is known as the "Yellow School," because of the yellow hats its monks wear during important ceremonies. Although the school has existed in China since the Yuan Dynasty (1271–1368), and its main monastery, Yonghegong in Beijing, was converted into a Tibetan-style monastery in 1744, the Gelugpa tradition was not widely practiced by Chinese Buddhists until more recently. Only during the last part of the 19th century did the school begin to attract Chinese devotees. During the first half of the present century, it began to be practiced on a vast scale, particularly in Sichuan province.

The founder of Tiexiangsi Nunnery was a Chinese *bhikṣu*, Nenghai. Like many other Chinese monks of his era, Nenghai devoted his life to spreading Tibetan Buddhist teachings in China. Tiexiangsi has been in continuous existence for about 50 years. Since it is situated in Chinese territory, it reflects the Chinese Buddhist tradition of its cultural setting as well as the Tibetan influence of the Gelugpa school. Chinese influence can be seen in the daily life of the nunnery, the religious calendar, monastic discipline, ordination procedures, and certain other rituals.

Even against a Chinese Buddhist backdrop, the substance and content of the nuns' practice – meditation, chanting services, and *tantric* teachings – are all of Tibetan origin. Transmitted privately from master to disciple, these teachings were imparted directly to the first nuns of the community during the early 1940s by Tiexiangsi's founder, Nenghai.

"Iron Statue" Beginnings

According to the *Annals of Huayang District*, an iron statue of Śākyamuni Buddha was excavated on the site of the nunnery during the 18th year of the Wanli era (1590). In order to honor and worship this statue, the local people built a monastery and called it Tiexiangsi, the "Iron Statue Monastery." The monastery followed the Chan tradition and has survived for more than three centuries.

During the war with Japan (1937–1945), Tiexiangsi became the property of a neighboring monastery, Jincisi, which had been converted into a Tibetan-style monastery by Nenghai in 1938 and followed the Gelugpa tradition. Nenghai had many devotees and his Dharma talks attracted many followers, including many women and nuns. Since the Vinaya (Buddhist monastic code) does not allow nuns to live in the same buildings as monks, Nenghai decided that the nuns should live at Tiexiangsi. Thus he founded the first and only Gelugpa nunnery in China. Two nuns, Longlian and Dingjing, were appointed as the first leaders of the new nunnery, and Longlian eventually became the abbess.

The ordination procedures of Tiexiangsi follow the Chinese tradition. In 1949, on the eve of the founding of the People's Republic of China (P.R.C.), Longlian and Nenghai invited the Vinaya Master Guanyi to teach monastic discipline to the nuns. At the end of the teachings, Guanyi conferred the *śikṣamāṇā* (probationary) precepts on the whole community. According to the Vinaya texts, the term of these vows is two years, after which the nuns were supposed to receive full ordination in the Dharmagupta tradition, the Vinaya school followed by Chinese Buddhists.[1] Master Guanyi explained the dual ordination procedure, the correct way for nuns to receive full ordination, that was first introduced into China from Sri Lanka in 434 C.E. According to these rules, nuns should receive the *bhikṣuṇī* precepts first from the *bhikṣu* community and then from the *bhikṣuṇī* community. The Chinese term for this ordination ritual is called *erbu sengjie*, "ordination (conferred) by the two Saṅghas."[2] Unfortunately, the nuns did not follow this ritual when they received their own ordination, but later Longlian decided to resurrect this procedure in China. In 1982, she finally fulfilled her goal, ordaining 21 nuns at Aidaotang Nunnery following the rules prescribed in the Vinaya. Since then, she has participated in almost every *bhikṣuṇī* ordination conducted in China.

Tiexiangsi Nunnery has evolved in relation to government policy shifts toward religion in China.[3] During the first 15 years of the P.R.C., about 30 nuns lived in Tiexiangsi. They had to work in the fields to sustain themselves, and they devoted the rest of their time to religious practice as they had been taught by Nenghai. Since they followed the Tibetan tradition, some began to study Tibetan language. Others (particularly Longlian, already fluent in Tibetan) began translating Tibetan Buddhist works commissioned by Nenghai.

In 1966, at the onset of the Cultural Revolution, nearly all the nuns left the nunnery. Some disrobed and went back to their original homes, while others followed Longlian and moved to Aidaotang Nunnery in the center of Chengdu.[4] They stayed there until 1979, living side-by-side with workers who were employed in nearby factories or the government workshop in the nunnery complex.

During the Cultural Revolution, Tiexiangsi was occupied by eight farming families and an elementary school. In the beginning, eight nuns lived there also, but they eventually left as conditions deteriorated. Some of the buildings and sacred images sustained heavy damage, including the iron Śākyamuni statue that gave Tiexiangsi its name and had presided peacefully over the nunnery since its discovery.

In 1979, the government began to relax its policy toward religion. Monks and nuns were gradually allowed to return to religious life, and Longlian and her community regained most of the property associated with Tiexiangsi, although the nunnery's fields continued to be cultivated by farmers, and an elementary school continued to occupy a large building on the nunnery grounds. The returning nuns, assisted by government funds, began restoring the damaged buildings and Buddha images. By 1985 Tiexiangsi had regained much of its previous beauty and the nunnery began to function smoothly once again.

In 1983, the Sichuan Buddhist Higher Institute for Bhikṣuṇīs (*Sichuan nizhong foxueyuan*) was established at Tiexiangsi. It is the first and only institution of higher learning for *bhikṣuṇīs* in China.

Tiexiangsi is a "closed" nunnery, like many other monasteries in China. This means it is for the nuns only and is not open to laypeople for devotions. While other monasteries (Aidaotang Nunnery, for example) welcome laypeople for daily meditations and other activities, outsiders rarely come to Tiexiangsi. Lay worshippers are discouraged from visiting the nunnery because of the Tibetan tradition it follows. The nuns' daily practice can be performed only by initiated disciples. In addition, the chanting and other activities are not understandable to Chinese Buddhists who do not have any knowledge of Tibetan Buddhism. The few laypeople that one sees at Tiexiangsi are usually Gelugpa devotees.

At the time of my research, there were more than 60 nuns living in Tiexiangsi. Forty of them were young students who entered the nunnery to attend a three-, six-, or nine-year course of study at the Buddhist Institute. While some nuns stay after graduation, the majority return to their own nunneries or move to other Buddhist facilities in China. Many other nuns spend summer retreats at Tiexiangsi to hear Longlian give Dharma talks. As Longlian once told me, "There are many ways to continue spreading Gelugpa practice among Chinese Buddhists, according to the wishes of our lama Nenghai."

Life and Work of Nenghai

Nenghai (1886–1967)[5] was born in Mianzhu district, Sichuan province. An orphan, he was raised by his elder sister and worked as an apprentice in a workshop in Chengdu until he entered the army in 1905. About ten years later, he began to study Buddhism with Zhang Kecheng, professor of Buddhist literature and philosophy at Beijing University. He wanted to enter the Buddhist Saṅgha, but his sister persuaded him to wait until he had fathered a male child.

In 1924, at the age of 39, Nenghai received the novice vows under the guidance of Foyuan, his master and a teacher of the Linji school of Chan Buddhism. At Yonghegong (a monastery of the Gelugpa tradition located in Beijing), he became interested in Tibetan Buddhism and decided to travel to Tibet.[6] In 1926, he went to Kangding (located in the Tibetan area of Khams), where he studied Tibetan language and began reading Tibetan Buddhist scriptures, particularly Tsongkhapa's *Lamrim Chenmo*.[7] He believed that the Buddhist *tantras* contained the very essence of the Buddhadharma. To deepen his understanding of *tantra*, he twice visited Lhasa, where he became the disciple of Kangsa Rinpoche, a lama of Drepung Monastery. He remained in Lhasa studying for five years.

Nenghai founded seven monasteries in China. Tiexiangsi is the only nunnery among what he called these "*tantric vajra* monasteries" (*micheng jingang daochang*). Except for during the rains retreat, he rarely stayed in the same monastery for long, always traveling from place to place, preaching the Dharma, lecturing on the scriptures, and giving instructions on Gelugpa doctrines.

The principal *tantric* transmission he received from his lama is known as "the tradition of the *Yamāntaka-Vajrabhairava Anuttarayoga Tantra*." The *tantras* he then transmitted to his disciples were mainly those of two *yidams* (meditation deities): Yellow Mañjuśrī, which is a lower *tantric* practice, and Yamāntaka, which is *anuttarayoga tantra*.[8] Yamāntaka-Vajrabhairava is a wrathful manifestation of Mañjuśrī.[9]

While Nenghai asserted that the *tantras* and Tsongkhapa's *Lamrim* are superior to all other Buddhist doctrines, he still included the Chinese and Theravāda scriptures in his teachings. He explained these scriptures as an example of the exoteric teachings that form the basis for the practice of the *tantras* and without which the *tantras* could not be understood. Among the exoteric Buddhist scriptures, he had a preference for the Vinaya and the Prajñāpāramitā texts.

Nenghai is responsible for more than 90 books and articles. Some are translations of Tibetan texts, some are commentaries. Some were written by Nenghai himself, while others were authored by his disciples in accordance with his teachings. Of these, 54 are related to *tantra*.

Life and Work of Longlian

Longlian (b. 1909)[10] was born in Leshan town, Sichuan province. Her father and her two grandfathers were famous scholars. Brought up in this atmosphere, she received an education, which was unusual for a woman of her time. As a child, she studied secular subjects at home, including calligraphy, painting, math, physics, and Chinese medicine. She was able to recite ancient Chinese poetry at the age of three. In addition to these traditional subjects, she also studied English and Tibetan languages. Raised by her grandmother, a devout Buddhist as was her mother, she began to show an interest in Buddhism while still a child. At the age of 13, she began her Dharma studies. Five years later, she found employment as a teacher in Chengdu. While in Chendu, she took advantage of every opportunity to hear Buddhist lectures and teachings on the scriptures. In this way, she was able to study with many famous Buddhist masters, including Wang Enyang, Fazun, and Nenghai. At the age of 30, she took the entrance examinations for the local magistrateship and was successful, becoming the first woman active in the provincial government. Her interest in Buddhism was stronger than her interest in worldly affairs, however; two years later she resigned her job to enter Aidaotang Nunnery.

Not long after entering the nunnery, Longlian was invited to teach Buddhist literature at Lianzong Nunnery. She became the director of studies there in 1943. By the end of the 1940s, she was the abbess of two nunneries in Chengdu – Aidaotang and Tiexiangsi – and has maintained these positions ever since. She has taught Buddhism for decades and still teaches at the Sichuan Buddhist Higher Institute for Bhikṣuṇīs, which she helped establish in 1983. She declares, "I am destined to live with blackboards and chalk, as a teacher, my entire life."

At 88 the abbess is still active, shuttling between the two nunneries. Ordinarily she lives in Tiexiangsi and goes to Aidaotang on weekends to teach the scriptures to the resident nuns, as well as to lay Buddhist followers. Her daily schedule is full; sometimes she teaches for half a day without a break.

Longlian is the author of numerous books and essays. Some elucidate Nenghai's teachings; some are based on notes of teachings she received from other masters; some are translations from Tibetan, while others are related to the Vinaya and other Buddhist scriptures. An accomplished poet, painter, and educator, Longlian was awarded the Teaching Culture Award and a copy of the Taisho Buddhist canon by the Japanese Buddhist Association in 1982. She is generally regarded as the most exemplary *bhikṣuṇī* in contemporary China.

Life in Tiexiangsi Nunnery

Tiexiangsi Nunnery reflects an unusual mixture of elements from different Buddhist traditions. One meets Chinese nuns dressed in yellow robes, not the traditional gray or black Chinese Buddhist robes. The yellow color represents yellow Mañjuśrī, the *yidam* of the community. Walking through the facility, one sees halls, statues, images, and religious objects in Tibetan style juxtaposed with others in Chinese style. The main hall of the nunnery (*daxiongdian*) is typical of buildings of the Ming Dynasty, but inside the structure resembles the main hall of Tibetan monasteries. The Palace of Scriptures (*zangjinglou*) has recently been restored in Tibetan Buddhist architectural style, yet both levels of the structure are furnished in Chinese style. Similar examples of blending the two traditions are evident throughout the buildings. Alongside halls clearly belonging to the Chinese tradition – the Avalokiteśvara hall (*guanyindian*), where the ashes of the deceased nuns are kept, and the Soul Tablet Hall (*dajuetang*, the "Hall of Clear Perception") – there is a Great Master Hall (*dashidian*) devoted to Tsongkhapa, founder of the Gelugpa school. The meditation hall (*yufodian*, the "Jade Buddha Hall"), a structure built according to the Theravāda Buddhist tradition, stands out as another peculiarity. The entire facility reflects the many cultures that have influenced it.

Life in Tiexiangsi presents the same unusual juxtaposition of Chinese and Tibetan elements. Chinese tradition prevails in the organization of activities, while Tibetan tradition prevails in religious practice.[11] The nuns' monastic names derive from ancient Chinese *gāthās*,[12] and the various activities in the monastic day are also designated by Chinese words. Everyday life in Tiexiangsi follows the usual routine of Chinese monasteries. Two chanting services per day (morning and evening), a meditation session, two vegetarian meals (eaten in formal Chinese monastic style), and the recitation of monastic vows in the morning form the "devotions of the five halls" (*wutang gongke*). The religious calendar followed is also mainly Chinese, with the exception of days honoring Nenghai, Mañjuśrī, and Tsongkhapa, which follow traditional Tibetan forms.

The meditation and scripture chanting are Tibetan in origin, as is the rite performed on religious feast days, the *tsog* offering (*huigong*). In addition, the nuns celebrate the Ullambana festival, or Festival of the Hungry Ghosts, typical of Chinese Buddhism. The three-month summer retreat (*anju*) of early Buddhist practice is strictly observed. During this period the nuns may not leave the nunnery as they please, and must practice and study more than usual. In addition to intensified religious practice during this time, Longlian and other masters give daily lectures on the scriptures. Another early Buddhist practice followed at Tiexiangsi is the bi-monthly recitation of the Prātimokṣa vows (*banyue songjie*).

The nuns follow the Dharmagupta Vinaya, the tradition generally observed in China, while Tibetan Buddhists follow the Mūlasarvāstivāda Vinaya. Nenghai himself followed the Dharmagupta vows, and claimed that there is no substantial difference among the various traditions of Vinaya practice. In their great similarity, he perceived the heart of the Vinaya as taught by the Buddha.

Most of the nuns come to the nunnery to attend the Sichuan Buddhist Higher Institute for Bhikṣuṇīs. In addition to five hours of classes per day, studying such topics as Vinaya, meditation (*dhyāna*), wisdom (*prajñā*), Buddhist literature, and the history of Buddhism in China and other countries, students attend all religious activities of the nunnery. The curriculum includes the study of the ordination ritual, the doctrines of the various Buddhist schools, and languages (ancient and modern Chinese, English, and Tibetan), as well as more mundane subjects, such as politics, psychology, and history. In the institute's curriculum, the mingling of Chinese and Tibetan Buddhism is also evident: first course students mainly study Chinese Buddhism, whereas senior-level courses are organized like the *geshe* study programs of Tibetan Buddhist institutes.[13] At the post-graduate level, classes on Tibetan literature and Tibetan Buddhist texts are also offered. The result is a curriculum that reflects the cross-cultural nature of the nunnery.

Meditation, Chanting Services, and *Tantric* Teachings

Nenghai's goal was to make the Gelugpa teachings as accessible as possible to his Chinese disciples. This objective is evident in the combination of Chinese and Tibetan practices, and in the prayers, meditations, visualization techniques, and explanatory passages in his works describing the three basic *tantric* practices to be observed in his monasteries. These *tantric* practices are conferred gradually on the nuns as a group. First, they learn the general meaning of the meditation and chanting texts, next they receive deeper instructions, and eventually they receive the prescribed initiations. The nuns are also privately initiated by their master into other *tantric* teachings.

The meditation practiced every afternoon by the community is called "Contemplation on the Three Refuges" (*sanguiyi guan*).[14] This teaching, transmitted orally by Nenghai to his disciples, follows a tradition he learned from his mentor Kangsa Rinpoche. Longlian, in turn, has written a handbook describing this method, which is the only written reference for practitioners. She describes this method as "a basic practice of Tibetan meditation." Taking refuge in the Three Jewels is fundamental to all Buddhist practice, but the "Contemplation of the Four Refuges," or "Secret Refuge," also involves taking refuge in the *guru* and the assembly of *maṇḍala* deities in the context of the *tantric* path.[15]

The text divides the meditative path into three stages: a preparatory practice; an analytical concentration (*liguan*) on the Three Jewels, the Four Noble Truths, and impermanence; and a long esoteric concentration (*shiguan*) consisting of many intertwined visualization practices. The practitioner begins by visualizing his or her body decomposing until it becomes a white skeleton. The skeleton then emits white light that evolves into a new body, the body of young Mañjuśrī.[16] This is referred to as the "self-generation," visualizing oneself in the form of one's *yidam*.

The practitioner then visualizes the *guru* and begs pardon for any misdeeds. The *guru* then bestows inspiration and purifying energy upon the practitioner. This energy, in the form of light, is then transmitted to all living beings. The same procedure is followed with respect to the Buddha, Dharma, and Saṅgha, visualizing them, one after the other, surrounding the *guru*. After this, the merit field is dissolved; the visualized images are gradually absorbed into the body of the practitioner, who then meditates on emptiness, acquires the "illusory" body, and finally returns to his or her ordinary "emanation" body, which concludes the meditation practice.

At 5:30 each morning, the nuns assemble in the main hall of the nunnery to chant a Chinese translation of the Guru Pūja (*Shangshigong*), a popular *guru yoga* text in the Gelugpa school.[17] Translated by Nenghai in the 1940s, the text has inspired many commentaries by the master himself, as well as by his disciples. Among these commentaries is a work by Longlian explaining *tantric* practices associated with the Guru Pūja. At the heart of this practice is the realization that one's own root *guru* is identical with the Buddha.[18] The practitioner visualizes his or her own *guru* as the meditational deity, who usually appears as Lama Tsongkhapa, and then identifies with him. The text presents the main subjects of the *sūtras* and *tantras*, reflecting on themes such as the stages of the path (*lamrim*) and the theories of the stages of generation and completion typical of *anuttarayoga tantra*.[19] The *guru* is visualized in the space in front of the practitioner. On his form, the practitioner visualizes the merit field and the deities of the *maṇḍala*. The master is then visualized on the top of the practitioner's head, and then at the heart.

The text used during the evening chanting service is the *Original Five-syllable Mantra of Mañjuśrī* (*Wenshu wuzi genben zhenyan*), a text written by Nenghai which is said to have received the approval of Mañjuśrī himself as the master was absorbed in meditation on Mt. Wutai. This text is not a translation of a Tibetan work. It includes an esoteric section – an explanation of the esoteric meditation on Yellow (or Orange) Mañjuśrī, identified by Longlian as belonging to the *yogatantra* class – and an exoteric section, an explanation of the "three trainings" in Vinaya, *dhyāna*, and *prajñā*.[20]

The main deity (*yidam*) of the text is Arapacana Mañjuśrī. The five syllables of Yellow Mañjuśrī's *mantra* – *a ra pa tza na* – together with the syllable *oṃ*, encircle the syllable *dhī* in a rosary-like *mantra* at the heart of the deity. Each syllable is associated with a particular Dhyāni Buddha and the type of knowledge symbolized by each.[21] During the *tantric* practice the practitioner emerges as Mañjuśrī.

⋆ ⋆ ⋆

Observing Tiexiangsi Nunnery, one realizes the unusual co-existence of Chinese and Tibetan elements. The Tibetan elements appear to be more dominant, but Chinese Buddhism also plays an important role in the life of the nuns. One reason is purely geographic. Located in China, the nunnery is constantly in contact with the Chinese monastic world; it has virtually no contact with the Tibetan world. A deeper reason for Tiexiangsi's unusual character is linked to the teachings of Nenghai. In spreading Tibetan Buddhist doctrines in China, the master did not intend to change Chinese Buddhism, but only to complete and enrich it with new elements. He did not wish to impose his experience of Tibetan practice, nor did he believe that the two traditions were in conflict with each another. He did, however, believe that Tibetan Buddhist practice had elements that he found superior, which held the potential for great learning. By this, he meant that no other Buddhist doctrines could equal the *tantras* and the *lamrim* teachings.

Influenced by their master's teaching, the nuns of Tiexiangsi live side-by-side with Chinese Buddhists, observing the same rules, and embracing the same doctrines. Despite their unique Tibetan practices and the innovative nature of their nunnery, they do not really feel any disparity, but unity instead. Their everyday lives, studies, and practice are a daily affirmation of the universality of the Buddhadharma.

Glossary

Aidaotang	愛道堂
anju	安居
banyue songjie	半月誦戒
Chan	禪
Dajuetang	大覺堂
Dashidian	大師殿
dayong	大勇
Daxiongdian	大雄殿
Dingjing	定靜
erbusengjie	二部僧戒
Fahai	法海
Fazun	法尊
Foyuan	佛源
Guanyindian	觀音殿
huigong	會供

liguan	理觀
Lincisi	金慈寺
Linji	臨濟
Longlian	隆蓮
Micheng jingang daochang	密乘金剛道場
Nenghai	能海
Sanguiyiguan	三歸依觀
Sanguiyi guan chuxiu luefa	三歸依觀初修略法
shangshigong	上師供
shiguan	事觀
Sichuan nizhong foxueyuan	四川尼衆佛學院
Tiexiangsi	鐵像寺
Wang Enyang	王恩洋
Wenshu wuzi genben zhenyan	文殊五字根本眞言
wutang gongke	五堂功課
Yonghegong	雍和宮
Yufodian	玉佛殿
Zangjinglou	藏經樓

Notes

1 For the ordination rituals and the different Vinaya traditions for nuns in the various Buddhist traditions, see Chatsumarn Kabilsingh, *A Comparative Study of Bhikkhunī Pāṭimokkha* (Varanasi: Chaukhambha Orientalia, 1984); Sheng Yanyuan, *Jiexue jiangzuo* [A Lecture on the Study of Precepts] (Beijing: Zhongguo fojiao xiehui chuban, 1989); Shuyu, *Erbuseng shoujie yishi* [Ritual for Conducting Dual Ordination] (Guhang zhaoqingsi [Qing dynasty, no date]); and Karma Lekshe Tsomo, *Sakyadhita: Daughters of the Buddha* (Ithaca, N.Y.: Snow Lion Publications, 1988) and *Sisters in Solitude: Two Traditions of Buddhist Monastic Ethics for Women. A Comparative Analysis of the Chinese Dharmagupta and the Tibetan Mūlasarvāstivāda Bhikṣuṇī Prātimokṣa Sūtras* (Albany, N.Y.: State University of New York Press, 1996).

2 In China it often happened that nuns took the Prātimokṣa precepts with *bhikṣus* only. While neither Tibetan nor Theravādin monastic establishments consider such an ordination fully legitimate, in the Chinese tradition ordination conducted by monks alone is considered valid. The dual ordination ritual (*erbu sengjie*) is described in Shuyu, *Erbuseng shoujie yishi*, op cit. For the *bhikṣuṇī* ordination issue, see Tsomo, *Sakyadhita: Daughters of the Buddha*, op cit.

3 For a discussion of Buddhism in the P.R.C., see Holmes Welch, *Buddhism Under Mao* (Cambridge: Harvard University Press, 1972); and Donald MacInnis, *Religion in China Today: Policy and Practice* (New York: Orbis Books, 1989).

4 Only nuns from farming families were allowed to stay in Tiexiangsi; others, who belonged to "citizen" status, had to move to urban areas.

5 For Nenghai's biography, see Zong Shunjin, *Nenghai shangshi zhuan* [Biography of Lama Nenghai] (Chengdu: Sichuansheng fojiao xiehui hongfalisheng huiyin, 1995); and Shi Zhimin and Fu Jiaoshi, "*Nenghai fashi zhuan* [Biography of Ven. Nenghai]" in *Fayin yuekan* 2 (1984): 23–28.

6 During the first part of the twentieth century, it was common for Chinese monks to go to Tibet to study Tibetan Buddhism. Their intent was to restore in China the tantric tradition

that had disappeared there after the Tang dynasty. Among these monks were Fazun (1902–1980), Dayong (1893–1929), and Fahai (1919–1991).

7 *The Path to Enlightenment* (Tibetan: *Lamrim*) is a comprehensive arrangement of the stages of practice from the beginning (attainment of a human life) up to the end (enlightenment or Buddhahood). Tsongkhapa composed three versions of the *Lamrim*, including the *Lamrim chenmo* [The Great Exposition of the Stages of the Path to Enlightenment]; a medium-length version; and a short version composed in verse, titled *Lamrim nyamgur* [Songs of Spiritual Experience]. See Tenzin Gyatso, *Path to Bliss: A Practical Guide to Stages of Meditation* (New York: Snow Lion Publications, 1991), pp. 20–22; and for a translation of the short version, Robert A. F. Thurman, ed., *The Life and Teachings of Tsong Khapa* (Dharamsala: Library of Tibetan Works and Archives, 1992), pp. 59–66.

8 Tibetans arrange the Buddhist *tantras* in four classes: (1) *kriyā* ("action"), (2) *caryā* ("performance"), (3) *yoga*, and (4) *anuttarayoga* ("highest *yoga*"). The first three classes together are called the "lower tantras." See Panchen Sonam Dragpa *Overview of Buddhist Tantra: General Presentation of the Classes of Tantra, Captivating the Minds of the Fortunate Ones*, trans. M. J. Boord and Losang Norbu Tsonawa (Dharamsala: Library of Tibetan Works and Archives, 1996); and Alex Wayman, *The Buddhist Tantras: Light on Indo-Tibetan Esotericism* (Delhi: Motilal Banarsidass, 1993).

9 On Yamāntaka-Vajrabhairava, see Hans Wolfgang Schumann, *Buddhistische Bilderwelt* (Köln: Eugen Diedrichs Verlag, 1986).

10 For the biography of Longlian, see Hua Chuan "*Zhongguo diyi biqiuni: Sichuan nizhong foxueyuan zhang longlian fashi* [The Most Outstanding *Bhikṣuṇī* in China: Ven. Longlian, President of the Sichuan Buddhist Higher Institute for Bhikṣuṇīs]," *Zhongwai wenhua jiaoliu zazhi* (1994): 104–6; Lawei Bandite, "*Jinri zhongguode biqiuni* [Bhikṣuṇīs in Contemporary China]," trans. Er Che, *Fayin yuekan*, no. 1 (1982): 43–45; Li Yuchuan, "*Dangjin zhongguo diyi ni: Longlian fashi* [The Most Outstanding Nun in Contemporary China: Ven. Longlian]" *Xianggang Fojiao*, no. 387, (1992): 19–22; Liu Qian, "Dharmacarya Longlian: A Chinese *Bhikṣuṇī* with High Prestige and Respect," trans. Jane Shaw, *Women of China*, no. 11 (1995): 29–30; Qiu Shanshan, *Dangdai diyi biqiuni: Longlian fashi zhuan* [The Most Outstanding *Bhikṣuṇī* in Contemporary China: Biography of Ven. Longlian] (Fanyu xinhua shudian jingxiao, 1997); *Sichuan nizhong foxueyuan chengdu tiexiangsi aidaotang* [Sichuan Buddhist Higher Institute for *Bhikṣuṇīs*, Tiexiangsi, Aidaotang] (Chengdu: Sichuan nizhong foxueyuan, 1988); Wen Qing, "Walking Into the Temple Gate," trans. Xiao Hongliu, *Women of China*, no. 11 (1995): 22–27; and the works of Longlian.

11 For life and practice in Chinese monasteries, see Holmes Welch, *The Practice of Chinese Buddhism* (Cambridge: Harvard University Press, 1967).

12 A *gāthā* is a religious poem. Chinese monastics' names are often taken from *gāthās* written by some master of the past, and these names were used character-by-character to name monastics from generation to generation. See Holmes Welch, "Dharma Scrolls and Succession of Abbots in Chinese Monasteries," in *T'oung Pao* (Leiden, 1963), pp. 93–149.

13 A *geshe* is a learned scholar who has successfully completed a Buddhist monastic education in the Tibetan tradition. In Gelugpa monasteries this usually requires 20 or 25 years of study.

14 See Longlian, *Sanguiyi guan chuxiu luefa: Nenghai shangshi chuanshou* [A Handbook on the Beginning Practice of the "Contemplation of the Three Refuges" According to Master Nenghai] (Chengdu: Jincisi huguo jingang daochang yin, 1946). This type of meditation practice is also described in Tenzin Gyatso, *The Union of Bliss and Emptiness* trans. Thubten Jinpa (New York: Snow Lion Publications, 1988); and in Tenzin Gyatso, *Path to Bliss: A Practical Guide to Stages of Meditation*, trans. Thubten Jinpa (Ithaca, N.Y.: Snow Lion Publications, 1991). In these two texts, the description of the practice is not as long

or detailed as in Longlian's work, however. In his teaching on the "Contemplation of the Three Refuges," Nenghai has incorporated other basic tantric practices, so as to provide his disciples with a fundamental knowledge of Tibetan contemplation methods.

15 Tibetan Buddhism distinguishes three different types of refuge: "outer," the practice of refuge that is common to the lesser vehicle; "inner," the unique refuge of Mahāyāna; and "secret," the unique refuge of *tantra*. See Gyatso, *Path to Bliss*, pp. 43, 221–22.

16 At the beginning of Mahāyāna scriptures, homage is frequently paid to Mañjuśrī. He is generally shown as a youth of 16, an eternally young crown prince of the Buddha dynasty. Hans Wolfgang Schumann, *Buddhistische Bilderwelt* (Koln: Eugen Diedrichs Verlag, 1986), p. 137; and Alex Wayman, *Chanting the Names of Mañjuśrī: The Mañjuśrī-nāmā-saṃgīti. Sanskrit and Tibetan Text* (London: Shambhala Publications, 1985), p. 3.

17 See Nenghai, *Shangshi wushang gongyang guanxingfa* [Contemplation Techniques of the Guru Pūja] (Shanghai: Shanghaishi fojiao xiehui, 1990); and Longlian, *Shangshi wushang gongyang guanxingfa jiangji: Nenghai shangshi jiang* [Notes on the Explanation of the Guru Pūja Contemplation Techniques According to Master Nenghai] (Chengdu: Chengdushi xinwen chubanju, 1995). For an English translation of the Guru Puja, see Gyatsho Tshering, *The Guru Pūja and The Hundred Deities of the Land of Joy* (Dharamsala, Library of Tibetan Works and Archives, 1995); and Gyatso, *The Union of Bliss and Emptiness*. For a different Chinese version, see Li Wuyang, *Zangyuxi Fojiao Niansongji: Zanghan Duizhao* [A Collection of Tibetan Buddhist Chanting Scriptures, Chinese-Tibetan Bilingual Versions] (Beijing: Zongjiao wenhua chubanshe, 1995), pp. 43–54.

18 Within the Buddhist *tantric* tradition, devotion to one's *guru* is crucial, because progress on the path to enlightenment cannot be made without relying upon the *guru*; hence, the strong emphasis on *guru yoga*, considered to be the foundation of Buddhist tantric practice.

19 *Anuttarayoga tantra* practice consists of two stages: the stage of generation and the stage of completion. The former necessarily precedes the latter. "The purpose of the stage of generation is to 'ripen' the mental continuum for the stage of completion. ... One passes from the stage of generation to the stage of completion by bringing one's imaginative vision to such a height of clarity and power that what one has imagined begins to become real. The stage of completion 'completes' the vision by effecting the transformation of the trainee into a Buddha." Daniel Cozort, *Highest Yoga Tantra* (Ithaca, N.Y.: Snow Lion Publications, 1986), pp. 39–114.

20 See Nenghai, *Wenshu wuzi genben zhenyan niansongfa* [How to Recite the Original Five Syllables Mantra of Mañjuśrī] (Chengdu: Chengdu Zhaojuesi Yinxing, 1995); and Nenghai, *Wenshu wuzi genben zhenyan niansongfa jianglu* [Explanatory Notes on How to Recite the Original Five Syllables Mantra of Mañjuśrī] (Chongching: Chongching Jingangdaochang, n.d.). The meditation on Orange Mañjuśrī has been translated into English by Glenn H. Mullin in *Meditation on the Lower Tantras: From the Collected Works of the Previous Dalai Lamas* (Dharamsala: Library of Tibetan Works and Archives, 1983), pp. 87–89.

21 Mañjuśrī is prominently associated with the number five (Sanskrit: *pañca*). The term *arapacana* probably refers to the five Dhyāni Buddhas and to the five kinds of knowledge: (1) pure *dharmadhātu* knowledge, associated with Vairocana; (2) mirrorlike knowledge, associated with Akṣobhya; (3) discriminating knowledge, associated with Amitābha; (4) "sameness" knowledge, associated with Ratnasambhava; and (5) "procedure-of-duty" knowledge, associated with Amoghasiddhi. These five kinds of knowledge are associated with five of the seven *maṇḍalas* in the Tibetan work *Mañjuśrīnāmasaṃgīti*. See Alex Wayman, *Chanting the Names of Mañjuśrī, Sanskrit and Tibetan Text* (London: Shambhala Publications, 1985), pp. 30–35.

CHAPTER THIRTEEN

Birth, Death, and Resurrection of Shim Ch'ông

Mistress of the Spiritual Domain

Chan E. Park

Round, round, 108 rounds.
Namu amit'abul, kwanseûm posal.

The eighth day of the fourth month
Is the day for lighting lanterns.

Round, round, 108 rounds.
Namu amit'abul, kwanseûm posal.[1]

Korean Cultural Synthesis

From time immemorial Koreans have believed that every object in nature is a temple housing a presiding spirit. As different faith systems entered the peninsula from the continent, they blended with one another and with indigenous animistic beliefs. A unique mosaic of rituals resulted, manifested in a wealth of tangible and intangible legacies, including temples, shrines, murals, oral chants, rituals, and performative expressions. During the Three Kingdoms period in Korea (57 B.C.E.–668 C.E.), Confucian ideology was introduced to the peninsula and found strong consonance with Korean perspectives on humanity. In the fourth century C.E., Buddhism, with its concept of enlightenment, found its way to Korea from India, via China.

Hyujông, a prominent monk of the Chosôn Dynasty (1392–1910), notes the spiritual diversity among ancient Koreans:[2]

> The ancients said, "Confucianists plant the root; Taoists grow the root; Buddhists yield the root." You see the sequence. At this moment, for beginners, I briefly opened the three gates [of the three traditions] and thereby directly communicated. [However,] on another day, if someone's mind eye might be opened, then he or she might laugh loudly and criticize it.[3]

Catholicism, referred to as "Western learning," first entered Korea four centuries ago through European Jesuit missionaries residing in Ming China.

It, too, set up its altars next to earlier arrivals that had already blended with the indigenous culture. As indicated by the "Rites Controversy," a 1742 papal ruling declaring that Confucian ancestor worship and Christian doctrine are incompatible,[4] Christianity from the beginning challenged the existing eclectic order in Korea, resulting in a series of religious persecutions. Korean Christians' exclusivistic approach has yet to seek harmony with earlier beliefs and practices.

In the course of 5,000 years of history, assorted faith systems have become successfully rooted in the Koreans' devotional consciousness, which is more comfortable with spiritual diversity than with religious confrontation. Deities from multiple pantheons share their abodes, ritual procedures, sacred chants, ceremonial music, and efficacy, evolving as a harmonized whole perceived as distinctly "Korean." A pantheon of otherworldly characters is portrayed on the walls behind the altars in Buddhist temples and shaman shrines alike. The presiding spirits in native shamanistic ritual systems regard the Buddhist deities as neighbors and invoke them in their ritual ceremonies. A common scenario dictates that, when a person departs this world, the family first observes the proper Confucian rites of mourning, then goes to a Buddhist temple to perform 49 days of prayer for an auspicious rebirth. After that, a shaman is entrusted with performing a purging ritual to acknowledge and confirm the inevitable divide between the living and the dead.

Cross-gender, Cross-genre Narrative

Feminist folklorists in the West, agreeing that women's traditions have had their own part to play "in countering the patriarchal tradition that has marginalized and silenced women," frequently discuss women, their roles, and their identities in the context of religious practices.[5] Locating women's power in religious practices finds rich resonance in Korea, where women publicly and privately have acted as mediators between the human world and netherworld. As the pillar of the family, whether visibly or not, a woman is usually the main supplicant, praying for the peace and prosperity of the household. Silhouetted by the light of a lone candle, and forever chafing her hands in humility, with deep devotion, she offers a bowl of purified water to invoke her guardian spirits in a traditional prayer:

I pray, I pray,
To Heaven I pray.
O, Guardian Spirits of Heaven, Earth, Sun, Moon, Stars,
Omnipotent Buddha,
Dear ancestors,
Pray, come down and have pity on me.

One subject of active feminist debate centers on locating woman's domain (including reproduction) in nature, away from the male domain of culture.

But there is another option: culturally marginalized, she may create a new center which metaphysically undermines the established "reality system," inventing and maintaining traditions that signal the viability and appropriateness of a different system.[6] As keeper of the altar, she locates her center in "the spiritual," beyond the dyadic hierarchy of "culture" and "nature." It is no mere coincidence that most shamans in Korea are women.

Women's devotion finds another powerful voice in the world of storytelling, especially in *p'ansori*, an oral narrative story-singing art whose origins lie buried in the ancient past, sometime before the 17th century. Perhaps *p'ansori* represents a rediscovery of women's own voice "defeminized" by male use, for history relates that *p'ansori* originated among the male musicians who accompanied shamans' ritual chant and dance. Only in the latter half of the 19th century did women officially enter the all-male *p'ansori* world. In a Neo-Confucian society structured on strict distinctions between male and female roles, mannerisms, and expectations, a unique vocal gender was evoked. "His" singing emerged from "her" chanting, to be recaptured in "her" singing.[7]

In the context of Korean culture, "masculinity" is represented as action, confidence, and aggression, whereas "femininity" is represented as hesitancy, modesty, and delicate passivity. Correspondingly, the male voice should be "deeply resonant," ringing metallically to prove leadership and strength, while the female voice should sound clear and high "like a jade ball rolling on a crystal tray," appealing for male protection. Against this cultural background, a woman singing *p'ansori* on stage becomes a kind of masculinized female, delivering a new expression of gender – a pioneer challenging the prescripted matrix of "masculine" and "feminine." In essence, she creates another dimension to gender without having to abandon her own.[8] Shaping a multi-dimensional cross-gender, cross-genre intertextuality, *p'ansori* has become a voice for women. For over 100 years, it has been a medium of expression for Korean woman's poetic and narrative sensibility, her faith, and her worldview.

Storytelling as narrative can be defined as the unity of two mutually reflexive realms, that is, the tale and the telling. Some see these as two events aptly juxtaposed: "the event that is narrated in the work and the event of narration itself."[9] It is also two intertwined worlds – the "taleworld" of characters and the "storyrealm" of the discourse of tellers who inhabit another space and time.[10] Just as women protagonists in the stories went against the social current that regarded women as hardly more than a male's dependent, in the "telling," women in *p'ansori* go against the current of existing gender delineation by venturing into the vocal range of men. Often invoking the name of Lord Buddha, their artistic expression is grounded on an unwavering faith in the ethical principles of humanity and its cosmic relationship with an omniscient being.

The Song of Shim Ch'ông

One example of this unwavering devotion unfolds in the panorama of birth, death, and mythical resurrection of the filial daughter Shim Ch'ông in "The Song of Shim Ch'ông," a *p'ansori* narrative. The story is also told as shaman narrative in the annual Kangnûng Tano Fest observed in the eastern coastal municipality of Kangnûng.[11] Here I attempt a Buddhist interpretation of the narrative as a tumultuous process of Shim Ch'ông's "de-cycling" of her own karma.

Since ancient times in East Asian cultures, filial piety has been revered as the supreme principle of "being human." Outside ancient tales, such as that of Princess Pari abandoned at birth due to her gender, daughters were virtually absent from the prescribed "human" categories:

> To be a son, one must do one's filial duty until death. To be an officer, one must be loyal until death. If someone has no mind for filial duty and loyalty, there is nothing else worth considering about him.[12]

The criteria for women's humanity were never so explicitly stated, leaving women's position in society considerably more ambiguous and compelling women to extremes in their efforts to demonstrate their worth and their humanity. Striving her utmost to be devoutly "human," Ch'ông sacrifices her own life to help her father keep his promise to Lord Buddha. Following the will of Heaven, she returns to the world to live the rest of her life as an empress. Ch'ông's exemplary filial piety results in her becoming immortalized in folk tales, folk songs, shamanic chanting, and *p'ansori*. Her resurrection from the realm of the dead is often invoked in shamanic rituals of healing and purification for both the living and the dead.

Ch'ông's suffering begins in Heaven and she is transported to the world of the living in answer to the ardent prayers of Kwak-ssi, the devoted wife of Blindman Shim of Peace Blossom Village. Diligent and resourceful, Kwak-ssi takes good care of her husband, but the couple is afflicted by the ultimate misfortune – they have no son to carry on the family name, a disgrace most unpardonable by his ancestors. Abjectly depressed by her failure to produce progeny, Kwak-ssi prays for a son.[13]

(*Chungmori*)[14]

> Kwak-ssi, from that day on,
> With her savings from her tireless labors,
> Prayers and donations she ungrudgingly offered
> Famous mountains, great temples, sacred shrines,
> Ancient altars, roadside shrines, and the Temple of Lord Buddha,[15]
> Stone Buddhas, Maitreya, wherever she may be,
> Ever so busily she went about offering

Robes to monks, lantern oil to light temples, paper for temple windows, and more.
Offerings to the Seven Stars, offerings to the Water Guardians,
Every imaginable offering she performed.
Would a tower built with devotion collapse?
Would a spirit-tree break?

In the *kapcha* year,[16] on the eighth night of the fourth month,[17]
She begets a dream.
An auspicious air envelops the sky,
The five colors reflect everywhere,
From heaven, a fairy, riding a jade branch, descends.
On her head a flower crown, on her body a round-armed robe,
Holding a sprig of laurel, to Kwak-ssi she performs her bow and sits beside her.
As if the spirit of the moon
Suddenly rose atop the mountain,
As if the Goddess of Mercy rose from the South Sea,
Mind and body, engulfed in ecstasy,
Kwak-ssi cannot be calmed; then the beautiful fairy
Half parts her mouth showing her beautiful teeth, and
With a voice resounding like jade balls
Clinking while being washed, speaks:
"This insignificant girl is the daughter of the Queen Mother of the West.
On my way to offer the Heavenly Peach,[18]
I met up briefly with Okchin Pija.[19]
We chatted about nothing in particular,
A tardiness at the offering ceremony I committed,
Angering our Heavenly Emperor,
Hence, he banished me to the world of humans,
Whether going or coming, I knew not.
T'aesang Nogun,[20] Hut'o Puin,[21]
Śākyamuni and the many Buddhas and *bodhisattvas*,
To your home directed me, so I found my way here.
Pray, have pity on me!"

Into her bosom the fairy rushes, and Kwak-ssi wakes up with a start,
A passing dream it was.

Kwak-ssi's dream comes true, but to the couple's great disappointment, the child is a girl. From elders in the *p'ansori* tradition, I heard the following explanation: Shim Ch'ông is conceived on the Buddha's birthday, which signifies that she is a child of the Buddha. The fact that she is born as a girl – the unwanted gender – predestines her to a difficult path. Her unfortunate destiny unfolds, starting with Kwak-ssi's death soon after Ch'ông's birth. Blindman Shim is left alone to care for the newborn baby, but thanks to the kind women of the village who take turns nursing her, Ch'ông grows up to be a beautiful girl with a filial heart. Blindman Shim finds great joy and happiness "watching" her blossom into womanhood.

Eventually Ch'ông turns 15 years of age. Having heard of her beauty and virtue, one day Lady Chang, the widow of Minister Chang, summons the girl to her mansion in Arcadia Village. As Ch'ông is enjoying her visit with Lady Chang, the sun begins to set. Meanwhile, sitting home alone, Blindman Shim anxiously awaits Ch'ông's return. Cold, hungry, and worried, he begins to grope his way out into the drifting snow to look for her. He accidentally slips into an icy stream and is about to drown, when suddenly a Buddhist monk passes by:

(*Onmori*)[22]

A Buddhist monk is ascending,
A monk is ascending.
That monk, of what temple is he?
Of Mongun Temple, a mendicant monk is he.
For rebuilding his temple,
He came down to town to collect donations door-to-door.
The day is ending and darkness is falling.
Taking a shortcut through the western slope,
Hurriedly he ascends.

Look at that monk's clothing:
Straw hat on his head,
Long-sleeved robe on his body,
A rosary of 108 beads round his neck,
A short rosary hung from his wrist,
Dragon's head carved on his six-ringed staff,
With added metal rings:
Chô-jôl-ch'ôl, ttuk ttuk ... tapping the ground,
Swinging, rocking, swaying,
He ascends.

The faraway mountains wrapped in darkness,
Snowy moon rising,
His white hemp robe
Flutters in the wind, *pôllông*, *pôllông* ...
Chanting a *sūtra*, he ascends.

"*Ah* ...
Ha ...
Ha ...

Ohû . . .
Hô . . .
Hô ;. . . ohô . . .
Oho . . . hô . . . ahù-û-aha. . . .

The mind of Buddha is transmitted,
Emulated in human practice.
Enlightenment is
As wide and deep as the ocean.

Return to the mind of Buddha,
The past, present, and future,
Hô-uh . . .
All are in the round circle. . . .

Let me be born again in *nirvāna*, let me return to *nirvāna*,
Let me not be reborn in this world, I chant:
Namu amit'abul,
Kwanseûm posal."

He comes to a spot,
A sudden cry
He hears on the wind.
The monk is startled:
"What cry is this? What cry is this?

At Maoe Horse Station,[23] at dusk,
Pleading her sad situation,
Is it the weeping of Yang T'aejin?[24]
What cry is this?
Is it a fox transforming
To lure me into disaster?[25]
What cry is this?"

Lifting his bamboo staff over his shoulder,
The monk looks this way and that.
Peering at one place,
He sees a person,
Drowning mid-stream,
About to be lost.

(*Chajinmori*)[26]

The monk is in a hurry,
The monk is in a hurry,
He takes off his hat and robe,
Throws them about at random,

Unfastens his leggings and pant-leg ties,
Takes off his socks,
With the legs of his quilted pants,
Rolled and rolled
All the way up to his privates,
Like a white heron wading into a flooded rice field,
Carefully, carefully,
Carefully approaches the scene.
He grabs Blindman Shim's topknot,
And pulls him out at once!

"There, I have him!"
Who was it, but Blindman Shim!

Feeling sorry for Blindman Shim, the monk tells him that the omnipotent Lord Buddha would return his sight within three years, if he pledged 300 gunny sacks of offering rice to the temple. Though penniless, Blindman Shim jumps at the chance. He makes his pledge for the full amount, despite the monk's warning that he will never walk again if he does not keep his pledge to Lord Buddha. It is not until after the monk has gone that Blindman Shim realizes the senselessness of his momentary blunder, but he also realizes that the pledge is final and rescinding his commitment to Lord Buddha would bring tragic punishment.

When Ch'ông returns home, Blindman Shim tells her about his near-drowning and his pledge to the Buddha when saved by the monk. Instead of scolding her father for his pledge, Ch'ông comforts him and tells him not to despair. She sets up an altar in the backyard, and from that day forth faithfully prays to her guardian spirits for their help in procuring the sacrificial rice.

(*Chinyang*)[27]

I pray to you, I pray to you,
Lord of Heaven, I pray to you.
Heaven, Earth, Sun, Moon, and Stars,
Pray come down and have pity on me.

Eventually her prayers are answered:

(*Chungmori*)

One day, outside the gate, a loud shouting.
"We are merchant sailors from the Southern Capital.
At the Water of Imdangsu, a human sacrifice we want to offer,
A 15- or 16-year-old,
A virgin we wish to buy.
Anyone interested in selling yourself?"

The sound of their announcement
Hovers over the village.

The sailors' announcement was shocking, but no surprise, for in ancient Korea sailors were said to perform an annual human sacrifice to the Dragon King of the four oceans to ensure their safe passage and prosperous journeys. Ch'ông decides to sell herself to fulfill her father's pledge to the temple. Leaving her grief-stricken father and the sympathetic villagers behind, she follows the sailors to the sea and hence to her death.

Fortunately, virtuous deeds do not pass unnoticed by Heaven. After her sacrifice, Ch'ông is sent back to the human world, afloat on the surface of the sea in a magical lotus bud, a symbol of her resurrection by the grace of Lord Buddha. The sailors, returning from another profitable journey, approach the place where Ch'ông's ceremonial sacrifice had been staged. Stricken with remorse, they offer a memorial service to her spirit hovering over the water. Drums and chants invoke her spirit, and suddenly it appears – a magical lotus bud floating from afar. The captain lifts it out of water and returns home.

Meanwhile the recently widowed emperor of the country, instead of remarrying, is trying his hand at horticulture. Cultivating plants from all over the world, he is delighted when the captain presents him with the mysterious lotus bud retrieved from the sea. One night, as the emperor strolls through his flower garden, the lotus bud opens, revealing the beautiful Ch'ông. She becomes his new empress, enjoying his love and his boundless wealth. She misses her father, however, and the emperor agrees to help her find him. He issues a decree inviting all the blind men of the country to attend a royal banquet for the blind that will last for 100 days.

Since Ch'ông's departure, Blindman Shim had been living with grief and remorse until one day a woman named Ppaengdôgine appeared and he married again. When the invitation to the royal banquet arrives, Blindman Shim sets out on the road to the capital accompanied by his wife. One night while staying at a roadside inn, she takes everything and runs off with a younger blind man.

After a lengthy journey filled with adventures, Blindman Shim arrives at the banquet. A commotion erupts as his name is announced. Several officers rush out to escort him to the inner palace where Empress Ch'ông anxiously awaits the good news of her father's arrival. At long last, father and daughter are reunited. In the intensity of his joy and surprise, Blindman Shim regains his sight. Not only that, but due to the blessing of Empress Ch'ông's filial piety, all the blind people of the country regain their sight. The story ends with great jubilation.

Transcending Illusions

> When water is clean, pearls can be seen brilliantly [in the water]. When clouds disappear, the moon shines brightly. When the three karmas are purified, all happiness is achieved together.[28]

Any analysis of cause and effect in Blindman Shim's healing is fraught with ambiguity. Is it mere coincidence that Blindman Shim regains his sight at the end? Or, in a scientific analysis, does the shock of events work a cure? Was the monk an imposter or an enlightened one? Did he realize that the pledge he exacted would take such a drastic turn, involving human sacrifice? The legitimacy of these questions pales beside the efficacy of Shim Ch'ông's faith. Armored with an unshakable devotion to Lord Buddha and her guardian spirits, she performed an act of "annihilate self, serve parent" (*salshin songhyo*),[29] heroically facing the faceless world of death. She applied her faith not only to life's enterprises, but also to meet her own death. Thus, she became one of the few women in history to become deified in prayer and legend.

A feminist analyst cannot help but question whether a son would be similarly sacrificed. In other words, is filial piety a universal value in East Asian societies or is it gender-specific? Are daughters more beholden to parents than sons? Are daughters more likely to be expected to make the ultimate sacrifice to prove their filial piety? And did Buddhist concepts of human enlightenment help mitigate these biased expectations or, by adding the concept of merit accumulation to the virtue of filial obligations, perhaps reinforce them? On the one hand, narratives such as Shim Ch'ông's confirm that gender discrimination exists in societal expectations and expressions of filial piety. On the other hand, by valorizing acts of filial piety performed by the "wrong gender," they reveal the illusory nature of those expectations and expressions.

Notes

1 From *T'apdori*, the "Pagoda Circling Song."

2 Also widely known as Sôsan Taesa. During the Japanese invasion of 1592–1598, he led the "hit and run thrusts of the Korean guerrilla forces" against Japanese military operations. Ki-baik Lee, *A New History of Korea* (Cambridge: Harvard University Press, 1984), p. 212.

3 From "The Ideal Mirror of the Three Religions (*Samga Kwigam*) of Ch'ônghô Hyujông," trans. Young-ho (Jinwôl) Lee, in *Buddhist-Christian Studies* 15 (1995): 164.

4 Lee, *A New History of Korea*, pp. 239–40.

5 Susan Tower Hollis, Linda Pershing, and M. Jane Young, eds., *Feminist Theory and the Study of Folklore* (Chicago: University of Illinois Press, 1993), p. 13. For example, in that volume, Kay Turner and Suzanne Seriff examine Sicilian-American women's elaborate tradition of "giving an altar" at the St. Joseph's Day feast and the communal power of women's work both in the St. Joseph story and in everyday social practice (p. 93). M. Jane

Young observes the "unofficial" but "central" role of women in Western Puebloan religious practice and concludes that "the private pilgrimages of the women to fertility shrines is as crucial a focus of religion as the public rain dances performed by the men." (pp. 219–220) Elaine J. Lawless studies Pentecostal female pastors in southern Indiana who challenge the Biblical message (1 Cor. 14: 34–35) that says, "Let your women keep silence in the church: for it is not permitted for them to speak: but they ought to be subject, as also the Law saith. And if they will learn any thing, let them ask their husbands at home: for it is a shame for a woman to speak in the church." (p. 259).

6 Ibid., p. 17.

7 In "Playful Reconstruction of Gender in *P'ansori* Storytelling," I focus on the latter phase of this vocal transition from male singers to female singers in the 19th century. *Korean Studies* 22 (1998): 62–81.

8 Ibid., p. 77.

9 Mikhail M. Bakhtin, *The Dialogic Imagination*, trans. Caryl Emerson and Michael Holquist (Austin: University of Texas Press, 1981), p. 255.

10 Katharine Galloway Young, *Taleworlds and Storyrealms: The Phenomenology of Narrative* (Dordecht: Martinus Nijhoff Publishers, 1987), p. 16.

11 *Tano* is the traditional Mayday, celebrated regionally.

12 From "The Ideal Mirror," of the Three Religions (*Samga Kwigam*) of Ch'ônghô Hyujông," trans. Young-ho (Jin Wol) Lee, in *Buddhist-Christian Studies* 15 (1995): 144.

13 The songs introduced here follow the late virtuoso Chông Kwônjin's version. He taught me *p'ansori* singing from 1976 until his passing in 1986. The translations of this and the following songs are mine. In an attempt to capture a trace of the flavor of "orality," I have translated the Korean words of each rhythmic cycle in one English line. In my "narrative translation," I have also chosen to retain as much as possible the original Korean sentence structure.

14 Medium 12-beat rhythmic cycle, the most standard among several rhythmic cycles in *p'ansori* singing and drum accompaniment.

15 Name of the ancestral grave of Yi Sônggye, founder of the Chosôn Dynasty (1392–1910).

16 Lit., "the year of the first stem of the rat branch." Along with the western calendar, Korea has continued to use the lunar calendar and the traditional system of reckoning years: a 60-year cycle of the twelve earth "branches" and the ten celestial "stems." *Kap* is the first of the ten celestial stems; *cha* is the year of the rat, first of the twelve earth branches (followed by the ox, tiger, rabbit, dragon, snake, horse, ram, monkey, rooster, dog, pig, then cycling back to the rat).

17 The eighth day of the fourth month is the Buddha's birthday. My teacher Chông Kwônjin once explained that Ch'ông's conception on this day symbolizes that her life is destined to be difficult, like the life of the Buddha himself. People who are born with such karma either suffer in the secular world or "enter the mountain," i.e., regiment their suffering via the asceticism of monastic life. By sacrificing security, sexuality, and possessions in pursuit of peace and enlightenment, they gain an objective perspective on suffering and are thereby freed from it.

18 The Queen Mother of the West (Sôhwangmo, Chinese: Hsiwangmu), a mythical Taoist character, is "first mentioned by the third- or fourth-century B.C.E. Chinese philosopher Lieh-tzu. The fruit of the heavenly peach tree, which she is said to have planted, ripens only once in three thousand years and is eaten by the immortals when they gather for their feast at Yao Lake, the abode of the Queen Mother of the West." Marshall Pihl, *The Korean Singer of Tales* (Cambridge: Harvard University Press, 1994), p. 252.

19 Yüchen Feitzu in Chinese, also known as Yang Kuei-fei (719–756), is the legendary concubine of the T'ang Emperor Ming Huang.

20 Taishang Laochün in Chinese; another name for the ancient philosopher Lao-tzu. In Chang Chiyông's text, Pihl finds that the title was given by the Emperor Chen Tsung of the Sung dynasty. *The Korean Singer of Tales*, p. 252.

21 Referred as the "Queen of the Earth."
22 In this "asymmetrical drive," each rhythmic cycle is composed of two parts (3/2 + 2/3). This creates an asymmetrical tension, provocatively used to signal the mysterious appearance of a Buddhist monk or a Taoist mystic in the narrative.
23 Yang Kuei-fei was murdered here.
24 I.e., Yang Kuei-fei.
25 In Korean folklore, the appearance of a fox symbolizes the lure of sex, a wicked witch metamorphosed. This "foxy lady" is a potent rouser of libido, sometimes with "tails as many as nine." Structurally delineated, "she" is the ultimate challenge to the heroic integrity of a male protagonist. In Korean society outside folktales, sexual experience is forbidden for unmarried women; an "experienced" one is disqualified as a bride and should be avoided. "His" often contradictory reading of "her" manifests as inevitable ruin to be heroically vanquished, on the one hand, and a virgin island to be conquered, on the other. This social and psychological contradiction may be more a symptom of "his" ineptitude in dealing with his own sexuality than a symptom of "her" schizophrenia, as is commonly assumed.
26 "Frequent drive," a four-beat cycle used in describing rapid motions.
27 A slow, six-beat cycle.
28 The three *karmas* (actions) performed by body, speech, and mind produce their results. Lee, "The Ideal Mirror," p. 184.
29 Traditionally the ultimate expression of filial piety.

CHAPTER FOURTEEN

Lineage or Family Tree?

The Implications for Gender

Miriam Levering

The publication of *Buddhist Women on the Edge*, a collection of pieces by women about their experience in American Buddhist communities, has made me think afresh about whether Buddhist "theologies," fundamental Buddhist accounts of the world, practice, and realization, need to be interrogated from a feminist standpoint.[1] It seems that there is a real question whether women in Buddhist communities in the West are being supported, empowered, and seen with complete respect and appreciation for who they are as they seek religious goals. If they are not, then even though basic Buddhist theologies do not seem to support any kind of discrimination on the basis of gender, perhaps those theologies are not free of a "gender problem" after all.

In *Buddhist Women on the Edge*, Buddhist lay teacher and author Sallie Jiko Tisdale tells of her frustration and pain as other members of her religious community, usually males, tell her that she should forget about her gender and the genders of others, not make an issue of the apparently gendered nature of practices and representations of the tradition in ritual, because to a Buddhist gender really does not matter. The reality, she wants to say, is that here, in this practice community, gender does matter. Male voices respond that the problem lies in her own dualistic mind, her attachment to conventional categories: "Stop making male, stop making female," one male says in print, and the problem will go away of itself. "Here," her fellow practitioners say, "we are not men or women. Gender is just an illusion."

"In the absolute, the vast, the One," she writes, "my concern – the concern of many women – that sexism is deeply harmful and must be addressed – is a chimera.... Femaleness and maleness are simply social constructs, to be let go, to let go."[2]

Tisdale's account of her experience is telling:

> And I have let them go; sometimes the particular construct falls away entirely, and we are truly not many, we are truly bound, he is not he and I am not she, and we sit together in intimate silence. Then my Dharma brother weeps beside me in the zendo and when I breathe in,

> I breathe in his outward-flowing breath, and when I let my breath go, he and I sigh together. We are unstirred by the relative, by the moving, evanescent world.
>
> Then we stir again.
>
> Stirring – not stirring – two, not two. Femaleness and maleness come into the world along with everything else, in a cycle of ignorance and movement and change. Shaping the world and being shaped in return.

"Gender is not illusion. Gender is karma," she concludes.[3] As karma, it is both illusion and reality. As in the case of racism and poverty, it is a reality that needs to be understood and addressed as we live together.[4]

The patriarchal nature of much of Buddhist literature and history, and the potential resources which basic Buddhist Mahāyāna and Vajrayāna theologies offer to those who wish to create non-patriarchal, androgynous Buddhisms, have been masterfully surveyed by Rita Gross in her *Buddhism After Patriarchy*.[5] One might conclude from reading Gross's book that Buddhist theology, in its fundamental concepts and insights, its fundamental account of what is most real and important, does not have a gender problem even though historical Buddhist communities have shown gender bias, have given little attention to women's spiritual needs and aspirations, and have silenced women's voices to a remarkable degree.

Again, one wonders if there is not a contradiction. What can one think of the concepts and insights of a theology that apparently has little purchase against practices that limit or silence half of the participants?

My own thinking on these matters has changed as I have come to realize, along with other American Buddhists and friends of Buddhism, that participating in Buddhist practices and experiencing deeper realizations may at some point make one qualified to teach, but they do not necessarily make one a perfect human being. Buddhist practice frees and deepens the intuitive wisdom and compassion of ordinary people with flaws and limited points of view. As with any other religion, Buddhist theologies and their appeals to authority need to be critically interrogated and creatively reshaped to remedy blind spots that prevent the realization of the highest goals of Buddhists and to reflect the best thinking of current members.

Lineage as a Theological Construct

Turning to Ch'an and Zen Buddhism in particular, at the heart of what we might call "Ch'an/Zen theology" is the fundamental idea that one can rely on there having been a transmission of awakened mind down to one's present teacher and to oneself through a lineage of awakened teachers. In early Ch'an, various authors went to considerable trouble to name the members of the lineage through which awakened mind had been transmitted from the Buddha Śākyamuni in India to Hui-neng (Eno), the

Sixth Chinese patriarch. Authors of genealogical histories in the Five Dynasties and the Sung Dynasty continued to work on recording and constructing the transmission lineage, the family tree rooted in Śākyamuni Buddha that authorized the claim to awakened insight of all of the contemporary members in all of the branches. In Japan, Zen teachers and their students continued to emphasize that participation in a true lineage meant that in one's present teacher one faced a mind identical to that of Śākyamuni Buddha himself.

Every morning at the San Francisco Zen Center the assembled group of priests and laypeople chants in gratitude the lineage of teachers who have transmitted the awakened mind of the Buddha from Śākyamuni to the present students, invoking the presence of these ancestors to receive the homage of the group. From Śākyamuni Buddha to Mahākāśyapa, from Mahākāśyapa over 28 generations to Bodhidharma, the Indian patriarch who brought the transmission to China, from Bodhidharma to Hui-k'o, from Hui-k'o to Seng-ts'an and so forth to Hui-neng, from Hui-neng to Ch'ing-yüan Hsing-ssu (d. 740) and so forth to Tung-shan Liang-chieh and then to Fu-jung Tao-k'ai, from Fu-jung Tao-k'ai to Ju ching, from Ju-ching to Dōgen, from Dōgen to Suzuki Shunryu, the founder of the San Francisco Zen Center.

Let me reproduce just a small but crucial part of this lineage:

Tung-shan Liang-chieh (Tōzan Ryōkai) (807–869)
|
Yün-chu Tao-ying (Ungo Dōyō) (d. 902)
:
:
(four generations)
:
:
T'ou-tzu I-ch'ing (Tōsu Gisei) (1032–1083)
|
Fu-jung Tao-k'ai (Fuyō Dōkai) (1043–1118)
|
Tan-hsia Tzu-ch'un (Tanka Shijun) (1064–1117)
|
Chen-hsieh Ch'ing-liao (Shingetsu Shoryo) (1088–1151)
|
T'ien-t'ung Ta-hsiu Tsung-yu (Tendō Sōyu) (1091–1162)
|
Tsu-an Chih-chien (1105–1192)
|
T'ien-t'ung Ju-ching (Tendō Nyōjō) (1163–1228)
|
Dōgen Kigen (1200–1253)

Why such emphasis on the lineage of teachers, guru and disciple (*guruparampara*), in the Ch'an/Zen tradition?

There is, of course, a practical problem that Buddhists and Hindus around the world have faced. Where what one is to learn is something that one cannot teach oneself, one especially needs to know that one has a good teacher, a master of that which one seeks to learn. There might be as many people claiming to teach as there are web sites – some are sources of good information and interpretation; some are full of misleading, false, unauthenticated information, speculation, and legend. Some teachers are able to recognize and enable the desired gnosis, and some are not. How does a beginner know which are which? This makes it important to know where exactly one's teacher learned what he teaches, and from whom. The authority of the teacher rests in part on how and by whom the teacher was taught, trained, and certified, and on when and where this took place.

The idea of a transmission lineage as a way of assuring the authenticity of teaching and practice and of authorizing the current teacher seems such a simple and practical idea, but in fact in the Ch'an/Zen tradition it is also a theological idea, an article of faith that grounds practice in an important way. This is clear from the way in which it resists alteration even in the face of a number of challenges. For example, what happens if you know that the lineage of the teacher is fictional? Twentieth-century scholars have pointed out that the claims of authors from early Ch'an and in later periods in China to have traced their lineage back to Śākyamuni do not withstand historical scrutiny. In recent decades it has come to be accepted that the notion of a single unbroken line of transmission from mind to mind from Śākyamuni to Bodhidharma, and the similar notion of a single line of transmission from Bodhidharma to Hui-neng, are at least to some extent fictions.[6]

These fictions were very useful to heirs of these lineages in the Sung Dynasty (and perhaps earlier), for they authorized members to make an extraordinary claim – they were heirs to the very awakened mind of Śākyamuni and not merely heirs to his verbal teachings and publicly promulgated practices. Therefore they had more authority as sons of the Buddha and as transmitters of the Buddha's awakening than members of others schools. If one really wanted to become a Buddha, one had better study with them, for they were the only ones who really knew what a Buddha is and how to become one. That a part of what was going on was a bid for power is clear from the way masters in T'ien-t'ai and other non-Ch'an Buddhist schools in Sung Dynasty China resented and attacked the claim of Ch'an/Zen Buddhists to have received the only authentic transmission of Śākyamuni Buddha's highest teaching and awakened mind.

In constructing this warrant to their claims to authority, Ch'an historians in China carried simplification to an extreme. Śākyamuni had one heir who understood him, Mahākāśyapa. Mahākāśyapa also had only one heir, and so forth. Bodhidharma likewise had only one heir who fully understood awakened mind, as did each of his successors down to Hui-neng. This simplification is another demonstration that what was at work here was authorizing myth rather than history.

And there is yet another challenge from historians to the notion of "authenticity" attached to the idea of an unbroken lineage of Dharma transmission: perhaps Dharma transmission was always to some degree political. This is of course made likely by the fact that Dharma transmission was required for a person to become the abbot or abbess of a Ch'an or Zen monastery. Dharma transmission was likely to be given to one whom the institution could trust to advance the good of the institution. There must have been times when the head of an institution who needed a successor simply had to settle for the best available candidate for transmission, rather than wait for a deeply awakened Dharma-heir to come along.

What are the implications for contemporary Ch'an and Zen communities if there can be little doubt that the transmission lineages that have come down to us are in part fictional? Does the situation in which one cannot be sure that one's awakening would be recognized as such by the Buddha Śākyamuni or by Dōgen eat away at the structure of authority and faith within these communities? Apparently not. How central then is lineage to the authorization and interpretation of the current practitioner's practice? And, seen from a contemporary, feminist perspective, how central should it be?

I asked these questions of Michael Wenger, a long-time practitioner and scholar who directs the San Francisco Zen Center's scholarly and education projects and programs. Wenger replied that the notion of a lineage of Dharma transmission is a *sine qua non* of Zen practice. He said that Zen practice is so much in and about the present moment, that Zen practitioners "need to have lineage as an anchor into the past. Even knowing that it is fictional," he said, "we have to have it."[7]

Hearing this, I remembered that I had recently seen an episode in the TV series *Nothing Sacred* in which a young parish priest says to an older priest, "What kind of a priest am I? I can't get a husband to attend his wife's funeral. All that I have is that my hands were touched by hands that had been touched by hands that had been touched by hands all the way back to hands that had been touched by Jesus." The efficacy of the priesthood is entirely a matter of the present moment. That efficacy at a given moment may seem feeble – but there is behind it that transmission in which one can have faith and trust, that anchor into the source. The line of apostolic succession from Jesus and Peter may also have its fictions, but they are authorizing fictions that may channel the mystery of divine presence and effective faith.

Yet from the point of view of a critical examination of Ch'an Buddhist theology, it is important to notice that no women appear in the list of ancestors chanted every morning at the San Francisco Zen Center – the ancestral line is a patriline. It names the one person in each generation who is the direct teacher of the direct teacher of Dōgen and Suzuki Shunryu. Eighty-three names – all of them men. Sallie Jiko Tisdale writes that, in her irritation with the failure of her Dharma-brothers to see that gender matters, she imagined "chanting an ancestral line of women every day, a matrilineal transmission eighty-three names long, without a single male name – imagined my *saṅgha* brother catching on to how isolating that imbalance can be."[8]

Some members of the San Francisco Zen Center community also feel the absence of women's names, women's presences, as they chant their ancestral line. They are trying various options. At one of their monasteries, Green Gulch Farm, they chant the names of nuns of the Buddha's time given in the early Indian scriptures – most notably, the names of the women in the Therīgatha. But these are Indian women, not Ch'an or Zen Dharma-heirs.

How did this lineage come to be all men? From its origins in India, Buddhist monastic practice was intended to be gender segregated, so it is not surprising that by and large in Ch'an and Zen, male teachers had male students. Yet because this was not always the case in China or in Japan, historical study gives us access to some moments in which the constructors of the lineage excluded women candidates. One important example is the case of the nun Ts'ung-chih, student of Bodhidharma.

We have said above that in constructing the notion of a lineage of mind-to-mind transmission as a warrant to their claims to authority, Ch'an historians in China carried simplification to an extreme. Śākyamuni had one heir, that heir also had only one, and so forth. Bodhidharma likewise had only one heir who fully understood awakened mind, as did each of his successors in the five generations down to Hui-neng (Eno).

Along the way later Ch'an authors brushed aside the idea that a woman, the nun Ts'ung-ch'ih, was a full heir to Bodhidharma – or so it seems from the texts. It is curious that Ts'ung-chih's name and those of the other two unsuccessful students of Bodhidharma are retained in the later texts at all. Later texts say that Ts'ung-chih was a sister of an important king. They imply that her being a woman would normally have caused her name to be forgotten, but the importance of her rank caused her name to be remembered, and the royal connection claimed. But this is an explanation far after the fact. It seems rather probable that at the time of the compilation of the earliest texts in which the story of her membership in a group of three or four disciples of Bodhidharma was told, her own disciples or Dharma-heirs were important enough as a group that their claims to a lineage founded by a woman who studied with Bodhidharma could not be denied. As long as they remained important, her link as a disciple who had learned much from Bodhidharma could not be erased. Only later, after her group had ceased to matter in the internal politics of Ch'an, was it possible to give her expression of her attainment ever decreasing status and to deny that she was a full Dharma heir to Bodhidharma. As the stories of Bodhidharma's transmission to his disciples were retold in the Five Dynasties and the Sung, in the context of the ideal that Bodhidharma and the other early patriarchs should each have a single legitimate heir, Bodhidharma's other students were demoted so that Bodhidharma, too, should have only one heir: the monk Hui-k'o.

Dōgen and the Story of Bodhidharma and Ts'ung-ch'ih

As every student of Sōtō Zen knows, Dōgen had an immense belief in mind-to-mind transmission – an esoteric transmission, from teacher to student, Dharma-father to Dharma-son, generation to generation – as a guarantee of the authenticity of his claim to have inherited the Buddha's mind. Yet he was uninterested in preserving the conception of awakening that underlay the notion that Bodhidharma had only one heir. In a number of places in his sermons and other writings he brought up the story of Bodhidharma and his four disciples (including the nun Ts'ung-ch'ih) and interpreted it quite differently from the way it was apparently interpreted in China. All of Bodhidharma's students who were asked by him to express what they had learned, including Ts'ung-ch'ih, expressed awakened understanding.

Lineage and Gender

Did Ch'an/Zen historically go through a period of finding it difficult or impossible to accept the notion of women teachers, women Dharma-heirs? My own reading of Southern School Ch'an texts through the Sung Dynasty suggests that this was largely the case in the Southern School up through the eleventh century.[9]

Most early texts reflect the view that women do not have what it takes to belong to the lineage of teachers who transmit the Dharma. In the *Chodang-chip* (Chinese: *Tsu-t'ang-chi*) of 952 C.E., for example, there is a story about the famous monk-master Huang-po Hsi-yün (?–850). When he was traveling as a Dharma-student he begged for food at the home of a woman. She met him with a Dharma challenge, then allowed him to come in. She continued to challenge him to display greater insight, and he gained a realization. He then asked her formally to be his teacher. She replied, "I am a woman (lit., "a five hindrances body"), and therefore not a vessel of the Dharma," and declined his request, recommending instead that he go to see Pai-chang, a male teacher, whose Dharma he inherited. This story holds two messages. First, there is the message that a woman may be herself awakened and informally useful in a teaching capacity to a man. Second, there is the message that whether because of society or *karma*, a woman is not suited to take a position of authority as a formal teacher.[10] These are the views reflected in the texts of the Ch'an world as the Sung Dynasty began in 960 C.E.

After that point, male teachers by and large had male students, and male students male teachers. For a long time the texts show us only one woman, Mo-shan Liao-jan, teaching a male. Nonetheless, more and more male teachers had women students, and there came to be women teachers and Dharma-heirs connected to the lineage through a male teacher.

Dōgen and Mo-shan Liao-jan

Dōgen knew that in Ch'an there were women Dharma-heirs. He brought it up in his discussion of the Five Dynasties nun-teacher Mo-shan Liao-jan, the first woman teacher and Dharma-heir given her own entry in the official Ch'an Dharma transmission family tree. The monk Chih-hsien is said to have studied with her. Dōgen said in his essay "Raihaitokuzui" that Chih-hsien's Dharma-father was Lin-chi and his Dharma-mother was Mo-shan Liao-jan. Dōgen's comment might be seen as a slight opening in the direction of a more complex application of the metaphor of family to the Ch'an/Zen situation. If Dōgen's statement had even been construed as a genealogical possibility, the lineage chart of Chih-hsien's descendants would be more complex, for those descendants would have a grandfather and a grandmother. But the Sung dynasty compilers of the Ch'an family tree in the "Record of the Transmission of the Flame (of Awakened Mind) in the Ching-te Era" (Ching-te ch'uan-teng-lu) of 1008 C.E. stuck to the notion of a single teacher transmitting Dharma in each generation of a single patriline: they saw Chih-hsien as Lin-chi's Dharma-heir, and attributed no heirs to Mo-shan.[11]

Women Dharma-Heirs

By the beginning of the thirteenth century, near the end of the Sung Dynasty, the genealogical Ch'an historical text called *The Record of the Universal Flame [Compiled in] the Chia-t'ai Era* of 1204 recognized 16 women as Dharma-heirs of Sung Ch'an teachers, as full members of the lineage who received the flame of awakening and were trusted to be qualified to transmit it. Some of these women had Dharma-heirs of their own who were recognized in *The Record of the Universal Flame [Compiled in] the Chia-t'ai Era* and later genealogical histories.

This fact has implications for the Ts'ao-tung/Sōtō school. If we look again at the ancestral lineage, the single patriline from Bodhidharma and Hui-neng to Dōgen, we notice that if one were to chant a bit more of the family tree beyond the single line, one would become aware of the presence of women.

Let us look at the lineage of which Dōgen became a member when he received Dharma transmission from Ju-ching. A detailed lineage chart, starting from Tōzan Ryōkai (Tung-shan Liang-che), makes it clear that there were women Dharma-heirs in Dōgen's lineage. From a historical point of view, a pivotal person in this lineage was Fuyō Dōkai (Chinese: Fu-jung Tao-k'ai), who had a major role in reviving the Sōtō (Ts'ao-tung) lineage in China at a time when it was in great decline. He had a relatively large number of Dharma-heirs, one of whom was a woman, the nun Tao-shen. She had two Dharma-heirs, one of which was the nun Chih-an, but we have no record of her lineage beyond those two.

Tao-shen and her woman Dharma-heir are examples of the women teachers and abbesses in Ch'an/Zen whose lineages were broken, but the point to notice is that Dōgen in fact had several women Dharma-heirs on his family tree. Tanka Shijun – one of Fuyō Dōkai's Dharma-heirs, through which the lineage was transmitted eventually to Dōgen – had a Dharma-sister and through her at least one Dharma-niece.

A second of Fuyō Dōkai's Dharma-heirs, Komoku Hōjō (Chinese: K'u-mu Fa-ch'eng), also had a woman Dharma-heir, the nun Hui-kuang, who headed the Miao-hui monastery, an important convent at the capital of the Northern Sung Dynasty, present-day Kaifeng. Hui-kuang received a purple robe from the emperor. Tanka Shijun, Dōgen's direct ancestor, had in her a second Dharma-niece. What Hui-kuang started at the Miao-hui monastery her Dharma-first-cousin, the nun Chih-an, continued when she became abbess of this same convent after Hui-kuang.

A third of Fuyō Dokai's Dharma-heirs, Shih-men Yuan-I, had a woman Dharma-heir named Fo-t'ung of Hsiang-shan. She was Tanka Shujun's third Dharma-niece. So, while Dōgen's direct patriline is all male, his family tree has women as well as men.

One Possible Solution: Why Not Chant the Family Tree?

In a Soto Zen context one never chants the name of a woman as one chants the traditional direct ancestral line. Sallie Jiko Tisdale recently suggested a way to address the problem. She suggests that one could chant the traditional patriline at some times and at other times chant a list of women Ch'an and Zen Dharma-heirs such as the ones mentioned above who either did not found lineages of their own or have suffered the loss of the knowledge of their lineages. This seems a creative and worthwhile suggestion, since it acknowledges the reality and value of women who have practiced Ch'an/Zen in the past.

I would like to suggest a way to solve the problem that, on the one hand, does not depart quite as far from traditional practice as chanting the names of nuns in the *Therīgāthā*, but on the other hand, challenges even more radically the theology of lineage as it is now conceived. I would suggest that Ch'an and Zen Buddhists chant more of the family tree than merely the direct line. How about recognizing the Dharma-sisters, the Dharma-aunts, the Dharma-nieces, of members of one's direct lineage?

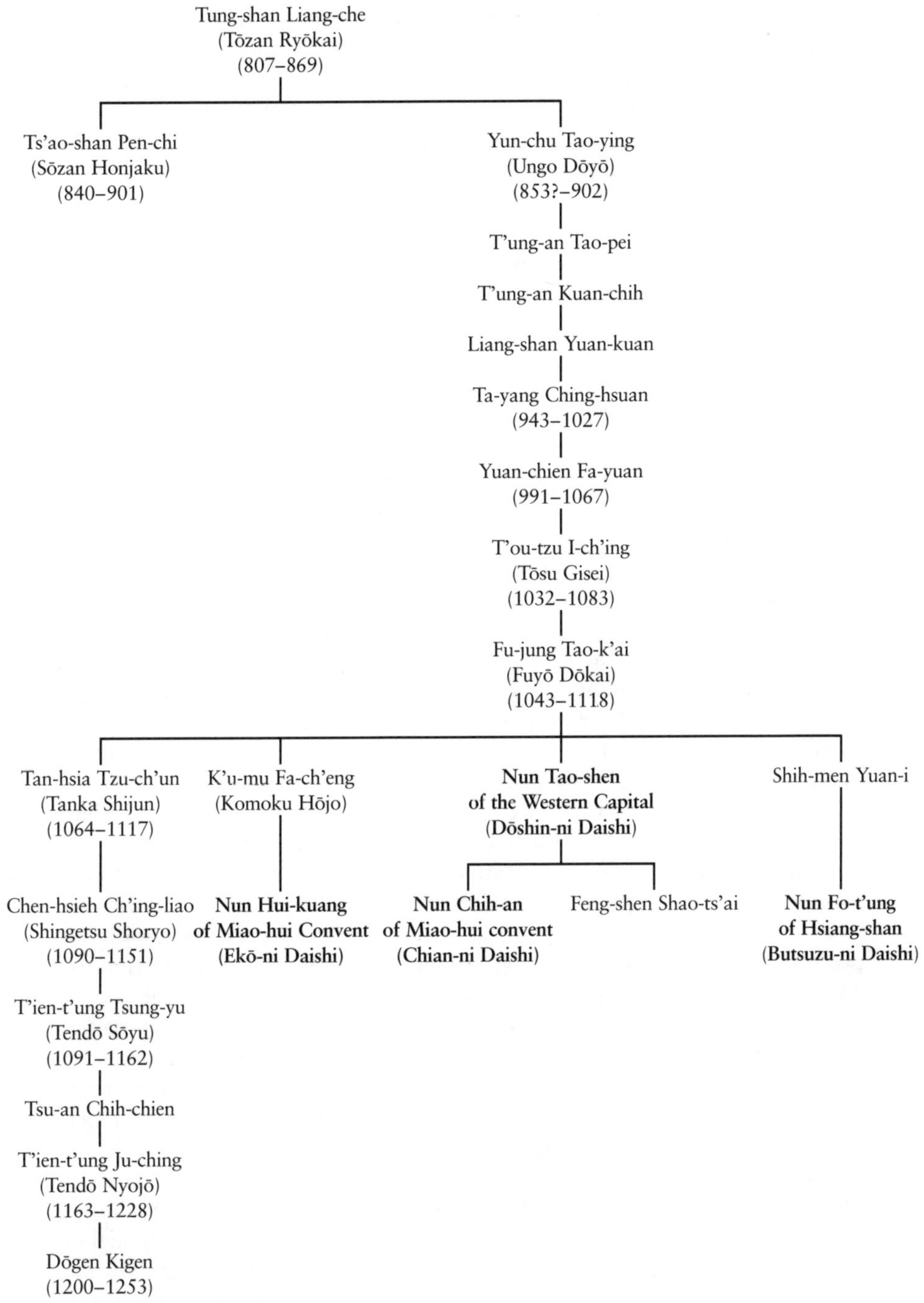
Tung-shan Liang-che
(Tōzan Ryōkai)
(807–869)
Ts'ao-shan Pen-chi
(Sōzan Honjaku)
(840–901)
Yun-chu Tao-ying
(Ungo Dōyō)
(853?–902)
T'ung-an Tao-pei
T'ung-an Kuan-chih
Liang-shan Yuan-kuan
Ta-yang Ching-hsuan
(943–1027)
Yuan-chien Fa-yuan
(991–1067)
T'ou-tzu I-ch'ing
(Tōsu Gisei)
(1032–1083)
Fu-jung Tao-k'ai
(Fuyō Dōkai)
(1043–1118)
Tan-hsia Tzu-ch'un
(Tanka Shijun)
(1064–1117)
K'u-mu Fa-ch'eng
(Komoku Hōjo)
Nun Tao-shen
of the Western Capital
(Dōshin-ni Daishi)
Shih-men Yuan-i
Chen-hsieh Ch'ing-liao
(Shingetsu Shoryo)
(1090–1151)
Nun Hui-kuang
of Miao-hui Convent
(Ekō-ni Daishi)
Nun Chih-an
of Miao-hui convent
(Chian-ni Daishi)
Feng-shen Shao-ts'ai
Nun Fo-t'ung
of Hsiang-shan
(Butsuzu-ni Daishi)
T'ien-t'ung Tsung-yu
(Tendō Sōyu)
(1091–1162)
Tsu-an Chih-chien
T'ien-t'ung Ju-ching
(Tendō Nyojō)
(1163–1228)
Dōgen Kigen
(1200–1253)

As one chants the ancestral lineage one could add the horizontal connections that would make one aware that there were women among those who studied and taught this Dharma that Dōgen and one's teacher inherited. One could chant: "Fuyō Dōkai Daio-sho; Tanka Shijun Daiosho; Dōshin-ni Daishi (Chinese: Ta-shih, the title given to nuns of attainment in the Ch'an school); Shingetsu Shoryo Daiosho; Ekō-ni Daishi; Chian-ni Daishi; Butsuzu-ni Daishi, Tendō Sōyu Daiosho," and so forth.

From the standpoint of women who are pained by the fact that not many women were included in the Ch'an and Zen transmission lineages as men passed them on, this might only be a modest improvement. Whether the Ch'an and Zen movements and institutions were in fact very largely male, or whether the way stories were told and records kept left out of the picture many women who were active, vital keepers of the flame of awakened mind – these are questions for which historians are now seeking answers and making educated guesses. But it is liberating to give proper place to the women in the lineage whose names are known and to name their names aloud.

This is not just a practical suggestion, but a theological one as well, for I would contend that the theological treatment of transmission as a matter of the direct patriline should be subject to a critical reexamination. The family of those who have gone before is larger than the emphasis on direct lineage allows contemporary practitioners to imagine.

Ch'an and Zen Buddhists, unlike Tibetan Buddhists, do not take refuge in the guru, but only in the Buddha, Dharma, and Saṅgha. The teacher may stand formally in the place of the Buddha, but the Saṅgha also plays important roles in deepening one's practice and occasioning awakening.

Emphasizing the patriline in China was no doubt a reflection of Indian culture's emphasis on the guru lineage. It was also a way in which Ch'an Buddhism conformed itself to native Chinese secular culture by appropriating the contemporary Chinese metaphor of family to authorize relations within the Saṅgha. Social historian Pat Ebrey writes of the profoundly male-centered ideology of the Sung Dynasty Chinese family: "The descent line from father to son to grandson was taken to be the core of the family: obligations to ancestors, family property, and family names were all transmitted along the patriline. Texts that can be broadly labeled Confucian presented family and kinship as at bottom a set of connections among men; indeed, people could and did compile family histories that failed to mention any women."[12]

The Chinese concept of family may be why knowledge of so few lineages of women Ch'an practitioners was preserved. In Ch'an, as in the Chinese family system, what men did was the important thing. The Chinese patriline as a model for imagining the Saṅgha of the past has not only been harmful to women in the same way as the Confucian family histories Ebrey mentions, it has ultimately had a non-Buddhist result in the way it has left women out of view. The Buddhist notion of *saṅgha*, going back to India, is of a two-fold or four-fold body that, wherever there is a Bhikṣuṇī Saṅgha and wherever there are laywomen, always consists of both men and women.

The lineage metaphor supports the notion that the crucial interaction through which one learns Dharma is with a single teacher. But if we look at Ch'an/Zen history, we can see that a person's teacher, one's official Dharma-father or -mother, is often simply the person of sufficient authority who recognizes an attainment that is already a *fait accompli*. The actual insight and maturation has taken place through one's own introspection and/or in interaction with others – the authors of words in texts, awakened laypeople (often laywomen) that one meets on one's travels or begging rounds, fellow students, somewhat more advanced students, holders of other teaching positions in the monastery.

The Western notion of the hermeneutic situation can be helpful in understanding this argument. At the moment of understanding and interpretation, who you are as you understand and interpret, and thus what it is that you understand, are influenced by all that takes part in the constituting of you. It includes all who take part, as well as your historical moment. It is not simply a patriline, a single father who creates you as a son, but embraces your Dharma-sisters, your Dharma-cousins, your students, your fellow students, and so forth.

The chanting of the patriline, giving one an opportunity to express one's deep gratitude to teachers of the lineage for making possible one's own study of the authentic Dharma, reflects an important truth. But a second truth – that one owes one's insight to all of those who have practiced together, supported one another's practice, become awakened together, and created the conditions that made each other's practice possible – is obscured in the chanting of the patriline. Fu-jung Tao-k'ai may have learned much from his own nun disciple Tao-shen who became his Dharma-heir. Tan-hsia Tzu-ch'un and Chen-hsieh Ch'ing-liao may have learned much from their Dharma-sisters, Dharma-nieces, and female Dharma-cousins. That dimension of the transmission of the awakened mind of the Buddha is obscured by the patrilineal chant. It could be brought back into awareness by chanting more of the family tree.

The recent experience of various Buddhists groups (including Zen groups) with the failures and blind spots of abbots who are Dharma-heirs has called attention to the possibility that awakened awareness is not a single, perfect, total, and monolithic thing. Rather, as Dōgen pointed out, practice and awakening, cultivation and authentication are one, yet complete only at the level of principle. One can be quite fully awakened and still blind to the suffering caused by one's own acts of gender discrimination. It seems important to chant a family tree that includes women as a way of recognizing the likely possibility that, in societies where gender is a marker of inferiority and a cause for segregation, women have contributed most to the awakening of male teachers to the spiritual potential of women. To chant the family tree of Dōgen and Suzuki Shunryu with this kind of understanding would represent a fundamental shift in the Ch'an/Zen "theology" of lineage transmission. This shift could awaken us all to more dimensions of the reality of gender and of *saṅgha* in the lives of practitioners.[13]

Notes

1 Marianne Dresser, ed., *Buddhist Women on the Edge: Contemporary Perspectives from the Western Frontier* (Berkeley: North Atlantic Books, 1996). I would like to express my gratitude to my colleagues Griff Foulk of Sarah Lawrence College and Jim Fitzgerald and David Linge of the University of Tennessee for their part in helpful conversations on this topic.

2 Sallie Jiko Tisdale, "Form, Emptiness: Emptiness, Form," ibid., pp. 14–15.

3 Tisdale, ibid., p. 16.

4 Sallie Jiko Tisdale's words here remind me here of the discussion of Dōgen's message that Japanese Zen scholars have conducted recently Is cultivation/authentication simply a way of releasing all illusions in the present moment, noting that something is an illusion and ceasing to pay attached attention to it? Or is it that a positive way of acting in which doing all good things and not doing evil things, turning evil things into good things, is the important cultivation/authentication? The latter has been the message of the Japanese scholarly/political movement called "critical Buddhism" – that Dōgen in his last writings turned away from emphasizing the actualization of an enlightened mind that everyone already possessed and toward urging students to give importance to karma and its fruits, to cause and effect.

5 Rita Gross, *Buddhism After Patriarchy: A Feminist History, Analysis and Reconstruction of Buddhism* (Albany, N.Y.: State University of New York Press, 1992).

6 The scholarship on this subject is ably summarized by Philip Yampolsky in the introduction to his translation of the *Platform Sutra*, in *The Platform Sutra of the Sixth Patriarch* (New York: Columbia University Press, 1967).

7 Personal communication, San Francisco Zen Center, San Francisco, California, Oct. 1997.

8 Tisdale, op. cit., p. 14.

9 Miriam Levering, "Dogen's *Raihaitokuzui* and Women Teaching in Sung Ch'an," *Journal of the International Association of Buddhist Studies*, 1998. The historical information given briefly below about the development of women teachers and Dharma-heirs in China, and about Dogen, is given in greater detail and with more detailed references in this *JIABS* article.

10 *Chodang-chip*, chuan 16, *Fo-kuang-shan ta-tsang-ching*, Ch'an-tsang, shih-chuan pu, vol. 16, pp. 818–19.

11 If Dōgen and Suzuki Shunryu had been descended from Chih-hsien, then the community at the San Francisco Zen Center would have a woman to recognize and thank for the gift of the transmission of awakened mind. Unfortunately, Dōgen's ancestral descent from Buddha Śākyamuni, Bodhidharma, and Hui-neng does not pass through Chih-hsien and Lin-chi, so there is no way that the outstanding woman teacher Mo-shan Liao-jan could turn up in the chanted lineage at the San Francisco Zen Center so long as Dōgen's and Suzuki Shunryu's direct lineage is chanted. If one does as Tisdale suggests, one could definitely add her to one's list.

12 Patricia Ebrey, *The Inner Quarters: Marriage and the Lives of Chinese Women in the Sung Period* (Berkeley: University of California Press, 1993), p. 7.

13 I have not spelled out here in lineage charts the ways in which a slightly expanded vision of the "family tree" would allow us to notice women in the Lin-chi/Rinzai lineages important today. This will have to wait for another occasion. Suffice it to say for the moment that the cases are quite parallel.

CHAPTER FIFTEEN

Ordination, Legitimacy, and Sisterhood

The International Full Ordination Ceremony in Bodhgaya

Yuchen Li

In February 1998, a momentous international full ordination ceremony was held in the religious metropolis of Bodhgaya, India, site of the Buddha's enlightenment. Among the newly ordained were 134 female practitioners from various Buddhist traditions, most of which had long since lost their own *bhikṣuṇī* lineages. Chinese Buddhists claim that their nuns are ordained according to a lineage introduced from India to Sri Lanka in the fourth century B.C.E. and subsequently to China in 432 C.E.[1] Unfortunately, the *bhikṣuṇī* lineage disappeared in Sri Lanka as a result of the 11th-century Coḷa invasions,[2] and apparently never reached Tibet. Buddhist monks from these traditions joined the 1998 ceremony, conferring blessings and lending support to the nuns. Their participation effectively restored the lineage of full ordination to these traditions, a milestone in Buddhist history.

The current movement to introduce full ordination for Buddhist nuns involves a significant reconstruction of religious traditions. The process of gaining legitimation for their own nuns in the eyes of the global Buddhist community is effecting changes in attitudes and institutions in various monastic communities. The historical tension among the Buddha's ordination of women, textual ambiguity, and *de facto* exclusion of women from full ordination in certain traditions, may soon be replaced by the principle of universal equality, from which a vital new tradition can emerge.

The impetus to establish an order of fully ordained nuns is fueled by three primary factors. First, monastic organizations attempting to expand in the West require many dedicated nuns for their success. Some competition for Western nuns has already surfaced between Tibetan and Taiwanese institutions. Second, there is competition between the traditions to demonstrate their commitment to social equality by recognizing women's equal right to full ordination. This competition is most evident between Tibetan and Theravādin institutions in the West. Third, there is competition between the *bhikṣuṇī* orders in Taiwan and the People's Republic of China to prove their legitimacy and pedigree. This competition, involving Tibetans in exile, the PRC, and Taiwan, is closely tied to political concerns that may be far removed from Buddhist doctrines and ideals.

Given the extremely complex nature of the controversy over full ordination for women in the international Buddhist community today, the ceremony in Bodhgaya provides a vantage point from which to view gender issues within Buddhist communities worldwide: the construction of Buddhist women's identity, Buddhist nuns' struggle to improve their status within the monastic framework, and the role of women in reforming monastic regulations. From this vantage point, I shall discuss the full ordination in Bodhgaya, the process of becoming a *bhikṣuṇī*, the crucial role of nuns in Taiwanese Buddhist monasteries, and the gender issues that are emerging globally in Buddhist communities.

The Full Ordination in Bodhgaya

My research began in Ithaca, New York, in September 1996, when I first learned that the exiled Tibetan authorities had permitted Western nuns of the Tibetan tradition to receive full ordination in Taiwan. After that, I had many opportunities to discuss the *bhikṣuṇī* issue with leading Taiwanese nuns, during both the Dalai Lama's first visit to Taiwan in March 1997 and the November 1997 visit of Bhikṣu Tashi Tsering, representative of the Tibetan Government-in-Exile's Ministry of Religious and Cultural Affairs. When members of Foguangshan, Taiwan's largest monastery, told me about their plans to conduct an international full ordination ceremony in Bodhgaya in February 1998, I made plans to travel to India to witness this historic event.

I arrived in Calcutta on February 14, in the company of about 40 ordination candidates. A team of organizers and workers from Foguangshan had already proceeded to Bodhgaya a week earlier. Traveling with us was a large group of Taiwanese lay Buddhists participating in a pilgrimage arranged by Foguangshan. After a press conference, we took an evening train that arrived in Bodhgaya around midnight. It was election time, and all local vehicles had already been commandeered by the local government. The nuns and prosperous Taiwanese pilgrims were very visible as they boarded their designated buses in this impoverished, crime-prone town.

My status in Bodhgaya was rather ambiguous. The organizers carefully maintained boundaries between the ordination candidates and the laity to make sure that the candidates, already exhausted by their busy schedule, could concentrate on the ordination, a crucial turning point in their lives. To experience the event as fully as possible, I volunteered my help as a Chinese-English translator, serving as a bridge between the nuns, ordination candidates, and visiting scholars. As a layperson, I was excluded from the gatherings of ordination candidates, but because there were only 30 nuns to tend to the needs of more than 1,500 participants (including pilgrims and candidates), my help as a translator was welcomed. During the nine days the ordination lasted, I often worked up to 16 hours a day. Except for the ordination itself and the lectures on Vinaya, which were restricted to monks and nuns, I participated in all aspects of the ordination. When I was not needed at ceremonies and events at the Chinese Temple or the Mahābodhi Stupa,[3] I was usually helping at the main office a block away from the Chinese Temple.

The village of Bodhgaya became crowded with the arrival of 1,200 Taiwanese pilgrims and 300 Buddhist monks and nuns participating in events connected with the ordination. This was one of the few times in history that Buddhist women in the Indian, Sri Lankan, and Tibetan traditions have had an opportunity to take full ordination. Out of more than 300 applicants, only 148 (134 nuns and 14 monks) were selected to participate. From February 15 to 23, candidates were ordained at three levels: novice monk or nun (*śrāmaṇera/śrāmaṇerikā*), fully ordained monk or nun (*bhikṣu/bhiksuṇī*), and *bodhisattva*. Meanwhile, lay applicants received the five precepts at the Mahābodhi Stupa.

The daily schedule of the ordination candidates was very similar to monastic life in Taiwan: waking at dawn, morning prayers from 5:00 to 6:00, meals at 6:00 and 11:10 a.m., evening prayers from 5:00 to 6:30 pm, and retiring at 10:00 p.m. Ceremonial training, lessons on the *Bhikṣu* and *Bhikṣuṇī Prātimokṣa Sūtras*, and the actual ordination ceremonies occupied most of the candidates' time. They were only allowed short breaks for resting at noon and for bathing in the evening. The first stage of the full ordination (*upasampadā*) for *bhikṣuṇīs* was conducted by ten *bhikṣu* precept masters on the evening of February 20. Candidates entered the ordination hall after 11:00 p.m., and the ceremony lasted until nearly 4:30 the next morning. After a very brief rest, the newly ordained *bhikṣuṇīs* then went to request the next stage of the *upasampadā* ordination, conducted by ten *bhikṣu* precept masters at 7:00 a.m. The process of ordination was very intensive, with intermittent kneeling, bowing, and recitations, but sincere in their determination, the exhausted ordination candidates concentrated their attention on the training and ordination procedures.

Following Chinese custom, the ordination was divided into five sections: (1) ceremonial training in small groups, (2) lessons on the Prātimokṣa precepts, (3) repentance rituals, (4) the formal ordination procedures, and (5) a large *saṅghadāna* (meal offering to the monastic community). The Chinese method of conducting the ordination differs from the Tibetan and Theravādin traditions, in which ordination is completed in a single day. By contrast, a Chinese ordination ceremony can take up to 90 days. During this time, the ordination candidates are not only taught the precepts, but also acquainted with monastic regulations and protocol, culminating in the ordination ceremony toward the end. Tashi Tsering commented that the Chinese style of ordination is more complex and ritualized than in Tibet.[4]

For example, in Bodhgaya the ordination hall was elaborately decorated with colorful flags and fabrics, and Buddhist music was broadcast loudly. In contrast, a Tibetan ordination ceremony is relatively simple and quiet. The highly decorative style of the Chinese ordination ceremony seems directed toward the lay devotees and guests rather than the candidates, who are required to be silent and stay in restricted areas during the ordination. The laity, including the family and friends of ordinands, were permitted to attend certain activities – to serve at the *saṅghadāna*, participate in repentance ceremonies, and receive the lay precepts – but were strictly excluded from the ordination procedures.

Taiwanese lay followers believe that by participating in these activities, they share the great merit accumulated by the ordination masters and candidates. Often they contribute the ordination fee for the candidates and contribute toward the organizing expenses. For instance, each Taiwanese layperson who received the five precepts in Bodhgaya not only paid an ordination fee and her own pilgrimage expenses, but also donated a certain amount for a nun at the ordination. One Taiwanese woman referred to her support for the newly ordained monks and nuns as "making a Buddha." In this way, a strong sense of religious community and reciprocal relationship is created between the monastics and the laity.

Another characteristic that distinguishes the Chinese system of ordination from the Tibetan and Theravādin is incorporating novice (*śrāmaṇera/śrāmaṇerikā*), full (*bhikṣu/bhikṣuṇī*), and *bodhisattva* ordinations in sequence, in what is known as a Triple Platform Ordination. Until 1987, Taiwan had a centralized ordination system in which only ordinations sanctioned by a national committee of Buddhist representatives and verified by an official ordination certificate were permitted. A probationary training period in a monastery, equivalent in some ways to the *śikṣamāṇā* (probationer) idea in early India, precedes the Triple Platform Ordination.[5] Some novices may need more than six months to adjust to their new religious identity. Others might spend several years in a monastery waiting to get their parents' permission to be ordained. Some monastic groups have their novices delay their ordination until their tonsure master is invited to serve as the *śīla-upādhyāya* at the national ordination ceremony.

Incorporating the *bodhisattva* precept ceremony into the Triple Platform Ordination procedure illustrates how Chinese Buddhism integrates Mahāyāna doctrine and Dharmagupta Vinaya into the ordination. The Prātimokṣa ordinations (*śrāmaṇerikā* and *bhikṣuṇī*) demonstrate that the Chinese Saṅgha maintains the orthodox monastic lineage as descendants of Śākyamuni Buddha. Incorporating the *bodhisattva* ordination as an integral part of the Triple Platform Ordination Ceremony demonstrates the importance of the *bodhisattva* ideal for their Mahāyāna identity. The sectarian implications of this ideal and its centrality in the ordination procedure were not lost on the Theravādin participants. Indeed, once the ordination candidates had received the *bhikṣuṇī* ordination, the Theravādin *ācāryas* pointedly led all of their disciples out of the ordination hall and only returned for the closing ceremony two days later. They clearly had no intention of becoming Mahāyāna Buddhists.

Ordination Masters and Witnesses

The Bodhgaya ordination brought together *bhikṣus* and *bhikṣuṇīs* from diverse Buddhist traditions. Since transmission of the *bhikṣuṇī* lineage to the Tibetan and Theravādin traditions can only come via the Chinese tradition,[6] preceptors and recipients of all these traditions must come to terms. In some ways, recognition of the ordination as valid and legitimate is as important as full ordination itself, because the future survival of the newly ordained *bhikṣuṇīs* rests on continual support from their local monastic communities, and this will only be forthcoming if their ordination is recognized as valid.

Three main *bhikṣu* precept masters officiate at a full ordination ceremony: the *śila-upādhyāya*, the *dharma-ācārya*, and the instructing *ācārya*. At the ordination in Bodhgaya, all three were from the Chinese tradition: the *śila-upādhyāya* was Foguangshan's founder, Xingyun; the *dharma-ācārya* was Wuqian;[7] and the instructing *ācārya* was Yongxing.[8] The ordination in Bodhgaya was largely driven by the personal charisma of Xingyun. He is one of the most renowned, if controversial, Buddhist teachers in Taiwan, with a high international profile. He has been a leading proponent of *bhikṣuṇī* ordination internationally since at least 1988. In Calcutta, just before the ordination in Bodhgaya, he pointed out that to exclude women from *bhikṣuṇī* ordination was to waste half of the Buddhists' potential energy worldwide. Despite historical and social differences between the different Buddhist schools, he argued, the Bodhgaya ordination would demonstrate that international cooperation on this issue is possible.

In addition to the three principal *bhikṣu ācāryas* already mentioned, 22 witnessing *ācāryas* also attended the Bodhgaya ordination. They came from Malaysia, Sri Lanka, Nepal, Thailand, India, Great Britain, Cambodia, and Tibet, thereby representing both the Tibetan and Theravādin traditions. Many of these monks live and promulgate Buddhism abroad. *Bhikṣu* witnesses served four distinct roles at the Bodhgaya ordination. The first group of five monks – Tep Vong (Supreme Patriarch of Maha Nikaya, Cambodia) and four monks from Thailand – served as witnesses rather than participants because the ordination of women is illegal in their own monastic communities.[9]

The second group of *ācāryas* consisted of monks active in the Bodhgaya Buddhist community: Dhammānanda Mahā Thero (the Chief High Priest of Malaysia), Dr. Mapalagama Wipulasara Mahā Thero (President of the

Mahā Bodhi Society in India), Dr. Rastrapala Mahāthera (Founder and President of the International Meditation Center), and Nyaneinda Mahāthera (Abbot of the Burmese Temple). Also participating were Ashvaghosh Mahāthera (Editor-in-Chief of *Dharmakīrti*, a Nepalese Buddhist monthly) and Inamaluwe Sumangala Nayaka Thera (Chief Secretary of Rangiri Dambulla Chapter, Sri Lanka). All of these monks are influential in the important movement to revive Buddhism in India. They come from different countries and wear different styles of robes, but their mission to revitalize Buddhism in the place of its birth has joined them in longterm cooperation.

The third group of *ācāryas* consisted of ten Sri Lankan monks, a meaningful number considering that ten *bhikṣus* are required to perform the full ordination. This group of respected senior *bhikṣus* was arguably the most important for re-establishing the Theravādin *bhikṣuṇī* lineage; some of the monks had devoted themselves to the advancement of Buddhist women for a long time.[10] Most had participated in the ordination of ten Sri Lankan nuns in Sārnāth, India, in October 1996. They conducted a Theravādin ordination ceremony for the 20 Sri Lankan nun candidates the morning before they received *śrāmaṇerikā* precepts from the Chinese monks in Bodhgaya. In a special meeting with Xingyun in Bodhgaya these ten *ācāryas* invited Foguangshan to conduct a *bhikṣuṇī* ordination in Sri Lanka in January 1999. This demonstrated their strong commitment to full ordination and established a connection between them and Foguangshan toward this goal. They expressed their belief that the re-establishment of *bhikṣuṇī* ordination would provide women greater access to Buddhism, both in Sri Lanka and in the West. Subsequently, however, rather than wait until January 1999, they went ahead and organized three ordinations in Dambulla, Sri Lanka, on their own: in March, July, and December 1998.

The fourth group of monks included just one *ācārya*, Lama Yeshe Losal Rinpoche, Abbot of Kagyu Samye Ling, Scotland, who brought eleven Western nuns from this center to Bodhgaya to receive full ordination. In comparison to other Western nuns, who often have to struggle to earn their living by working at jobs unrelated to spiritual practice, these nuns were privileged. They had received monastic training in an institutional setting and were able to settle down for longterm retreats. Satisfied with their situation in Scotland, they had not been particularly concerned about receiving full ordination. Their motivation for receiving it was discussed in general terms: personal satisfaction, the welfare of all sentient beings, the transmission of the Buddha's lineage to others, and the importance of correct monastic discipline. On the one hand, they regarded spiritual cultivation as primarily dependent on individual effort, regardless of ordination status. On the other hand, one told me that she understood the meaning that this international ordination held for her center (although if her master had told her there was no need to come, she would have followed his advice). In this case, the institutional advantages and protection of living in a monastic community become clear. It is significant that even a Dharma master as well-established as Lama Yeshe, with a relatively strong institutional base, considered full ordination an important direction for the development of Buddhism in the West.

The ten *bhikṣuṇī ācāryas* who assembled in Bodhgaya reflected the contemporary development of the *bhikṣuṇī* lineage in the various Buddhist traditions. Three senior *bhikṣuṇīs* from Foguangshan assumed the positions of *śila-upādhyāya*, *dharma-ācārya*, and instructing *ācārya*, indicating the important role that the Taiwanese Bhikṣuṇī Saṅgha played in the Bodhgaya ordination. Kuang Woo, head of Bhikṣuṇī Affairs of the Chogye order in Korea, represented the next largest *bhikṣuṇī* lineage in the world, lending its approval to the ordination. The appointment of Karma Lekshe Tsomo and Thubten Chodron as witnessing *ācāryas* demonstrates the emergence of the Western Bhikṣuṇī Saṅgha. Tsomo and Chodron are American *bhikṣuṇīs* practicing in the Tibetan tradition; both are active internationally. The combination of the three components – Taiwanese, Korean, and American – among the ten *bhikṣuṇī ācāryas* reveals the important emerging links between the various *bhikṣuṇī* groups.

The Ordination Candidates

Of the 134 nuns who arrived in Bodhgaya to receive ordination, all but three – one Korean, one Indian, and one Spanish – fulfilled their aspirations to receive *bhikṣuṇī* ordination.[11] Candidates were selected from among roughly 300 nuns who had applied, on the basis of health examinations, personal recommendations, and interviews. According to a Taiwanese male candidate, the competition to participate in the ordination was keen and Bhikṣu Xinding, abbot of Foguangshan, conducted the interviews quite strictly. First, the applicants had to provide evidence that their own Dharma masters and communities approved of their participation. Then, during interviews conducted by Xinding, the applicants were evaluated on the basis of their monastic experience and responses to questions about their motivation, their subsequent plans, and so on.[12] Foguangshan insisted upon accepting only those applicants whose participation in the ordination was approved by their monastic communities, reasoning that this approval was crucial for validating the Bodhgaya ordination.

To get a more comprehensive picture of the 134 female candidates, I have categorized them according to the location of their monastic communities: Taiwan, South Asia, and the West. The Taiwan group consisted of 25 members of Foguangshan and eleven Taiwanese nuns from other Taiwanese Buddhist institutes. The Foguangshan group included not only ethnic Taiwanese, but also four Ladakhi novices of the Tibetan tradition, two Chinese Australians, one Chinese American, and one

Singaporean, most of whom had studied at Foguangshan. The ages of the nuns in the Foguangshan group ranged from 20 to 42, with an average age of 25 – relatively young in comparison to other groups. The ages of the eleven other nuns from Taiwan ranged from 28 to 54, with an average age 41, representing a difference of 16 years from the Foguangshan group. Although these nuns were older than the Foguangshan candidates, they had been nuns for about the same length of time. Except for one who had been a nun for more than ten years, the Taiwan nuns had all taken vows within the last five years.

The religious identities of the Taiwan group were complex. They represented different practice lineages: Chinese, Tibetan, and Theravādin. The Ladakhi nuns and three non-Foguangshan nuns from Taiwan belonged to the Tibetan lineage, while two others identified themselves as Theravādins. In private interviews, they expressed the view that the Bodhgaya ordination was "more appropriate" for them than the annual ordination in Taiwan, conducted in a school to which their masters generally did not belong. Their explanation indicates a significant current phenomenon in Taiwan. Both the Tibetan and Theravādin traditions have been attracting more and more women followers, yet these traditions do not offer women *bhikṣuṇī* status. The absence of *bhikṣuṇī* ordination may eventually become problematic for these nuns as they conduct their activities in Taiwanese society, where people take the availability of *bhikṣuṇī* ordination for granted.

The second category of female candidates consisted of 18 Western nuns – 17 practicing in the Tibetan tradition and one German nun practicing in the Theravādin tradition. Of these nuns, seven were from the United Kingdom, three from the United States, two from Denmark, two from Belgium, two from Canada, one from Germany, and one from Spain. The educational backgrounds of the Western candidates included one Ph.D., eight M.A.s, three B.A.s, and four who had completed post-secondary vocational training. Their ages ranged from 28 to 59. Almost all of them had been nuns for more than ten years.

The third category included 66 South Asian candidates, ranging in age from 19 to 80. Their educational backgrounds included five M.A.s, six B.A.s, and five who had completed post-secondary vocational training. Some had been nuns for as long as 30 years, while others had been nuns for only four years. This relatively high level of education indicates a recent shift in the status of nuns.

Translating the Dharma: Nuns at Work

During the ordination proceedings, most monks relied on interpreters to communicate their ideas, and most of the interpreters were nuns. Whenever invited scholars explained the proceedings to monks and journalists from various countries, and whenever the senior monks of the various Buddhist traditions sat down for discussions – whether on monastic regulations, the establishment of the *bhikṣuṇī* lineage, or the future of the newly ordained nuns – communications were almost always facilitated by interpreters who were nuns or laywomen. All ideas needed to be expressed in at least six different languages: Hindi, Nepali, Tibetan, Sinhalese, Mandarin, and English.[13] At times, Burmese, Malaysian, Japanese, Hakka, Taiwanese, Cantonese, Cambodian, and Thai were also used. As more and more Asian nuns receive Western educations and assume important monastic positions, they become indispensable in organizing and administering international Buddhist events.

Because the nuns who translated had access to key discussions and planning meetings, they generally had a more complete picture of the proceedings than other participants. In addition, because of their more cosmopolitan training and experience, these nuns understood the concerns of different groups more fully than some of their monolingual superiors. Nevertheless, when the leading monks met to decide the future of the *bhikṣuṇī* lineage in their countries, the nuns were remarkably reticent and were not encouraged to express their views. On the surface at least, they seemed to place their fate in the hands of monks. The authority of leading monks at the conference was never questioned; it was assumed that monks would decide the future of nuns. Yet indirectly, nuns played key roles and gained insights into the issues at stake, insights that they can pass on to other nuns.

The importance of nuns as translators and international administrators was not lost on their male counterparts. Far from feeling threatened by the nuns' competence, the monks seemed proud of their female disciples' qualifications and capabilities. Obviously, a command of English provides greater access to resources, and more nuns than monks in this generation seem to have recognized the urgency of this. Some Western Buddhist nuns even earn their living by teaching English at Asian Buddhist monasteries. In Asia, more and more college-educated women have entered the Buddhist order. To many of these nuns, English represents a practical tool for promoting both Buddhism and their own religious careers. More than simply a tool for communicating traditional ideas, English also brings a new worldview, a new sense of community with nuns from other cultures, and a new self-identity for Buddhist women.

The Vitality of Taiwanese Nuns

To organize and administer an event as large and complex as the ordination ceremony in Bodhgaya, Foguangshan asked a working team of 30 Taiwanese nuns to take the main administrative responsibilities. Although many non-Chinese nuns came to help out periodically, in a location so far from modern conveniences it was still a challenge for the core group of nuns to arrange all the details of the ordination, including accommodations for two weeks for 50 masters, 160 novices, and countless journalists and pilgrims. These nuns woke up early, retired late, and held daily meetings to evaluate the day's events and delegate responsibilities for the next day. The main office was a frenetic hub: attending to medical needs, travel arrangements, public relations, and the daily schedule of events. A sign on the wall that read, "Speak in a Friendly Voice with a Gentle Mind," reflected the nuns' determination to keep their composure.

The nuns of Foguangshan are generally very capable administrators and skilled at communicating with the laity. They excel in teamwork and financial management. Because of their educational qualifications, their ability to work in groups, and their numbers, the nuns are essential for administering large international events and monastic life in Taiwan. The nuns' capabilities and solidarity may even make the monks uncertain of their role. Foguangshan monks are charged with important liturgical and spiritual responsibilities, of course, but are far less active than the nuns. The popular monks at Foguangshan are kind and considerate listeners and, outnumbered by the nuns, are willing to be almost invisible.

Nuns as a Community of Women

In addition to the pivotal role of nuns in formal, public settings at the ordination, nuns also related to each other in more informal, private settings, establishing and strengthening their identity as Buddhist women. The night before I left Bodhgaya, I attended an informal get-together of nuns on the work team, occasioned by the birthday of a particular nun. Eight people gathered, including nuns from Taiwan, Burma, the United States, Nepal, and myself. In addition to celebrating a birthday, these nuns were celebrating a reunion, since most of them had received full ordination together at Xilai Temple in Los Angeles in 1988. Ten years later, they were together again as part of an efficient work team to help other nuns receive ordination. In their various languages, they discussed the Bodhgaya ordination and reminisced about their own ordination at Xilai Temple.

These nuns agreed that one of the most significant events of the ordination was the appearance of nine Indian nuns who suddenly arrived for the ordination without previous registration. These nuns belong to a large community of over six million people from scheduled castes, primarily ex-"untouchables," who have converted to Buddhism since 1965 under the influence of B. R. Ambedkar.[14] The nuns explained that they had walked for five days, all the way from central India, and would rather die than leave Bodhgaya unordained. In the beginning, no one understood their language (Marathi), but the nuns conveyed their sincerity through gestures. Although their robes were tattered and some did not even have shoes, their sincerity impressed the Taiwanese abbot in charge. After much discussion on women's limitations in India and their potential to help revive Buddhism, the nine nuns were admitted. At the birthday party, the nuns discussed with great appreciation the hardships these Indian nuns had endured. Indeed, the oldest, a nun over 80, became very popular, even though she was hardly able to communicate a word.

At the party, the nuns mentioned their masters, colleagues, mothers, and friends. At one point they tried imitating the different styles of chanting practiced in the various Buddhist traditions. They reflected on the joys and challenges of the ordination, too, especially the frustrating communication difficulties. One Taiwanese nun even said she found her Ph.D. useless in taking care of the candidates. The cultural differences, often brokered by gestures and nods, had been a learning experience for all, now recalled with good humor. This final gathering was a warm, relaxed, and enjoyable way of creating and maintaining their strong sense of shared identity as Buddhist nuns.

Women's Full Ordination: Focus of International Competition

Nuns play a crucial role in communicating Buddhist teachings and attracting female followers, but their importance to Buddhist institutions goes beyond this. Although most influential Buddhist intellectuals are still elderly monks, young nuns are increasingly the most educated and sophisticated members of the Buddhist community, especially in Taiwan. This trend was well-illustrated by events in Bodhgaya.

There is an integral relationship between ordination, discipline, monastic administration, and financial support. Full ordination for women has become a focal point in the Buddhist women's movement because it provides women with full membership in the monastic community, entitling them to monastic training and support. It also allows them to participate in monastic procedures such as ordinations, bi-monthly confession ceremonies, and other rituals. Ordination therefore provides not only a means to individual spiritual cultivation, but also access to the benefits of a collective administrative system. Buddhist nuns without full ordination are excluded from the core of power, including the right to manage their own spiritual training. Unfortunately, at present this is the case for most Buddhist nuns of the Tibetan and Theravādin monastic communities.

By contrast, in the Chinese tradition currently flourishing in China, Hong Kong, and Taiwan, Buddhist nuns have access to *bhikṣuṇī* ordination and enjoy the full benefits of monastic life. The vitality of Taiwanese nuns, in particular, has created a paradigm for Buddhist women. Many Tibetan and Theravādin Buddhist nuns attribute the success of the Taiwanese nuns' community to the fact that they are able to receive full ordination.

Recent efforts by traditional Buddhists to spread Buddhism in Western countries and in India have highlighted the urgency of establishing full ordination for women. This enthusiasm is complicated by the cultural contradictions nuns encounter as they attempt to disseminate Buddhism abroad. For instance, the dilemma of preserving their own cultural heritage from Westernization is unavoidably complex in the area of gendered division of religious labor. On the one hand, Buddhist women raised in Western countries represent valuable human resources for international propagation activities. On the other hand, these "foreigners" with their feminist ideas often challenge the male-dominated ecclesiastic power structures of Asian Buddhist traditions. The competition for followers among the various Buddhist traditions makes full ordination for women an urgent concern; if one tradition does not attract female followers, a rival tradition will. Buddhists from Taiwan have used their well-established *bhikṣuṇī* lineage to advantage in promoting and revitalizing their traditions in other parts of the world.

The establishment of the *bhikṣuṇī* lineage among Tibetan and Theravādin Buddhists has become a focus of much Buddhist activity today. With the current Chinese Buddhist revitalization, particularly as institutionalized by Foguangshan, four major international full ordination ceremonies for women have been conducted in the past decade. In 1988, 250 female ordination candidates from 16 countries gathered in Los Angeles to receive full ordination under the auspices of Xilai Temple, the American headquarters of Foguangshan.[15] The ordination was organized to coincide with the opening of Xilai Temple to demonstrate that Buddhism had arrived in the West with both a large monastery *and* a *bhikṣuṇī* lineage. Foguangshan claimed that this was the first dual ordination held in the West and, as such, represented the revival of Śākyamuni Buddha's tradition of full ordination for women.[16]

Even before the *bhikṣuṇī* ordination was held at Xilai Temple, many nuns of the Tibetan tradition had pursued full ordination in the Chinese Buddhist tradition. For instance, in 1982 four Western women received *bhikṣuṇī* ordination at the annual ordination ceremony hosted by Ven. Wuming at Hae Ming Temple in Taiwan.[17] In 1983, four Tibetan nuns from Karma Drubgyu Targye Ling, India, received full ordination at a 45-day ceremony in Hong Kong.[18] Other nuns of the Tibetan tradition, both Westerners and Tibetans, have been ordained in Hong Kong and Taiwan, both before and since.

The Korean tradition provided some competition in the race to establish a *bhikṣiṇī* lineage by arranging the full ordination of ten Sri Lankan nuns in Sārnāth, India, in October 1996.[19] The next year, after the Dalai Lama publicly expressed his continuing interest in the Taiwanese *bhikṣuṇī* lineage during his first visit to Taiwan, Buddhist authorities in mainland China conducted an international ordination for 400 monks and nuns, including both nuns from the Theravādin tradition and Himalayan nuns of the Tibetan tradition.[20]

The Role of Foguangshan

Foguangshan organized the ordination of 134 Buddhist nuns from 19 countries in Bodhgaya in response to a suggestion made at the 4th International Monastic Seminar held at Foguangshan in 1997.[21] Xingyun maintains that the *bhikṣuṇī* community in Taiwan is the most legitimate institution to conduct full ordination for nuns of the Tibetan and Theravādin traditions because it has inherited and transmitted the Chinese *bhikṣuṇī* lineage of dual ordination since 1953. In addition, Foguangshan has the financial resources and a remarkable team of nuns with the administrative skills to organize such a huge event. Of course, the success of an ordination depends on more than inspiration; social and economic factors also play a significant role.

The presence of Thai, Cambodian, Indian, British, American, Tibetan, Korean, Sri Lankan, Indian, and Taiwanese ordination masters was arranged to lend credibility to the proceedings. As mentioned, the Sri Lankan representatives who attended reached an agreement with Foguangshan to hold a full ordination for nuns in Sri Lanka in January 1999. Meanwhile, in March 1998 in Dharamsala, the Tibetan government-in-exile organized a conference designed to conclude its 13-year investigation of the *bhikṣuṇī* ordination.[22] To understand the historical significance of these events for gender studies, first we must unravel some fairly complex issues of Buddhist monastic law.

The *Upasampadā* Ritual for Nuns

The *bhikṣuṇī upasampadā* is the ritual that transforms a female practitioner into a *bhikṣuṇī* or fully ordained nun – the highest status a woman can achieve in the Buddhist monastic framework. The first step in the ritual is to gather the precept masters and candidates. If the monastic community agrees, the number of ordination masters and teachers may be adjusted under certain conditions. For instance, in border areas of the Buddhist world, Śākyamuni Buddha allowed the number of both male and female ordination masters to be reduced from ten to five.[23]

After assembling the participants, the teachers define the ritual arena (*sīmā*) by means of a purification ceremony. In the Chinese tradition, the *sīmā* is generally an ordination platform or altar. Setting the boundaries of the ordination altar not only protects the participants, but also symbolizes the boundaries of the monastic community. Once these boundaries are set, the ordination becomes recognized as having been approved by the monastic community.

However, in most Buddhist countries, including Burma, Cambodia, Sri Lanka, Thailand, and Tibet, the *bhikṣuṇī* order died out long ago or was never established. The lineage survives only in China, Korea, Taiwan, and Vietnam. According to monastic regulations, a *bhikṣuṇī* should be ordained in the presence of other *bhikṣuṇīs*, in what is termed a "dual ordination procedure." Therefore the re-establishment of an order of *bhikṣuṇīs* ideally should involve the participation of *bhikṣuṇīs* ordained in an existing lineage. This inevitably gives rise to two questions: which nuns from which traditions are best qualified to carry out these ordinations, and whether or not *bhikṣuṇī* ordinations should be carried out at all.[24]

For some traditional ecclesiastics, the idea of reintroducing full ordination for women is as absurd as changing the Buddha's gender from male to female. Full ordination has been a male-exclusive privilege in the Tibetan and Theravādin Buddhist traditions for centuries. It is widely believed and stated in some canonical texts that women are incapable of achieving Buddhahood.[25] This belief has had the effect of keeping women in subordinate positions and away from monastic resources.

However, even the staunchest critics of the ordination of nuns admit that Śākyamuni Buddha himself ordained women and made contributions to social equality. When confronted by a *bhikṣu* opposed to the ordination of nuns, one Sri Lankan nun recently replied, "How can you [monks] take vows of serving all sentient beings, but turn your backs on your own Dharma sisters?"[26] Such contradictions leave much room for debate, and the controversy is greatly compounded by complex power relations and vested interests within and between the Buddhist traditions. Nevertheless, as the constraints placed upon women have come to light in recent years, the need to rectify the situation has created substantial cooperation between Buddhist nuns of the various traditions. International associations of Buddhist women, notably Śākyadhitā ("Daughters of the Buddha"), have emerged to promote full ordination.[27]

Buddha Śākyamuni's purported words and the account of his establishment of the *bhikṣuṇī* order, which are preserved in the canon, provide an external authority validating women's right to ordination. Ranking in the monastic hierarchy depended not on gender, but on the status of its members as determined by the number of years they had been ordained. Men go through two stages: *śrāmaṇera* (novice monk) and *bhikṣu* (fully ordained monk). Women go through three stages: *śrāmaṇerikā* (novice nun), *śikṣamāṇā* (a two-year probationary period created to exclude pregnant women), and *bhikṣuṇī* (fully ordained nun).[28]

The lineage and format of Śākyamuni Buddha's monastic community have been transmitted for generations, up to modern times. The existence of the *bhikṣuṇī* lineage is certain, but the circumstances of its establishment have always been somewhat controversial. The early texts portray Śākyamuni as reluctant to allow women into the order and state that he predicted that their admission would shorten the life of the teachings (*sāsana*).[29] On the other hand, some early Buddhist groups believed that the *bhikṣuṇī* community would bring prosperity to Buddhism.[30] Today, at least, many view the benefits of having both male and female monastic lineages as more important than the potential dangers.[31] Significantly for the history of nuns, after the Buddha ordained Mahāprajāpatī, it was stipulated that the full ordination of women requires the presence of both *bhikṣuṇīs* and *bhikṣus*, implying that monks or nuns alone should not ordain nuns.

In India, the order of nuns died out along with the order of monks and Buddhism in general in the 11th century. The order of nuns also disappeared in Sri Lanka when the Buddhist monastic community was destroyed there around the same time. Although the Sinhalese re-established their *bhikṣu* order by inviting Siamese and Burmese monks to carry out ordinations, it was impossible to revive the *bhikṣuṇī* lineage because there were no *bhikṣuṇīs* available to perform the ordination. These events were later interpreted in light of the Buddha's earlier prediction of the decline of the *sāsana*. The presumption was that the suppression of Buddhism under the Muslim invaders was related to the decline of the Dharma, which in line with the Buddha's prophecy was hastened by the admission of women into the order. Even today, some Buddhists claim that the order of fully ordained nuns will not reappear until the arrival of Maitreya, the future Buddha.

The order of nuns did survive in China, however, and eventually made its way to Taiwan, Korea, and Vietnam. In Taiwan, before a woman makes the decision to enter the order, she usually lives in a monastic community for quite some time and is referred to as *jinfanyu*. Next, she requests the tonsure, a ceremony that involves shaving the head and entering into a disciple relationship with her master. After receiving the tonsure, she undergoes a probationary period to adjust to monastic life, during which her master and colleagues observe her character and depth of commitment. After a period of six months to two years, her master sends her to receive full ordination in a Triple Platform Ordination.

The full ordination ceremony is the highlight of the whole procedure. Many Taiwanese nuns refer to full ordination as "a rite of rebirth."[32] Just as *bhikṣuṇī* ordination is received, the master announces the specific time of the ordination, down to the second, symbolizing the beginning of a new life. Thus, after a long period of intensive training and scrutiny, the nun finally becomes a full-fledged member of the monastic order – an "offspring of the Buddha." Unlike tonsure, which is performed by individual masters and monasteries, full ordination usually involves an array of important ecclesiastic leaders and representatives. Full ordination for nuns requires ten *bhikṣuṇīs* in addition to ten *bhikṣus*; the three central precept masters of each category must have been ordained for twelve years or more.

The Dual Ordination Controversy

The controversy over *bhikṣuṇī* ordination usually centers on the necessity of dual ordination. According to the Vinaya (Buddhist monastic texts), full ordination for nuns requires 20 qualified precept masters: ten *bhikṣus* as well as ten *bhikṣuṇīs*, or at least five of each in remote areas.[33] The purpose of this requirement is to make sure the nuns are well prepared for ordination and to avoid embarrassment when certain personal questions are asked.[34] Throughout history, Buddhist communities have encountered difficulty finding qualified *bhikṣuṇīs* to perform the dual ordination. This difficulty stems in part from prevailing social conditions, which confined most women to the family. Among the accounts of hundreds of Indian teachers who traveled to the East Asia to spread Buddhism, there are no records of nuns. Importantly, the two documented incidents of dispatching nuns abroad – from India to Sri Lanka in the fourth century B.C.E. and from Sri Lanka to China in 432 C.E. – were state-sponsored missions for the specific purpose of transmitting the Bhikṣuṇī Saṅgha abroad.

When members of the Bhikṣuṇī Saṅgha were not available to conduct the ordination, nuns were often ordained by monks alone. For instance, before the Sri Lankan *bhikṣuṇīs* arrived in China, the monastic community allowed women to be ordained by *bhikṣus* alone. This ordination procedure was considered legitimate, as a passage in the *Biographies of Bhiksuṇīs* attests. Huimin explains:

> According to the biography of Guṇavarman in the *Biographies of Eminent Monks*, monks initiated the *bhikṣuṇī* ordination. If a nun did not receive dual ordination, her ordination by monks was also valid. Although the ordination masters commit a misdemeanor, the ordination is valid. This ordination has never been proclaimed invalid because the monastic regulations do not discuss the lack of dual ordination in the procedures.[35]

Baochang, author of the *Biographies of Bhikṣuṇīs*, traces the origins of the Chinese Bhikṣuṇī Saṅgha to Mahāprajāpatī. By the fifth century, the Chinese Saṅgha recognized Jingjian as the first Chinese *bhikṣuṇī*, ordained by a procedure similar to Mahāprajāpatī's, that is, by *bhikṣus* alone.[36] This type of ordination is not necessarily invalid, for although the Vinaya literature explains the dual ordination procedure as the ideal, nowhere does it declare a single ordination procedure invalid. In fact, many contend that it is the *bhikṣus*, rather than *bhikṣuṇīs*, who constitute the final authority on the ordination of nuns. Although feminists might dispute the reasoning behind this contention, the fact remains that when members of a particular monastic order endorse Buddhist nuns ordained by *bhikṣus* alone, the ordination is considered valid. In other words, the legitimacy of monastic ordination is dependent upon decisions reached by local Bhikṣuṇī Saṅgha communities. Therefore, as the Taiwanese *bhikṣuṇī* Zhaohui has stated, if it is monks who are authorized to conduct *bhikṣuṇī* ordinations, then it is monks who must be held accountable for the absence of a lineage of full ordination for women, not the nuns.[37]

The deep concern for receiving ordination according to the orthodox dual ordination procedure expressed by authorities in the Theravādin and Tibetan traditions may indicate their intention to establish a core group of nuns capable of ordaining others in the future. The same concern for orthodoxy was in evidence at the ordination held at Xilai Temple in 1988. Originally ten Sri Lankan nuns applied to receive full ordination, but were unable to get their passports in time. Among the twelve Sri Lankan nuns who eventually made the trip to Los Angeles, only five candidates successfully received ordination.[38] Some speculate that the lack of support these five new *bhikṣuṇīs* received after they returned to Sri Lanka was an indication that the Buddhist community preferred to have a full quorum of ten nuns ordained, instead of just five.[39]

The promotion of the *bhikṣuṇī* ordination at present is a result of efforts by international Buddhist associations, primarily initiated by Western nuns. The most important of these is Śākyadhitā: International Association of Buddhist Women, which has encouraged research and publications on the topic of ordination through conferences and seminars since 1987.[40] These endeavors are a reflection of the significant role women are playing in the dissemination of Buddhism in the global community.[41] For instance, about 80 percent of Tibetan Dharma centers in the West are maintained, and sometimes led, by women. Women, especially nuns, are also the strongest force propelling Chinese Buddhist activities abroad.

The Care and Training of Nuns

Tibetan and Taiwanese Buddhist nuns receive very different treatment in their endeavors, however. The Foguangshan authorities already know how productive Buddhist women can be. Gender equality is one of the most important dimensions of what Master Xingyun calls "humanistic Buddhism." Taiwanese and overseas Chinese women who enter the monastic order at Foguangshan become skilled in social service activities and qualified to create a sense of cultural identity among women in overseas, particularly immigrant, Chinese communities.[42] Recognizing this, Foguangshan offers free education for foreign students and monastic positions after their graduation. Graduates of these programs enhance Foguangshan's competitive edge in Buddhist propagation activities due to their language abilities and personal connections. For many Buddhist nuns, Foguangshan provides opportunities for education and career advancement that few, if any, other Buddhist organizations can match.

In Taiwan, Buddhist masters are generally very careful to select reliable representatives to ordain their disciples. They contribute time and financial support to ordination ceremonies; some even accompany their disciples to the temple and stay throughout. The relationship between a novice and her tonsure and ordination masters is likened to the relationship between a child, her parents, and the clan patriarchs. The tonsure master brings his "children" to the ordination master to solicit their admission into the larger monastic family. In this way, traditional monastic structures replicate familiar family structures and traditional patterns of behavior.

In contrast, there is hardly any institutional support for Western female monastics in the Tibetan tradition. This is due both to a lack of resources and to the lack of full ordination which traditionally provides recognition. The monastic role of nuns is usually limited to a supportive function, both in exile Tibetan and Western settings. Although their abilities as English teachers, fundraisers, and translators are socially acknowledged, there is no financial support, and these volunteer activities often conflict with these nuns' personal commitment to spiritual practice. Their lack of full ordination status means that the monastic community places the nuns' needs behind those of male monastics, and sometimes even behind the laity. For instance, a layman who is interested in monastic discipline will be encouraged and supported to study in Dharamsala, while a Western nun has to pay her own expenses and usually finds no monastic facilities available at all.[43]

The structure of Tibetan and Taiwanese Buddhist communities in the West is also quite different. Taiwanese Buddhist temples serve as important social institutions for maintaining cultural continuity. Although Taiwanese nuns may not be as active as Western nuns in teaching, they are well-integrated into overseas Chinese communities and are appreciated for the traditional ritual services they provide.[44] Economic dependence may have its drawbacks, but the ethnic integrity of these communities and the respect traditionally accorded to monastics in Chinese Buddhist societies ensure that nuns are appreciated and protected from financial difficulties.

In contrast, Tibetan Buddhists in the West offer very little support for monastics individually or for the establishment of monastic institutions. The Tibetan tradition has expanded rapidly in the West over the last two decades owing to the accessibility and flexibility of its spiritual training, particularly meditation. Tibetan Buddhism is very open to lay practitioners, but has not yet given sufficient support to developing monastic communities in the West.[45] What support is available is generally channeled to refugee monasteries in India and Nepal, mostly to monks. In Tibet, although monasteries for nuns and monks were established separately, both communities were considered part of local society, and supported at least at subsistence level. At this stage, however, Western nuns of the Tibetan tradition benefit neither from the Western notion of religious community, nor do they find an appropriate place in the Tibetan religious community.[46] As Tibetan Buddhism becomes better established in the West, it is important that the Tibetan Buddhist authorities help integrate Western nuns into their monastic systems. Endorsing the *bhikṣuṇī* ordination is one of the most effective strategies the Tibetan Buddhist authorities could use to accomplish this task.

Dharma and Gender Politics

The competition to gain recognition and support for *bhikṣuṇīs* among Buddhists in the West is only one aspect of the ordination controversy, however. Another aspect is the competition to establish the *bhikṣuṇī* lineage that has emerged among Tibetan Buddhists in exile and Theravādin Buddhists from Sri Lanka, Thailand, and Burma. In addition, there is competition surrounding the *bhikṣuṇī* lineage within Chinese Buddhism itself.

Following the Cultural Revolution, the survival and revitalization of Chinese Buddhism relied heavily on financial support from Buddhist followers in the Chinese diaspora and Taiwan. Buddhists in China lack the resources to compete with Taiwanese efforts to spread Buddhism abroad, yet they were anxious to assert their legitimacy and orthodoxy.[47] During the tumultuous years of the Cultural Revolution, Buddhism in the People's Republic suffered many setbacks. Buddhists in Taiwan rose to the task of representing Chinese Buddhism at conferences abroad, often supported by the government of the Republic of China. Buddhists in China have struggled valiantly to restore their traditions in the aftermath of the Cultural Revolution, but it will take decades to recover from the devastating losses of Buddhist literary, architectural, and human resources. Although it may be impossible to replace the Taiwanese as representatives of Chinese Buddhism internationally, mainland Chinese Buddhists can claim that their *bhikṣuṇī* lineage is more orthodox than Taiwan's. Buddhist authorities in China have therefore shifted their focus to claims of historical orthodoxy for their monastic traditions and their "sovereign right" over all *bhikṣuṇī* lineages.

Political issues are also involved. The Tibetan Buddhist authorities in exile are aware that claims to religious sovereignty may affect their claim to political sovereignty, the key factor in maintaining ethnic, religious, and cultural identity in the Tibetan exile community. In the past, Tibetan authorities have avoided any type of formal association with the Taiwanese authorities, and the Guomindang government in Taiwan has also been very sensitive about the issue of Tibetan independence. Coincidentally, however, during the Buddhist revival in Taiwan over the last two decades, so many Taiwanese Buddhists have become attracted to Tibetan Buddhism that the Tibetan Government-in-Exile has altered its stance and cautiously begun relations with the Taiwanese Buddhist authorities.[48] If the Tibetans intend to continue cultural communications with Chinese Buddhists, the Tibetan leadership will eventually have to choose between the Chinese and Taiwanese Buddhist orders. If this choice carries weighty political implications, however, it may be simpler to reject them both.

In the present bid to reestablish the *bhikṣuṇī* order in Sri Lanka, the Buddhist leadership there has the option of cooperating with Buddhists in either China or Taiwan, with potential advantages either way. Apart from the *bhikṣuṇī* issue, however, because Theravādin Buddhist practice is popular in the West its future is inextricably linked with Tibetan Buddhist activities there. Although communications with other Buddhist traditions have been minimal in the past, since settling in India the Tibetan Government-in-Exile has also established relations with Theravādin Buddhists there. Earlier certain *bhikṣus* were concerned that Tibetan Buddhist recognition of the *bhikṣuṇī* lineage might attract censure from Theravādin Buddhists, who are generally considered more conservative, particularly on women's issues. Now the tables have turned somewhat; if the Tibetan authorities do not respond appropriately to demands for full ordination for women in its monastic system, the Theravādins will gain recognition as being more socially enlightened on the international scene.[49]

His Holiness the Dalai Lama's first visit to Taiwan in March 1997 shows that the Tibetan Government-in-Exile has gradually realized the urgency and influence of *bhikṣuṇī* ordination. In fact, His Holiness has expressed interest in the *bhikṣuṇī* lineage publicly many times. Although he has stopped short of officially recognizing the *bhikṣuṇī* lineage, he has consistently affirmed the benefits of full ordination for women and the right of nuns in the Tibetan tradition to receive it. During his trip to Taiwan, he specifically requested a meeting with Taiwanese *bhikṣuṇīs* to discuss this issue and, moreover, declared that this was one of his purposes in making the trip. Procedures for decision-making in the Tibetan ecclesiastic system are cumbersome, however; decisions concerning monastic law require formal consultations among senior Bhikṣu Saṅgha members. For this reason, the Dalai Lama has said that it is not within his power, as a single *bhikṣu*, to formally recognize the Chinese *bhikṣuṇī* lineage.[50] This may explain why he did not respond immediately to Foguangshan's suggestion of a full ordination ceremony in Bodhgaya, as proposed at the May 1997 International Federation of Buddhist Saṅgha Conference.

In November 1997, His Holiness sent Bhikṣu Tashi Tsering to Taiwan to investigate the Chinese *bhikṣuṇī* lineage. During this visit, Taiwanese scholars frankly informed Tashi Tsering about the potential competition between the Buddhist authorities in China and Taiwan to establish the *bhikṣuṇī* lineage in the Tibetan tradition. However, it seems that the Tibetan authorities were unable to make a decision at that time. On December 20, 1997, just 36 days later, the Chinese Buddhist authorities in mainland China held their first international ordination, which was attended by nuns of both the Tibetan and Nepalese traditions. The timing suggests a conscious effort by the mainland Chinese authorities to demonstrate their stature on the international Buddhist front.

Nuns and Buddhist Monastic Legitimacy

Ordination reproduces the monastic continuity. The traditional notion of monastic community, requiring three principal precept masters (*ācāryas*) and at least seven witnesses to officiate, provides legal recognition and legitimacy to ordinations. In this way, the ordination ritual repeatedly integrates the community and guarantees its continuity. Traditionally, precept masters who performed ordinations belonged to the same monastic community, or at least the same Vinaya lineage. The traditional system is designed to establish ties and lines of authority between monastics and their own communities by maintaining sectarian boundaries.

The model used by Foguangshan at the Bodhgaya ordination – inviting instructors and witnesses from different monastic communities to preside together at the ordination of nuns from different monastic communities and Vinaya lineages – is something new, initiated only in the last two decades by monasteries in the West.[51] From the perspective of Buddhist nuns today, however, the notion of community is unified and globalized by the full ordination itself. Monks of the various Vinaya traditions also have a historical connectedness. For example, Tibetan monastics sew a blue cord on their vests to remember their indebtedness to the Chinese masters who assisted them in reviving their own *bhikṣu* lineage in the tenth century in northeast Tibet (Amdo). This sense of mutual connectedness may be expanded upon to create a more broadminded and flexible international monastic community.

The full ordination of women may promote cooperation among ordination masters of different monastic communities, yet taking full ordination in the Chinese tradition may also alienate women from their own monastic communities. For this reason, it is necessary to develop relations with sympathetic elements in each country to help sustain newly ordained nuns and help them reintegrate into their local communities. As more and more Buddhist nuns devote themselves to full ordination, they acquire a broader sense of monastic community, one which is unified rather than divided by sectarian identities. In this sense, they function to reaffirm the underlying unity of the Buddhist traditions and exemplify the Dharma taught by Śākyamuni Buddha, a doctrine of universal salvation and social equality.

The Bodhgaya ordination demonstrated that most monastic groups recognize the urgency of establishing full ordination in terms of Buddhist dissemination activities rather than the gender issue *per se*. In the context of expanding Buddhism internationally, nuns are a valuable resource, representing not only a powerful pool of talent for spreading the Buddha's teachings, but also a key to modernizing different Buddhist groups.[52] The *bhikṣuṇī* ordination creates a common dilemma for all monastic orders, however: how to regulate these nuns' membership and how to transmit the *bhikṣuṇī* lineage from one Buddhist tradition to another. The present strategy of Foguangshan is to assemble monks of various Buddhist traditions and schools. This is why the appointment of the three central ordination masters is important in the current international competition for *bhikṣuṇī* ordination. Particularly owing to political conflicts, it is possible that some groups attempt to maintain their religious sovereignty by claiming orthodoxy for their *bhikṣuṇī* lineages. The movement to re-establish full ordination for women in the Tibetan and Theravādin traditions is one that requires mutual cooperation among various Buddhist traditions and schools. The establishment of the Bhikṣuṇī Saṅgha therefore necessitates crossing sectarian boundaries. Moreover, *if* monks are recognized as the legitimate authorities for validating *bhikṣuṇī* ordinations, the movement relies on mutual recognition among the male-dominated ecclesiastic hierarchies.

Ecclesiastic authority usually represents the institutionalized legitimacy of its founder and canon. Therefore, the discourse on full ordination for women is complicated by ambiguities intrinsic in the Buddha's attitude toward women (first hesitating, then agreeing to ordain *bhikṣuṇīs*) and in the canon (which both supports and denigrates women). Moreover, there are various interpretations of the historical events surrounding the creation and transmission of the *bhikṣuṇī* lineage. The procedures used to ordain women in the various Buddhist traditions shed light on how Buddhists traditionally dealt with notions of membership and legitimacy in the monastic community, but these procedures can be applied and interpreted differently, depending on circumstances and ideology.

For instance, ecclesiastical authorities in Tibet traditionally insisted upon the dual procedure for ordaining *bhikṣuṇīs*. A 15th-century Tibetan monk's attempt to conduct a *bhikṣuṇī* ordination with *bhikṣus* alone was an anomaly and never gained official acceptance. Nevertheless, his efforts to ordain *bhikṣuṇīs* demonstrate his commitment to equal religious rights for women. Even though there apparently were no *bhikṣuṇīs* available to conduct an ordination by the orthodox procedure, this monk was willing to take personal and political risks to help nuns get fully ordained. The reluctance of Tibetan ecclesiastical authorities to recognize full ordination for women in modern times, then, naturally raises questions. When the acceptance of Buddhism in the modern world requires an egalitarian approach, what explains their hesitation? If the Tibetan monastic community wishes to avoid interference by Chinese Buddhist authorities in their internal ecclesiastic affairs, why insist on dual ordination?

The case of Sri Lanka also indicates the crucial role of historical connections. Despite canonical regulations, the lack of a Bhikṣuṇī Saṅgha since the 11th century, and vocal opposition on the part of some monks, the Sri Lankan monastic community is discussing how to regain its lost heritage by restoring the *bhikṣuṇī* lineage. Many Sri Lankans are committed to reviving this lost lineage of Śākyamuni Buddha and are ready to back an international ordination conducted by Foguangshan and its well-established *bhikṣuṇī* order. In the process of organizing the Bodhgaya ordination, Foguangshan transcended traditional boundaries posed by canonical and historical differences. In the name of revitalization, Foguangshan is creating a new tradition by aligning internationally with traditional authorities.

The ordination in Bodhgaya was not the first time a Buddhist monastery in Taiwan had exported Vinaya. In the last three decades, there have been many activities related to ordination led by Taiwanese Buddhist organizations. For instance, the annual ordination ceremonies organized by the Chinese Buddhist Association of the Republic of China and held at monasteries throughout Taiwan have attracted both overseas Chinese and Western candidates from a range of countries since 1970. Bhikṣuṇī Wuyin of Xiangguangsi (Luminary Buddhist Society) in Chiayi, Taiwan, was a featured lecturer on Bhikṣuṇī Vinaya at a three-week monastic training seminar for 100 nuns and laywomen in Bodhgaya in 1996. It is noteworthy that all these activities focused on full ordination for women. Quite clearly, Taiwanese Buddhist monasteries are earnest about reintroducing the *bhikṣuṇī* lineage into other traditions.

As representatives of the Tibetan tradition challenge the validity of the Chinese *bhikṣuṇī* lineage, the question that arises is whether the *bhikṣuṇī* community in Taiwan legitimately represents the Chinese *bhikṣuṇī* lineage. Xingyun claims orthodoxy for the Taiwanese *bhikṣuṇī* lineage by counting the beginning of the Taiwanese *bhikṣuṇī* lineage from the ordination reforms introduced by Chinese monks in post-war Taiwan. However, Xingyun's stance, which represents the popular perspective of Chinese refugee monks, takes the legitimacy of the Chinese lineage for granted and also ignores ordination ties between mainland Chinese and Taiwanese Buddhists from before the war. Prior to 1949 some Taiwanese Buddhist nuns received full ordination in China, but the post-war ordination system controlled by the Chinese Buddhist Association in Taiwan has consciously or unconsciously ignored this historical connection, hoping to legitimize its status as the only official Buddhist representative on the international scene.

Moreover, there is clearly more than one interpretation of the concept of lineage in the creation of Buddhist monastic identity.[53] The Chinese system of ordination needs to be understood in the context of a particular Mahāyāna country's adaptation of pre-Mahāyāna monastic regulations in establishing its Buddhist identity. By performing dual ordination for *bhikṣuṇīs* and by maintaining the monastic format initiated by Śākyamuni Buddha, the Chinese monastic community feels that it has authentically preserved the lineage. Moreover, the Dharmagupta Vinaya which the Chinese Saṅgha uses to conduct ordination rites is very similar in structure both to the Mūlasarvāstivādin Vinaya followed by the Tibetans and to the Theravādin Vinaya followed in Burma, Cambodia, Laos, Thailand, and Sri Lanka.

Taiwanese scholars such as Bhikṣuṇī Hengqing, Bhikṣuṇī Zhaohui, and Bhikṣu Huimin have compared the Chinese Dharmagupta and the Tibetan Mūlasarvāstivādin renditions of the *Bhikṣuṇī Prātimokṣa Sūtra* and discussed the close resemblance between them with Bhikṣu Tashi Tsering.[54] Comparative analysis shows that, despite small differences in monastic regulations, these two Vinaya systems are extremely similar.[55] It is the historical and cultural differences reflected in the format of ordination that distinguish the various systems of ordination far more than the monastic regulations or textual narratives explaining them.

Buddhist Nuns and Gender

Although monks have traditionally been in charge of presiding at ordinations, this does not mean that Buddhist nuns have been passive in the movement to establish *bhikṣuṇī* ordination. On the contrary, since Mahāprajāpatī initiated the *bhikṣuṇī* movement two and a half millennia ago, the lineage has continued by virtue of women's commitment to ordination and to the Dharma. The process of dual ordination entails the transmission of the lineage from senior *bhikṣuṇīs* to novices, confirming a sense of shared identity and commitment among women from generation to generation.[56] Because the *bhikṣuṇī* lineage is absent in the Tibetan and Theravādin traditions, however, these Buddhist nuns need to borrow, or recover, the lineage from the Chinese Buddhist tradition. This creates a special situation – a potential space for intra-Buddhist communications and an urgent need for Buddhist nuns to network internationally.

The current discourse on *bhikṣuṇī* ordination is unprecedented in Buddhist history. It may be the first and only time that Buddhist women have transcended sectarian identities to form a distinctive group. The issue of ordination therefore represents a unique opportunity for encouraging sectarian cooperation. *Bhikṣuṇī* ordination not only represents full membership in the Buddhist family, it establishes Buddhist nuns as a distinctive social and religious circle. It symbolizes nuns striving to gain legitimacy for themselves and it is also a visible banner uniting Buddhist nuns of the various schools.

The Buddhist nuns involved in this movement are markedly different from previous generations because of their experience in manipulating new knowledge and creating an international sisterhood. In this situation, the capacity to speak English not only opens the way to new realms of experience for Buddhist nuns and teaches them the importance of access to information, but also opens new channels for community development and the cross-fertilization of ideas. In the process of promoting full ordination, nuns are expanding their horizons through exposure to diverse Buddhist traditions and to feminist ideas. In the process, they are consciously or unconsciously re-evaluating their traditions and their own religious, ethnic, and gender identity. For Buddhist nuns in traditions without *bhikṣuṇī* status, the vital and confident order of Taiwanese nuns serves as a rare and inspiring role model which holds promise for their own future.

Reintroducing full ordination for women has its irony, however. The emphasis on *bhikṣuṇī* status and dual ordination as the key to legitimizing Buddhist nuns oversimplifies the problem of nuns in the various Buddhist traditions. For one thing, no canonical statement specifically pronounces the single ordination invalid.[57] In fact, there is a clear statement allowing this procedure: "*Bhikṣus*, I permit you to confer full ordination on *bhikṣuṇīs*."[58] Second, male ecclesiastics in Sri Lanka, Thailand, and Tibet have long ignored the absence of a *bhikṣuī* order in their traditions. Therefore, introducing dual ordination in these traditions is not simply a matter of creating something new, but entails institutionalizing and according official recognition to an order of nuns that is already functioning outside their own traditions. This potentially complicates not only Saṅgha relationships in their own countries, but also patriarchal international Buddhist relationships. Third, if dual ordination is advanced as the only valid method of ordination for *bhikṣuṇīs*, it calls into question those ordinations already authorized by *bhikṣus* alone. Ordination procedures vary in the different Buddhist traditions, and each assumes it is orthodox, so to pronounce as invalid the *bhikṣuṇī* lineages that currently exist in East Asia, as some conservative *bhikṣus* do, raises significant questions about different notions of monastic lineage and legitimacy among the various Buddhist traditions. In addition, there are power dynamics at work that must be taken into account. Conducting ordinations may be symbolic of privilege and status for the tradition that assumes leadership. Underlying the peaceful, festival atmosphere of the full ordination activities in Bodhgaya, therefore, a symbolic international struggle for power, prestige, and legitimacy was taking place.

Regardless of political nuances, because of their strong economic and institutional base, Taiwanese Buddhists have been able to create a strong international movement for the full ordination of women. This is due primarily to the commitment and determination of the nuns themselves. It demonstrates that the more economically independent Buddhist nuns are, the more autonomy and power they have to transform attitudes and institutions. In comparison to the nuns of Thailand (*mae chi*), whose survival depends on the largess of monks' monasteries,[59] and the ten-precept nuns of Sri Lanka (*dasasilmātā*), who live independently and administer their own nunneries but are nonetheless financially constrained,[60] nuns in Taiwan are economically independent and powerful. In Taiwanese Buddhist circles, it is an open secret that Buddhist nuns are generally better at raising and administering finances than monks. Coincidentally, it is these relatively self-sufficient nuns, rather than nuns in economic straits, who confidently pursue a more appropriate religious status for themselves. The vitality of Taiwanese nuns, therefore, has been a significant force in the endeavor to introduce full ordination to nuns of the Tibetan and Theravādin traditions.

The *bhikṣuṇī* community is well-established in Taiwanese society. Even though the division of religious labor and leadership reflects the conventional, patriarchal expectations of Chinese society, the religious identity and relatively equal status of nuns and monks is recognized both in the monastic community and society at large.[61] Both the ritual and economic autonomy of Taiwanese nuns are solidly institutionalized. In Taiwan, Buddhist nuns virtually control monastic education, and they wield a powerful influence on lay education as well. The success of the Ziji Foundation, a Buddhist charity organization with 3,500,000 members, has established Bhikṣuṇī Zhengyan as the most influential Buddhist leader in Taiwan.[62] Also in the top ten are Bhikṣuṇīs Xiaoyun (Shig Hiu Wan), Zhaohui, and Hengqing – all leading Buddhist educators. The remarkable achievements and institutional success of Buddhist nuns in Taiwan make them logical role models for modern Buddhist women.

Based on their experience of a monastic culture in which nuns function at least as effectively as monks, Taiwanese society regards Buddhist education and full ordination for women as axiomatic. The Taiwanese, both lay and ordained, thus naturally support education and ordination for women in the Tibetan and Theravādin Buddhist traditions. Against this background, Foguangshan has been able to motivate Taiwanese Buddhists to donate time, energy, and money to support their international ordination activities. One might assume that Taiwan's sound economic system is the primary ingredient for success, but this explanation ignores the religious motivation of Taiwanese Buddhists. Although many Taiwanese Buddhists may be oblivious to the complex issues of gender equality and monastic law behind the *bhikṣuṇī* ordination movement they support, most interpret their generosity as religious merit accumulated by "making a (future) Buddha." They make no gender distinctions in their religiosity, acquiring merit through supporting the ordination of monks and nuns equally, implying that the Bhikṣu and Bhikṣuṇī Saṅghas are equally respected and equally capable of achieving Buddhahood. This unbiased social support for the Saṅgha has been a key factor in promoting full ordination for women and the advancement of Buddhist women as a whole.

The vitality of Buddhism in Taiwan, the dedication and competence of Taiwanese *bhikṣuṇīs*, and the religious commitment of Taiwanese Buddhists in supporting the establishment of a recognized *bhikṣuṇī* lineage beyond the boundaries of their own tradition combine to make the Taiwanese Buddhists pioneers in establishing full ordination for women. The nuns of Taiwan who have benefited from the unbiased support of their lay followers have returned manifold benefits to the laity and the Dharma, becoming examples of the tremendous potential the *bhikṣuṇī* order holds for Buddhism globally. Whether they are aware of it or not, their success represents a major restructuring of Buddhist institutions that has profound significance for hundreds of millions of women.

Notes

1 Kathryn A. Tsai, "The Chinese Buddhist Monastic Order for Women: The First Two Centuries" (*Historical Reflections/Réflexions Historiques* 8, no. 3 (Fall 1981): 1–20; Richard W. Guiss and Stanley Johannesen, eds., *Women in China, Current Directions in Historical Scholarship* (Youngtown, N.Y.: Philo Press, 1981); and Yuchen Li, *Bhikṣuṇīs of the Tang Dynasty* (Taipei: Xuesheng Bookstore, 1989).

2 The consequent monastic reform initiated by the Sinhalese king Vikramabahu I (r. 1111–1132) played a key role of the disappearance of the Sri Lankan Bhikṣuṇī Saṅgha. See Bardwell L. Smith, *Religion and Legitimation of Power in Sri Lanka* (Chambersburg, Pa.: ANIMA Books 1978); Nancy Auer Falk, "The Case of Vanishing Nuns: the Fruits of Ambivalence in Ancient Indian Buddhism," in Nancy A. Falk and Rita M. Gross, eds., *Women's Religious Lives in Non-Western Cultures* (Chicago: University of Chicago Press, 1989), pp. 207–24; and Amarasir Weeraratne's "The Bhikkhunī Order in Ceylon," *Journal of the Maha Bodhi Society* 10 & 11 (1970): 333–37, and "Welcome More Towards Reviving Bhikkhuni Order," *The Island*, Colombo, June 4, 1987. Weeraratne's articles have been translated into Chinese and published by both Chinese and Taiwanese Buddhist journals.

3 Almost all the branches of Buddhism have a representative temple in Bodhgaya. The Chinese Temple, supported largely by Taiwanese Buddhists, represents Chinese Buddhism.

4 Interview conducted in Bodhgaya on February 21, 1998.

5 This probationary period for nuns, which is not required for monks, is discussed in Karma Lekshe Tsomo, *Sakyadhita: Daughters of the Buddha* (Ithaca, N.Y.: Snow Lion Publications, 1988), pp. 237, 256–57; and Akira Hirakawa's *Monastic Discipline for the Buddhist Nuns* (Patna: K. P. Jayaswal Research Institute, 1982), pp. 53–55.

6 The *bhikṣuṇī* lineages extant in Korea and Vietnam today also derive from the Chinese lineage.

7 Wuqian is the abbot of Xuanzang Temple in Calcutta and abbot of the Chinese Buddhist Temple in Bodhgaya. In the eyes of Taiwanese *bhikṣuṇīs*, Wuqian is a very special figure: a well-respected monk who has devoted himself to Buddhist missionary activities in India, adapting himself to all the difficulties of life there. The overseas Chinese community in Calcutta is the main support for the two temples under Wuqian's leadership. As more and more Buddhists from Taiwan have come to visit the Buddhist pilgrimage places in India in the last ten years, their generous donations have made the remodeling of these two temples possible.

8 Yongxing is President of the Hong Kong Buddhist Association and is very experienced in ordination training. Generally speaking, the monastic community in Hong Kong has preserved the Chinese Buddhist heritage better than in mainland China. A large number of Chinese monks escaped to Hong Kong both during and after World War II, some using Hong Kong as a base before moving further afield, to the United States, Taiwan, or Southeast Asia. Because of Hong Kong's unique geographical and political circumstances, overseas Chinese Buddhists have continued their connection with the Chinese monastic community through Hong Kong. For this reason, the monastic community in Hong Kong plays an important role in the Chinese Buddhist world.

Yongxing's participation as a representative of the Chinese *bhikṣuṇī* lineage in Hong Kong is also quite justifiable due to the large number of nuns in Hong Kong. Since Hong Kong had already established its position as a route of passage for monastics from Canton and Shanghai to Southeast Asia before World War II, many Chinese nuns fled to Hong Kong both during and after the war. After the war also, many Chinese women refugees entered the Buddhist order in Hong Kong. The ratio of nuns to monks in Hong Kong after 1949 was approximately 10 to 1.

The earliest documented record of *bhikṣuṇī* ordination in Taiwan was the ordination of more than 100 nuns at Daxian Temple in Baihe (Tainan County) in 1953. Only a few Chinese nuns fled from mainland China to Taiwan, but many Taiwanese women entered the Buddhist order after World War II. It was generally not until after the riots in Hong Kong in 1968 that nuns fled to Taiwan from China. Bhikṣuṇī Xiaoyun (Shig Hiu Wan), founder of Huafan University, is the best-known example.

9 No female candidate ordained in the Cambodian or Thai traditions participated in the ordination in Bodhgaya. The only Thai nun to receive ordination had been ordained in the Sri Lankan tradition. She was quite aware of the difficult reception she might receive in her own tradition and planned to pursue graduate studies abroad instead. For background on nuns in Thailand, see *Thai Women in Buddhism* (Berkeley: Parallax Press, 1991), pp. 36–66, especially pp. 46–48. It would appear that Cambodia has simply replicated the Thai custom regarding nuns.

10 For instance, Inamaluwe Sumangala Nayaka Thero, who initiated a special monastic school in Sri Lanka in 1974 aimed at preparing nuns for full ordination.

11 Before the ordination began, the Korean nun became so ill from drinking contaminated water that she had to be hospitalized for several days and missed the ordination. In a controversial decision, the ordination committee allowed the Tibetan nun to receive *śrāmaṇerikā* precepts but, citing orthodox Vinaya regulations, did not allow her to receive *bhikṣuṇī* ordination because she was handicapped. The Spanish nun Karma Chopel Dronma, who had worn a pacemaker for 15 years, passed away peacefully during morning prayers under the *bodhi* tree, with her teacher, Lama Yeshe, by her side. Because this is the site of the Buddha's enlightenment and because she had received fresh *śrāmaṇerikā* precepts just the night before, the incident was regarded as extraordinary and her funeral procession attracted several hundred Buddhists, who offered prayers in their various languages: Pāli, Tibetan, and Chinese.

12 Topics discussed in these interviews included family background, educational and occupational background, special skills, personal interests, motivation for entering the order, religious commitment, monastic experience, motivation for receiving full ordination, teaching experience, future plans, economic support, relations with friends, and health.

13 Bhikṣuṇīs Yifa and Manke interpreted for Chinese; Bhikṣuṇī Yihua for Chinese, Hindi, and Tibetan; Dr. Hema Goonatilake and Bhikṣuṇī Kusuma for Sinhalese; Dr. Chatsumarn Kabilisingh for Thai; and Bhikṣuṇī Karma Lekshe Tsomo for Tibetan.

14 See Dhananjay Keer, *Dr. Ambedkar: Life and Mission* (Bombay: Popular Prakashan, 1990); Christopher S. Queen, "Dr. Ambedkar and the Hermeneutics of Buddhist Liberation," and Alan Sponberg, "TMBSG: A Dhamma Revolution in Contemporary India," in *Engaged Buddhism: Buddhist Liberation Movements in Asia*, ed. Christopher S. Queen and Sallie B. King (Albany, N.Y.: State University of New York Press, 1996), pp. 45–71, 73–120.

15 "The Honor of the Chinese: A Collective Report on the Three Refuges, Five Precepts, Bodhisattva Vows, the Triple Platform Ordination, Practicing Dharma, and the International Federation of Buddhists," in *The Opening of Xilai Temple* (January 11, 1989): 12–23; also, Yongyuan, "A Collective Report on the Three Refuges, Five Precepts, Bodhisattva Vows, the Triple Platform Ordination, and Practicing Dharma," in Xilai Temple's *Universal Door Monthly*, 114 (March 1989): 36–43.

16 *The Memorial Issue of the 30th Year of Foguangshan Monastery* (Gaoxiong: Foguangshan Monastery, 1997), p. 51.

17 Tenzin Yeshe from New Zealand, Tenzin Dawa from Australia, and Guoxian (Karen Zinn) and Karma Lekshe Tsomo from the United States.

18 Kunzang Wangmo, Wangchuk Palmo, Karma Tsultrim, and Nordzom. See Hanna Havnevik, *Tibetan Buddhist Nuns: History, Cultural Norms and Social Reality* (Oslo: Norwegian University Press, no date), pp. 199–200; and Tsomo, *Sakyadhita: Daughters of the Buddha*, pp. 153, 246.

19 Interview with Bhikṣuṇī Kusuma, Sri Lankan Buddhist scholar and leading nun at the full ordination ceremony held in Sārnāth, conducted in Bodhgaya, February 19, 1998.

20 This is not the first time that the Chinese Saṅgha has worked to bring the dual ordination to Tibetan Buddhist nuns. In mainland China, Bhikṣuṇī Longlian, abbess of Tiexiangsi in Chengdu, is the most well-known proponent of this movement. See Miaochang, "Introducing Buddhist Women on International Women's Day."

21 "Record of the Fourth I. M. S. Seminar, May 6 to 8, 1997: The Moment We Created History: A General Report on Preparations for the Bodhgaya International Triple Platform Ordination," *Universal Gate Monthly* 218 (November 1997): 35–48.

22 Interview with Bhikṣu Tashi Tsering, Ministry of Religious and Cultural Affairs, Tibetan Government-in-Exile, Dharamsala, conducted in Bodhgaya, February 21, 1998.

23 The Mūlasarvāstivādin Vinaya requires 12 *bhikṣuṇīs*, or a minimum of six in a border area. Huimin Shi, "The Chinese Bhikṣuṇī Lineage and the Re-establishment of the Tibetan Bhikṣuṇī Saṅgha," *Journal of the Center for Buddhist Studies* 3 (July 1998): 6–7.

24 Peter Skilling, "A Note on the History of the Bhikkhunī-saṅgha (II): The Order of Nuns after the Parinirvana," *World Fellowship of Buddhist Review* 31, no. 1 (January-March 1994): 29–49.

25 For a discussion of this claim, see Cheng-mei Ku, "The Mahayanic View of Women: A Doctrinal Study," doctoral dissertation (Ann Arbor, Mich.: University Microfilms International, 1984), and Haeju Sunim (Ho-Ryeon Jeon), "Can Women Achieve Enlightenment? A Critique of Sexual Transformation for Enlightenment," *Buddhist Women Across Cultures: Realizations*, ed. Karma Lekshe Tsomo, (Albany, N.Y.: State University of New York Press, 1999), pp. 123–41.

26 This sentence is the title of an essay by a Sri Lankan nun published in the institutional newspaper of the national association of the Sri Lanka Saṅgha in 1997. Dr. Hema Goonatilake provided and translated this article for me.

27 See Maha Upasila Visakha Gunadharma, "First Buddhist Women's Organization Congress," *NIBWA* 11 (April-June 1987): 27–28; and the proceedings of this conference in Tsomo, *Sakyadhita: Daughters of the Buddha*.

28 Huimin, "The Chinese Bhikṣuṇī Lineage and the Reestablishment of the Tibetan Bhikṣuṇī Saṅgha," p. 18.

29 Li, *Bhikṣuṇīs of the Tang Dynasty*, pp. 117–26.

30 The Mahāsāṅghika Vinaya is relatively friendly toward the Bhikṣuṇī Saṅgha. Different sectarian attitudes toward the Bhikṣuṇī Saṅgha reflect the different processes of their doctrinal development. See Cheng-mei Ku, "The Mahayanic View of Women: A Doctrinal Study (Ph.D. diss., University of Wisconsin-Madison, 1983).

31 These also include the danger of sexual assault on female mendicants and the danger to celibacy among monks and nuns living side by side.

32 Observations during fieldwork at the Xiangguangsi, Chiayi, Taiwan, June, 1996.

33 See Li, *Bhikṣuṇīs of the Tang Dynasty*, pp. 126–130; and Nakamura Hajime, *The History of Chinese Buddhism*, trans. Wanchu Yu (Taipei: Tianhua Publications, 1984), pp. 113–16.

34 That is, they should have received training from *bhikṣuṇīs* before receiving ordination from *bhikṣus*. Huimin, "The Chinese Bhikṣuṇī Lineage and the Re-establishment of the Tibetan Bhikṣuṇī Saṅgha," p. 7.

35 Ibid.

36 Li, *Bhikṣuṇīs of the Tang Dynasty*, pp. 127–28.
37 Statement during discussions on the *bhikṣuṇī* lineage held between Chinese and Tibetan scholars held on November 2, 1997, Taipei.
38 "Removing Geographical and Sectarian Boundaries through the Xilai Ordination," *Awakening* 1114 (January 11, 1989), p. 4.
39 Others dispute this, contending that the lack of support and acceptance they experienced was due to other factors: the independent initiative the nuns took in seeking ordination, the lack of support for their initiative from the Bhikṣu Saṅgha, their lack of academic qualifications, and their subsequent failure to establish a *bhikṣuṇī* community to observe monastic rites.
40 Sakyadhita's website is at http://www2.hawaii.edu/~tsomo.
41 Letter written by Sister Sucinta of the Bhāvanā Society, High View, West Virginia, to Foguangshan on October 1, 1995.
42 Personal observations at Xilai Temple, Los Angeles, January 1997; Tetsuden Kashima, *Buddhism in America: The Social Organization of an Ethnic Religious Institution* (Westport, Conn.: Greenwood Press, 1977).
43 Thubten Chodron, "You're Becoming a What? Living as a Western Buddhist Nun," *Buddhist Women on the Edge: Contemporary Perspectives from the Western Frontier*, ed. Marianne Dresser (Berkeley: North Atlantic Books, 1996), pp. 223–34.
44 Yihua, "The Social Contribution of Modern Bhikṣuṇīs," a report to the Fourth International Federation of Buddhist Sangha Seminar, May 7, 1998. According to Xingyun, most Chinese immigrant communities overseas request that Foguangshan appoint nuns rather than monks to establish and administer local Buddhist temples for them.
45 Stephen Batchelor, *The Awakening of the West: The Encounter of Buddhism and Western Culture* (Berkeley: Parallax Press, 1994).
46 Jan Nattier, "Visible and Invisible: The Politics of Representation in Buddhist America," *Tricycle: The Buddhist Review* 5, no. 1 (Fall 1995): 42–49.
47 The Chinese government repeatedly emphasizes this religious policy in the official annual reports of the PRC's Chinese Buddhist Association.
48 "The Dalai Lama to Accept Bhikṣuṇī System," excerpt from *United Daily News* (March 1, 1997), p. 5; Liang Yufang, "The Dalai Lama to Gather Information on Bhikṣuṇī System," *United Daily News* (March 1, 1997), p. 5; Liang Yufang, "Women's Self-Awareness and the Flood of Scholarly Bhikṣuṇīs," *United Daily News* (March 1, 1997), p. 5.
49 I will investigate the complex discourse on the Taiwanese lineage and its relationship to the Chinese *bhikṣuṇī* lineage in another article.
50 Tsomo, *Sakyadhita: Daughters of the Buddha*, p. 269.
51 Precedents include ordinations organized by the City of Ten Thousand Buddhas, in Talmadge, California, and by The International Buddhist Meditation Center in Los Angeles. The latter, held in December 1994, is reported in *Sakyadhita: International Association of Buddhist Women* 6, no. 1 (1995): 12.
52 Xingyun, "Buddhism Should Be Modernized," *Buddhist Light Age Biweekly* 2 (June 1, 1991): 2.
53 The emphasis on the purity and continuity of the *bhikṣuṇī* lineage expressed by Tashi Tsering, the Tibetan representative, during discussions at the Bodhgaya ordination, reveals Tibetan rather than Chinese priorities. For the Tibetans, the transmission of an ordination lineage does not depend merely on a centralized ordination system, such as the one established in Taiwan, but instead emphasizes the continuity of an uninterrupted lineage of ordination that can be traced to Buddha Śākyamuni. This unusual emphasis on lineage and continuity is a natural result of the unique link between religion and political patronage that is the Tibetan inheritance. Unlike the separation of Buddhist monastic institutions and government in Taiwan and Republican China, and also unlike the PRC,

where the state-controlled Chinese Buddhist Association finds it advantageous to include monk leaders from as many schools as possible to enforce governmental control over the ordination system, the Tibetan ecclesiastic authorities place great importance on maintaining the purity of an ordination lineage traceable to the time of the Buddha. From a Tibetan point of view, this difference in perspective on the nature of lineage makes it is difficult to verify a 1,500-year-old ordination lineage in China. Li, *Bhikṣuṇīs of the Tang Dynasty*, pp. 185–95; and Nakamura, *The History of Chinese Buddhism*, pp. 185–234.

54 Wanding Cai, "Daughters of the Buddha," *Sinorama* 22, no. 12 (December 1997): 85–86.

55 See Karma Lekshe Tsomo, *Sisters in Solitude: Two Traditions of Buddhist Monastic Ethics for Women, A Comparative Analysis of the Dharmagupta and Mūlasarvāstivāda Bhikṣuṇī Prātimokṣa Sūtras* (Albany, N.Y.: State University of New York Press, 1996).

56 Such important *bhikṣuṇī* teachers as Hengqing, Zhaohui, and Wuyin all pointed out this important dimension of dual ordination to me.

57 After comparing the Dharmaguptaka *Bhikṣuṇī Prātimokṣa Sūtra*, *Dge slong ma'i so sor thar pahi mdo*, and *Dge slong ma'i 'dul ba rnam par byed pa*, Bhikṣu Tashi Tsering, Bhikṣuṇī Hengqing, Bhikṣuṇī Zhaohui, Yuchen Li, and Bhikṣu Huimin agreed with this finding on November 3, 1997. See Huimin, "The Chinese Bhikṣuṇī Lineage and the Re-establishment of the Tibetan Bhikṣuṇī Sangha," pp. 4–6; and Chatsumarn Kabilsingh, *A Comparative Study of Bhikkunī Pātimokkha* (Varanasi: Chaukhambha Orientalia, 1984).

58 The Pāli reads, *Anujānāmi bhikkhave bhikkūhi bhikkhuniyo upasampādetun ti. Cullavagga* 257.

59 See Kabilsingh, *Thai Women in Buddhism*, p. 41; and Niwa Nori, "Asceticism of Female Buddhists: A Report of the Preliminary Research on Thai Mae Chii," *Yakara: Studies in Ethnology* (Institute of History and Anthropology, University of Tsukuba) 23 (March 1994), pp. 30–42.

60 I am grateful to Dr. Hema Goonatilake for sharing her Bodhgaya fieldnotes.

61 Bhikṣuṇī Zhaohui, a well-known and outspoken Buddhist social critic in Taiwan, attributes this phenomenon to: (1) advances in education for women in Taiwan; (2) increased open-mindedness toward women in Taiwanese society; and (3) nuns' economic self-sufficiency. Also see Tsai, "The Chinese Buddhist Monastic Order for Women: The First Two Centuries," pp. 86, 89.

62 Chien-yu Huang and Robert P. Wellner, "Merit and Mothering: Women and Social Welfare in Taiwanese Buddhism," *Journal of Asian Studies* 57, no. 2 (May 1998): 379–96.

BUDDHIST WOMEN IN THE HIMALAYAS

CHAPTER SIXTEEN

Of Birds and Wings

Tibetan Nuns and their Encounters with Knowledge[1]

Yolanda van Ede

From a sociopolitical perspective, history can be viewed as a succession of unifying and diversifying events. Solidarities and loyalties adhere and then shatter, generating new communities with new loyalties. This ebb and flow results when the balance of power shifts from one sphere to another, creating inequalities between groups and individuals in a constantly changing world.

Such changes have affected monastic communities throughout the world. Ethnic and political conflicts, gender differentials, geographic issues, and their economic consequences, create diversity among Buddhist monastic communities in relation to the socio-historical contexts from which they emerge. These factors can also cause dissension and internal fractures.

The remote Tibetan Buddhist nunnery in the Nepal Himalayas described here was once isolated in its own culture. By the 1970s, the nunnery experienced dramatic changes as it encountered the globalizing forces of the modern world.[2] At this new stage, Western Buddhists with their money and knowledge became the agents of inequality. The influence wielded by these Westerners became a unifying force between the nunnery and the rest of the world. Conversely, the same power provoked dissension within its very walls.

In the spring of 1992, I visited Bekung Gonpa[3] to conduct preliminary research for my doctorate. During my visit I became friends with a 16-year-old *ani* (nun) named Dawa Chöden, who openly shared her experiences as a nun with me. Two years later, when I returned for a year of fieldwork, I found that my young friend had "run away" with another *ani* who was also her cousin. Given the commitment she had expressed when we first met, this new development surprised me. I could not imagine that she wanted to return to secular life, nor could I believe that she had fallen in love. Neither the other nuns nor their families would explain why Dawa Chöden left the nunnery or where she might have gone. This curious reluctance to disclose her (and her cousin's) reason for departure pervaded the nunnery.

It took four months before I finally won the confidence of an *ani* who would reveal the address of my young friend and her cousin. The nun nervously pleaded with me not to let anyone know that she had disclosed this information declaring, "Please do not tell anyone I gave you their address. Dawa wrote me to ask whether I could send her personal belongings. Write her that this is impossible. Now that she left the Rinpoche, the lama, and the *gonpa*, all her things belong to the *gonpa*. Then you can ask her herself why she left, too." I wrote and a few weeks later I received her answer, written in English:

> We two decided to come down to South India because we ... felt so unhappy that we did not have to study, [and] we heard that in South-Indian monasteries, especially of the Nyingma sect, we would get nice education. So, we thought that man without education is like a bird without wings. So, we decided to leave Bekung and come here.

This declaration highlighted Dawa Chöden's declared motivation to become an *ani* – the opportunity to learn to read and write and to study religious texts (*pecha*). As she matured, her family provided little support for her and her ambitions, and the Hindu teachers of Bekung's local school proved disappointing. Education provisions of Bekung Gonpa and its *khenpo* (abbot) also did not suffice for this earnest young girl. This urge to learn required that she leave the nunnery without permission and thus break with the lineage she adhered to, her lamas, her fellow nuns, and her family as well.

At the end of my fieldwork in March 1995, Bekung Gonpa's *khenpo* invited me to a farewell dinner in Kathmandu. On this occasion he confided that three other *anis* had left for Mysore. He subsequently received a letter from them, stating they had followed Dawa Chöden's example. Among the "disappeared" was Dawa Chöden's former neighbor, the nun who had previously revealed her whereabouts to me.

These departures, very unusual for an organization such as this nunnery, no longer surprised me. My young friend's letter had inspired me to redirect the focus of my research to the importance of knowledge – both religious and secular – in this particular community. Knowledge turned out to be a major theme in the *gonpa*'s history, as it probably is in the history of many other monastic communities. Problems surrounding educational opportunities and spiritual guidance had already surfaced in its past. The discovery of the background of these upheavals intrigued me from an anthropological standpoint. And I also wondered whether my presence two years earlier had sparked an interest in the outside world that might not have emerged had I not visited.

Information and Discontent

In 1951 after the fall of the Rana regime, Nepal became accessible to the rest of the world. In 1959, when the Dalai Lama escaped into exile, the

Tibetan diaspora began. During the late 1960s and early 1970s, young people from the West began heading to the East searching for religious alternatives and philosophies to compensate, or substitute, for the inadequacies they felt in their own cultures. Since the 1980s technological innovations – particularly media and communications systems such as telephone, fax, e-mail, and the internet – and the availability of inexpensive airline tickets, created networks among people – East and West – who had previously been ignorant of one another's existence. Now communication in a small world affected even this remote nunnery high up in the Himalayas.

With all this information comes the thirst for more knowledge and education. These wishes affected even a young 16-year-old in Nepal named Dawa Chöden. The lamas' plans for the future, plans that will avoid situations such as the disappearance of young nuns from the monastery, revolve around Western money – the same source from which the dissension originated.

In the light of this growing emphasis on learning we begin to understand Dawa Chöden's action. However, her quest for learning, along with that of her fellow *anis*, will only mark a phase in their nunnery's history, as its Rinpoche and its *khenpo* search for solutions before all the young *anis* run off. Nevertheless, the future plans for the community depend on the same global network that originally prompted the departures. Although in one sense the plan is logical, in another it also emphasizes a web of dependence. Unless the Western Buddhists involved remain aware of the deeper role they play, realizing the long-term impact their presence inherently creates, the future of the nunnery may be irretrievably altered. Here my role as an anthropologist emerges – to analyze the situation so that potentially damaging consequences may be avoided.

To comprehend the importance of knowledge in the history of Bekung Gonpa, another distinction remains to be made. This distinction concerns knowledge itself, namely, as a process of spiritual development either through meditation or through study. Geoffrey Samuel has already elaborately described how the shifting emphasis on the path of *sūtra* or the path of *tantra* has guided parts of the Tibetan world.[4] My historical ethnography of Bekung Gonpa, in fact, supports Samuel's analysis, describing how the shifts in emphasis upon the two paths (meditation and learning) have evolved on a micro level. This level is directed by very basic, practical choices made by individuals responding to social circumstances, not only in the *gonpa*'s past, but also in its near future. In this same way, the plans of the Rinpoche and the *khenpo* conflict in their emphasis on either meditation or learning.

The History of Bekung Gonpa

Bekung Gonpa was started in 1933 by a Drugpa Kagyu Rinpoche from Bhutan at the request of a village headman from Bekung.[5] This headman competed with a local, high-caste Hindu family for the position of tax collector. To obtain that position he had to consolidate the cultural dominance of the Sherpas, the Tibetan ethnic group to which he belonged. The idea of founding a monastery slumbered in his mind. This monastery would tower over the Bekung valley and be a visual symbol of Sherpa dominance. "A center of religious learning and arts," it had to counter the Hindu assertion that their culture was more civilized and knowledgeable than the Sherpas'. Only when the Drugpa Rinpoche appeared in Bekung, as he journeyed on a pilgrimage, did the Drugpa Kagyu Rinpoche attain the religious authority to put the headman's dream into practice.

A few years earlier the Drugpa Rinpoche had founded a *gonpa* in Kyirong, Tibet. In Bekung he realized the opportunity to extend his lineage. Bekung, however, was not a religious and economic center like Kyirong. The primary industry of the region was agriculture and the small Tibetan Buddhist population had no monastic heritage. To ensure the population's backing and their economic support for the new *gonpa*, the Drugpa Rinpoche decided to initiate a religious community composed of both women and men.[6] The focus of the community was to be meditation and individual retreats. Due to his recruitment activities, the new community soon had about 40 monks and nuns.

The restricted economic resources of the area and the limited Buddhist population stalled the process of building the *gonpa*, however. It took five years to finish the temple hall, the *dukhang*, and altogether nearly 20 years to construct housing for the monastics. By that time, all the monks and the younger nuns had left Bekung Gonpa – and often left the robe as well. By 1952 the religious community consisted of only 12 elderly nuns. How did this happen?

The monks and nuns had been recruited with promises of a life of study. Instead, they had to work day in and day out on the *gonpa*'s construction. At night, they were too tired to concentrate on the lamas' teachings in Tibetan, an unfamiliar language. The Drugpa Rinpoche had left Bekung one year after the *gonpa*'s founding to establish monasteries in two other areas so the original inspiration for residing in the *gonpa* was no longer there, and it did not provide the opportunities they yearned for. Fed up with a life that seemed worse than the hardships of a layperson, the monks soon followed their guru, the lama, to his other new *gonpas*. The *anis*, however, had no option but to stay in Bekung and make the best of their new way of life. In this culture, women only left home if they had specific, compelling reasons to do so. For many women, the quest for religious learning and an aversion to hard labor do not constitute compelling reasons.

Some monks remained at the other *gonpas*, while others returned with the Drugpa Rinpoche when the *dukhang* was ready for consecration. When the Rinpoche went into solitary retreat, Bekung Gonpa's community still had not received proper education in monastic discipline, and he died soon after, in 1942. The Drugpa Rinpoche had left his nephew in charge of the *gonpa*, but this young lama soon fell in love with an *ani* and left the *gonpa* and the robe behind. Many other monks and nuns also decided to marry and return to secular life. Bekung Gonpa degenerated from its original dream, a "center of religious learning and arts," into a "place of refuge" mainly for widows, divorced women, and orphans, without a lama in charge and without an experienced *lobön* to lead *pūjas* or provide instruction in either meditation or textual studies.[7]

During the 1950s, the remaining 12 *anis* lived largely as "village *anis,*" that is, women who "were recognized as individuals with a legitimate religious purpose, but who maintained a close association with their natal families and took part in its productive activities."[8] The *anis* of Bekung lived at the *gonpa*, but returned to their parents' homes daily to work in the fields and gather firewood and fodder. Only on the eighth, tenth, fifteenth, and twenty-fifth days of the Tibetan months did they gather in the *dukhang* to perform *pūjas* by reading the few *pechas* they knew. On special occasions, such as funeral observances, they assisted the village lama, a former Bekung monk.

Everything changed in 1959. A lama from Sera monastery, one of the major monasteries of Tibet, fled the Chinese occupation of his country along with the Dalai Lama and thousands of monks and laypeople. Unlike most of them, this Gelugpa lama headed not for India, but for Bekung, where he had met the Drugpa Rinpoche 20 years earlier, around 1940. On that occasion, the Drugpa Rinpoche offered him the position of *khenpo* of Bekung Gonpa, but at that time the young lama chose to follow his own path and return to Sera. Years later, when he reached Bekung Gonpa and saw the poor state of affairs there, he resolved to infuse the community with a new sense of religious esteem. This included practical matters. He supervised the building of a kitchen and a storeroom as well as a nicely decorated *simchung*, a small residence where he could live and receive visitors seeking his blessing and advice. Moreover, he ordered *pechas* from Kathmandu, taught nearly every day, and initiated the *anis* in meditation practices such as *nyungne* (the fasting ritual) and Dorje Semba. His activities caused him to become known as "the Guru Lama."

In 1970 a delegation of villagers from a town two days' hike away from Bekung arrived and requested help from him in founding a monastery. By now Bekung Gonpa had been transformed from a monastery into a nunnery, and the Guru Lama favored the idea of a *gonpa* for boys and young men seeking to lead a monastic life. Agreeing to help, the Guru Lama changed the focus of his attention and began to devote most of his attention to supervising construction at the new monastery.

Because of the strong impetus he had given to religious practice at Bekung Gonpa and the systematic monastic organization he had introduced – with offices such as head nun (*unze*), head cook (*niermu*), and disciplinarian (*kutum*) – his absence should not have been problematic. However, the *anis* of the 1950s preferred to spend their time on what they had finally managed to learn: *tsam*, meditation practices that prepared them for death. Organizational matters fell by the wayside. The older residents hoped to leave these responsibilities to the younger nuns, about 20 in number, who had taken their vows under the Guru Lama. But the younger generation had not experienced Bekung Gonpa's difficult past, and did not wish to focus on meditation. Instead, they wanted to pursue those activities they had been promised when recruited, including educational opportunities.

In 1951, Nepal had opened its doors to the world, launching modernization and state-organized educational programs. Because of its remote location, these changes filtered slowly into the Bekung valley. Only some 20 years later did these initiatives actually affect the lives of the Sherpa population. By that time, the Hindu family mentioned previously had obtained funds for a local primary school in the area. Many Sherpas sent their sons to attend this school during the late 1960s and early 1970s.

By 1969, the road between Kathmandu and the Chinese/Tibetan border had been completed. This launched a stream of labor migration by young Bekung Sherpa men to Nepal's capital and from there to India. Girls and unmarried women were excluded from these new opportunities, however. Not allowed to attend school, nor to travel to the big city, they fulfilled traditional roles at home. Under the circumstances, Bekung Gonpa became a respectable alternative, not only because of the Guru Lama's efforts, but also because a national Buddhist committee created networks among the monasteries in Nepal, organizing pilgrimages to spiritual sites such as Bodhgaya, Vārāṇasi, Lumbini, and Dharamsala. Religious life in Bekung Gonpa therefore offered women opportunities they would otherwise not have. Many a young girl opted for the chance to become an *ani*.

After becoming *anis*, however, these young women discovered the shadow side of "going into the world." At pilgrimage sites and other large religious gatherings, they encountered monastics from urban *gonpas*. They had more financial resources, knew more *pechas* by heart, had received more initiations, and done more retreats than the Bekung *anis* could even imagine. Although the older generation maintained an indifferent attitude toward these discrepancies, the younger *anis* began to realize that their rural, underdeveloped nunnery, with an absent Guru Lama, provided inadequate resources for their needs and desires. In 1976, 12 nuns departed for Dharamsala searching for a life of religious learning and Western sponsors to support them.[9] This initiative failed and eight of the nuns returned home to Bekung after a few months; the four who remained in

Dharamsala ended up leaving the robes within a year. This exodus was concealed in a manner similar to Dawa Chöden's departure.

After the incident of the 12 nuns, the Guru Lama began reorganizing the community, which now consisted of 35 *anis*. Individual retreats and pilgrimages were regulated, terms of office for the administrators were shortened, and a *lobön* from Tsum Gonpa moved in to organize instructions for novices and young nuns. Peace returned. For the first time since its inception, Bekung Gonpa earned a reputation as a serious Dharma facility for women of all ages. In 1980, the Drugpa Rinpoche's reincarnation (referred to henceforth as the Tulku) arrived at Bekung Gonpa with a Kangyur, or set of the Tibetan canon. He stayed almost an entire year and the nunnery's star as a Dharma community continued to rise. Within five years, the number of residents increased from 35 to 60 *anis*.

The Guru Lama suffered a heart attack and died in 1986 after his *gonpa* for monks was plundered by local members of the Communist Party. In his place as *khenpo* of Bekung Gonpa, the Tulku appointed a *geshe*, a lama with the highest degree of Buddhist education, Lama Tenzin. With his appointment, the current phase in the history of Bekung Gonpa began.

The Search for Religious Alternatives

The Tulku had an uncle, also a Rinpoche, who had never paid much attention to the rural *gonpas*. His interests revolved around the growing popularity of Tibetan Buddhism in the world at large. When the Tulku took over the supervision of his *gonpas*, his uncle became chairman of the Nepal Buddhist Committee. In this position, he traveled the world contacting other Buddhist leaders, giving lectures and teachings, leading initiations, and inaugurating *gonpas* and stupas. Lama Tenzin accompanied him as his caretaker and interpreter, and continued these activities even after being appointed as Bekung Gonpa's *khenpo* in 1986. As a result, he now spends only two months a year in Bekung, supervising the change in officers and leading the yearly *nyungne* retreats in late spring.

For the Bekung *anis*, Lama Tenzin represents the larger world they yearned for. Compared to the 1970s, when the *anis* emigrated to Dharamsala, more and more foreigners now visit the *ani gonpa* and the *anis* have also begun to wander far afield. In addition, tourists have begun to venture into the beautiful small valley and trekkers have turned Bekung into a popular destination. Although the tourists make small donations to the *gonpa*, most go on their way. However, five young Western women – presumably rich, well-educated, and able to travel alone – have stayed for longer periods of time. As one of these young women, I realize that we are perceived by the young *anis* as role models; from their perspective, we are everything they long to be. We are envied for our good karma. One of the *anis* even volunteered the information that she no longer hopes to be reborn as a man, but as a woman in the West!

Since the late 1980s Lama Tenzin has sent several Western Buddhists to practice short retreats (Vajrasattva meditation) at Bekung Gonpa. These visitors impressed the *anis* with the amounts of time and money they could spend on Dharma practice, including the financial means to attend large ceremonies far away from their home countries. In addition, these Western practitioners seemed to be knowledgeable about many different lamas, gods, *bodhisattvas*, initiations, and texts unknown at Bekung Gonpa. "Good karma," a young *ani* sighed. "We are born Buddhists, but we Sherpas don't even pronounce the *pechas* as beautifully as they do."

These encounters with Western travelers also affect those outside the Bekung valley, particularly in Kathmandu. Many residents now travel back and forth to Kathmandu, and some have even moved there to work in the tourist industry, so now these excursions have become a normal feature of life in the valley. The *anis*, too, now travel more often, usually with the intention of following Lama Tenzin, much as the monks had done in Bekung Gonpa's early years. He has little time for them, however, since his residence is overcrowded with Western Buddhists whom he has met on his travels abroad. The *anis* serve his guests silently, observing both the guests and the monks carefully. Many of the monks now have personal sponsors among the Westerners. They chat, sightsee, and travel about with the new visitors in a manner that excludes the *anis*. However, the *anis* are included whenever a large ceremony is organized in Nepal, usually sponsored by Westerners, Taiwanese, or Japanese. Lama Tenzin sends them to these events, which they appreciate, though they still hope to have the opportunity to travel with Lama Tenzin. So far, no *ani* has been asked to do so. In addition to travel, the *anis* also wish to meet a Westerner willing to be their personal sponsor. Nearly all monks living in Kathmandu have sponsors.

Many Westerners feel the limitations of Bekung Gonpa's physical facilities. The small comforts the *gonpa* offers, and the very simple meals the *anis* provide, have their charm during the first few days. But after a week of daily prostrations, the lack of luxuries becomes very inconvenient. The silence of the mountains, together with the communications barrier with the *anis*, soon becomes claustrophobic. Within two weeks most Westerners pack their bags and leave.

Lama Tenzin recognizes the lack of comforts at Bekung, in comparison to the luxurious circumstances he himself has experienced when visiting the West. Consequently, he dreams of enlarging the *gonpa* complex to provide retreat studios, each with its own bath and toilet facilities; a larger kitchen; and a team of porters permanently employed by the *gonpa* to bring food from the town so that a greater variety of familiar foods will be available for Western guests. In addition, he dreams of a "man-sized wall surrounding the *gonpa* complex to secure its peace and silence."

When Lama Tenzin related these dreams to me as we walked through the *gonpa* complex, I could not help but ask, "And what about the *anis*?" He replied, "Well, they will never have to suffer problems of money and food anymore. They can earn enough by serving the Dharma *injis* (foreigners)." I persisted, "But what about their education?" He responded, "They can come to Kathmandu in winter to listen to teachings. But it is not good for them to stay in the city too long. They will become spoiled by movies and television. Foreign people have already learned that television is no good. That's why they come here, to go into retreat, to look into themselves instead of looking to the bad world."

The plans of the Tulku remain localized. He sees opportunities in the changing, larger world that could be beneficial to the local people, both to the *anis* and the laity, in both the religious and the secular spheres. He does not seem to emphasize retreat and meditation (the path of *tantric* meditation), but would like to see his nuns studying – not only religious texts, but also languages and medical sciences.[10] However, he lacks the contacts with the larger network of people to promote his case. Lama Tenzin, on the other hand, is a representative of a larger, globalizing process. He views Bekung Gonpa as a retreat from those secular forces, with the goal of preserving and promoting the Dharma. The *anis*, from his perspective, have a good position now, away from the destructive elements of the modern world, with a chance to fulfill their intended purpose in life, as "servants"[11] of the Buddha, the Dharma, the Saṅgha – and, eventually, Western practitioners.

Although Lama Tenzin's plan includes many laudable characteristics (creating a perfect place for Westerners to do retreat), it bypasses the *anis*' wish to be included in the modern, global processes their lama exemplifies. Although his wish is to shut out the outside changing world (by building a high wall around Bekung Gonpa), in effect he himself is bringing that world into the *gonpa*, by inviting Western practitioners and catering to their requirements. A further dilemma revolves around money. Bekung Gonpa needs the financial support that, for now, can only be provided by wealthy Western Buddhists. Without this money, the Tulku's plans cannot be implemented.

During the last few months of my stay in 1995, I observed the two generations of nuns clashing over such things as pilgrimage plans, my language course, the time spent on homework, everyday tasks and how best to complete them, who should participate in *pūjas*, and so on. The differences among them were also revealed in how conflicts were mediated. The older *anis* called upon Lama Tenzin for moral support, while the younger ones went to the Tulku.

Solving this generational conflict requires that both plans be implemented – that of the Tulku and that of his *khenpo*. The current disharmony not only undermines the implicit intention of a harmonious Saṅgha, but may also precipitate more departures by the unhappy younger generation. These conflicts can best be solved when Western practitioners take their experiences at Bekung a step further than most have done so far. Instead of running away when the facilities and atmosphere do not satisfy their images of "mythical Tibet," they might offer not only their money, but their time and knowledge as well. Most Westerners visiting Bekung Gonpa are knowledgeable about texts and reciting *pechas*. In addition, they could help with basic labor, using their hands to build retreat houses for the *anis* as well as themselves. With this attitude, they would gain the respect of the local people for their concrete assistance in time and effort. Participation and exchange on this level would create better understanding among people already inevitably linked. Each group would gain more insight into the other's worlds, more compassion, and therefore more Dharma. Without this understanding, instead of learning from one another, diversity will only produce and maintain greater inequalities. Shared efforts can unite both groups as followers of the Buddha, creating an even stronger sense of Saṅgha.

Global Streams

Globalization entails two tendencies: in one, the local becomes assimilated into the global, while in the other, the global is absorbed into the local. At Bekung Gonpa, these two tendencies manifest themselves as the *anis* go into the outside world, while Westerners arrive at Bekung from that very same world. Linked to these two streams of contact are the two conceptual paths of spiritual development: the path of *sūtra* and the path of *tantra*. Generally speaking, when a monastic community (such as the young generation of nuns at Bekung Gonpa) orients itself outward (from the local to the global), the path of *sūtra* (learning) tends to be the preferred path. Conversely, when a monastic community (or part of it, such as the older nuns) is more inwardly oriented (from the global to the local), the path of *tantra* is generally preferred. All this diversity – geographic, economic, and spiritual factors – can be transformed into a sense of unity if the motivating factor is devotion to the Dharma. Westerners, with their greater external advantages, need to maintain an awareness of and respect for the processes occurring on the local level so that the unifying factors can emerge.

Peoples and their cultures have changed through interaction since the beginning of humankind. In this era, interactions have accelerated, and the balance between give and take must be carefully weighed so that one does not overwhelm the other. Only by sharing money, knowledge, and others' worlds – while maintaining respect for the other – can these interactions succeed. As these steps toward unification evolve, each side can maintain its integrity while increasing its togetherness as a Saṅgha with the purpose of experiencing the Dharma.

Notes

1 This paper, written for the 5th Śākyadhitā Conference, is based upon my doctoral research, for which I wish to thank the Centre for Asian Studies Amsterdam (CASA), the Amsterdam School for Social Research (ASSR), and my supervisor Prof. Peter van der Veer and his Research Centre for Religion and Society, all at the University of Amsterdam, for their financial, institutional, and personal support.

2 On globalizing forces see, for instance, A. Appadurai, *Modernity at Large: Cultural Dimensions of Globalization* (Minneapolis: The University of Minnesota Press, 1996) and Ulf Hannerz, *Studies in Social Organization of Meaning* (New York: Columbia University Press, 1992).

3 For ethical reasons, all names mentioned in this paper are pseudonyms.

4 Geoffrey Samuels, *Civilized Shamans* (Washington and London: Smithsonian Institution Press, 1993).

5 See Christopher von Fürer-Haimendorf, who visited Bekung Gonpa in 1974 when this village headman was still alive. "A Nunnery in Nepal," *Kailash* 4, no. 2 (1976): 121–54.

6 See Hanna Havnevik, *Tibetan Buddhist Nuns: History, Cultural Norms and Social Reality* (Oslo: Norwegian University Press, 1990).

7 See also von Fürer-Haimendorf, "A Nunnery in Nepal," p. 123.

8 See Kathryn March, "The Intermediacy of Women: Female Gender Symbolism and the Social Position of Women among Tamangs and Sherpas of Highland Nepal," doctoral dissertation, Department of Anthropology, Cornell University, 1979, p. 274; and Melvyn Goldstein, "Growing Old in Helambu: Aging, Migration and Family Structure Among Sherpas," *Contributions to Nepalese Studies* 8, no. 1 (1980): 53.

9 I only found out about this Dharamsala event after I met one of the ex-*anis* who had participated in it and finally left the robe.

10 In a flyer, written in English and thus presumably meant particularly for Westerners, the Tulku requests the help of readers in teaching the *anis* English, Nepali, and Tibetan language. During an interview he stated his wish that the *anis* would get their "school-leaving certificate" so they would be able to study medical sciences at the university. In his opinion the local population lacks proper medical care. The *anis* should be able to fill this vacuum.

11 The expression is taken from Anna Grimshaw's diary on her stay in a nunnery in Ladakh, *Servants of the Buddha: Winter in a Himalayan Convent* (Cleveland: Pilgrim Press, 1994).

CHAPTER SEVENTEEN

Yeshe's Tibetan Pilgrimage and the Founding of a Himalayan Nunnery[1]

Kim Gutschow

The three heroines of our story first came to a solitary cliff to build their meditation cells nearly six decades ago, before the Buddhist principality of Zangskar was a part of the nation we now know as India.[2] One by one, nuns came to piece their tiny meditation cells out of rocks and mud mortar, laboriously hauled to the site basket by basket. In the mid 1950s, three of the founding nuns traveled several thousand kilometers to be ordained as novices by the venerable Ganden Throne Holder in Tibet. Before they went to Tibet, Yeshe and her companions were no more than celibate spinsters living on a cliff. After their ordination, they founded a full-fledged nunnery in Karsha village, one of the oldest and most prominent villages in Zangskar. Karsha proudly hosts ancient temples dating back to the 11th century and ruins dating back even earlier, yet it appears never to have hosted a nunnery. How could a group of women achieve in this century what others had failed during the previous millennium? We shall examine how ordination can spark both individual and collective transformation, just as it transformed the inner and the outer landscape of one Himalayan Buddhist community.

> Life's what you see in people's eyes. Life's what they learn, and having learnt it, never, though they seek to hide it, cease to be aware of ...[3]

The lines around Yeshe's piercing eyes indicate the tremendous determination which has enabled her to weather countless hardships in her lifetime. Like most nuns in Zangskar, Yeshe first learned to read and memorize Buddhist texts with relatives at monastic institutions. In Yeshe's case, these apprenticeships were of two different sects, which do not operate exclusively in the Tibetan Buddhist tradition but may share initiations and revere the same teachers. After spending several winters at the 18th-century Drugpa Kagyud (*'Brug pa bKa' rgyud*) temple in Sani village, Yeshe moved to a Gelugpa (*dGe lugs pa*) nunnery called Dorje Dzong, supposedly founded by a disciple of the 15th-century Tibetan saint, Tsongkhapa. In order to be closer to home, Yeshe returned to a site steeped in antiquity in her natal village of Karsha. She moved in with her childhood friend Angmo, the first nun to build a retreat cell near an 11th-century temple high above Karsha village. Unlike Angmo, who had been orphaned as a child and had built her cell laboriously without assistance from any family members, Yeshe received generous help from her father and mother when it came time to build her cell. Yeshe still recalls how her parents held "begging beers" in Karsha to solicit the beams for her cell and how her relatives volunteered their services as carpenters and masons.

Yeshe, Angmo, and a third nun, Deskyid, spent their first years on the cliff memorizing the Guru Pūja (*bLa ma mchod pa*) and the Vajra Offering (*rDo rje gchod pa*). At this time, they lived mostly at home as "lay nuns" with five precepts – not to kill, steal, lie, commit sexual misconduct, or take intoxicants. They were not qualified to wear monastic robes, for they lacked ordination, which was a rare privilege for Zangskari women in those days. After receiving ritual instruction from an elderly monk at Karsha monastery, they decided to join him on a pilgrimage to Tibet in 1956. It was to be a turning point in their lives.

Setting out on foot, Ani Yeshe and her companions traveled some 5,000 km to Tibet, a distant and fabled place of learning and spirituality they had never seen. The first challenge was gathering provisions for the lengthy journey. They each packed a few pounds of butter and nearly 60 lb. of flour, fearing they would be unable to carry much more. They begged relatives for money and pulled together whatever savings they had: Yeshe collected 500 rupees, Angmo had 300 rupees, but poor Deskyid raised only 250 rupees. In late November, they set off with seven other Zangskari villagers, heading south over the 16,400 ft. Shingo La pass. After walking 400 km to the neighboring region of Lahaul, they took the first bus ride of their lives. In Delhi, they caught a train that took them clear across northern India to Kalimpong. They begged for food and free spots on the train, and eventually made their way to Gangtok. In Sikkim, they split into smaller groups for the last leg of their journey on foot. Crossing the Himalayan ranges into Tibet in late December, they faced a freezing wind beyond Phari village. All of them suffered severe frostbite, which bothers them to this day. Along the way, they slept in the courtyards of Tibetan farmhouses and begged for flour or butter. After several weeks, they reached Tashilhunpo Monastery, where they rejoiced in a reunion with the Zangskari monks. For the first time in months, they ate their fill and could chat freely in their local dialect. After recuperating for several days and visiting the resplendent monastic halls, they set off once more for Lhasa.

They reached Lhasa in time to see the 14th Dalai Lama preside over the annual Great Prayer Festival during the Tibetan New Year. Afterward, they were ordained as novices (*dge tshul ma*), the highest ordination available to women in Tibet at that time.[4] They received the 36 novice precepts from the Ganden Throne Holder (*dGa' ldan khri pa*), who held the throne built for

Tsongkhapa, the 15th-century founder of both Ganden Monastery and Lhasa's Prayer Festival. They could not have guessed that 40 years later they would be among the last Zangskari novices ordained in Tibet by this venerable teacher.

After being ordained as novices, nuns are expected to abide by the same 36 precepts and wear the same robes as novice monks (*dge tshul*). The day of ordination is the first time they may wear the three sacred robes (vest, lower robe, and yellow outer robe)[5] which signal their new androgynous state. Novices of both sexes are expected to wear their robes until the day they die, for the robes are deeply invested with symbolic import. Representing poverty, chastity, and purity, they symbolize the Buddha's teachings and the path of renunciation that was his main legacy. The robes are fashioned out of pieces of cloth sewn in such a way as to recall the scraps of cloth the Buddha and his disciples collected from cremation grounds.[6] Imbued with an aura of sanctity, they are worn in a ritually prescribed manner that Yeshe and her companions learned only years later. Yeshe recalls how she rarely wore the robes at all in the first years after her ordination, because she simply did not know how to tie them! Eventually, a kindly monk taught her the required number of folds and the rules that apply to wearing the robes. The upper garments must never touch the lower extremities of the body. Just as one avoids stepping over food, religious books, and other sacred objects, one is forbidden to step over the robes. Yet the robes alone cannot sustain a novice nun. Renunciation also requires practice and learning to retreat from the daily demands of worldly life.

Initial Hardships of Spiritual Practice

When the newly ordained novice nuns returned home in late spring of 1957, after crossing many mountain passes and the teeming north Indian plains, they were pulled back into the routine work of agrarian life. After working most days on their family farms in the village, they hastened back up to their cells each night to recapture the warm bonds of their nine-month pilgrimage. As their new-found spiritual companionship at the nunnery grew stronger, they decided to devote the next winter to religious austerities.

Working double shifts during the harvest season, they earned enough grain in wages to stockpile for a lengthy period of meditative seclusion. As the snow began to fall, they repaired their stone cells on the cliff which had been largely neglected during their absence. While the villagers let loose with revelry and feasting, turning the ordinary world upside down in their customary New Year (*lo gsar*) celebrations during the winter solstice, the nuns retired to their cells to perform the preliminary practices (*sngon 'gro*). A certain degree of stamina is required to complete the required 111,111 repetitions of these practices in sub-zero winter temperatures. The nuns took solace and warmth from each other as they repeated their prayers of refuge (*skyabs 'gro*), full-length prostrations (*phyag chen mo*), *maṇḍala* offerings (*dkyil 'khor*), and the prayer of generation (*bdag skyed*).[7] Although laypeople occasionally complete these practices late in life when they have fewer household obligations, monastics perform them in their youth.

Yeshe described the full-length prostrations to me by leaping off her cushion, throwing her full body along the floor, and sliding her hands until her arms were fully extended above her head. As she pushed herself back up on her knees, she grimaced and joked that she was getting too old for this sort of thing. Pointing to her elbows, palms, and knees, she recalled the blood that had stained her freshly plastered floor as she did prostrations years ago. She described her sensations as if they had occurred just yesterday, noting, "Although I felt pain at first, after a while I didn't even feel the bleeding sores anymore." Unlike Tibetan pilgrims, who often wear leather aprons, or wooden blocks on their forearms, Yeshe wore no protective pads during her repeated slides along the floor. The preliminary practices are a training in the arts of mindfulness and awareness. The hypnotic effect of the repeated physical rigors and prayers create the conditions for single-pointed concentration and a gradual emptying of the mind. The practices force the practitioner to focus on her body and breath, while ignoring her pain, exhaustion, and the daily distractions of village life.

Yeshe's reminiscences were not intended as exaggerated bravado, but rather as poignant reminders of time spent training herself in the art of detachment. Self-inflicted pain may help mask the wrenching pain of separation as novices psychologically, if not physically, detach themselves from the mundane sphere of village life. Although they may continue to participate in their family's domestic life, nuns learn to rise above the mundane desires and dreams shared by their village sisters. Nuns take up a shadow life on the cliff above that involves more intense physical deprivation than that ordinarily experienced by village women. After their winter meditations, Yeshe and her companions emerged from their cells with much more than scars on their palms and knees. They had found a sustaining vision for their spiritual life and for the community of nuns that would slowly follow them to the nunnery atop the cliff over the next decades.

Daily Praxis and The Art of Detachment

After taking ordination, Yeshe's religious rituals became merged with her mundane daily life. As a novice, she is required to adhere to the *bodhisattva* vow: to maintain an awakened mind (*sems skyed*) attuned to compassion at all times.[8] The vow demands a profound altruism that places the welfare of others before one's own at every moment. Yeshe knows how difficult it is to practice perfect generosity. Rather than trying to live up to an unattainable ideal of infinite compassion, she makes a vow to take up the pain of those less fortunate than herself through a practice known as *gtong len* ("sending and receiving"):

> May the suffering of all those who are hungry come to me. May all of my happiness go to them. May those without clothes receive from those who have clothes. Just as we now drink tea and eat bread, we think, "May all those without food also receive food." If I go hungry, it is okay. If I have no clothes and am cold, it is no problem.[9]

Like most nuns, Yeshe performs her daily ritual recitations almost unthinkingly while cooking tea or carrying water. Yet these recitations should not be confused with secular rituals like brushing one's teeth. As symbolic or aesthetic acts, the recitations express a profound shift in the way the world is perceived. Non-attachment is far more than a philosophical principle; it is lived bodily praxis. Even a simple act such as going to sleep may be infused with profound meditative import. Every night after dinner, as Yeshe completes her evening prayers and visualizations, she mixes the last sip of tea in her cup with a pinch of barley flour. The dough cleans out the butter left in her cup and serves as a bedtime snack. She then turns her cup upside down, for in Zangskari idiom an empty cup invites a host to fill it. When Yeshe places her cup face down every night, it signals that she might not arise the next morning to break her fast:

> By next morning, if I open my eyes, it is by the mercy of the Three Jewels and my root teacher that I have not died, that I am not sick, that I have a sound body. Will my consciousness return tomorrow morning or not? Will I rise again tomorrow morning or not? If I die, it is by the mercy of the Precious Buddha. If we die, it is all right for us old ones.[10]

With this contemplation, Yeshe – 73 years old in 1999 – tucks herself in and sleeps soundly one more night. By preparing herself emotionally for death every evening, she infuses her days with meditative awareness. Her evening ritual expresses the credo of Tsongkhapa's *Great Exposition of the Stages to the Path of Enlightenment* (*Lam rim chen mo*). In this text, the practitioner is urged to meditate upon the inevitability and possible immediacy of death as a reminder of why merit-making is the most urgent task in this lifetime.[11] Although Yeshe has never read the text, she has heard oral commentary on it from both Ladakhi and Tibetan monks who tour Zangskar in the summer to give teachings. Yeshe also prays every evening to Maitreya and Samanthabhadra, to remind herself of the impermanent, conditioned, and interdependent nature of all things.[12] She tries to maintain a state of mental clarity in which only good thoughts (*kun slong bzang po*) arise.

> To say "perfectly pure thoughts" means good thoughts, white thoughts. We do not send others evil thoughts or black thoughts. "Perfectly cleansed thoughts" means we generate only the "*bodhisattva* mind," a straight mind which doesn't wish harm upon others, doesn't feel jealous, doesn't feel anger and pride, and doesn't covet another's wealth. And in Buddhism, we imagine all sentient beings of the six realms to be our father or mother, and say, "May they be reborn in the Buddha fields."[13]

Yeshe explains that suffering is inescapable within the six realms of existence. In the hells one feels the sufferings of heat and cold; in the hungry ghost realm, hunger and thirst; in the animal realm, the suffering of carrying heavy burdens; even in the god realm, one suffers because pleasures cannot last. Yeshe admits that she does not know whether she will be blessed with another human rebirth, but nonetheless she prays fervently to be reborn as a monk. To explain why she feels it is fortunate to be born as a human, Yeshe told me a parable from a Buddhist *sūtra*:

> Imagine the entire world covered with a stormy ocean. Deep in this vast ocean, long before the continents emerged, there was a single tortoise who only surfaced once every hundred years for air. Along with the tortoise, there was one other object in this ocean: a wooden yoke, like one puts on a yak. The probability of the tortoise surfacing and putting its neck through the yoke is greater than the probability of our attaining a human rebirth in our next lifetime.

Given that human rebirth is so rare, it would be a shame not to study Buddhism in this lifetime.

Many Zangskari nuns dedicate themselves to the practice of *tantra*, an advanced path which offers a shortcut to esoteric truths that might take lifetimes to learn by the study of the *sūtras*. Yeshe and the other nuns at Karsha practice the *Vajrayoginī Tantra*, an advanced *tantric* text.[14] After receiving a Vajrayoginī empowerment, a nun dedicates herself to meditative austerities and a daily regimen of prayers and prostrations. *Tantric* practice demands intensive motivation and discipline, because it offers a shortcut on the path to awakening. The daily practices of most Karsha nuns include an evening meditation (*rDo rje rnal 'byor ma'i bdag skyed*) in which the practitioner generates and dissolves an image of her protective deity (*yi dam*), Vajrayoginī. The same deity is called forth twice a month in a special ritual in the monastic assembly. On this occasion, all those who have not completed the obligatory meditation retreat (such as the ethnographer and the younger nuns) are required to leave the assembly.

All but one of the Karsha nuns have completed the solitary three-month retreat of Vajrayoginī.[15] In this concentrated set of visualizations and recitation, the practitioner focuses on, and eventually becomes, the guardian deity. During the retreat a nun does not leave her cell, nor does she receive any visitors except her meditation assistant (*mtshams g.yog*) and her meditation instructor (*mtshams rgan*). For nearly 18 hours a day, she meditates, prostrates, and performs the *maṇḍala* offering. This practice entails the creation and destruction of a tiny three-dimensional structure created of rice, which symbolizes the universe. Except for four breaks for tea and meals, the practitioner spends the entire day focused on the ritual performance of movement, posture, breathing, thinking, sleeping, and rising. Even her sleep is regulated in terms of posture and meditation.[16] Ultimately, these practices aim at the realization of *yoga* (*rnal 'byor*), a "non-duality of action and awareness" which is both the goal and the starting point of the practice.[17] The yogic practitioner unites with the ultimate, primordial nature of existence, which obliterates the conventional duality between mundane and ultimate truth.

Ordination as Collective Transformation: Founding Karsha Nunnery

> Liminality may perhaps be regarded as the Nay to all positive structural assertions, but as in some sense the source of them all, and, more than that, as a realm of pure possibility whence novel configurations of ideas and relations may arise.[18]

For Yeshe and her companions pilgrimage and ordination marked a shift in personal status and served as a catalyst for the collective development of the nunnery. Although they left home as simple renunciants, Yeshe and her companions returned from Tibet as novices with an extraordinary blessing. Their ordination under the third highest Gelugpa hierarch in Tibet (after the Dalai Lama and Panchen Lama) gave them a certain clout and courage in the eyes of their immediate community. In one pilgrimage, they had seen more of the world than most of their relatives would see in a lifetime. On their return, the three nuns had the audacious dream of expanding their community of nuns in the direct shadow of the powerful monastery which had dominated Karsha for centuries.

For nearly two decades, a tiny community of nuns struggled with limited economic resources to found a ritual program. As Yeshe and her companions completed their preliminary practices, they incorporated the abstract truths of impermanence into a bodily habitus of self-denial.[19] And as they visualized the vast, interdependent emptiness of which they were a part, they began to think in broader terms than ordinary village women. To build an assembly hall on the cliff, the nuns needed both a powerful patron and widespread support from the community. Not a single stone in the village could be moved without permission from the village leaders. The nuns were only able to accomplish this remarkable feat due to the initiative and intervention of a charismatic Ladakhi monk who came to live at Karsha monastery.

Geshe Lobzang Zodpa and Vajrayoginī Practice

When Geshe Lobzang Zodpa came to Zangskar in 1972, he gave a series of initiations including Tsongkhapa's *Great Exposition of the Path* (*Lam rim chen mo*) and a Kalachakra initiation (*dus 'khor dbang chen*). In the tradition of scholars from centuries past, the Geshe also wrote a short history of religious establishments in Zangskar while residing at Karsha monastery.[20] His teachings were so powerful that four women renounced lay life and took the five precepts, while the older nuns were ordained as novices (*dge tshul ma*) under the Geshe's tutelage.[21] In the summer of 1975, the Geshe gave the Profound Teachings of Vajrayoginī (*rDo rje rnal 'byor ma'i zab khrid*) to a select group of nuns and monks in Karsha. The Vajrayoginī empowerment is an esoteric rite transmitted orally only to serious initiates who commit themselves to certain precepts and meditations.[22] While only a few monks participated, all of the nuns from Karsha did. As a result of this initiation, the Karsha nuns found both a spiritual practice and their root teacher (*rtsa ba'i bla ma*).

After holding the week-long Vajrayoginī empowerment at the monks' monastery, the Geshe crossed the Karsha gorge to visit the cluster of nuns' cells on the opposite cliff. When he saw the nuns diligently performing their humble practices in the dark, windowless temple with its ancient paintings and crumbling walls, he was deeply moved. The nuns told him how they prepared their tea and meals on a makeshift outdoor hearth, despite blizzards and hailstorms in the winter. They spoke about the difficulty of gathering in a temple they could not call their own, where they were never certain to have access. In response, the Geshe suggested it was time to build a new assembly hall. The nuns spent the next decade converting this vision into reality. While the construction was driven by powerful and persevering women, the catalysts and engineers were men.[23] Before he left Zangskar in 1975, the Geshe urged the nuns to begin collecting rocks from the surrounding hillside. Although the Geshe did not return until two years later, the nuns never gave up their dream of an assembly hall on the site he had selected.

The nuns worked as menial laborers on the site for the next ten years. For two summers, they gathered stones from the surrounding cliff, conveniently littered with the remnants of Karsha's earliest settlement, which dates back to well before the tenth century. In the summer of 1978, when the nuns held the ritual to open the earth (*sa'i cho ga*), the entire congregation of nuns and most senior monks of Karsha monastery were present. After they performed the ritual to mollify local spirits of the earth (*sa bdag, gzhi bdag*), the foundation of the new assembly hall was laid. The construction proceeded slowly, since silt and water had to be hauled from the stream bed far below the clifftop. A monk from Karsha proved indispensable as construction manager, for he bought construction supplies (central beams, glass, wood for framing the windows and doors) from the neighboring district capital of Kargil. He called masons and carpenters from Karsha village, and well-known artisans from the distant monastery of Lingshed. With his initial loan, the nuns began to build, and as the walls took shape, they began to solicit contributions for the work in progress. In gratitude for his assistance, the nuns spun his wool for two winters and helped build him a house in the village. One might say they inadvertently wove this monk into their female company, for he abandoned his monastic robes thereafter. First he married a woman in Karsha and settled into the house the nuns helped build. Later he took a second wife, an ex-nun who left the order to tend his house and sheep in a neighboring village.[24]

After four years of hard labor, the nuns had exhausted their supplies as well as the generosity of villagers who worked largely without pay. Although some of the beams had been donated from neighboring villages, thanks to Geshe Zodpa's solicitations, most had been bought on credit.[25] When funds ran out, several nuns traveled on foot throughout Zangskar and Ladakh to beg for donations. Three nuns who went to the upper Indus valley in Ladakh recall the difficulties they faced, far from kin networks and the natural generosity of their region. Sometimes they were turned away from houses with angry insults and only a cup of roasted barley flour (*rtsam pa*) for their efforts. Since the Ladakhi villagers appeared to have little respect for nuns, they were often refused beds and had to sleep in courtyards under the stars. After several winters of soliciting donations, the nuns sold the barley flour they had earned and returned to Zangskar with a lighter and more useful commodity: cash. Meanwhile other Karsha nuns had been soliciting donations up and down the three major river valleys of Zangskar: Stod, Lungnag, and Sham. At a total cost of nearly 30,000 rupees, the completed nunnery complex included an assembly hall, guest room for visiting dignitaries, winter and summer kitchens, assorted storage rooms, and a bathroom. After 15 years of labor, the wall murals in the assembly hall were painted in the summer of 1990.[26] The finished monastic complex, known as the Land of Oral Accomplishments and Propitiation (*bKa' spyod sgrub gling*), stands as testimony to the perseverance of the remarkable Karsha nuns.

Evolution of the Ritual Calendar at Karsha Nunnery

After their ordination in Tibet, the founding nuns had the courage and ability to take on greater ritual responsibilities. Instead of gathering only once a year, they began to gather to take the eight Mahāyāna precepts (*theg chen gso sbyong*) every month. This was suggested by an elderly monk from Karsha, Meme Khachen, who had lived in Tibet for many years. If they had not been to Tibet themselves, the nuns might not have merited the attention of this monk or had much success gathering donations of food and cash for their rituals. Angmo's family gave each nun five rupees as principal, to start monthly prayers on the full moon of every month. The rupees were pooled as a fund on which to collect interest, while supplies for the actual ceremony were contributed by individual nuns. At first, each nun brought 1 kg butter, 5 kg roasted barley flour, a handful of tea, and a pinch of salt. They borrowed the cooking implements – a fat copper pot, a brass ladle, and tea strainer – from a village temple at the base of the cliff. Eventually, as membership grew, the original fund was abandoned. Now that the nunnery had 20 members, a rotation system was organized; one by one, the nuns took turns sponsoring the various rituals.[27] At present, one or two nuns serve as stewards (*gnyer pa*) and sponsor the tri-monthly ritual assemblies at the nunnery by soliciting the requisites from their families.[28]

Many years after her pilgrimage to Tibet, Angmo decided to initiate a Great Prayer Festival (*smon lam chen mo*) modeled upon the one that impressed her so greatly in Lhasa. Lhasa's Great Prayer Festival had been imitated throughout Tibet and its borderlands, though none could match the original celebration in Lhasa, where until 1959, 21,000 monks maintained law and order for an entire month each year.[29] At Karsha monastery today, the Great Prayer Festival involves 150 monks and over 440 residents of Karsha village, plus hundreds of donors from near and far who come to celebrate for nearly a month. When the nuns first initiated their own Great Prayer Festival, they invited monks to lead it and to teach them the ceremonies and prayers. By the late 1960s, Yeshe and her companions no longer needed assistance from the monks and began to organize the festival on their own. The nunnery's Great Prayer Festival has become the single largest nunnery-based festival in Zangskar and it attracts hundreds of donors every year.[30]

As the nunnery's largest ritual expense of the year, each Great Prayer Festival requires year-long preparation. Twelve months before the festival begins, one nun is chosen to be steward (*gnyer pa*). Each nun must take her turn in the dreaded position, which requires her to feast her colleagues at the nunnery for nearly a month. In the spring, the steward collects dung and firewood to feed the cooking fires during the festival. In summer, she travels to Zangskar's high pasture camps (*'brog sa*) to collect cheese and butter (*dkar slong*) from the shepherds. During the fall harvest and all winter, she begs for alms (*bsod snyoms*) of grain and flour. In early spring, she gives a series of "begging beers" (*slong chang*) in nearby villages to request donations in cash or kind. In each village she selects, every household may send one adult to the party, where barley beer (*chang*) is the only fare. As the evening wears on and the guests become sufficiently inebriated, the sponsoring nun or her male relative solicits donations. Every guest must stand up and orally proclaim the exact gift he or she will make to the upcoming festival. In return, the steward hosts the sponsors when they deliver the promised goods during the festival.

Membership in the nunnery involves serving in a number of ritual offices, which the nuns take up by turns. Each nun serves as conch blower (*dung ma*), ritual assistant (*chos g.yog*), sacristan (*dkon gnyer*), assistant chant master (*dbu chung*), and chant master (*dbu mdzad*), a post that doubles as head nun. Except for the sacristan, all these positions involve a three-year tenure. The ritual assistant is responsible for making the dough and butter sculptures, offering cakes, and other aspects of the ritual altar whenever there is a collective ritual. The main ingredients of the ritual sculptures (butter, roasted barley flour, milk, beer, buttermilk, yogurt, saffron and other ritual spices) are provided by the sponsoring villager. The ritual assistant must procure auspicious spices such as *bzang drug* which are required for esoteric rites. She takes care of the nunnery's ritual items: the colored powders for dying butter sculptures, the woodblock and orange powder used to create the Vajrayoginī *maṇḍala*, plates for tossing *gtor ma*, butter lamps, offering bowls, and other ritual paraphenalia. The door-keeper must go at dawn and dusk to the assembly hall to light butter lamps, refill offering bowls, and offer a litany of sounds and smells to the protective spirits: juniper incense, a ritual shake of the bell (*dril bu*) and hand drum (*da ma ru*), a quick crescendo of beats on a large drum (*rnga*).

The most important post at the nunnery is that of head nun and chant master (*dbu mdzad*). This post is filled by each nun in turn, in order of seniority. According to the seating order, based on when she joined the assembly, each nun must serve her turn as chant master for a term of three years. Prior to serving as chantmaster, she spends three years training as assistant chant master, memorizing chants, and learning the innumerable details of running a religious institution of 20 women. The chant master has memorized scores of texts which she can recite on call, and bears sole responsibility for the nunnery's collective resources, works and projects, ritual calendar, and annual investments or expenditures. The chant master combines the roles of C. E. O., principal shareholder, and office manager. When necessary, she even prepares the tea or meal requested by a donor before leading the necessary chants of a given rite. Although final adjudication of disputes and any disciplinary measures are decided by the abbot or by a unanimous vote of the entire assembly (*dge 'dun*), she must also handle the internal politics and negotiate complaints registered by other nuns.

The Economic Basis of Female Renunciation

As a collective, the nunnery owns two small fields which yield a crop of 80–100 kg of grain per year, depending on the climate and on the crop sown (wheat, peas, or barley). The communal grain is used to feed visiting guests or the nuns on days of communal labor such as repairing the walls and path at the nunnery compound after each winter's damage. When the next year's seed and other expenses have been subtracted, each nun receives a lump sum of eight kg of grain every three years.[31] The grain is distributed once every three years when the position of head nun shifts. At that time, a collective audit is conducted by the head nun in front of the entire community of nuns. All outlying accounts, loans, and expenses are cleared before the new incoming head nun takes office. Two nuns serve as field stewards (*zhing gi gnyer pa*) each year to organize the tilling of the nunnery's fields. Karsha villagers are not obliged to participate in this process, although individual nuns may ask a male relative to assist with plowing in early spring, a task customarily forbidden to women. At that time the two stewards smooth the furrows; during spring and summer they are responsible for weeding and watering the fields. In the autumn half of the nuns are selected to perform the harvest, threshing, and winnowing.

The nunnery is relatively impoverished compared to most monastic establishments in Zangskar. Whereas Karsha monastery annually collects nearly 10,000 kg of grain and 450 kg of butter in tithes, and has a herd of 30 or more cows and crossbreeds, Karsha Nunnery does not own a single cow nor does it collect an ounce of grain in taxes or rent. Even butter lamps in the assembly hall are filled by the largesse of the sacristan (*dkon gnyer*) and other nuns, rather than from random village donations. The nunnery owns 40 goats, which are farmed out to the 20 member nuns who keep them at a relative's home. Twice a year, during the Vajrayoginī burnt offering[32] and at the springtime Thousand Offerings of an Auspicious Era,[33] every nun delivers to the nunnery a kilo of butter, which will be used to fill the substantial number of butter lamps required on these occasions. The rest of the butter produced by the goats is kept by the nun's family in exchange for their daily care of the livestock. When a nun passes away or leaves the nunnery, the two goats must be returned to the collective (or other goats as substitutes if the original goats have died). Unlike the monks' monastery, Karsha Nunnery does not receive obligatory loads of dung or thistles from surrounding villagers. Every year each nun must collect four or five loads of thistle wood and two loads of dung as communal cooking fuel for the nunnery's hearth.

The effect of the nunnery's meager economic resources is twofold. First, collective rituals only occur when nuns solicit sufficient donations. Second, individual nuns must seek their own subsistence. The nunnery performs *ad hoc* rites for villagers, who provide the ritual expenses in the interest of making merit. Such rites include commemorative prayers for the deceased within the 49-day period between death and rebirth (*bar do*) and readings from selected texts.[34] Individual nuns collect donations to sponsor all regular rituals on a rotating scheme, yet the nunnery's calendar clearly is limited by the skill of the stewards and the generosity of the villagers. For instance, the duration of the Great Prayer Festival each year depends on the sponsoring nun's fundraising abilities. A successful sponsor will hold the festival for 20 days or more, while a less proficient nun may only manage 15 days. As the nunnery has grown more prominent, the duration and donations for the Great Prayer Festival have increased tremendously.[35] The sharp increase in village donations over the last five years may reflect rising living standards or the nunnery's increased status. Since 1991, Karsha Nunnery has received some foreign sponsorship from the Ganden Choling Center in Toronto, Canada. The funds were pooled collectively to build a classroom, and initiate a modern study curriculum in Tibetan grammar, math, and English. The nuns also bought butter, tea, salt, and rations to serve a simple meal daily and tea during ritual assemblies held between December and May each year.

Although such foreign money has supplemented the nunnery's capital costs in terms of ritual expenses, it remains an insufficient endowment. In short, money is no substitute for the basic elements of Zangskari subsistence: butter, barley, and fuel. While the male monastery is maintained by extensive relations of patronage and privilege, the nunnery must rely on the generosity of its members and their families. A nun's life is a vocation, but not an occupation. Most nuns still descend to the village most days to perform domestic chores in exchange for their daily bread. They remain caught between two worlds – esoteric ritual and mundane production – which are essential to Zangskari livelihood. Nuns are pushed and pulled between nunnery and household, but can depend fully on neither.

A Fragile Economy of Merit

The hippo's feeble steps may err
In compassing material ends
While the True Church need never stir
To gather in its dividends. . . .[36]

Religious practice is fraught with the uncertainty of subsistence. While Zangskari monasteries are supported by sharecroppers and endowments, most nunneries are either landless or forced to till their small land holdings by themselves. The nunneries do not receive grain tithes, but are supported mainly by voluntary donations. The stark contrast between the landed wealth of the monasteries and the few token fields owned by the nunneries is testimony to centuries of Zangskari patronage and a belief in the innate superiority of the monks as ritual mediators. This economic disparity has magnified the differences between the male and female establishments. While monks belong to an endowed institution which guarantees their future, nuns are part of institution which demands loyalty but cannot guarantee survival. Thus, while monks are urged to sever their domestic obligations, nuns are bound to hearth and home. Due to more patronage, monks may pursue higher studies, which legitimize their status as ritual officiants, while nuns do not receive higher education nor any advanced ritual instruction. It should not surprise us that monks are called upon to serve as ritual officiants more often than nuns. While both monastics may practice similar visualizations and meditations, their public roles are dramatically different. The significant advances of Yeshe and her colleagues in the latter half of this century bode well for the status of nuns in the next millennium. Indeed, several new nunneries have been founded recently in Ladakh, while membership at Zangskari and Ladakhi nunneries continues to grow and may eventually outpace the declining membership at monasteries. Centuries of disproportionate patronage cannot be undone overnight, yet the dedication of a few nuns has altered the religious landscapes in one Himalayan region beyond their, and our, expectations.

Notes

1 I thank all of the Zangskari nuns whose infinite kindness and limitless patience have provided a living picture of the *bodhisattva* of compassion upon whom they meditate. I especially thank Sarah Levine, Karma Lekshe Tsomo, Jan Willis, Michael Aris, Nur Yalman, Arthur Kleinman, Henry Osmaston, and John Crook for conversations and correspondences relating to my research in Zangskar. My fieldwork between 1991 and 1997 was supported by the Jacob Javits Foundation, the Mellon Foundation, and Harvard's Department of Anthropology. I have used the standard Wylie system of transliteration for Tibetan terms.

2 Zangskar is a subdistrict of the Indian State of Jammu and Kashmir, which lies amidst the Greater Himalayan range. With an area of 7,000 square km., Zangskar is slightly smaller than Sikkim. It is inhabited by only 12,000 people, making it one of the least populated sub-districts in India.

3 Virginia Woolf, *An Unwritten Novel. In Monday or Tuesday: Eight Stories* (New York: Harcourt, Brace and Co., 1921), p. 19.

4 See Kim Gutschow, "A Novice Ordination in Tibet: The Rhetoric and Reality of Female Monasticism in Zangskar, Northwest India," in *Women Changing Contemporary Buddhism*, ed. Ellison Findly (Boston: Wisdom Books, 1999), as well as several of the contributions in this volume on the politics of ordination. The debate about reviving full ordination for women in Sri Lanka is addressed in Tessa Bartholomeusz, *Women Under the Bō Tree: Buddhist Nuns in Sri Lanka* (Cambridge: Cambridge University Press, 1994); Richard Gombrich and Gananath Obeyesekere, *Buddhism Transformed: Religious Change in Sri Lanka* (Princeton: Princeton Unversity Press, 1988); and Karma Lekshe Tsomo, *Śākyadhitā: Daughters of the Buddha* (Ithaca: Snow Lion Publications, 1988), as well as the newsletter *Śākyadhitā: International Association of Buddhist Women.* Hanna Havnevik describes the pilgrimages and ordination of notable Tibetan nuns in *Tibetan Buddhist Nuns* (Oslo: Norwegian University Press, 1990) and "On Pilgimage for 40 Years in the Himalayas: The Female Lama Jetsun Lochen Rinpoche's (1865–1951) Quest for Sacred Sites, "*Pilgrimage in Tibet*, ed. Alex McKay (London: Curzon Press, 1998), pp. 85–107.

5 *sTud thung, sham thabs, chos gos.*

6 The proportions of the robes are ritually specified. The upper robe (*gzan gos*, *nam za*) has 25 lengthwise folds and nine widthwise folds. The outer yellow robe (*chos gos*) has seven folds lengthwise and 2.5 folds widthwise. Both these robes are 6 x 3 cubits in size. The

lower robe (*sham thabs, thang gos*) has 5 folds lengthwise and 2.5 folds widthwise. It is 5 x 2 cubits, but can be shortened to 1.5 cubits.

7 In theory, a nun need only do 100,000 repetitions of each meditational practice; however, she performs an additional 11,111 of each practice in case her attention has lapsed at any point in the process.

8 *Bodhicitta* denotes the state of mind in which practitioners seek enlightenment for the sake of all sentient beings. According to Lhalungpa, it is "at once an enlightening attitude and a state of awareness, each of which is both a means to the goal and the goal itself." Lobsang Lhalungpa, *The Life of Milarepa* (Boston: Shambhala, 1984), p. xv.

9 Yeshe said: "*Khong ba tshang ma ltogs ri yong mkhan po'i [dug bsngal] nga la yong zhig. Nga'i skyid po tshang ma khong ba cha zhig. De khong gos lag med mkhan po, yod mkhan po tshang ma yong zhig. Nga zha dag sa ja thung byes, te gir za byes: te 'o do tshang ma khong ba za byes yong zhig. Rang ltogs na sgrigs byes. De gos lag med na drang mo yong na sgrigs bsam byes.*"

10 Yeshe simply stated: "*De snga mo mig phye, 'di bla ma dkon mchog la thugs rje, bla ma sangs rgyas dang rtsa ba'i bla ma thugs rje, nga ma shi, nga zur mo me rag, gzugs po bde mo rag, tho res snga mo nga rang rnam shes yong ni mi yong, tho res snga mo lang byes yong ni mi yong, nga shi nas, ci byo en, bla ma dkon mchog gi thugs rje, shi cha nas, khams bzang yin nog, nga ja rgan mo gun.*"

11 See Donald Lopez, *Religions of Tibet in Practice* (Princeton: Princeton University Press, 1997), pp. 421–41, for a translation of a part of Tsongkhapa's text.

12 Michael Diener, et. al., eds., *The Encyclopedia of Eastern Philosophy and Religion* (Boston: Shambhala, 1994), pp. 296. Note that Samanthabadra (*Kun tu bzang po*) is "venerated as the protector of all those who teach the Dharma and is regarded as an embodiment of the wisdom of essential sameness, i.e., the insight into the unity of sameness and difference." Ibid., p. 377.

13 Abbi Yeshe explained: "*Sems rnam par dag pa zer nas sems bzang po, rgyal ba, sems dkar po. Gzhan mi sems pa ngan pa mi bcos. Sems pa nag po mi bcos zer te zer re nog. Sems rnam par dag pa ni don 'di yin. Phad byang chub sems zer nas, sems drang po, mi gnod pa mi bcos, khra dog mi byos, zhe sdang nga rgyal mi bcos, mi nor na thob byes mi bsam. De rang chos phad bzhugs nang la pha ma 'gro ba rigs drug sems can thams cad dag pa sangs rgyas zhing du skyes zhig zer byes.*"

14 *rDo rje rnal 'byor ma'i brgyud.*

15 Retreat practices involve four elements (*bsnyen pa bzhi*): (1) a complete ritualization of all movements and posture of the body (*lus kyi bsnyen pa*); (2) the counting of *mantras* (*grangs kyi bsnyen pa*); (3) visualizing and dissolving oneself into the deity (*mtshan ma'i bsnyen pa*); and (4) the generation and (ultimately) completion stages of the yoga practiced (*sems brtan gyi bsnyen pa*).

16 The yoga of sleep specifies that the practitioner should sleep with her head to the north and facing west where the *ḍākinīs* reside.

17 Cited from Herbert Guenther, *Tibetan Buddhism in Western Perspective* (Boston: Shambhala, 1989), p. 85. Vajrayoginī practice is described in Geshe Kelsang Gyatso, *Guide to Dakini Land: The Highest Yoga Tantra Practice of Buddha Vajrayogini* (London: Tharpa Publications, 1996); and Chögyam Trungpa, "Sacred Outlook: The Vajrayogini Shrine and Practice," in *The Silk Route and the Diamond Path: Esoteric Buddhist Art on the Trans-Himalayan Trade Routes*, Deborah Klimburg Salter, ed. (Los Angeles: UCLA Art Council, 1982), pp. 226–42.

18 Victor Turner, *The Ritual Process: Structure and Anti-Structure* (Ithaca: Cornell University Press, 1969), p. 97. Monasticism may well exemplify the liminal state Turner so exhaustively catalogued. Total obedience is required towards ritual norms and sacred instruction, kinship rights are suspended, and uniform clothing is adopted. Novices are expected to submit to a certain suffering, simplicity, silence, unselfishness, sexlessness,

anonymity, homogeneity, and equality. Vows to fast, maintain lifelong celibacy, and eschew romantic attachments to others require absolute adherence. Ibid., p. 106.

19 I refer to Bourdieu's definition of habitus as "the durably installed generative principle of regulated improvisations . . . history turned into nature (and denied as such)." P. Bourdieu, *Outline of a Theory of Practice*, trans. by R. Nice (Cambridge: Cambridge University Press, 1977), p. 78.

20 dGe bshes Zod pa and Ngag dbang Tshe ring Shags po, *Zangs dkar gyi rgyal rabs dang chos 'byung* [The Royal Chronicles and Religious History of Zangskar] (Leh: Ladakh Buddha Vihar, 1979).

21 Although their vows forbid them from killing, most Zangskari monastics do eat meat. They justify this by eating meat which was slaughtered by passing Muslims or meat from an animal that has died a "natural" death, such as falling off a cliff or dying suddenly in its stall.

22 The Geshe had received the Vajrayoginī empowerment from the head of Ganden Monastery, who had transmitted the same initiation to his foremost pupil, the 14th Dalai Lama.

23 Compare Sherry Ortner's descriptions of the founding of a Sherpa nunnery in Nepal which indicate that although local nuns initiated the fundraising, they first needed to secure the legitimation of a male monastic, the head of Tengboche monastery. "The Founding of the First Sherpa Nunnery and the Problem of Women as an Analytic Category," *Feminist Revisions: What Has Been and Might Be*, ed. V. Patraka and L. Tilly (Ann Arbor: University of Michigan Women's Study Program, 1983), pp. 93–134; and *High Religion: A Cultural and Political History of Sherpa Buddhism* (Princeton: Princeton University Press, 1989).

24 The nuns still quip: "We carried every rock in Tandzin's new house on our back. Maybe we should call the house *bcu gcig zhal bla brang* instead. . . ." They pun by calling Tandzin's private house a *labrang*, a term ordinarily reserved for monastic institutions founded by important monks. Unlike monasteries, most nunneries do not have a *labrang*, since they have such small endowments.

25 After the Geshe had made his pleas, the nuns held so-called "begging beer" parties (*slong chang*) in three nearby villages in order to solicit wood for the subsidiary beams and wooden lattices used in constructing traditional Zangskari roofs. The nuns carried this wood on their backs for up to 30 km. to their construction site, as there was still no vehicular transport within Zangskar in those days.

26 These murals include the Buddha Śākyamuni, the 16 *arhats*, Tsongkhapa and his two disciples, the lineage holders for the nun's Vajrayoginī practice, and a group of protectors (*chos skyong*), including Phyag na rdo rje, 'Jigs byed, mGon po phyag drug pa, and rDo rje rnal 'byor ma.

27 I compare the ritual calendars of the nunnery and monastery in Karsha village in "Unfocussed Merit Making In Zangskar: A Socio-Economic Account of Karsha Nunnery," *Tibet Journal* 22, no. 2 (1998): 30–58; and "An Economy of Merit: Women and Buddhist Monasticism in Zangskar, Northwest India."

28 Turn by turn, a single nun serves as sponsor for the rituals held on the 10th and 25th days of each Tibetan month, while two nuns serve as sponsors for the more extensive rite on the 15th. Each ritual roughly demands: 1.3 kg of butter for tea and butter lamps, 7 kg of roasted barley flour for the communal offering cakes (*tshog*), 10 kg of wheat flour for the breads (except on the tenth when no breads are served), one bottle of beer or buttermilk as leavening agent for the breads, a handful of salt, two handfuls of loose green tea, and a plateful of *tshogs zas*, which is an assortment of fried dough, sweets, biscuits, and dried meat to go along with the offering cakes.

29 According to Li An-Che, at Labrang Monastery in Amdo, the Great Prayer Festival of 1940 involved a population of 3,600 monks who consumed 45 yaks, 6,000 kg of rice,

10,000 kg of butter, and 12,000 kg of raisins. The total cost of running the festival for 15 days was estimated at $46,710 in 1940 terms. Li An-Che, Li, *History of Tibetan Religion: A Study in the Field* (Beijing: New World Press, 1994).

30 In the course of the Great Prayer Festival, both the monastery and the nunnery hold their annual fasting ritual (*smyung gnas*). A comparison of the economic outlay for the monastery's rite versus the nunnery's rite may illuminate the disparity between the two institutions. In 1994, the monastery's fast consumed 1,500 kg grain for the beer, 7,000 rupees worth of meat, 930 kg butter, 1,700 kg local flour, 700 kg baking flour, 400 kg rice, and 2,000 flat breads. In contrast, the nunnery's fast used only 60 kg of grain for beer, 1,000 rupees worth of meat, 31 kg of butter, 200 kg local flour, 20 kg baking flour, 20 kg rice, and 100 flat breads.

31 Karsha Nunnery fares worse than a comparably sized Sherpa nunnery described by Fürer-Haimendorf and Aziz. The fields of Tashi Gonpa provided 2,025 kg of grain annually which was divided amongst the 23 nuns and their teacher. Each nun received about 84 kg of grain per year, equivalent to 1/5 of her annual grain consumption. The 2.6 kg of grain which Karsha nuns receive per year from the collective is a pittance in contrast. Fürer-Haimendorf, "A Nunnery in Nepal," *Kailash* 4, no. 2 (1976): 127; and Barbara Aziz, "Views From the Monastery Kitchen," *Kailash* 4, no. 2 (1976): 155–67.

32 *rDo rje rnal 'byor ma'i sbyin sreg*, held on the tenth day of the twelfth month.

33 *bsKal bzang sTong mchod*, held on the 15th day of the fourth month.

34 *'Bum, sGrol chog, sGrol ma, rNam rgyal stong mchod*, and so on.

35 The length of the festival has increased from its initial run of five days to an average of 20 days in recent years. The total monetary donations (*'gyed*) a single nun earns in the course of the entire Great Prayer Festival has increased sharply. In 1995, each nun received 206 rupees, while five years earlier, she may have earned only 100 rupees. More than ten years ago, she might have earned 30 rupees, while 30 years ago she earned less than 10 rupees.

36 T. S. Eliot, "The Hippopotamus." The hippo in Eliot's poem serves as an apt metaphor for the community of nuns, who may appear substantial but are indeed quite fragile. While the monastery receives its donations from far afield, the nuns must strike out far and wide on foot to build and maintain their monastic community.

CHAPTER EIGHTEEN

Born Buddhist is Not Enough

Tashi Zangmo

I feel very fortunate to have been born in a Buddhist country where Buddhism is very much alive and valued. The Royal Government of Bhutan is trying its best to give equal opportunities for both women and men to get an education and Buddhism continues to flourish throughout the country. Nevertheless, there is a strong preconception in Bhutanese society that profound religious and philosophical studies are meant only for men. The nuns lag far behind in traditional Buddhist learning, to say nothing of the laywomen. The monks receive pride of place in the monasteries and Buddhist institutes of the land.

My vision is to serve nuns and laywomen who wish to receive a traditional Buddhist education. With this vision in mind, I went to Vārāṇasi in 1987 to study Buddhist philosophy at the Central Institute of Higher Buddhist Studies. I was the first woman from Bhutan to study Buddhist philosophy there. When I arrived, there were eight Tibetan women students. All of them had been studying since 1985. Since then, all of these women have completed their studies, and some have gone on to do graduate studies, too, usually in philosophy. They are now serving as teachers in Tibetan refugee schools in settlements all over India.

There is a quota for women students at the Central Institute of Higher Buddhist Studies. Only a certain number of women are accepted each year. Originally the Institute was only for monks, but gradually this has changed. Now that a new hostel has been built, the number of women accepted has grown. Except for one other Bhutanese student, who joined the year after I did, all the women students are Tibetan. Although many of us are laywomen, at the Institute we live like nuns.

The curriculum at the Institute focuses on philosophy, both Indian and Tibetan. The courses are taught in Tibetan, but we study Sanskrit and other languages as well. Learning all these languages was a struggle for me and I had to race to keep up. Because the courses were very intensive, I learned many new things that I otherwise would have missed in my life. This fortunate opportunity, not easily gained, taught me many useful things.

I learned that being a Buddhist means much more than simply one's cultural identity. Recognizing this, I feel, was a great accomplishment. My eyes were opened in many new directions and I learned to be a more responsive human being.

I come from a very religious family, and both of my parents are serious Buddhist practitioners. This background, especially the strong influence of my mother, fueled my own strong inclination to further my spiritual education. Until I was sent to school, I received my spiritual education at home. My father taught me how to pray, how to memorize the texts, and instructed me on the merits of practicing the precepts.

As a child, I did not realize the very limited opportunities girls had to receive a Buddhist education. As I grew older, my interest in advancing my studies increased. I especially wished to immerse myself in the study of Buddhist philosophy, but the people in my community did not understand my longing. They did not even know that the subject of Buddhist philosophy existed, much less that a woman could be worthy of studying it.

Women in Bhutan today have a much better chance of getting a systematic Buddhist education than when I left for Vārāṇasi. There are hopes that a traditional learning institution for women will open its doors in the near future. There is already a traditional grammar school for female students, which began in 1995. More and more women in traditional societies are beginning to recognize the importance of understanding one's own religious heritage on a deeper level. We recognize that we must do our share in preserving our culture and realize that we have some catching up to do. As one of my Tibetan teachers in Vārāṇasi used to say, "We must chew our own share, even if it is stone. We musn't touch another's share, even if it is cheese."

Things have begun to change for Buddhist women, however. Perhaps now is the time for women to grab our own share. Especially because Buddhism is a path for all sentient beings, how can gender distinctions persist? Buddhism is not only for men. Buddhism is something to be shared, regardless of gender differences.

Fortunately, in 1985 the Central Institute of Higher Tibetan Studies finally decided to accept women. I stumbled upon this information while I was working in offices at the Bhutan Government's Planning Commission and Ministry of Agriculture in 1987. The same day I heard that the policy had changed and the Institute was accepting women, I resigned from my job and left for India.

Even though I was delighted that my wishes had been fulfilled, I soon discovered there were also problems. The policy of admitting women was just a trial and the eight women candidates were applying along with 250 men. There were no separate facilities for female students and we lived in temporary housing until proper facilities could be built. In our temporary quarters, the monk professors observed our every move. We were constantly cautioned to behave in an exemplary manner and warned that any misstep would not only mean our own dismissal, but jeopardize future admissions for women.

For me, the most difficult problem was language. I did not speak a word of Tibetan when I arrived. I had to begin at the beginning and dive in with all the diligence I could muster. I was determined to fulfill my dream of studying philosophy. At that time everybody thought it was impossible for a woman to study philosophy and found my blind faith peculiar. I ignored their opinions and proceeded to accomplish what I wished.

I experienced great difficulty gleaning the deeper hidden meanings in the special, secret teachings, especially the Vajrayāna teachings. Because only *khenpos* (highly qualified ordained monks) impart these teachings, many communications problems arose. Among Asian women, the social norm is to believe everything a teacher might say. Penetrating questions are avoided. But in these highly esoteric studies, many curious questions are asked. Because of their different social conditioning, Western women are less likely to feel inhibited about questioning monks and teachers, and less likely to accept everything they hear. But for us young Asian women, it required tremendous fortitude.

It is my great hope that nuns and interested laywomen will excel in these teachings and, in turn, impart them to others. In this way, many eager women will have an opportunity for open dialogue. Although there may already be nuns accomplished in these studies, so far they are unknown to me.

The crucial question in my personal narrative – and the narratives of many Asian women, especially Tibetans and Bhutanese – is simply: Shall we continue to accept the limitations that society places upon us? Shall we blame others for withholding opportunities from us? Or shall we step forward and take those opportunities for ourselves so that we can determine our own future?

My suggestion, confirmed through my own experience, is that no matter what others tell you or who may discourage you, you must believe in yourself. If you have faith, trust in yourself and keep going, somewhere, somehow, you will reach your goal. If I had been aware of all the difficulties and limitations I would face at the institute, I might not have been able to proceed. I received neither moral nor financial support. Many pressures – social, cultural, and from family – were pressing in on me from all sides. But I am happy I persevered, despite all the hindrances. We must create support for other women who wish to continue their studies, so that others will not have to endure these hardships.

BUDDHIST WOMEN IN HAWAI'I

CHAPTER NINETEEN

Mary Foster

The First Hawaiian Buddhist

Patricia Lee Masters and Karma Lekshe Tsomo

Mūlagandhakuṭi Vihāra in Sārnāth commemorates Buddha Śākyamuni's first teachings, "the turning of the wheel of Dharma." When we first visited this exquisite temple, we each had a similar experience. As residents of Hawai'i, we were astonished to see a marble plaque to the right of the door that read:

Mulagandhakuti Vihara
erected by The Anagarika Dharmapala
Founder and General Secretary of
The Maha Bodhi Society
with the generous help of Mrs. Mary Elizabeth Foster
of Honolulu and others
on the site where
Our Lord Buddha
promulgated the teachings
2500 years ago.

The name "Mary Foster" is familiar to everyone who has visited Foster Botanical Gardens in Honolulu. Each of us had spent hours gazing at a large bronze statue of the Buddha placed in the center of a tranquil arbor and had also attended Buddhist weddings conducted at this spot.

When we visited Sārnāth together in November 1996, we were curious to discover more about the *vihāra*'s connection with Mary Foster.[1] We entered the temple and greeted the young monk working at a small table next to the altar with folded hands, with "Ayubowan." Startled to hear himself addressed in Sinhala, he came out to greet us. After the formalities, we queried him on the connection between the temple and Mary Foster of Hawai'i. He related the story of how Mary Foster, a native Hawaiian woman and a follower of Theosophy, had met the great Buddhist teacher Anagarika Dharmapala as he passed through Honolulu on his way back to Sri Lanka after the Parliament of World Religions held in Chicago in 1893. His ship, the *U.S.S. Oceanic*, made a one-day stop in Honolulu Harbor, and he and Mary Foster spent the day in conversation about Buddhist meditation practices, ethics, and Hawaiian spirituality. This brief meeting was to be the beginning of a long and fruitful relationship between the two, and the opening of new vistas for Mary Elizabeth Foster.

Elites and Resistance: Hawai'i in the 1890s

To understand Mary Foster better, it is useful to draw a picture of the social and political climate of Hawai'i in the late 1800s. The year she and Dharmapala met, 1893, was a year of devastating changes in the Hawaiian Islands, with the illegal overthrow of the Hawaiian monarchy and the imprisonment of Queen Lili'uokalani.[2] Resistance to American and European social and economic domination bubbled under the surface of supposed compliance and acceptance. One result of that resistance was the development of an underground religious organization called Ho'omana Na'auao, comprised primarily of native Hawaiian *ali'i* (nobility) and a group of Euroamerican supporters.[3] Mary Foster was an important member of this group, which combined Christianity and Hawaiian spirituality and was searching for an identity that reflected the shared understandings of the members. It was spearheaded by a Dr. Auguste Marques, a prominent physician and member of the Territorial government.

Mary Elizabeth Mikahala Robinson Foster, born September 21, 1844, was herself part Hawaiian royalty, a descendant of the *ali'i* of Maui on the side of her mother, Rebecca Prever Robinson. She was the eldest child of James Robinson, a shipwrecked Englishman who became one of Honolulu's most prominent shipbuilders. Although Mary was raised under the watchful gaze of Christian missionary relatives, she turned away from the dominant Christian belief system to explore Theosophy, her own native Hawaiian beliefs, and eventually Buddhism.

Exactly what transpired between Mary and Anagarika Dharmapala in 1893 is unknown, but this shipboard meeting was to change both their lives forever. We know that Dharmapala offered her a reading from the *Visuddhimagga*, a text with useful advice on how to control negative emotions. This fateful encounter inspired her to support his work for the next 40 years. She became his primary and most faithful patron and friend.

Spiritualism in Hawai'i

The spiritualist movements that emerged in Hawai'i in the late 1800s were part of a larger movement that began on the east coast of the United States among intellectuals, artists, and naturalists. Some of the key figures associated with this movement were Sir Edwin Arnold, Madame Helena Petrovna Blavatsky, Colonel Henry Steel Olcott, Henry David Thoreau, Ralph Waldo Emerson, and Walt Whitman. One purpose of the movement was to address major philosophical issues of the time, notably the relationships between religion, science, and technology. It also offered alternatives to the dominant Christian discourse. Some groups, such as the Theosophical Society, were instrumental in the introduction of Asian philosophies to America and Europe. Ironically, through the work of Olcott and Blavatsky in particular, the Theosophical Society had a far-reaching impact in the revitalization of Buddhism in Asia.[4]

In Hawai'i, related types of spiritualism began to grow. At least in part, these developments were a response to the attempts of New England missionaries to ban the Hawaiian language, indigenous religious beliefs, and cultural practices in the 1820s. The Christian missionaries who settled in Hawai'i were interested in reproducing the rigid boundaries, dogmas, and religious categories they had brought with them from Europe and the United States. These exclusivistic religious traditions and categories stood in contrast to the eclecticism of local Hawaiian and Asian customs. Among the diverse spiritualist groups that arose in Hawai'i in response to Christian conversion efforts were the Theosophical Society, the Anthroposophical Society, Ho'omana Na'auao (the Hawaiian-Christian group mentioned above), and the Baha'i movement. A subtext of these developments and their later bonding together was a more or less subversive critique of the dominant Christian socio-religious structures that had been superimposed upon the Hawaiians by outsiders.

Another reason for the development of such groups was the marginalization of Asian and Pacific peoples by Christian missionaries and Euro-American political elites. Chinese and Japanese laborers who continued their native religious practices on the plantations were perceived as alien and threatening to Christian missionary activities. "Whites must create a form of government through which they can rule the natives, Chinese, Japanese, and Portuguese in order to prevent being 'snowed under,'" said the scion of one missionary family.[5] On the plantations, Christian missionaries attempted to convert Chinese and Japanese laborers, but even if they converted, these workers were forced to worship in locations separate from white worshippers. This had the effect of rekindling interest in Buddhism among many plantation workers; they used the opportunity to revive their Buddhist beliefs, albeit cloaked in Christian trappings. As the workers were exposed to Christianity and its methodologies, a Christian veneer – complete with hymnals, pews, and Sunday services – was gradually appropriated by Asian plantation workers to lend legitimacy to their own Buddhist belief systems.[6]

The Theosophical Movement

The Theosophical Society was founded by Helena Petrovna Blavatsky and Henry Steel Olcott in New York in 1875. It relocated to India in 1880 due to opposition from Christian groups who labeled it blasphemous and dangerous. Theosophy combined elements of Buddhism, science, and the occult. According to one writer, it "offered solutions to two important challenges to religion in the modern world: the need to harmonize conflicting religious belief systems and to integrate spiritual belief with science and technology."[7] The problem of harmonizing conflicting religious belief systems arose, or came into greater prominence, with the arrival of immigrant groups who brought new religious and philosophical belief systems to the Americas from Europe and Asia. The problem of integrating religion and science led some to reject religion altogether, but that created a spiritual vacuum that spiritualist traditions spontaneously filled. There are historical as well as philosophical reasons for this trend, as Rick Fields notes: "Spiritualism occupied a central place in post-Civil War America, where it not only soothed the grief of bereaved relatives, but also gave assurance that there was, in fact, a world beyond death – a belief which science, with its insistence on tangible evidence, had called into serious question, and which religion, in its reliance on dogma and form, had failed to defend convincingly."[8]

What Theosophy offered was the premise that truth is to be found in all religious belief systems, that among the traditional world religions and the various articulations of spirituality, there is a universal truth from which each draws and which each expresses in its own unique way. The primary objective of the Theosophical Society, enunciated by Colonel Olcott at the founding meeting of the Society on November 17, 1875, was "to collect and diffuse knowledge of the laws that govern the universe"[9] and "to study the ancient and modern religions, philosophies and sciences, and the demonstrations of the importance of such study; and to investigate the unexplained laws of nature and the psychical powers latent in man."[10]

When Blavatsky met Olcott she was critical of the materialistic tendency of American spiritualism, which she felt failed to recognize the philosophical truths behind the appearance of occult phenomena. As sources for her eclectic, more philosophically grounded approach, Blavatsky drew from the Masons, the Vedas, Sinhalese Buddhist monks, and information that she claimed to have channeled from certain "Divine Masters," or spiritually evolved "Adepts," in India and Tibet. Although Blavatsky drew significantly from Buddhist ideas and went so far as to become the first Westerner to publicly take refuge in Theravāda Buddhism, her universalistic approach ranged far beyond orthodox Buddhist tenets. Part of her appeal was no doubt her articulation of parallels between a Darwinian model of human evolution and an "Eastern" model of spiritual evolution based on cause and effect.

There was a social dimension to Theosophy's universalism, too, for among the stated goals of the new society was "to form the nucleus of a new universal brotherhood of humanity without distinction of race, creed, sex, caste or color."[11] Perhaps this universalistic social model was appealing to people like Mary Foster, who had experienced racial discrimination and cultural domination at the hands of white colonialists in Hawai‘i.

Theosophy in Hawai‘i and its Influence on Mary Foster

In 1894, Mary Foster and Auguste Marques established the Aloha Branch of the Theosophical Society in Hawai‘i. Although the roots of Theosophy in Hawai‘i are difficult to trace, we do know that Colonel Henry Steel Olcott, a pivotal figure in the Theosophical Society, visited Hawai‘i in 1901. According to Ruth Tabrah, the first Caucasian ordained as a Jōdo Shinshū priest in Hawai‘i, Colonel Olcott was the first Caucasian visitor invited to speak at Honpa Hongwanji Buddhist Temple.[12] His talk, entitled "Buddhism, the Superior Religion," drew a crowd of more than 400 people and received an enthusiastic response. Olcott's unorthodox message to the Japanese Buddhist immigrant population and other audiences in Honolulu constituted a direct challenge to normative social and religious forms – and to the Christian mission.

Although Theosophy never attracted a large following in Hawai‘i, a stellar coterie of spiritually inclined residents was drawn to its philosophical approach. For example, Marques, himself of Portuguese ancestry, was so inspired by his reading of Madame Blavatsky's *Isis Unveiled* that he dropped his earlier activities with the Anti-Asiatic League, which aimed at limiting the numbers of Chinese and Japanese immigrants because they were perceived as a threat to earlier arrivals, including Portuguese immigrant laborers. Not only was Marques a scholar, writer, physician, and member of the Hawaiian legislature before the monarchy was overthrown, he was a thoughtful person who saw the integration of new ideas as an important part of his own spiritual awakening.

Marques, who was with Mary Foster when she met Dharmapala during his stop in Honolulu in 1893, was a prominent figure in the campaign to remove the *haole* [outsider]-dominated cabinet. He was one of Queen Lili‘uokalani's allies during the events that led to the overthrow of the monarchy. In 1892, he was also the person who warned Lili‘uokalani about the planned coup against her government. Marques publicly condemned the plotters and, in a series of newspaper editorials, defended the institution of the monarchy and declared annexation to be of "no possible benefit to the Hawaiians."[13] Marques not only had deep feelings about the monarchy, but was also keenly interested in Hawaiian spirituality. He worked with Mary Foster to integrate traditional Hawaiian myths and symbols with Theosophical and Buddhist beliefs. This amalgamation led to a new interpretation of Theosophy – an interpretation that had its critics among Theosophists in the U.S. and Asia. Regardless of their political or philosophical leanings, the backing of prominent individuals such as Marques lent a certain credibility to the nascent Theosophical movement.

The Life and Spiritual Evolution of Mary Foster

Mary Robinson's early upbringing, similar to that of other upper-class Hawaiian women of her day, yields few specific clues to explain her religious change of heart. She was educated at the Fort Street Catholic School and O'ahu Charity School, a prestigious school for English-speaking children.[14] On May 4, 1861, when she was 16, she married Thomas R. Foster in Honolulu. Her husband was a shipbuilder from Nova Scotia who had arrived three years earlier and worked for her father. Thomas Foster became prominent as a landowner, investor, philanthropist, and major shareholder in Hui o Kahana, a partnership of landholders with properties on O'ahu and the island of Hawai'i, as well as President of the Inter-Island Steam Navigation Company, which he founded in 1882.[15] Mary assisted her husband in many of his business interests, in addition to managing the large tracts of land she had inherited from her father. In 1876, he commissioned the building of a ship named the *Mary E. Foster.*[16]

This period of Hawaiian history was a time of cultural and political interaction between the Hawaiian royal family and Britain. King Kalākaua preferred the British style and the shared monarchical traditions to the aggressive style of the Americans who were asserting themselves in the economic and religious lives of the Hawaiian people. King Kalākaua objected to the moralistic tone and attempts at Christian hegemony that accompanied American offers of education and economic gain in the Islands.

The contradictions and divided loyalties implicit in Hawaiian society at this time are revealed in Mary's relationships within her own family. The family was closely connected with the Hawaiian monarchy, both through royal blood lines and economics. Her father, James Robinson, "lent substantial sums of money to the Hawaiian government during the 1850s and maintained a close relationship to the kingdom's leaders until his death in 1876."[17] Her mother, Rebecca Prever, was a direct descendant of the chiefs of Maui, one of the major lines of Hawaiian royalty. Mary's brother, Mark Robinson, served as a member of Queen Lili'uokalani's cabinet, but the queen felt that he abandoned the monarchy during the crucial period leading up to the takeover.[18] Mary and her sister, Victoria Ward, on the other hand, were staunch supporters of the queen before, during, and after the illegal overthrow of the monarchy. A variety of Hawaiian political and cultural causes sought Mary's support throughout her adult life, especially during the two years leading up to the January 1895 attempt to restore the monarchy. Mary was seen as an advocate of preserving Hawaiian values and culture. She gave financial support for the education of many young Hawaiians. Her promotion of greater understanding of Hawaiian cultural and religious ways often brought her into conflict with members of her own family. Not only were political allegiances tested, but religious loyalties as well. Mary's rejection of Christianity undoubtedly strained relations with some family members, but Mark Robinson supported his sister's involvement with Theosophy and even hosted several Theosophical gatherings at his own estate.

It is interesting to speculate upon why Mary Foster became interested in Theosophy and eventually embraced Buddhism. There is some evidence that the spiritualist, esoteric approaches of Theosophy resonated with her unwavering interest in preserving traditional Hawaiian spirituality. She was also melanacholy due to her husband's death in 1889 and had found no solace in the missionary Christianity around her. By comparison, Theosophy envisioned a world with fewer boundaries – ethnic, religious, and political – in contrast to the approach of the missionary elite that imposed its own standards of moral behavior upon the Hawaiian people. Theosophy's inclusive approach was refreshing in an era of increasing religious polarization. All these factors may have contributed to Mary Foster's strong support of Theosophical ideas.

An account of Mary Foster's first meeting with Dharmapala aboard ship in Honolulu provides some insight into her family, her temperament, and the transformation she experienced as a result of Buddhist practice:

> The Parliament of Religions closed on September 27th, and after delivering a number of lectures at Oakland and San Francisco, on October 10th Dharmapala left the shores of America for India by way of Japan and China. At Honolulu Dr. Marques and two lady Theosophists came on board to see him, bringing with them gifts of brilliant South Sea flowers and fruits, all of which he distributed among the passengers. One of the visitors, a stout, middle-aged woman of about fifty, confessed that she suffered from violent outbursts of temper which were a source of misery to herself and her relations, and asked Dharmapala how they could be controlled. As a student of Buddhist yoga, Dharmapala was able to give her the help for which she had sought in vain elsewhere, and by following his few simple words of advice she was eventually able to overcome her failing altogether. The name of the hot-tempered lady was Mrs. Mary E. Foster. ...[19]

Although she also may have met Marie de Souza Canavarro, who arrived from California in the 1890s to share a deeper understanding of the Buddhist teachings, the meeting with Dharmapala was definitely the catalyst for Mary's conversion to Buddhism.

Hawaiian Beneficence

After meeting with Dharmapala, Mary Foster became his most generous patron, contributing to schools, hospitals, orphanages, and temples throughout South Asia.[20] Between 1902 and 1913, her contributions to the Maha Bodhi Society alone amounted to Rs. 3,000 a year. When Dharmapala made a special visit to Honolulu in June 1913 to express his appreciation, she donated the equivalent of Rs. 60,000 for constructing the Foster Robinson Memorial Hospital in Colombo in memory of her late husband and parents.[21] Pleased with Dharmapala's work, she donated another $50,000 to the Maha Bodhi Society in 1919, on the day the Armistice was signed, apparently to celebrate the end of World War I. Among other projects, she helped Dharmapala construct Sri Dharmarajika Vihar in Calcutta in 1920, fulfilling his longstanding dream. This and another gift of $100,000 in 1923 expressed her wish to support Dharmapala's projects in perpetuity. For her generosity to projects in India and Sri Lanka, she became immortalized as "verily a Visakha reincarnate" and "one of the greatest benefactors of Buddhism that have ever lived:"[22]

> There were innumerable *dayakas* [benefactors] of Buddha and His disciples but the names of Anathapindika and Visakha will ever remain as the outstanding supporters of the Buddhist Sangha. The way in which Visakha alone rendered succour to the Buddhist Sangha might well be compared to the timely and substantial aid rendered by Mrs. Foster singlehanded for the cause of Buddhism and the Maha Bodhi Society.... It was Mrs. Foster's donation alone that materialised the dream of the Anagarika, who repeatedly expressed his unbounded gratefulness to the twentieth century Visakha for offering aid at the right moment.[23]

Mary Foster's family was not pleased with her Buddhist charity. In fact, the family reportedly destroyed many relevant letters and journals, and has steadfastly refused to speak of Mary's penchant for Buddhism even up to the present day.[24] Although her family found her new spiritual direction an embarrassment, even an anathema, Mary found sympathy in another quarter. In 1901, during Queen Lili'oukalani's incarceration, at Bishop Yemyo Imamura's invitation, Mary took the queen from Iolani Palace to attend the birthday celebration of Saint Shinran and a special reception afterwards.[25]

Mary Foster's philanthropy was not limited to India and Sri Lanka; she also supported the development of Japanese Buddhism in Hawai'i. In 1899, she raised money to buy land on Fort Lane to construct Honolulu's first Jōdo Shinshū temple, which immediately became a valuable community resource during an outbreak of plague and subsequent conflagrations in the downtown Chinatown area. There was a famous legend that Mary Foster contributed a bag of gold dust toward the construction. In 1902, she set up the Foster-Robinson Foundation to facilitate her charitable activities. About once a month on a Sunday afternoon Bishop Imamura and his family would formally call on Mary Foster to express their appreciation for her generosity to the Japanese Buddhist community.

In 1906, Mary donated a large piece of land covered with kiawe trees, now bisected by the Pali Highway, which was used to construct Hongwanji High School in 1907 and the new Honpa Hongwanji Betsuin in 1918.[26] This temple, a white stucco *stūpa*-like structure located on the Pali Highway, even today serves as the locus of the Jōdo Shinshū sect in Hawai'i, with a reported membership of 80,000. Mary Foster's patronage may explain why the building was constructed in Indian rather than Japanese architectural styling.[27] The temple, which blends Indian, Japanese, Hawaiian, and American elements, is an apt reflection of Hongwanji's eclectic and innovative way of propagating the Buddha's teachings.[28] The architecture is classical Indian, the altar is traditional Japanese, the pews and hymnals are American, and the half-ton boulder transported from the Fort Lane temple on a silk cushion sewn by members of the Fujinkai (Buddhist Women's Association) could be taken to symbolize the temple's connection with the *aina*, its new Hawaiian soil. The auspicious falling of a "sweet rain" during the lowering of the cornerstone at the groundbreaking ceremony for the new building on July 30, 1916, could be interpreted as a blessing by the local deities (*'uhane*). Despite continuing charges of anti-Americanism, the large number of respected non-Japanese residents who attended the temple's dedication ceremony in July 1918 indicated Buddhism's increased acceptance in public life in Hawai'i.

Mary Foster's Legacy

Mary Foster died on December 19, 1930, at the age of 86, at Victoria Ward estate on O'ahu. From a postscript to a letter from C. H. Hunter to Shunzo Sakamaki, we know that her funeral services did not proceed as she had wished: "Shortly before she died, Mrs. Foster asked Rev. Hunt [a Caucasian Sōtō Zen Buddhist priest] to preside at her funeral services. Unfortunately she did not follow his advice by putting this request in writing – so, of course, when she passed on, the 'heathen priest' was ignored altogether and her family saw to it that she got the one thing she didn't want – a Christian burial."[29]

Despite Mary Foster's generous donations to projects in India and Sri Lanka during years of charitable activities, her estate was still valued at $3,018,000 at the time of her death. Among the properties included in her estate was Hillebrand Gardens, formerly the estate of Thomas Hillebrand, who traveled the world in connection with his position as horticultural specialist. Wherever he traveled, he collected tropical plant species which he then planted on his estate. Mary Foster acquired the Hillebrand Estate in 1880 and later bequeathed 5.687 acres of it to the City of Honolulu for the express purpose of a public tropical park.[30] The property was accepted by the city supervisors as a public botanical garden on October 6, 1931, and has been maintained by the city ever since as Foster Botanical Garden.

The horticultural collection includes a *bodhi* tree (*ficus religiosa*), believed to be a descendant of the tree under which the Buddha achieved enlightenment, and an orchid named the Vanda Mary E. Foster.[31] A temple dedicated to the *bodhisattva* Kuan Yin stands on one corner of the property.[32]

It was no doubt because of the extent of Mary's philanthropy that Dharmapala nicknamed her "Queen of the Empire of Righteousness."[33] Although this is probably simply a feminization of the traditional epithet Dharmarāja, "King of the Dharma" (denoting a paragon of the Buddhist teachings on right living), it is a curious coincidence that he applied the terms to a Hawaiian of royal blood. Ironically, in Sri Lanka this native Hawaiian daughter is exalted by the people as Sudu Amma, "White Mother."[34] The maternal epithet was a natural expression of gratitude for her nurturing qualities: "Anagarika Dharmapala was always the first to admit that if he was the father whose fiery will had engendered the Maha Bodhi movement, Mrs. Foster was the mother who fed and sustained it with the milk of her charities, and that it could no more have come to maturity without one 'parent' than without the other."[35] Her charitable influence continues to inspire Buddhist generosity in Asia and the West. In 1995, the monks of Dharmavijaya Vihāra in Los Angeles commemorated the 65th anniversary of Mary Foster's passing with a distribution of food to the hungry and homeless in the downtown area.[36]

A Relaxing of Boundaries

Although there is at present insufficient documentation to explain Mary Foster's conversion to Buddhism, a combination of historical and cultural circumstances, and random clues among the literature and oral narratives at hand, allow us to entertain some tentative hypotheses. The three most likely reasons for her conversion are: (1) resistance to Christian hegemony; 2) the influence of religious systems introduced to Hawai'i with Asian immigration; and 3) resonance with elements within indigenous Hawaiian spirituality. Most probably, her Buddhist sympathies were an amalgamation of the three.

First, the embrace of Asian spirituality by Mary Foster and other elite Hawaiians was in part a response to Protestant domination – a religion and culture that had been forcibly imposed upon the Hawaiian people at the expense of their own indigenous beliefs and practices. Rather than seeking confrontation with Protestant mores, however, certain Hawaiian women chose a path of accommodation that was consistent with their own cultural values. Although their interest in Asian spirituality represented a conscious rebuff of a tradition connected to colonial rule, it was not simply a matter of replacing one particular belief system with another, but a move toward a more universalistic approach. This response was consistent with the Hawaiian proclivity for openness and sharing, the same tendency that ironically had cost the Hawaiians their culture and their lands.

Second, Mary's embrace of Asian spirituality may have been influenced by Asian immigration to Hawai'i. As Chinese and Japanese workers settled into life on the plantations, they brought with them a range of diverse religious traditions and beliefs, including Taoism, Buddhism, and Shintō. By the late 1890s, immigrants from China and Japan were reaching the Hawaiian Islands in such numbers that the impact of their cultures and customs could no longer be ignored. The Asian religious traditions that these immigrant laborers brought with them were reviled as "the devil's work" by Christian missionaries, including some Japanese converts.[37] And while Asians might be forgiven their "heathen" beliefs since they "did not know any better," a Christian converting to Buddhism was bizarre. As Ruth Tabrah notes, "In the eyes of Hongwanji's haole detractors a Buddhist converting to become a Christian was fine. A Christian becoming a Buddhist was not. Mary Foster's having become Buddhist continued to earn her the label of eccentric in the community."[38] For some, Asian religious traditions clearly constituted a dreaded "other," whereas for others, they represented a viable alternative to prevailing religious options. The sympathetic response of certain Causasians and other "elites" to Asian spirituality signaled a new openness to diverse peoples and religious traditions in Hawaiian society. Mary Foster's participation in Hongwanji's activities was a notable example. Not only did her involvement lend credibility to the temple at a time when Buddhism was openly vilified as heathen, it also suggested that Buddhism offered something of value to people beyond the Asian immigrant community.

Third, it is possible that Asian spirituality touched something deep in the psyche of Mary Foster and other Hawaiians that was not being adequately acknowledged in Christian beliefs. At least some Hawaiians, like Mary Foster and Queen Lili'uokalani, were foraging beyond the accepted religious norms of their time. Despite the social risks involved in exploring alternative religious traditions, they looked to traditions that were inclusive enough to validate rather than deny Hawaiian spirituality. For instance, in 1885 when Auguste Marques wrote several articles on Hawaiian mythology and symbolism for the Theosophist journal, he drew connections between these ideas and those presented by Madame Blavatsky in *Isis Unveiled*.[39] Mary Foster shared Marques' penchant for integrating Hawaiian spirituality with Theosophy and Buddhism to create a new spiritual fusion within the Aloha Branch. It appears that Theosophy helped certain iconoclastic women express elements of their spirituality that were being suppressed, denied, or ignored, even by Hawaiians themselves, under Christian domination.

The story of Mary Foster is thus a narrative of how one Hawaiian woman utilized imported Asian religious traditions to express indigenous spiritual sentiments in response to cultural domination. With the limited avenues of expression available to women of her upper-class Hawaiian socio-cultural background, she chose a unique path, embodying a material and spiritual magnanimity that encompassed and also enriched many cultures and traditions. Her step beyond the boundaries has left a lasting impression.

Notes

1 On the occasion of the ordination of Sri Lankan *bhikṣuṇīs* in Sārnāth.

2 A useful introduction to this history is Haunani-Kay Trask, *From a Native Daughter: Colonialism and Sovereignty in Hawai'i* (Honolulu: University of Hawaii Press, 1999), especially pp. 1–21.

3 *Ho'omana Na'auao* "translates variously as The Enlightened Worship, The Enlightened Religion, The Learned Church, The Learned Religion, Buddhism, Christian Science. . . . The parishioners prefer to use the Hawaiian title without offering a translation." The church's beliefs and practices were largely Christian, including observance of the Sabbath, baptism, and "the sacrament of the Lord." Marion Morrison, *Ka Ho'omana Na'auao: The History of an Early Hawaiian Church*, University of Hawai'i Hamilton Library monograph, 1984, pp. 18–19.

4 Stephen Prothero describes the founding of the Theosophical Society in his book, *The White Buddhist: The Asian Odyssey of Henry Steel Olcott* (Delhi: Sri Satguru Publications, 1996), pp. 48–50. In fashionable New York society in the late 19th century, the Theosophical Society was one of a number of attempts at reconciling science and religion, one that leaned heavily toward the occult. A list of biographies of co-founder Madame Helena Petrovna Blavatsky is found on pp. 196–97 of Prothero's book.

5 W. N. Armstrong, son of Protestant ministers and a cabinet minister, quoted in "The Effect of the Alien," *Pacific Commercial Advertiser*, Honolulu, June 14, 1894.

6 This phenomenon is discussed in Louise Hunter's *Buddhism in Hawaii: Its Impact on a Yankee Community* (Honolulu: University of Hawaii Press, 1971).

7 Frank J. Karpiel, "Theosophy, Culture, and Politics in Honolulu, 1890–1920," *The Hawaiian Journal of History* 30 (1996): 177.

8 Rick Fields, *How the Swans Came to the Lake: A Narrative History of Buddhism in America* (Boston: Shambhala, 1992), p. 83.

9 Ibid., p. 89.

10 Ibid., p. 90.

11 Ibid., p. 90.

12 Ruth Tabrah, *A Grateful Past, A Promising Future* (Honolulu: Honpa Hongwanji Mission, 1989), pp. 24–25. She notes, "The discovery that there were serious followers of Buddhism even among the Caucasians lifted the inferior feeling among the Hongwanji members and gradually, the attendance increased."

13 Cited in Karpiel, "Theosophy, Culture, and Politics," p. 181.

14 When the school first opened on January 10, 1833, it was for educating native adults, including the king and other *ali'i*. Within a few years, virtually the entire Hawaiian population was going to school. Due to a lack of American schools in California and the lack of railroad transportation to east coast schools, some prominent families also sent their children to be educated there. "Strange as it may seem, some of the best-known California families in the days of the Forty-Niners, and immediately preceding, were sending their sons and daughters to the Sandwich Islands – 2100 miles away – for their primary and secondary education. Included in this number was the first child born of American parents in California." Charles T. Fitts, "Youthful Californians Seeking Education 1841–1844," *Pomona College Bulletin* 35, no. 10 (June 1938): 25.

15 Ibid., p. 178; and Rhoda Hackler, "A History of Foster Botanic Garden," University of Hawai'i Hamilton Library monograph, 1986, p. 37.
16 Hackler, "A History of Foster Botanic Garden," p. 39.
17 Karpiel, "Theosophy, Culture, and Politics," p. 178.
18 Ibid., p. 179.
19 Bhikshu Sangharakshita, *Anagarika Dharmapala: A Biographical Sketch* (Kandy: Buddhist Publication Society, 1964), p. 65.
20 Nalinaksha Dutt recounts: "The greatest benefactor of the [Maha Bodhi] Society was Mrs. T. R. Foster, who was by birth at [*sic*] Hawaiian belonging to the Royal Family, and who had married a North America banker. In October 1893, she met Anagarika Dharmapala for the first time at Honolulu, and from 1902 she became a steady supporter of his mission. In 1903 her first donation amounted to 44,000 dollars for educational works and publications in India and Ceylon, particularly in connection with the industrial education undertaken by the Maha Bodhi Society at Sarnath. For four years, 1905–1908, she contributed 1000 dollars annually for educational institutions at Rajagiri, Colombo, and other works of the Society. With the donations of this noble-hearted lady it was possible for the Society to have a printing press of its own in Colombo. . . ." "The Maha Bodhi Society, Its History and Influence," *Anagarika Dharmapala and His "Foster-Mother,"* University of Hawai'i Hamilton Library monograph, pp. 69–70.
21 *Anagarika Dharmapala and His "Foster-Mother,"* p. 37. The hospital, built in 1914, provided indigenous Sinhala medical treatment and "the street on which it was built, Deans Lane, was later renamed Foster Lane." Major Herby Seneviratne, "83rd Anniversary of Foster Robinson Free Memorial Ayurveda Slava," Colombo *Daily News*, June 7, 1997.
22 Sangharakshita, *Anagarika Dharmapala*, p. 65.
23 Nalinaksha Dutt, "The Maha Bodhi Society, Its History and Influence," pp. 70–71.
24 In a letter to John R. Hendrickson, dated February 1, 1965, Robert Aitken writes: "Mrs. Foster's generosity was nice for the Indian and Singhalese Buddhists, but it did not sit well with her family, and the Buddhist aspect of her life is scarcely spoken of locally, almost to the point of suppression." *Anagārikā Dharmapāla and his "Foster-Mother,"* p. 2.
25 In Bishop Imamura's words, "I had heard that the Queen of Hawaii, Liliuokalani, held good will toward Japan and had some interest in Buddhism. An invitation for her presence was presented through a mediator for the Gotanye Service to be held on May 19, 1901. Unexpectedly she accepted and was accompanied by Mrs. Mary Foster. This being the first instance where the Queen in person had attended a Japanese organization event, the publicity was enormous. Every land throughout the world telegraph noticed the event in large captions. In Japan, articles appeared in newspapers such as *Jiji Shimpo* in Tokyo, *Osaka Asahi*, etc. and the consequence was that Hongwanji found its self-esteem elevated tremendously." Tabrah, *A Grateful Past*, p. 25.
26 Bishop Yemyo Imamura received encouragement for his education project both from Abbot Kozui Ohtani and Honzan Headquarters in Japan, and an unexpected windfall to realize it: "Upon my return to Hawaii I went to see Mrs. Mary Foster, a warmly supportive patron in recent years, to explain to her the desire for a new school building. She immediately agreed with my idea and, on the spot, presented me the land for the school. Her graceful figure raising her arms to say 'this land is yours!' will always remain in my memory." Ibid., p. 42.
27 Another interpretation is offered by Shoji Matsumoto, who said that the choice of Indian styling was an attempt to expand the temple's appeal beyond Japanese Pure Land followers. Interview with Ramdas Lamb, University of Hawai'i, June 27, 1999.
28 "From its inception, the mission has sought to provide a religious atmosphere adapted to the dominant culture. Thus, the temple's interior, furnished with a pulpit, prayer pews, and hymnals, in many respects resembles a traditional Christian church. Sunday worship

service includes a sermon and a choir. The temple acquired the first pipe organ in the state and was the setting for the first non-Christian service in English." Ramdas Lamb, "Religion," *Atlas of Hawai'i*, 3rd edition, ed. Sonia P. Juvik and James O. Juvik (Honolulu: University of Hawai'i Press, 1998), p. 204.

29 Letter dated May 10, 1965. The postscript is signed by Louise Hunter. The letter, sent in response to an inquiry on behalf of J. R. Hendrickson, a student at the East-West Center interested in researching Mary Foster's life, is not encouraging: "If I were Hendrickson I'd quit while I was ahead. He doesn't want the Honolulu side of this picture. Mrs. Foster was one of the Ward sisters of Old Plantation fame. Her adviser, John Waterhouse, her family (the Hustaces, etc) were fit to be tied because of her financial activities and the story from this side would not win friends and influence people in India...." Included in *Anagarika Dharmapala and His "Foster-Mother,"* p. 3.

30 Hackler, "A History of Foster Botanic Garden," p. 39.

31 Ibid, p. 78.

32 Hackler contends that this was originally a Taoist temple. Ibid., p. 105–7. However, Hunter says that although Kwan-Ti, a martial god associated with Taoism, was earlier worshipped there, the temple (destroyed once by fire in 1886) was built to honor the *bodhisattva* Kuan-yin (*Buddhism in Hawaii*, p. 41). Because of the temple's historical value, Frank Hustace managed to preserve it by negotiating a settlement with a group of Chinese businessmen who hoped to acquire the property for development. Although the temple is now decidedly Buddhist, under the spiritual direction of nuns from Hong Kong, signs reminding visitors, "Don't put chickens on the altar [a Taoist custom]," appeared as late as 1984.

33 Sangharakshita notes, "It is hardly to be wondered at that the Anagarika, who had appealed in vain to the wealthy Buddhists of Ceylon, Burma, Siam and Japan, should behold with amazement the princely donations which poured in from the tiny Pacific Island.... His ardently grateful nature could not help believing that she had been born to assist his work, and that the subtle threads of destiny had knit the lives of a daughter of Hawaii and a son of Sri Lanka together for the sublime work of propagating the Dharma." Sangharakshita, *Flame in Darkness: The Life and Saying of Anagarika Dharmapala* (Pune: Triratna Granthamala, 1995), p. 121.

34 Dhammacari Sama Dede Whiteside, "Mary Elizabeth Foster: Sudu Amma," *Sri Lanka Express*, March 22, 1996, p. 9.

35 Sangharakshita, *Flame in Darkness*, p. 121.

36 Ibid.

37 For example, Takie Okumura. Hunter, *Buddhism in Hawaii*, pp. 56–59.

38 Tabrah, *A Grateful Past*, p. 58. Even Asian Buddhists encountered obstacles in achieving social acceptance of their faith. In 1906, Governor George R. Carter rejected Hongwanji's application to incorporate as a legal entity. His statement read, "The Constitution of the United States guarantees religious freedom to all men ... [but] I do not believe that the language of this charter is compatible with the best future interests of the Territory [of Hawaii]." Ibid., p. 33–34.

39 Helena Petrovna Blavatsky, *Isis Unveiled*, 2 vol. (New York: J. W. Bouton, 1977; Pasadena: Theosophical University Press, 1960).

CHAPTER TWENTY

Bishop Jikyu Rose

A Tendai Ajari in Hawai'i[1]

Joseph M. Gardewin

Koganji, a Buddhist temple, blends so well with its neighborhood in Honolulu's Mānoa Valley it would not be visible unless one knew precisely where to look. Beginning around seven o'clock in the morning, five to seven volunteers are already hard at work as they water the grass and ornamental shrubs, keep weeds from invading, rake the rock gardens, wash the windows, wipe the screens, check for dust in the main hall (*hondo*), and place flowers on the altar. Most of the volunteers are young, while some are gracefully aging. Many appear to be *nisei* and *sansei* (second- and third-generation Japanese Americans) and they are unfailingly polite.

Members of Koganji welcome visitors to their temple and, with a smile, explain that their temple belongs to Tendai, an esoteric form of Buddhism which is one of six major schools in Japan. If members sense a genuine interest, visitors may be invited to help prepare for a temple event: "We really could use some more help, especially with making *mochi* [pounded rice cakes] for the New Year. The *mochi* is really *ono* [Hawaiian: delicious]. Everybody helps. Of course, we offer the first *mochi* to O-Jizō-san [Kṣitigarbha Bodhisattva] as a good omen for the New Year, but there's enough for everybody." Besides being a temple with a beautiful main hall, a children's play area, and an exceptional rock garden, Koganji is a unique family home built by a charismatic woman.

Koganji's Founder: Jikyu Rose

Koganji was conceived by Jikyu Rose, a Japanese woman who emigrated to the United States as the bride of a U.S. naval officer. Bishop Jikyu Rose's Japanese heritage served as a wellspring, not only for the architecture, but also for the Tendai practice that is central at Koganji. Her strong determination was the driving force behind the temple's founding and construction.

Jikyu Rose was born Hisako Yamauchi and raised near Tokyo. Her father was a businessman who sized and cut pure white crystals to be made into jewelry. From her father, Hisako gained an appreciation for business and finance. As a young woman, she studied to be a seamstress, but her mother noted that she had another talent – as a healer. Her mother believed she was a reincarnation of her great-grandmother, a woman who also was a seamstress and a healer who instinctively knew what medicinal herbs to prescribe.

Although raised in the Buddhist tradition, Hisako was not schooled in those beliefs. She was familiar with the *Lotus Sūtra*, but was not affiliated with any particular sect. She encountered suffering at a relatively young age because of World War II. As a teenager, she experienced the horrors of war firsthand when her family's house was destroyed by fire bombs three times. She acknowledges with a shudder that this was "a terrible time."

In the early 1950s, as a young woman in her early 20s, Hisako began to practice her dressmaking trade. Through this trade she became known to the wives of American officers and was asked to teach them to draft patterns. As her concern for the less fortunate began to manifest itself, she helped build an orphanage for abandoned babies of mixed Japanese-American parentage. In addition to her charitable activities, she found time for her spiritual life, reflecting and praying regularly at Tsugamo, a temple near her home, where there was a statue of Jizō Bodhisattva. During this time, a priest at Tsugamo Temple predicted that she would meet a special man ten years her senior and marry him on the 25th of May or October. At the time, Hisako had little interest in sex or marriage, so she paid little attention to what the priest said.

In 1953, she met Lester Rose, a naval aviator stationed in Japan with the occupying U.S. forces. Actually, she had met him three times before they went out on a "date." When she recalls the first time she saw Lester, her memories are as fresh as yesterday. She was at a theater watching a Marilyn Monroe movie, when two officers came in with their dates. As Lester passed Hisako, she retrieved his handkerchief as it fell to the floor and he thanked her. Their second meeting was at a performance of Tchaikovsky's *Swan Lake* when Lester asked her to explain the program which was in Japanese. Shortly thereafter, they met formally at the home of an American officer whose wife was her friend. Their relationship now had an official beginning.

Jikyu recalls their frequent dates and Lester's gentlemanly behavior: pulling out chairs for her, bringing her home early, and never making physical advances. In fact, Lester was so much of a gentleman that one evening she couldn't refrain from asking whether he really liked her. A bit taken aback, Lester replied: "If I ever say I love you to any woman, that will be the first and last one!" Five months after they met, Hisako Yamauchi legally became Mary Rose. The date of their marriage was May 25.

On their honeymoon, the newlyweds traveled to Nikko and had their picture taken in front of Kegon waterfall. When the picture was developed, four or five strange figures were visible where only the newlyweds and the waterfall should have appeared. At first, they thought the processor must have tampered with the film, but checks of the Leica, film, and processor produced no explanation. The long-legged figures carried swords and appeared to be warriors, but were dressed in a fashion quite un-Japanese. One appeared to have a broken leg. Later, a Buddhist priest told them that the strange figures were warrior gods who protected Buddhas and bodhisattvas.

The Roses remained in Japan until 1955, when Lester was reassigned to New York. After 20 years of military service, he retired and found a job in a defense-related industry that required them to move every six months. As they traveled from place to place, Jikyu began to dream of a permanent home. In her dream there was a castle with a view of the ocean and mountains. Being a good military wife, the dream included a small airplane for her husband.

Before settling down, the Roses decided to travel once more, to Hawai'i and Japan. Once in Hawai'i, they quickly decided to stay. With a smile, Jikyu admits that they decided on Hawai'i because there she could get good rice and all types of Japanese food. At this point, her seamstress skills and business acumen came into full play. She opened a dress shop in Moanalua Shopping Center and, quite naturally, found she had a marriage counseling business going on the side. She also got a realtor associate's license and began investing in real estate though, she recalls, her penchant for investing ran counter to her husband's conservative financial bent. Like many military men, she says, he was a bit "square."

During this period, a near-tragic event reaffirmed her faith in Jizō Bodhisattva. A woman had ordered a wedding dress for the marriage of her niece. When the dress was ready for pickup, the woman arrived at the shop, paid for the dress, and turned to leave. Just as she was about to reach the door, Jikyu was shocked to hear the following words involuntarily come from her mouth, warning the woman, "Use the dress quickly. Your niece will attempt to commit suicide soon!" The woman froze in her tracks, then turned to face Jikyu in disbelief. "What did you say?" she demanded. Stunned by her outburst, Jikyu apologized profusely.

Three weeks later, the young bride-to-be took an overdose and lay in a coma at St. Francis Hospital. An irate early morning call to Jikyu confirmed that her words of warning had been true. Although the aunt had not mentioned the warning to the young woman, Jikyu felt a deep sense of responsibility for the young woman's fate. She rushed to the hospital and found her lying comatose on the bed in intensive care, connected to all kinds of tubes. Jikyu can still vividly see blood flowing from one tube in the young woman's nose. Overwhelmed by concern, and even guilt, she called on Jizō Bodhisattva for help and prayed intensely at the hospital for the next two days.

On the third day, in the midst of her prayers, Jikyu heard the young woman say, "I'm sorry, I'm sorry, I'm sorry." When she looked up and saw tears streaming down the woman's face, Jikyu immediately knew she would recover. Family members in the room had not heard the woman speak, but Jikyu told them everything would be fine. Later that day, in a phone call more pleasant than the first, the family confirmed what Jikyu already knew: the woman would fully recover. Later, the bride-to-be remembered that during her coma she had seen "a beautiful lady in white praying." Jikyu patiently continued to visit her. This series of events deeply confirmed Jikyu's belief in Jizō Bodhisattva's power and compassion.

Jikyu's Training as a Tendai Priest

In the early 1970s, Jikyu found herself attracted to the Tendai school of Buddhism, particularly to the teachings of Dengyō Daishi. To better understand the *Heart of Wisdom Sūtra*, she began studying calligraphy at the Tendai Mission of Hawai'i in Honolulu. Meanwhile, she continued her devotions to Jizō. She was attracted to the Tendai school, she says, because of its broad Mahāyāna view. She felt that Tendai offered a sense of freedom that was not restricted to specific doctrines. At this point, Jikyu never even thought of becoming a priest. She only wanted to deepen her understanding of Buddhism and to find a lifesize statue of Jizō Bodhisattva. Her desire for the statue was motivated by her love for Jizō's compassion and vow to protect children. In part, her affinity to Jizō Bodhisattva stemmed from the fact that her marriage, as happy as it was, had produced no children.

Jikyu's work at the Tendai Mission gave her the opportunity to meet Archbishop Haba, a special Tendai emissary from Enryaku Temple in Japan, when he visited in 1973. Never one to be intimidated in the presence of authority, Jikyu approached the Archbishop with something on her mind. She told the Archbishop she wanted to purchase a lifesize statue of Jizō Bodhisattva for her home. She asked him to help her locate a woodcarver who was sincere and strictly followed the traditional way of carving religious figures. After a moment's reflection, the Archbishop looked at her, smiled, and said she had a greater need. He was the first to encourage her to go to Enryaku Temple to train for ordination. Although she had never even considered ordination prior to that meeting, her life's work was now about to begin in earnest.

That same year, Jikyu went to Japan to begin several months of intense training and instruction. Archbishop Haba himself oversaw her training at Enryaku Temple on Mt. Hiei just northeast of Kyoto. Three progressively more difficult tests were required for ordination. In effect, the aspirant had to prove her worth before being allowed to proceed to the next stage of training. The first stage was designed to test whether the candidate had sufficient physical and mental discipline and stamina to be an *ajari* (fully ordained Tendai priest).

At the first stage, the daily routine began at 5 a.m. The candidates had five minutes of "private time" to wash and attend to their personal needs. The next 55 minutes were spent in meditation, prayer, and cleaning the temple, with a few minutes for a simple meal. The prayers included a ritual of facing east, west, north, and south to give thanks for blessings received. Meals were spartan – barely enough to provide nourishment. The morning meal, for example, might include two small slices of *takuan* (pickled radish), *miso* (fermented bean paste) soup, a small cup of *ojiya* (rice gruel), perhaps a small piece or two of *nori* (dried seaweed), and small amount of tea poured in to wash the bowl. A strict code of silence was maintained during meals: "Not one word could be spoken!" The crunchy *takuan* had to be ground with the teeth, rather than chewed, to avoid making a sound. From 6 a.m. on, the aspirants were on the move for most of the day, vigorously hiking up and down Mt. Hiei. Typically the group covered five or six miles in the morning, broke for a simple lunch (perhaps a sandwich, fruit, and tea), then covered another five or six miles of steep hiking along narrow mountain trails with steep drops and, occasionally, poisonous snakes. Jikyu recalls thinking that even a goat would have difficulty walking those trails. Except during lunch, silence was observed at all times.

After returning to the temple and taking an evening meal, the novices spent hours in study, reflection, and meditation. Sitting rigidly in traditional *seiza* position (on the knees), they studied and memorized *sūtras*, especially the *Lotus Sūtra*. Questions were permitted, Jikyu says, but it was better to concentrate on getting the answers right away, because the material was only presented once. Now, when she reflects on this first two months of training, she smiles and shakes her head in disbelief, as if to say, "How did I endure this? How did I survive?" She reminisces, "When I began this first stage of training, I had clear, well-tended, strong fingernails. By the time I finished, my nails were cracked, torn, and black and blue." Prior to beginning the process leading to Tendai ordination, she had no idea how severe the training would be.

Despite the tough physical and mental demands, Jikyu survived and through the strict religious training, acquired a deep appreciation for Dengyō Daishi (Saichō), Tendai's founder. With great conviction, she says, "Until then, I never knew how broad-minded and how compassionate Dengyō Daishi was." With a smile, she recalls that all three women in her group of 28 novices completed the first stage of training, but some of the men did not. After the first stage (*manjo*), they were ready to take the next step.

The second stage of training (*kanjo*) required something Jikyu found quite distasteful: the candidates had to shave their heads. For Jikyu, this was a real sacrifice. Much of her early life had been spent helping make women more attractive and she had seen the height of fashion on Fifth

Avenue in New York. Although she was unconcerned about clothes, hair and personal appearance were very important to her. Forcing herself to overcome her initial feeling of revulsion, she shaved her head.

To begin *kanjo*, the aspirants were blindfolded and had to drink a cup of purified water immediately and completely. In a ritual of purification, rainwater had been boiled with cloves, giving it the color of mud and an extremely pungent taste. Jikyu almost gagged as she choked it down and had to exert considerable mental discipline not to regurgitate the "mud tea" as the ritual continued. Next, the aspirants were led blindfolded through the temple for approximately 30 minutes. After this was a ceremony in which they, still blindfolded, were ordained as "guardians" of the Buddha. Each one was given flowers and instructed to gently toss them in the air. When the blindfolds were removed, the new "guardians" were able to see that they were standing in the middle of an elaborate *maṇḍala*. Jikyu's flowers had landed on the symbol of the Universal Buddha, a very auspicious part of the *maṇḍala*, which was considered to be an extremely favorable omen. She had completed the second step on her road to full ordination. She smiles and recalls: "There was only one bad side effect. As a result of drinking that 'mud tea,' I was constipated for three days."

Jikyu completed the first two stages of her training in 1973, but the third stage (*daiei*) involved an oral examination which was given only once every four years. She had to wait for two more years for the next test to be given. In September 1975, now in her mid-40s, she successfully completed the third stage. This took only 24 hours, but the entire time was spent with a high-ranking Tendai priest. The examination began at 2 a.m., when Jikyu, carrying a lantern in one hand, was admitted to a single room lit only by candles. Alone, she followed the candles to a platform where the master sat. For the next 24 hours, the master directed questions at her, all pertaining to the *Lotus Sūtra*. The examination was rigorous and both mentally and physically draining. Jikyu had been an exceptional student, however, and her responses were favorably received. By successfully completing this final examination, Jikyu achieved her goal and became authorized as a fully ordained Tendai priest with the rank of *ajari*. This rank entitles her to wear a white scarf with her Tendai robes. Along with degree of *ajari*, she was given the name Jikyu. When she reflects on the process of ordination, she is refreshingly honest. "You know," she says frankly, "When I first began this whole thing, it was as much as out a sense of curiosity as it was from a love of Buddhism." Listening to her, one can sense that she is genuinely amazed at her own achievements.

Constructing the Temple, Koganji

After completing the process of ordination, Jikyu set a new goal: to build a temple within two years. When she returned to Hawai'i, things began to move quickly. She expanded her Moanalua home to include a prayer hall for a very distinguished resident. On Jikyu's return flight from Japan in 1976, an exquisitely carved lifesize image of Jizō Bodhisattva sat in the seat next to her. Bishop Haba had kept his promise and commissioned a traditional artisan (*bushi*) to carve this beautiful wooden image.

The Moanalua residence was only temporary, however. Jikyu and Lester, her principal supporter, located an ideal two-acre parcel of land in Mānoa. The only obstacle was the $500,000 price tag. The money had to be raised quickly, because there was another prospective buyer, so the Roses put virtually everything they had into the deal. When their assets proved inadequate, Jikyu had to borrow the remainder at the best rate she could find.

The burden of meeting the mortgage payments forced Jikyu to live an extremely frugal lifestyle, but she found such sacrifices a small price to pay for realizing her dream. She bought whatever she needed at the annual temple sales and, for years after, temple members spotted her wearing dresses and shoes bought for a dollar apiece. Eventually the debt to First Hawaiian Bank was paid off, and when Jikyu reflects on those difficult times, she feels proud that building the temple was not hers alone, but a shared experience.

The investment Jikyu and her followers made in the temple was much more than monetary; they invested a lot of "sweat equity" in the project, too. Within five months they had cleared the completely overgrown parcel of land, and Jikyu and Lester had moved onto a small structure on the site that was quickly enlarged to serve as a temporary meeting hall for the congregation. Jikyu smiles as she recalls how much the many temple members contributed. Some of the members' teenaged children also helped. In one case, Jikyu arranged for a troubled young man to live at Koganji with her. Taking Jikyu's example to heart, he learned to appreciate what can be achieved through hard work. Recalling that young man, she says, "We must realize that life arises from a seed, is fed by rain, and fertilized by all the blessings from O-Jizō-sama. So appreciate life and your reward will be the fruits of all your labor."

Jikyu's efforts did not go unnoticed. In November 1976, the Chief Abbot (Geika) of the Tendai school, Etai Yamada, paid a visit to her fledgling congregation to personally bless the temple site. Over time, the temple construction became a $2 million endeavor. The fundraising, excavation, planning, design, solicitation of contractor bids, and all the other construction tasks took four years. The official groundbreaking was held in October 1980. On March 28, 1982, 18 months later, Geika Yamada returned for the formal dedication of Koganji Temple. The congregation had grown to 125 members. What Jikyu had envisioned and worked so hard to achieve had now become a reality. In building Koganji, Jikyu had proven herself as a wife, businesswoman, organizer, fundraiser, counselor, and healer, as well as an *ajari* of the Tendai school. Her achievements were manifest not only in the outer structures of Koganji, but also in the inner structures – the teachings and practices which form the spiritual foundation of Koganji.

Jizō Bodhisattva: Object of Devotion

Three *sūtras* provide the underpinnings of Jikyu's teachings: *The Sutra of the Eternal Life Jizō Bodhisattva* (*Bussetsu Enmei Jizō Bosatsukyō*), the *Lotus Sūtra*, and the *Heart of Wisdom Sūtra* (*Hannya Shingyō*). The first *sūtra* recounts the story of Jizō ("Earth Store") Bodhisattva (Chinese: Dizang, Sanskrit: Kṣitigarbha) who is regarded as "the bodhisattva who encompasses the earth" and preserves the Dharma until the advent of Maitreya Buddha. Some believers regard Jizō as an incarnation of Yama, the king of the hell realm, while others regard him a master of all six realms (hells, hungry ghosts, animals, humans, demi-gods, and gods). He is described as an intermediary between the human realm and the hells, a greatly compassionate bodhisattva capable of saving all sentient beings from suffering and helping them escape from the cycle of rebirth.

The Sutra of the Eternal Life that Jikyu teaches elaborates the qualities of Jizō Bodhisattva as follows:

> He calms the entire world. He causes the six paths to cycle (*deva*, human, animal, *asura*, *preta*, demon), relieves all suffering, and brings happiness to everyone.[2] If someone is cast on the shores of hell and sees an image of this Bodhisattva's body or hears His name, that person will be born again in the Pure Land.... By invoking Him, all of your wishes will be fulfilled, your eyes will be opened and you will attain absolute enlightenment. Also by invoking Him, the ten happinesses will you attain:
>
> 1. Women will bear children easily;
> 2. Your illnesses will be healed;
> 3. Your body will be healthy and complete;
> 4. You will attain long life (eternal life);
> 5. You will become bright and wise;
> 6. You will become wealthy and fulfilled;
> 7. You will be loved and respected by all;
> 8. Your harvests will be abundant;
> 9. Your spiritual life will be protected;
> 10. Great enlightenment will be yours.[3]

The *sūtra* declares that invoking or even hearing the name of Jizō Bodhisattva will guarantee health, wisdom, love, and happiness. The *sūtra* suggests that Jizō's power is so great that seeing (his image), hearing (his name), and praying (chanting his name) bring multiple material and spiritual blessings.

A Chinese version of this text recounts a discussion between Mañjuśri and Śākyamuni Buddha that helps trace Kṣitigarbha Bodhisattva's origins.[4] According to the account, long before the time of Śākyamuni, a resolute youth approached Lion Power Buddha and asked how he had achieved such a divine appearance. Lion Power Buddha responded: "If you want to gain such an appearance, you must attempt your utmost to relieve the sufferings of all sorrowful beings and continue this practice for a long, long time.[5] Later, Kṣitigarbha was reborn as a devout brahmin girl who had accumulated much merit from good practice in previous lives. This girl embraced the Buddha's teachings, but was criticized by her mother for doing so. When the mother died, she was reborn in Avīci, the worst of the eight hot hells. Her daughter gave up all her material belongings and devoted herself to the Buddha of her time, Flower of Meditation and Enlightenment Buddha. Seeing the young brahmin girl's absolute sincerity in wishing to help her mother, the Buddha acceded to her entreaties. He granted her the power to travel to Avīci Hell in meditation to successfully negotiate for her mother's release.[6] The *sūtra* also tells of Kṣitigarbha's other past lives, as he built up merit on the path to ultimately become a great bodhisattva.

Jikyu believes that Śākyamuni Buddha told Indra that, like the earth which nurtures things and makes them grow, "[Jizō] can produce a myriad of things and make them grow." Jikyu also holds the fundamental Mahāyāna belief that Jizō vowed, "Until the hells are empty, I will not become a Buddha." Based on these convictions, Jikyu has made Jizō the focus of devotion at Koganji. In the preface to *Tendai Shu Koganji*, she cites the deep compassion that Jizō has for each and every living human being. She writes, "Jizō Bodhisattva will help whoever has faith, and will relieve his suffering."[7] Elsewhere she amplifies the term "earth store" to declare that "anyone who believes in Him may obtain the treasures stored in the earth."[8] Among the members of Koganji, the *Jizō Bodhisattva Sūtra* is an article of faith.

Faith in Jizō is manifested in rituals performed during daily services at the temple. Devotions and *sūtra* readings follow a prescribed order and the chanting of certain words is accompanied by specific ritual gestures. For example, when devotees reach the word "*sanrai*" in the text, they make three bows, each with a silent declaration of faith in the Buddha, Dharma, and Sangha. At the words "*sange mon*," a confession of evil karma accumulated through one's greed, anger, and ignorance is made directly to "the compassion of Jizō." After this comes an expression of desire to hear, see, and realize the real meaning of the Tathāgata (i.e., the Buddha). Then Jizō's name is invoked seven times: *Namu jizō ganon son*. Although the role played by the *Lotus Sūtra* at Koganji is not as transparent as this, it is regarded as essential and complementary to faith in Jizō. To understand the link, it is necessary to look at Tendai's origins.

Foundations of the Tendai School

Jikyu frequently speaks of Dengyō Daishi, founder of the Tendai school, and honors him with these words:

> The immortal Teachings of Dengyō Daishi
> Shining brightly
> Even until the age of the Future Buddha
> The lantern of the Dharma.[9]

Dengyō Daishi is the honorific posthumous name for the Japanese monk Saichō, who became the first patriarch of the Tendai school in Japan. Saichō was from Omi, located in central Honshu on the Sea of Japan. Born into a devout Buddhist family named Mitsuomi, Saichō entered a Buddhist monastery at the age of 12, received novice ordination at 14, and full ordination at 19. Disenchanted with the type of Buddhism then practiced at Nara, he left and went to live in a hut on Mt. Hiei. Before long, he established a temple with Yakushi, the healing Buddha, as the central image.

Around 780 C.E., Saichō became interested in a Chinese form of Buddhism called Tiantai. Around this time, Emperor Kammu moved his capital from Nara to Kyoto and in 802, impressed with Saichō's interpretation of the *Lotus Sūtra*, became his patron. In 804, imperial sponsorship gave Saichō an opportunity to study with three important practitioners – Taosui, Xingman, and Huiran – at Mt. Tiantai in Chekiang province of China.[10]

The progenitor of the Tiantai school was the Chinese monk, Zhiyi (538–597), famous for his work on the *Saddharmapuṇḍarika Sūtra* (*Lotus of the Wonderful Law*). He interpreted this *sūtra* as a guide to salvation through practice and used it to elaborate the theory of the Three Truths: (1) all things (*dharmas*) are empty because they are produced through causation and therefore have no self-nature; (2) things do have temporary existence; and (3) the nature of things is both empty and temporary, which represents "the mean," or middle way. Because these three – emptiness, impermanence, and the mean – all entail one another, the one appears as three and the three appear as one.[11] In this way, ultimate truth, conventional truth, and the middle path are all expressions of one single integrated reality.

The theory of the Three Truths represents a paradigm shift in Buddhist thought. The new philosophy that developed spoke of the middle path in terms of "one-in-all" and "all-in-one." In place of "greater" and "lesser" vehicles, it posited "one vehicle" that traveled the middle path. Following this middle path brought enlightenment back into the temporary world, as expressed in the famous saying, "Every color or fragrance is none other than the middle path." This interpretation reaffirmed that every sentient being has Buddha nature and the potential to be saved.[12] This affirmation, foreshadowed by Zhiyi's interpretation of Nāgārjuna, validates every individual's Buddha nature and potential for enlightenment.

The *Lotus Sūtra* is taken as the source for a doctrine of universal salvation, in which not merely the extinction of *nirvāna*, but the attainment of Buddhahood is accessible to all. The *sūtra* specifies that meritorious actions such as installing an image of the Buddha, having such an image carved, worshipping, and singing the praises of the Buddha lead to Buddhahood. With this interpretation of the *Lotus Sūtra*, based on Zhiyi's understanding, Mahāyāna was in full flower. It was no longer simply a "great" vehicle, but "one" vehicle coming down from the "heavenly terrace" and landing squarely in the "middle" of the path.

It was on this core of teachings that Saichō founded Tendai. The young monk spent 92 months refining his knowledge of the *Lotus Sūtra* and other doctrines before returning to Japan. Not only did he refine his ideas and gain a greater appreciation for the *sūtra*, he also expanded them, becoming more inclusive than the Chinese. The Tiantai he studied in China was reserved for monks, but Saichō encouraged the laity to become practitioners as well.

The third *sūtra* that is central to Jikyu and Koganji is the *Heart of Wisdom Sūtra* (*Hannya Shingyō*). As the great Bodhisattva Avalokiteśvara studies the five aggregates (*skandhas*, i.e., form, feeling, recognition, karmic formations, and consciousness) and realizes they are empty, he overcomes suffering and reaches the allegorical "other shore." At Koganji, this *sūtra* is taught as a means of dealing with the sufferings of the world. Jikyu's interpretation is clearly reflected in one of her poems:

Higan ("Other Shore")

No matter how much you cry and regret,
The past is the past ...
See the ocean, the vast ocean,
See the sky, the endless sky.
Look ahead with confidence
Knowing that you are not alone.

Though it may rain, it will soon clear:
This is what is meant by the transitory world.
Dry your tears and open your eyes.
Spiritually enlightened, looking ahead it will be easy
To steer the ship to the Other Shore.

Having cried yourself, you can know the ache.
Help one another with a merciful heart.
Today, smilingly, put your hands together (in *gassho*),
Look forward with confidence
Knowing that you are not alone.[13]

To complete the picture of Koganji's spiritual foundations, it is important to understand Saichō's eclecticism. Rather than rejecting the indigenous Japanese deities (*kami*), the spirits or divine forces associated with the natural elements, Saichō is said to have taught the *Lotus Sūtra* to the popular Shintō deity Hachiman, protector of warriors and the community.[14] In a similar manner, Jikyu incorporates practices that have their roots in Shintō and other Japanese folk beliefs. An example is the *yakudoshi* ("critical, or unlucky years") blessing requested by women between the ages of 33 and 60 and men between 42 and 60. Koganji's blessings for houses and cars also seem to be rooted in folk belief. For example, a house blessing requires a fresh whole red fish, *sekihan* (rice with azuki beans), a small bottle of *sake*, an unopened bag of rice, and a new bag of rock salt. There is also a ritual for dealing with spiritual problems that requires throwing fresh blessed flowers over one's shoulder into the ocean without looking – taking care even to turn down the rearview mirrors to prevent catching a glimpse. All these practices have their origins in Japanese folk belief.

Jikyu's Sources of Inspiration

The figurative frame for this portrait of Koganji is the influence of Jikyu's teachers: Dengyō Daishi, Archbishop Haba, and Geika Etai Yamada. She frequently refers to Dengyō Daishi and his aim to "light up the world" by practicing devoutly and serving the community. She couples this with an injunction to "let your light shine." The quintessential advice she gained from these religious mentors is, "In this world you have to pray for peace and help each other."

A photograph of her third great source of inspiration, the great Geika Etai Yamada, has the place of honor on her shrine. Yamada, who died just a few years ago, returned to Hawai'i in 1991 to mark the 16th anniversary of Koganji. He was an active peace advocate, encouraging Buddhists to "lead the way to international harmony and world peace." In recognition of his efforts, he was honored with the Niwano Peace Prize in 1989.[15] On one of his last visits to Hawai'i, he conferred the title of *sōjō* (bishop) on Jikyu. He seems to have recognized a kindred spirit, brave enough to go forward on her own and speak out for what is right – a spirit totally committed to helping others and ready to light their way.

The Future of Koganji

Although Jikyu is now approaching 70, she still keeps up a busy schedule and only takes Mondays off. To conserve energy, she does her most demanding work from 8 a.m. to 2 p.m. Immediately after the daily morning service, she begins consultations with her temple members. Some may want advice on business deals, some may spread photographs on the table and ask which is the best potential husband, others may request memorial services for their departed loved ones or ask what offerings to make to Jizō Bodhisattva to handle a particular spiritual problem. Others may ask advice on medical problems.

Although Jikyu Sensei still graciously deals with each person and problem as it arises, she is beginning to feel a sense of urgency. The burden of caring for so many followers is beginning to show. Lester is afflicted with Alzheimer's disease and Jikyu's healing powers have not been able to reverse the condition. Financial concerns are also on her mind; Lester is no longer able to support her work and maintaining Koganji costs almost $10,000 a month. More important is the question of a successor.

Jikyu does not fear death, but openly worries about having the right person to care for her followers after she is gone. This question always seems to float just below the surface. There is an *ajari* in Japan that she would like to see succeed her, but Tendai politics and visa regulations have slowed the process of getting him to Hawai'i.

Koganji is a special place in the Tendai tradition, created by a remarkable woman. Jikyu has made this beautiful temple in Hawai'i a fitting place to honor Jizō, indelibly stamped with her own rich cultural heritage. When Jikyu attains the "Other Shore," perhaps Dengyō Daishi will be there to greet her. He might well pay tribute to this wise and compassionate woman who lets her light shine and relieves the sufferings of others.

Notes

1 I would like to express my appreciation to Bishop Jikyu Rose, who warmly welcomed me to Koganji, served me tea, and treated me like an honored guest during morning services and like an old friend during interviews. I also benefitted greatly from discussions with David W. Chappell, who patiently explained relevant doctrines and texts, and kindly lent me a copy of the *Kṣitigarbha Sūtra*.

2 *Devas* are longlived gods; *asuras*, demi-gods; *pretas*, hungry ghosts.

3 Jikyu Rose, *Koganji Temple Text One and Sūtras of the Jizō Bodhisattva* (Honolulu: Koganji, 1983), p. 20.

4 The benefits listed in the Chinese text differ slightly: (1) their soil will be rich and produce a good harvest; (2) the whole family will be in peace forever; (3) all deceased relatives will be born in the heavens; (4) all living relatives will have longevity; (5) all their aspirations will be achieved; (6) they will never suffer the dangers of flood and fire; (7) all bad becomings [states of rebirth] will be eliminated; (8) they will never have bad dreams; (9)

they will be protected by guardians wherever they go; and (10) they will always come across holy conditions. C. H. Pitt, trans., *Sutra on the Original Vows and the Attainment of Merits of Kṣitigarbha Bodhisattva* (Hong Kong: H. K. Buddhist Book Distributor, 1976), p. 27.

5 Ibid., p. 4.

6 Ibid., pp. 4–9.

7 Jikyu Rose, *Tendai Shu Koganji* (*Togenuki Jizō-son*) (Honolulu: Koganji, undated), p. i.

8 *Koganji Temple Text One*, p. 2.

9 Jikyu Rose, *Tendaishu Koganji: Koganji Temple 16th Anniversary* (Honolulu: Koganji, 1991), p. 1.

10 R. Tsunoda, W. T. DeBary, and D. Keene, *Sources of Japanese Tradition*, Vol 1 (New York: Columbia University Press, 1958), pp. 112–16.

11 Ibid., p. 310.

12 Ibid., 311.

13 Ibid., p. 24.

14 *Unity in Diversity: Hawaii's Buddhist Communities* (Kaneohe: Hawaii Association of International Buddhists, 1997), p. 240.

15 Ibid., p. 25.

PART II

Women in Compassionate Social Action

CHAPTER TWENTY-ONE

Buddhism and the Media

Elizabeth J. Harris

Are we victims or shapers of the media? Is the media our ally or adversary? What impression of Buddhism comes across in the media? Would we prefer to see it represented differently? These are the questions I want to explore with reference to radio, press, film, and television. These questions fall into two categories: How can we constructively engage with the media? And what message do we, as women, want to put across in a world of violence, war, and consumer madness? This is an exploration. I do not claim to answer these questions definitely, but rather to provoke further research and reflection. My point of view is as a writer for radio and the press. I wrote and presented a series of radio programs called *The Way of the Buddha* for the BBC World Service, a series that sought to convey the heart of Buddhism through the words of practitioners.[1] I first visited Cambodia to gather material for these programs, and some of the people I interviewed were there when I presented these ideas at the Śākyadhitā conference in Phnom Penh.

There are Buddhists in almost every country of the world and, in each country, the cultural and political context is different. Some Buddhists live in places where there is tight censorship of the press, radio, and television, and those who seek to publish what contravenes official policy may risk harassment and reprisals. Others live in countries where Buddhism is given a privileged place. Obtaining media coverage may be simple in Buddhist countries, but there can be dangers if some faces of Buddhism predominate at the expense of alternative or radical voices within the religious community, such as those of women.

Although many countries with large Buddhist populations have a sympathetic media which depicts Buddhism in a positive light, this same media can deliberately choose sensationalized headlines to tantalize readers. For example, Sri Lanka was my home for over seven years. I studied Buddhism and earned my doctorate there, forming a deep appreciation of Buddhism and Buddhist culture. Buddhism holds "foremost place" in Sri Lanka, according to the words of the present constitution, and will continue to hold this position if the Government's October 1997 proposals for constitutional reform eventually become law.[2] However, this privileged place does not prevent the media from deliberately choosing provocative headlines in its coverage of Buddhism. "All Ceylon Buddhist Congress crumbling on corruption charges,"[3] "Alleged rogue in yellow robes,"[4] and "Saṅgha flexes muscles,"[5] are but a few headlines randomly chosen from the Sunday papers. Of course, wholesome stories also appear. On the same day that the Saṅgha was reportedly flexing its muscles, the papers also highlighted a picture of a monk caught in the act of giving a bowl of food to a beggar, reversing the usual pattern of receiving alms.[6] There was also some positive reportage of the higher ordination of Theravāda nuns that occurred in Sārnāth on December 8, 1996.[7] Still, in Sri Lanka, as in Britain, coverage often depends on the political sympathies of each paper's editor. What is omitted can be as significant as what is reported.

The Western media especially seizes on scandal and the sensational without regard to context or complexity. Often such simplistic reportage downgrades religion as fit only for the mentally unsound. Here, let me take Britain as an example. "A religion is just a cult with more followers," is how one commentator dismissed the subject in a British paper not long ago.[8] In Britain, Buddhism is generally underreported in relation to its growing popularity.[9] More space is given to those religions that are immediately visible by external markers such as ethnicity or dress. When Buddhism does appear in the press, it usually hangs on a few well-worn pegs: the adoption of Buddhism by celebrities, Tibet, the Dalai Lama, or the scandalous.

Film portrayals of Buddhism often have not achieved success in the West. When the film *Little Buddha*, by Bertolucci, an Italian producer, was released in Britain several years ago, even Buddhists did not flock to see it, mainly because the film took a motif that did not speak to all schools – the reincarnation of a lama.[10] Even the CD of the music can hardly be found in the shops. Similarly, the film *Seven Years in Tibet* did little for Buddhism in Britain. Perhaps this was because the producer created a film to feature a matinee idol rather than a serious presentation of Tibetan Buddhist culture.

In print, *The Guardian*, a British national daily newspaper, seized on the scandalous by writing a hard-hitting article about the Western Buddhist Order. Entitled "The Dark Side of Enlightenment," it accused the order of damaging vulnerable people through sanctioning manipulative behavior in single-sex communities.[11] Individual cases cited included that of Mark Dunlop, who claimed that the founder of the order, Sangharakshita, had tried to force him, through repeated physical contact, to conquer his anti-homosexual conditioning with the argument that it blocked him from spiritual progress. The headlines and captions for the article – for example, "Sex and the Sect" – were deliberately provocative, casting a sinister light over meditation and the whole of Buddhist practice. Selected quotations from the writings of Sangharakshita implied that the aberrations highlighted sprang directly from emphases within his teaching.

Some of the allegations are founded on fact. Sexual misconduct occurred in one center of the order and members of the order never hid this. In fact, they closed the center down. However, the article's negative message has been used by anti-cult groups in universities and colleges to discredit the whole of Buddhism, even though the order dealt with the matter in an appropriate way. Having said all this, I nevertheless believe that, in Britain, Buddhism's message is potentially media-friendly, if presented with the full co-operation of Buddhists.

The dangers within media coverage of Buddhism include the presence of hidden agendas and the thirst for eye-catching headlines or ear-tantalizing soundbites. An additional danger is the projection of inappropriate categories onto Buddhism by journalists who know little about things religious, let alone Buddhism. An example of this came in a radio interview I heard by chance in 1997. An interviewer reported that a Buddhist monk in Hong Kong used the phrase, "personal practice." The interviewer then explained this to the listeners as a preoccupation with "the inner self." He went on to suggest that such a preoccupation lay in direct opposition to social involvement and compassionate action, revealing his ignorance of the basic Buddhist doctrine of *anatta* and the link between mental cultivation and social action.

The main danger in media coverage of religion is one of misrepresentation. At a practical level, whenever presenters, producers, and writers have inadequate information, misrepresentation will occur. At a philosophical level, wherever there is greed, hatred, and delusion, wherever observers of Buddhism and listeners to the Buddha's teachings observe and listen through senses clouded by the defilements (*kilesas*), there will be misrepresentation. Here I return to my original question. How do we deal with this misrepresentation?

A good place to start is with the *suttas*. The dangers of miscommunication and misunderstanding certainly existed in the Buddha's time. In examining passages in which the Buddha counters misrepresentation, we can find keys to handing problematic present-day reporting. This is not the place to discuss whether the words put in the mouth of the Buddha in the Pāli texts are words the Buddha actually spoke. Even if the texts we have are the result of a process of redaction, stylization, and systematization to meet the demands both of oral transmission and the social and religious context of the early disciples – not least of all, the inevitable dialogue with other religious groups[12] – this does not mean that the texts should be discounted, but rather that the wider context of transmission needs to be taken into account in the hermeneutical task. This is vitally important in examining passages in which the Buddha counters incidents of misrepresentation, for each example both relates to an actual incident and also to a wider context of contemporary dialogue with other religious groups. Seen in this light, they are not simply isolated events, but an integral part of the contemporary discourse with which the early followers were forced to engage.

The Pāli texts point to a context of debate, dispute, and quarrel between rival religious groups, a climate in which short, snappy stereotypes were accepted currency. The texts relate numerous instances where the Buddha is presented as misunderstood or the object of false rumors. Whether connected with reports of miracles, asceticism, coercion, or preaching annihilationism, the Buddha is portrayed as facing serious allegations due to misreportage.

In the *Kassapa Sihanāda Sutta*,[13] for instance, Kassapa, a naked ascetic, is shown coming to the Buddha and saying something like this: "Is it true, as I have heard, that the Buddha reviles and finds fault with every ascetic, with everyone who leads a hard life?" Kassapa is keen to know whether this is true or false, since it is a judgment on his choice of life. The question itself reveals that the Buddha's word have been distorted through retelling. The Buddha had, at one time, lived an ascetic lifestyle and subsequently rejected it. He had found through experience that a healthy body was necessary for a healthy mind and taught this middle way to others. His own serene, glowing appearance would have embodied the message. While it is true that at times he criticized asceticism as a way of life, to say that he reviled all ascetics is false and a gross injustice typical of the way the media works today.

A similar example from the *suttas* is the allegation by Vacchagotta[14] that the Buddha claimed the only alms that brought rewards were those given to him and his disciples, and that alms should not be given to followers of other teachers. Again, one can imagine the process. The Buddha's original words could have been that any giving is virtuous, but that giving to people who are virtuous is even better. In the media machine of the fifth century B.C.E.,[15] this concept was twisted until it proclaimed that only the Buddha and his own followers were virtuous and deserving of alms.

Another example comes from the Vinaya Piṭaka.[16] A brahmin comes to the Buddha and accuses him of being one "without enjoyment," of professing a doctrine of inaction, teaching annihilation and austerities.

A slightly different example is found in the *Majjhima Nikāya*.[17] A wanderer's son approaches a follower of the Buddha and reports that he had heard the Buddha say, "A deed of body is foolish, a deed of speech is foolish, only a deed of mind is truth." The Buddha's original statement no doubt referred to the importance of the mind and actions of mind, but was obviously misunderstood.

Can we learn from how the Buddha responds to these allegations, according to the Pāli texts? Are his methods relevant today? I think we can. I believe the methods he used are as relevant today as they were then. Anger and the wish to defend oneself or one's religious practice are two reactions to misrepresentation: "How could that possibly be said! How could that journalist or television reporter be so stupid! How dare they say that of us!" These thoughts come almost naturally to mind and are rooted in a sense of hurt and injustice. But they can lead to distorted thinking and unfruitful engagement with those who have misunderstood. They are in fact fruits of greed, hatred, and delusion.

At a very basic level, the Buddha engaged with those who questioned him. He did not seek controversy, yet he did not hesitate to correct distorted views, clearly and distinctly. Importantly, he did not demolish the point of the other with anger or defensiveness, but responded seriously, agreeing with the truthful aspects. For instance, in the example taken from the Vinaya, the Buddha agrees that there is some truth in each allegation. Yes, the Buddha *does* preach a doctrine of annihilation, but it is the annihilation of greed, hatred, and delusion, the annihilation of evil and wrong states of mind, not total annihilation at death. He agrees that the Buddha *is* one who is without enjoyment, but clarifies that he is without enjoyment of sense pleasures, not without an appreciation of beauty or the experience of happiness. He does not deny that the Buddha professes a doctrine of inaction, but explains that it is a non-doing of offenses of body, speech, and thought, not withdrawal of active concern for the world. It is as though the Buddha is saying in each case, "You have a partial truth, not the whole. You have ignored the total context of my words and have seized on half-truths."

In the *Kassapa Sihanāda Sutta*, the approach is different. The Buddha categorically says that it would be wrong to say that he reviles *all* ascetics. Yet he leads Kassapa to realize that asceticism is not an end in itself, that it is a questionable lifestyle if it does not lead to the destruction of the defilements and a heart which knows no anger and ill-will. Again, he is implying that Kassapa's original allegation had some truth in it, but not the whole truth.

On the evidence of the texts, the Buddha used methods which sought to uncover errors in understanding and, with respect and sensitivity, pointed the accuser to the full meaning of his own teaching. Although the context has changed, I believe the principle is still relevant. When the media highlights the negative within religion or seizes on the sensational, there is often some truth in the allegation. In practice, all religion has a dark side, Buddhism included. Religion has harmed the world as well as uplifted it. When the religious affairs correspondent of *The Guardian* uncovered abuses within the Western Buddhist Order, the order openly admitted that one of their centers had had to be closed down because it had gone wrong. It did not hide this from the media. But it was quick to add that it was unjustified to say that such abuses were continuing in an unbroken line from that event. In replies to the original article both in the national press and in their own journal, *Dharma Life*, they pressed this point.[18]

An important lesson to learn is that nothing is gained if what goes wrong within Buddhism is hidden. After all, at the very center of Buddhism is an image of the world entangled and on fire with craving, or *taṇhā*. It is not surprising that this craving enters religion itself sometimes.

One of the most important lessons that can be extrapolated from the Pāli texts is to engage seriously and openly with the media. This requires a willingness to recognize our mistakes. We must also encourage the media to consider the total context. In the Pāli texts the Buddha is shown doing this through asking questions such as: Does this allegation make sense? Is it rational? Does it accord with your experience of me? Does it match your experience of me? Does it agree with the totality of my teaching? The texts assert that he did not use the methods of some of his contemporaries who were "experienced in controversy, hair-splitters, who go about breaking into pieces by their wisdom the speculations of their adversaries."[19] He did not seek to demolish the arguments of others through polemic. He is shown to be the supreme embodiment of skillful means, meeting people where they are, drawing them on through compassion.

In contemporary society, when a television program or a newspaper presents distorted perspectives on Buddhism, a balanced conversation, in which distortions are revealed and righted, is not usually possible. After all, the damage has already been done. The words have been printed. The phrases have been uttered. Yet the general principle remains valid, that of constructively engaging with open-minded media representatives. Ordinary religious people need not be passive victims of the media but must help to mold it. There are sections of the media which are willing to listen, in every country. We all have a task in making Buddhism better understood, through approaching the media with suggestions and the potential resources to make those suggestions reality.

The Message We Wish to Communicate

Do we want to pander to the sensational soundbite and the simplistic story? Or do we want to challenge contemporary society with a message some might find uncomfortable? When I was asked to create a series of radio programs on Buddhism by the BBC World Service, it was not because I was a media expert but because I was teaching Buddhism at the time and had contacts with Buddhists around the world, who could actually give me the content of the programs. Writing those programs forced me to face some central questions about how to communicate Buddhism.

The aim of the radio programs was to communicate Buddhist principles and practice to people who knew very little about them. My approach was to use the words of others. I chose to let practitioners speak for themselves, using many different contexts, and the crucial question was "What aspects of Buddhism should be emphasized?"

Three categories emerged. First were the concerns of those who knew little about Buddhism. Giving talks to Christians about Buddhism in Sri Lanka and England had given me some experience of this. The intricacies of *Abhidhamma* within Theravāda Buddhism were certainly out, as were detailed explanations of the Vinaya. Questions took a more simple form: Is the Buddha worshipped? Is the aim of meditation to make the mind a blank? Why do monks and nuns wear the colors they do? What do Buddhists believe happens after death? Do Buddhists believe in God? Do Buddhists pray?

The next category involved stereotypes which seem prevalent in the West and need to be challenged. Last came the question of what Buddhism could do both to reinforce what was good in all cultures and to challenge what was unwholesome. The first category involved conveying basic facts in an accessible form and I will not concentrate on this here. I would like to focus on the last two, informed both by perspectives shared with me in interviews for the programs and my own appreciation of Buddhism.

Currently my work involves building inter-faith understanding. In this, I frequently encounter stereotypes of Buddhism. One of the most common, especially in the West, is that Buddhism is only about gaining self-fulfillment and inner peace. An extreme example of this can be seen in some words of Cardinal Joseph Ratzinger, prefect of the Roman Congregation of the Doctrine of the Faith at the Vatican. In a series of reflections which were reported in *The Tablet*, a Roman Catholic journal, he went so far as to link Buddhism with "a spiritual auto-eroticism."[20] In other words, he suggested that the practice of Buddhism could be reduced to the search for a feeling of almost erotic well-being. What a travesty! It is a horrible twisting of the peace which is the fruit of practice. This misrepresentation is the result of Buddhism being linked with other self-fulfillment therapies in the West in a post-modern society – one of many options to be taken off the shelf and used to create a better quality of life.

Inner peace is the result of practice, but it is not enough to refer to inner peace alone when speaking about the Buddhist path. Where inner peace alone is stressed as the essence of Buddhism, the cutting edge of the Dhamma is lost, for there is a cost to gaining inner peace or uncovering that purity of mind, and that is the elimination of the defilements, or *kilesas*. Greed, hatred, and delusion (*lobha*, *dosa*, *moha*) are the three defilements, but the *Visuddhi Magga* (*The Path of Purification*), an important compendium of doctrine within the Pāli tradition, written in the fifth century C.E. by Bhadantācariya Buddhaghosa, adds seven more: conceit (*māna*), clinging to opinions or speculative views (*diṭṭhi*), skeptical doubt (*vicikicchā*), mental laziness (*thīna*), restlessness (*uddhacca*), shamelessness (*arihika*), and the lack of moral dread (*anottappa*).[21] To eliminate these defilements is hard work and certainly has nothing to do with auto-eroticism. It has everything to do with the strenuous cultivation of "the heart of love that knows no anger, that knows no ill-will," in the words of the *Kassapa Sihanāda Sutta*.

The questions on meditation that I asked contributors in the programs elicited answers that could certainly help counter this stereotype. Helen Jandamit, a well-known meditation teacher in Thailand, set the scene:

> The teaching of the Buddha is, "Do good, avoid evil, and purify the mind." Meditation is about purifying the mind. It is very difficult to avoid evil if your mind is not pure because you're dragged in there whether you want to be or not. And it is the same for doing good. Sometimes we're doing good for all the wrong reasons, but if you purify the mind then you're able to see clearly what you are doing and determine how much or how little to do, and what is right and what is wrong.

Ven. Professor Dhammavihari in Sri Lanka added this:

> *Bhāvanā* (meditation) should not be the mere ability to fix your mind on the bulb that is burning on the ceiling or the glow of light on the wall. But it is to know that you have gradually peeled off the stains of contamination in your mind: conflict, ill-will, jealousy, rivalry. It is a question of how clean your inside is.

Aloysius Pieris, S.J., a Jesuit priest, committed meditator, and renowned scholar of Buddhism emphasized the hard work involved:

> The ultimate goal of meditation is greedlessness, which is really a definition of *nibbāna*. The purpose of meditation is that. It's not just an ego trip to another world. It is simply a hard, committed, continuous, uninterrupted effort at eradicating the egocentric building of a world around yourself. It is to break those barriers and to be free enough, not only to enjoy the freedom yourself, but to share it with others.

The goal of Buddhism is the liberation that comes when the defilements have been eradicated. There is joy. There is the peace that can enable the meditator to engage with others from a point of inner strength and equanimity. Voices such as these counter the distortion that comes when this peace is interpreted only as escapism or a form of erotic well-being.

Another stereotype linked to this is that Buddhism has little to say about society, that it is concerned with withdrawal and renunciation only. This erroneous idea is akin to the passage quoted earlier from the Vinaya. It has been around for a long time! The stereotype contains a half-truth. The Buddhist path most certainly involves renunciation. But it is renunciation of such things as greed, obsessive accumulation and consumerism, violence, arrogance, and competition. It is not renunciation of concern for society, but renunciation of all those traits that cause havoc in society, traits that flow from the *kilesas*. Again and again, this was expressed in the lives and words of those interviewed for the programs, particularly in Thailand, Cambodia, and Sri Lanka.

Bhikkhu Santikaro, an American monk resident in Thailand, spoke about the mandate to relieve suffering:

> To me, the main thrust of Buddhism is an approach to life that aims at ending suffering, and suffering the way the Buddha presented it was never modified by pronouns like "my" suffering or "our" suffering. He just talked about the reality of suffering in the world, analyzed its causes, and proposed responses that intelligent, committed people of good will could put into practice. He never limited it to just *my* suffering. I think many Buddhists have made the mistake of interpreting the teachings very personally. That, of course, is part of it, but there's suffering everywhere. Buddhism needs to be a vehicle for individuals and groups and, if possible, even societies to understand, confront, and dismantle the structures which create suffering, whether it's an inner personal ego structure or a structure in society such as capitalism, consumerism, or patriarchy.

Professor Gunapala Dharmasiri, a Sri Lankan Mahāyāna Buddhist, rooted his words in the concept of interdependence:

> Everything is part of an enormous web of interdependent relations. This contains an extremely sophisticated theory of morality. If you are related to others, that means you have obligations to everything else. Your existence is dependent on everything else in the universe. Therefore, everything in nature becomes your parent. You exist because of them and therefore you have this incredible moral obligation towards everything else.

Ven. Paisan Wisalo, a Thai monk, stressed that social action and mental cultivation are two sides of one coin:

> There are two aspects of the Buddha's teaching. The first is to act intelligently – the exterior act. The second is to enlighten your mind. To be detached means to be free from hatred, greed, and delusion. It doesn't mean that we should refrain from action, that we shouldn't do anything. The Buddha emphasized that we have to work hard, to be diligent, to accomplish what has to be done. This is the aspect of exterior behavior which is accomplished by our body. It is social work. But at the same time it has to be done together with mental work, and the mental work is to be detached. To be detached without working, without doing anything, is not the Buddha's teaching.

Among the women we interviewed, the emphasis was often searingly practical. Dr. Chatsumarn Kabilsingh, of Thammasat University, Bangkok, said:

> We have a population of 60 million. Ninety-four percent of the people are Buddhist. But the fact that the majority of people in this country are Buddhist doesn't help us to become better Buddhists. We have taken it for granted. We have become negligent of the real teaching. One sidetrack is that we tend to commercialize Buddhism. We observe the precepts. We go to the temple. We make a donation. But when we make a donation of 100 baht, we make a wish that we will become very rich or very successful in our business or that we will have a big house. We make a donation of a hundred baht and ask for so many things! Expecting things in return is not the Buddhist attitude. The Buddhist attitude is to let go.

Kim Leng, who works at the Dhammayietra Centre for Peace and Non-Violence in Cambodia, spoke about the teaching given to participants in the annual *dhammayietras*, or walks for peace. Such walks have taken place every year since 1992, often going right into the middle of the conflict zones, putting the walkers at considerable personal risk. Involvement with issues of peace and violence is central to her Buddhist practice, but she was quick to explain that such involvement would be impossible without mental culture. This is what she teaches participants in the *dhammayietras* in preparatory workshops:

> First, the *dhammayietra* teaches its own participants, the walkers, to have Dhamma – to walk in a spirit of meditation and to have peace within our own selves first, before we can have peace outside. So when we are walking, we are mindful at every moment, not allowing our thoughts to go in different directions. We teach all participants about nonviolence so that even if we enter dangerous areas we will not be afraid. We will know that even if we are risking our lives, we are risking our lives for peace. It is also important to teach participants how to deal with their own fear, how to deal with any danger that they might encounter so that they will not wait for others to solve problems for them.

Then there was Mae chi Khunying Kanitha, a Thai nun, who had spent a lifetime trying to better the lives of women. When still a layperson, she opened her own home as an emergency shelter for battered women:

> When I was using my home, I wrote to all the police stations and hospitals in Bangkok telling them to send any woman needing a temporary home because of distress. I will always remember the first time an ambulance came to my house. It happened to be a woman who was drunk. She had been unconscious on the roadside with a five- or six-month-old baby crawling on her body. The police had not known what to do with her. One eventually remembered, "Oh, there

> was one lady who offered her house!" So they brought her to me and I cleaned her with cool water and things like that. We helped her.
>
> Many men come to Bangkok from rural areas to work on building sites. These workers send the money to their family or ask their family to come and collect the pay. This woman had come several times to one construction site but, that particular month, the construction work had finished and everyone had moved away. So, she didn't know what to do. She told me, "I was so frightened. I got lost. I had no money – only three baht." And she had used that money to buy alcohol. This is the kind of thing that happens to many women. The men leave the family behind and they find other women in the big city.
>
> I have helped many kinds of women. One other case was an elderly woman who had several children. She told me she could not live with any one of them. They had made it obvious they did not want her. So she had to leave their homes and someone recommended she come to us. She was the first woman to move from my house to the new shelter.

All these excerpts show compassion in action, whether it be witnessing for peace, challenging consumerism, pointing to the dangers of a society overpowered by greed, or meeting the needs of individuals. I could have added many more. All challenge the stereotype that Buddhism encourages complete withdrawal from active concern for society. Put succinctly, they embody the message that there is a problem at the root of existence, caused by greed, hatred, and delusion, and the way to wholeness in society and the individual lies in eliminating these defilements. To root them out, both mental cultivation and action in society are needed. To live this message involves radical challenges to every society. This is the message that the media should be urged to portray.

It is not always a comfortable message. It is not as media-friendly as a picture of Buddhism as an easy path to peace. But it is a critical message in this age of global consumerism, ecological rape, and conflict. To communicate this message, constructive engagement with the media is essential. We need not be victims. We can be its shapers.

The important questions continue to be: What is the central message that we want to put across? What misunderstandings need to be rectified or false representations challenged? What is the challenge or model that Buddhist women should express to society through their lives and practice? I have given a personal perspective on these. It is only one perspective, but I believe it can help society understand what the Buddha meant when he said that his teaching concerned "suffering and the end of suffering."

Notes

1 Now published in book form: Elizabeth Harris, *What Buddhists Believe* (Oxford: Oneworld), 1998.
2 The Government's Proposals for Constitutional Reform, October 1997, state, "The Republic of Sri Lanka shall give to Buddhism the foremost place and, accordingly, it shall be the duty of the State to protect and foster the Buddha Sāsana while giving adequate protection to all religions and guaranteeing to every person the rights and freedoms granted by paragraphs (1) and (3) of Article 15."
3 *The Times*, May 8, 1997.
4 *The Times*, January 5, 1997.
5 *The Sunday Leader*, December 15, 1996.
6 Ibid.
7 For example, D. Amarasiri Weeraratne's "Revival of Bhikkhuni Order in Sri Lanka," *The Island*, March 2, 1997.
8 Polly Toynbee, "In Defence of Islamophobia," *The Independent* (U.K.), November 23, 1997.
9 For example, see David Scott, "Buddhism in the Media," in *Discernment*, New Series 3, no. 3 (1996/7): 12–23.
10 See Elizabeth Harris, "Little Buddha," ibid., pp. 24–29.
11 Madeleine Bunting, "The Dark Side of Enlightenment," *The Guardian*, October 27, 1997.
12 Useful studies relevant to this issue include: Richard Gombrich, *How Buddhism Began: The Conditioned Genesis of the Early Teachings* (London and Atlantic Highlands, N.J.: Athlone, 1996); K. R. Norman, *A Philological Approach to Buddhism* (London: School of Oriental and African Studies, University of London, 1997); and Greg Bailey, "Problems of the Interpretation of the Data Pertaining to Religious Interaction in Ancient India: The Conversion Stories of the Sutta Nipata," *Religious Traditions in South Asia: Interaction and Change*, ed. Geoffrey A. Oddie (Richmond, Surrey: Curzon, 1998).
13 *Dialogues of the Buddha*, vol. 1, 161ff.
14 *Gradual Sayings*, vol. 1, p. 160.
15 I take here the dating of the Buddha put forward by scholars such as Richard Gombrich who argue that the historical Buddha lived in the fifth century B.C.E., rather than the sixth. See, for example, "Dating the Buddha: A Red Herring Revealed," in *The Dating of the Buddha*, Part 2, ed. Heinz Bechert (Göttingen: Vandenhoeck & Ruprecht, 1992), pp. 237–59.
16 *The Book of Discipline*, vol. 1, no. 1 (*Pārājika* 1).
17 *Mahākammavibhaṅga Sutta*, *Middle Length Sayings*, vol. 3, 207ff.
18 See *The Guardian*, Nov. 8, 1997. For a reply by an order member, see Vishvapani's "Learning the Harsh Way," *Dharma Life* (Spring 1998): 56–61.
19 *Dialogues of the Buddha*, vol. 1, p. 162.
20 "Interview with the Panzer-Cardinal," in *The Tablet*, March 29/April 5, 1997, p. 447. It is probable that he drew this perspective on Buddhism from Hans Urs von Balthasar (1908–1988), a Swiss Roman Catholic theologian. See M. Kehl and W. Loser, eds., *A Von Balthasar Reader* (Edinburgh: T & T Clark, 1982), pp. 325–47.
21 *The Path of Purification*, trans. Bhikkhu Ñāṇamoli (Kandy: Buddhist Publication Society) XXII.49, p. 708.

CHAPTER TWENTY-TWO

Diversity as Practice

Thinking about Race and "American" Buddhism

Lori Pierce

Most Americans are now well aware of the diverse and heterogeneous nature of our past. American history is the history of the often violent encounter between native peoples, European explorers, immigrants, and enslaved Africans. The story of who we are today, people who speak different languages, who have different values, beliefs, and practices, is one we are growing increasingly comfortable with. Though the national discussion of racial oppression and the implications of ethnic diversity have lurched along fitfully, I see in my own teaching of undergraduate students that some progress has been made.

Many problems, however, remain unsolved. Many questions remain undiscussed, even unasked. The question I wish to raise here concerns the discussion of race in the sphere of religion. As an academician I began to ask these question as a method of furthering my own research; they have, I think, specific implications for other historians and researchers in the field of American religion. But the town/gown split never fully applies in the field of religion. Those who study religion, even the history of religion, tend also to be concerned with the implications of their study for the communities of belief. In this discussion of race and American Buddhism I am concerned with the implications of racial ideologies, both in the academic discipline of religious studies and in temples, *saṅghas*, and other sites of worship and practice. The notion of "diversity as practice" is peculiarly suited to American Buddhist practitioners as well as those of us who research and write.[1] Diversity – meaning racial and ethnic difference and the problems that have resulted from the hierarchical structuring of difference in American social and political life – has been America's recurrent *koan*. No era of American history has been free of the struggle for justice of those who have been marginalized by White supremacist notions of difference. These struggles have a particular resonance for Americans because our founding ideologies were so clearly articulated as expressions of equality and justice for all. The irony of the struggle between those who have held power and espoused liberty and justice for all, and those who have been distanced from centers of power but asserted their rights to liberty and justice, has created the opportunity for us. How can we as American Buddhists use this conundrum, this *koan*, which is at the heart of American life, as a meaningful way to engage what it means to be both "American" and "Buddhist"?

I cannot discuss all of these questions within the confines of this article; I wish only to take this opportunity to sketch out some of the ground rules, as it were, of what a discussion of race in American Buddhism must take into consideration. We must first consider the nature of race and racism and how these beliefs have structured American life; we must then re-evaluate the history of American Buddhism in order to be more inclusive and attentive to diversity; finally, we must find ways to push the discussion beyond "mere" diversity and toward the implications of racial ideologies on religious belief and spiritual practice.

Henry Louis Gates has called race "a trope of irreducible difference."[2] The history of the concept of race is entangled with the history of science and pseudo-science in the West.[3] Many cultures developed belief systems which assert their superiority over others, but the racial ideologies of Western Europeans have grown out of a specific philosophical system of thought.[4] The history of the concept of race in the West parallels the development of Western philosophy, science, and imperialism. Though many scientists were instrumental in creating the racial classification system we are now familiar with, the delineation of human races into a five-fold division was the creation of Johan Friedrich Blumenbach (1752–1840). Blumenbach surmised that there were five racial "types"; Caucasian (Europeans), Mongolian (Asians), Ethiopian (Africans), American (native inhabitants of the "new" world), and Malay (Polynesian or South Pacific Islanders). What is significant about these racial varieties is that they are not based on scientific logic, but rather upon casual observation and speculation. As such, they were necessarily informed by common thinking about human differences which was pervasive at the time. Blumenbach, whom we might consider "liberal" politically (he supported the abolition of slavery and believed in the equal capacity of all humans), based his taxonomy of racial type on aesthetics. Caucasians, those who were born in the region of Europe closest to the Caucasus mountains, were, in his opinion, the most beautiful people in the world. "Ethiopians" were, obviously, the least beautiful, so "Whites" and "Blacks"[5] came to represent the extreme ends of the racial spectrum.[6]

Our thinking about race has been informed by supposedly scientific and "objective" observations about the world. However, population biologists now know that the genetic difference *within* "racial" groups is as great as the genetic difference *between* groups. In other words, the difference of skin color, eye fold, and hair texture we see as "natural" markers of racial difference are "accidental" characteristics which cross over "racial boundaries" with stunning frequency. The seeming permanence of racial groups has been a function of geographic dispersal and isolation. All humans share the characteristics which make us fully human; the markers of difference represent an incredibly small portion of our DNA.

The concept of race that we have inherited from our European ancestors, then, is largely mythological and highly politicized. Though many European scientists were true to objectivist standards, it is impossible to avoid the political implications of difference. The enslavement of millions of Africans is only the most obvious example of the way in which racial ideologies rationalized a highly profitable economic enterprise. Though many slave traders and slave owners were twinged by their consciences, especially after their "property" became Christians, the profit they exacted more often than not outweighed their principles. Thomas Jefferson, whose political writing so clearly articulated our "American" values, was, of course, a slave owner who could never bring himself to square his principles with his practices.[7]

The belief in the inherent superiority of White Europeans is clearly implicated in American history. The first law defining American citizenship written in 1790 restricted the privilege to "free White European males." The restriction of citizenship to "Whites" led to a perverse series of court challenges by Asian Indian and Japanese immigrants to have their "race" designated "White" in order to conform to White supremacists' notions of who could be successfully assimilated.[8] The result of the belief in race as White supremacy has been profound. Racism, defined here as acts or policies which "create or reproduce structures of domination based on essentialist categories of race"[9] is integrally intertwined in the history of all our social structures. Our legal system, which denied minorities the right to testify against Whites and denied citizenship to Asians; our educational system, which rationalized segregation in all parts of the country; our political system, which denied voting rights to vote to Blacks, women, and legal immigrants, have all been profoundly racist in that they have all contributed to the creation of images of non-Whites as somehow unworthy of the privilege of American rights. Further, these and other institutions throughout American history have systematically denied access to economic advancement and political power to non-Whites.

Since Western racial ideologies assert the supremacy of "Whites," this creates a privileged "raceless" status for Whites implying that racial problems are "minority" problems. Race is not just a problem that "non-Whites" must deal with. Every act of discrimination against non-Whites secures some subtle form of privilege for Whites. For example, at the end of Reconstruction in the South, many state legislatures passed "Black Codes" which effectively denied African Americans the right to vote guaranteed them by the Fifteenth Amendment. Southern legislators saw themselves as "protecting" the franchise from abuse by ignorant ex-slaves. By ridding the rolls of Black voters, Southern Whites enjoyed nearly 100 years of uncontested hegemony over the South, even in areas where they were the minority population. Any act of discrimination against one person secures privilege for someone else. Race and racism, then, are problems for all of us – those who have been the victims of discrimination as well as those who have been the beneficiaries of racial privileges.

Churches, temples, synagogues – religious institutions of every type – are necessarily implicated by racial ideologies. Even a cursory knowledge of American history makes it impossible to assert that somehow religious institutions could be exempt from the influence of racial ideologies. From this perspective it is easy to see how we have gotten to a point where "American" Buddhism has been defined by the concerns, beliefs, and values of White Euroamericans. Just as citizenship was defined as the province of "Whites," so to has "American" come to be synonymous with "White." So the study of American Buddhism has come to be dominated by the study of White Euroamericans and is only peripherally concerned with Asian immigrants, in spite of the fact that Asian Americans have always been the majority of Buddhists in this country.[10]

Recovering the entirety of American Buddhist history would show that for the last 100 years the vast majority of American Buddhists have been Asian American. The single largest Buddhist institution in the United States has been the Buddhist Churches of America (BCA) which, prior to their forced closure due to the World War II-era internment of Japanese Americans on the mainland, encompassed a network of 44 Hongwanji temples or churches. The first Japanese Buddhist priests arrived in California and Hawai'i in the late 19th century (1898 on the Mainland and 1889 in Hawai'i) in response to the requests of immigrants who labored in the agricultural industries of Hawai'i and the western United States. Though the majority of Japanese immigrants belonged to Jōdo Shinshū sects (what came to be known as the Buddhist Churches of America), by 1941 Buddhist temples representing Nichiren, Shingon, Tendai, Sōtō, and Jōdo-shū traditions had been established. In 1930 it is estimated that there were as many as 11,000 member families belonging to the Buddhist Churches of America alone. In Hawai'i prior to World War II there were 39 temples throughout the territory. The headquarters in Honolulu had over 2,000 adult members in 1931.[11]

While Japanese immigrants and their children formed the bulk of these congregations, many Buddhist temples were open to the inquiries of Euroamericans and formed groups, variously known as "the Buddhist Brotherhood" or "the Dharma Saṅgha of the Buddha," to accommodate their interests. In Hawai'i, Bishop Yemyo Imamura presided over the conversion of dozens of "Haole" (White) Buddhists, many from among Hawaii's more prominent and wealthy families. This is, so far as I know, the only instance of Euroamericans converting to and joining a "minority" religious institution except in cases of intermarriage. These Haole Buddhists are also interesting because they demonstrate the fact that it was not inevitable that the Buddhist Churches of America become an "ethnic" religion, exclusively made up of Japanese American families. The very first generation of American Buddhists was nominally diverse and many Japanese priests made significant efforts to reach out to their Euroamerican neighbors, even as they ministered to their Japanese congregations.

The common objection to inserting ethnic history into "mainstream" history is that the concerns of "ethnic" institutions, especially religious institutions, are specific and peculiar to their community. The Italian American Catholic Church is not representative of the whole field of American religious history, and therefore it should not be presumed that if we talk about Italian American Catholics, we have sufficiently told the story of all American Catholics. Similarly, it might be argued that Japanese American Buddhism, represented by the Buddhist Churches of America, did come to exist within an ethnic enclave, and the beliefs and practices are specific to the Japanese American community and therefore only of limited help in understanding all of American Buddhism.

This is, of course, a convenient way of continuing to ignore the significance of Asian American Buddhism in the development of American Buddhism. Rather than focusing on the differences between these two communities, and seeing them as incompatible and therefore irrelevant to one another, we ought to broaden our conception of "American." We have only to look at the example of American history to see how scholarship can define how and what we think. It took a generation of minority, women, and working-class scholars to broaden the common understanding of American history beyond the concerns, ideals, and values of not just White Americans but the wealthy ruling class. What would it mean if our understanding of "American" Buddhism had to be widened enough to include Asian American practices as well as those that concerned and interested European Americans? Because of the focus on multicultural history, we ought to be able to look around and recognize a wide variety of Americans; to be American need not mean being White or conforming to "White" values or beliefs. Similarly, if we broaden our understanding of American Buddhist history to include a discussion of the growth of the BCA on a par with the significance of the Parliament of World Religions, it no longer seems necessary to talk about Asian American Buddhism separately from Euroamerican Buddhism. American Buddhist studies ought to reflect the diversity of America as a whole. In that way it becomes less problematic to talk about the vast proliferation of Buddhist thought and practice in the late 20th century. If in our history we see that American Buddhism has always been heterogeneous, then the vast diversity of belief, practice, and ethnicity that exists at the present moment is less problematic.

The study of religion has only just begun to address questions of race and diversity. Scholars in this field have been particularly successful in reinventing American religious history in such a way that is "inclusive" of Native American traditions, Hispanic Catholicism, the ethnic diversity of Christian Churches, the proliferation of Judaism, and the effect of political progressivism on religious activism. The field has become wonderfully multifarious. However, the field can also be seen as "merely" diverse. The problem with the mainstreaming of diversity is that we assume that we have "addressed" the problem of diversity merely by calling attention to it. For example, I recently attended a conference of younger scholars in religion. Many of the papers that were delivered during the weekend seemed to take race (as well as class and gender) as a necessary starting point in their studies. As the only person there presenting a paper on Asian American Buddhism, I was particularly keen to hear more about how other students were grappling with these issues. One person delivered a paper regarding Christian missionary contacts with Native Americans in the early colonial period. Since he mentioned that some Native Americans were slave holders and many intermarried with Whites, I expected that he would have quite a bit to say about the implications of racial ideology on the subjects of his study. What, I wondered, was the relationship between missionary attitudes toward enslaved Africans and Native Americans, and the growing scientific construction of race as an essential biological reality? At the same time Western Christians were beginning their missionary efforts to indigenous peoples around the world, Western European scientists were solidifying their understanding of the permanence of racial categories. It seemed to me that there might be some connection philosophically between these two movements: the sorting of humans according to racial categories and the Christianizing of humans newly "discovered" by the West.

It could be that I asked the question poorly, but the speaker seemed to suggest that his paper had nothing to do with "race." It occurred to me later that his understanding of "race" was limited to "mere" diversity. In other words, he had nothing further to say about race beyond a relatively superficial acknowledgment of the "differences" between Whites and Native Americans. He spoke about "cultural" difference, but could not speak at a deeper level about the ideological implications of race. If the "problem" of race is defined merely as inclusiveness, then the problem is dispensed with by merely being "inclusive" in our studies and in our practice. Widening the circle of our understanding is certainly important, but it is only a preliminary step, because it fails to acknowledge the ways in which race implicates everyone. African American theologians have always written about the impact that oppression and discrimination have had on the development of the Black Church, but they have also raised the question of racism in theological circles. Theology filtered through a racist mindset has implications for the theologian as well as the congregation to whom s/he preaches.

African American philosophers have also engaged the question of the influence of racial ideologies on the development of the Western philosophical tradition. These questions move us beyond the merely inclusive. Feminists began their inquiry into the "problem" of gender and religion by addressing basic questions of equity and sexual harassment, but have moved on to discuss the relevance of gender construction and the body to our understanding of self. If feminists can assert the importance of the gendered body in discussions of religious belief and spiritual practice, what would happen if we were to assert the importance of the racialized body in discussions of religious belief and spiritual practice? What would it mean to affirm the body, as feminists do, as a worthy site for practice and enlightenment? How do my experiences in this body that is maligned and discriminated against change my attitude toward practice? If my body represents privilege and political power, and inspires resentment and anger in others, how does my practice begin to resolve these issues?

Koans do not have answers; they are "unsolvable" puzzles which resolve themselves in the life of the meditator, but only after intense effort and close attention. Those who resolve their *koans* do so not through intellectual acumen, but by developing a felt sense of the problem and melting into it. These questions of diversity and difference ought to be at the heart of American Buddhist practice. These questions ought to be at the heart of research, both philosophical and historical, concerning American Buddhism. Creating an understanding of diversity as practice must encompass inclusiveness and acceptance as well as the struggle for justice for all beings. Engaging these questions at a level deeper than politics has the potential to actually make a difference. The problem of diversity has defied solution, emerging in each historical era as an increasingly difficult series of dilemmas which belie our best intentions. Diversity is our *koan*; diversity is our practice.

Notes

1 I am indebted to Rosa Zubizarretta, co-founder of the Mindfulness and Social Change Saṅgha in Oakland, California, for coining this rich conceptual phrase.

2 Henry Louis Gates, "Writing, 'Race,' and the Difference it Makes," in *Loose Cannons: Notes on the Culture Wars*. (New York: Oxford University Press, 1992), p. 47.

3 There are a number of fine studies on the history of the concept of race in America. See, for example, Winthrop Jordan, *The White Man's Burden: Historical Origins of Racism in the United States* (New York: Oxford University Press, 1974) and Thomas Gossett, *Race: The History of an Idea in America* (New York: Oxford University Press, 1963). For a discussion of race and the history of the scientific community see Jonathan Marks, *Human Biodiversity: Genes, Race and History* (New York: Aldine de Gruyter, 1995); and Stephen Jay Gould, *Mismeasure of Man* (New York: Penguin Books, 1984).

4 For an extended discussion of the relationship between racial thinking and Western culture see: Robert J. C. Young, *Colonial Desire: Hybridity in Theory, Culture and Race* (New York: Routledge, 1995).

5 It is commonly understood that "Black" and "White" refer to specific groups of people and are not descriptive adjectives. Therefore "Black" and "White" are capitalized here in the same way that "Japanese," "Jew," or "European" would be capitalized.

6 Stephen Jay Gould explains that Blumenbach used what he considered to be a more "objective" criterion for organizing human variety. Other scientists at the time who believed in the innate inferiority of non-Whites argued that Caucasians were "naturally" superior to other humans because of their superior mental capacity. Ironically, Blumenbach was looking for a classificatory scheme which presumed the equal mental capacity of all humans because he believed racial variation to be arbitrary. See Stephen Jay Gould, "The Geometer of Race," *Discover Magazine* (November 1, 1994): 65–69.

7 The recent announcement that DNA testing has all but proved that Jefferson fathered several children by his "slave" Sally Hemmings further complicates the politics of slavery.

8 Ian Haney-Lopez, "White by Law," *Critical Race Theory: The Cutting Edge* (Philadelphia: Temple University Press, 1995), pp. 542–50.

9 Michael Omi and Howard Winant, *Racial Formation in the United States* (New York: Routledge, 1992), pg. 71.

10 This is not the place to reproduce a review of the literature on Buddhism in America, but as a student researching the field for at least the last ten years I can say with some certainty that the literature by, for, and about Euroamerican practitioners vastly outweighs literature by, for, and about Asian American Buddhists. For example, there are still only three book length studies of Asian American Buddhism – two on Jōdo Shinshū, which is the dominant practice in the Japanese American community, and one on two Thai Buddhist temples in Chicago and Los Angeles. Very few of the commonly cited histories of "American" Buddhism talk about the existence of Japanese or any other Asian Buddhists in the U.S. prior to World War II. Emma McCoy Layman and Charles Prebish are the exceptions. Layman's *Buddhism in America* and Prebish's *American Buddhism* make note of the existence of the Jōdo Shinshū sect, but these writers are still largely concerned with the conversion of Euroamericans to Mahāyāna meditation-based groups. On Asian American Buddhism, see Tetsuden Kashima, *Buddhism in America: The Social Organization of an Ethnic Religious Institution* (Westport, Ct.: Greenwood Press, 1977); and Louise Hunter, *Buddhism in Hawai'i: Its Impact on a Yankee Community* (Honolulu: University of Hawaii Press, 1971). Paul David Numrich's *Old Wisdom in the New World: Americanization in Two Immigrant Theravada Buddhist Temples* (Knoxville: University of Tennessee Press, 1996) deals with two immigrant temples in Los Angeles and Chicago, but also discusses the role Euroamericans have played in these communities.

On Euroamerican Buddhism, see Rick Fields, *How the Swans Came to the Lake: A Narrative History of Buddhism in American* (Boston: Shambhala Press, 1992) and Thomas Tweed, *An American Encounter with Buddhism: 1844–1912 Victorian Culture and the Limits of Dissent* (Bloomington, Ind.: Indiana University Press, 1992).

11 Statistics regarding the exact numbers of Japanese Buddhists in America prior to World War II may be unreliably reported, because member families are counted rather than individual members. Researchers have suggested that the 11,852 member families represented approximately 35,000 individuals. As stated, this figure represents only the largest Buddhist group, the BCA; counting the total number of Japanese American Buddhists in all sects before World War II would obviously reveal a higher number.

CHAPTER TWENTY-THREE

Sexual Conduct and Misconduct

Buddhist Ethics in the West

Gabriele Küstermann

Since Buddhism emerged as a significant philosophy in the West, the integration of Buddhist practice into daily life has brought meaning and joy to countless practitioners. Newly aware of this practical spiritual path, many practitioners have unexpectedly experienced some rough spots along the way. Among the difficulties experienced by new practitioners, problems of sexual misconduct stand out as a painful reminder of the very human failings the Dharma aims to eradicate.

Guidelines for Ethical Living

Buddhists begin by taking refuge in the Three Jewels (Buddha, Dharma, and Saṅgha), taking the Buddha's life, the Dharma teachings, and the inspiration and companionship of the Saṅgha (the spiritual community), as their guides and examples on the spiritual path. Refuge is seen as a sensible means of embarking on a meaningful way of life, taking responsibility for ourselves, and becoming mindful of the causes of happiness and misery.

Central to the practice of the Dharma is a core of ethical conduct taught by the Buddha which is relevant for beginners and advanced practitioners alike. These ethical guidelines are evident, implicitly or explicitly, in all the Buddhist teachings. For example, they are clearly implied in the key to daily living, the Noble Eightfold Path: Right View, Intention, Speech, Action, Livelihood, Effort, Mindfulness, and Concentration. Ideally, Buddhists strive to earnestly follow this path.

In addition to these ideals and principles are specific guidelines that reinforce the practice of ethical conduct, explained in a number of books on Buddhist ethics.[1] Buddhist laypeople traditionally practice the five precepts, to refrain from destroying living creatures, taking that which is not given, sexual misconduct, untruthful speech, and intoxicating drinks and drugs. Monastics add many more precepts to these and are naturally expected to abide by them. Failure to do so creates uneasiness in the minds of practitioners and can undermine their confidence in the Buddhist way of life, melting their respect like snow in the sun.

Ethics for Teachers

After taking refuge, practitioners rely on the help and example of qualified teachers. Teachers of Buddhism, whether Western and Asian, lay or ordained, are expected to practice the precepts and live wholesome lives. By following ethical guidelines, Buddhist teachers serve as examples to society, demonstrating the beneficial effects of leading a wholesome life. The central place these guidelines hold in all Buddhist traditions demonstrates the importance of sincere adherence to them. Those who choose to become ordained have an especially great responsibility. If they transgress the precepts, the psychological effects are devastating, especially for their students.[2]

Who are these teachers? Many arrive in the West from Asia, brought up in a culture very different from the 20th-century Western world. When they arrive, they encounter eager students plunging into unfamiliar territory. The ability to communicate the Dharma effectively, and the beauty of the message, can often erroneously convey the impression that these teachers are saints above normal human temptations. When Western students and their Asian teachers cannot communicate fluently, due to linguistic and cultural differences, the problems and dangers are compounded.

In the West, it is first necessary to explain that Buddhism is not an unknown sect, but a major world religion, and that Buddhists aspire to lead a peaceful way of life, not harming anyone and setting a good example. Most people in the West expect Buddhist monks and nuns to be non-materialistic, living simple, wholesome, spiritually directed, celibate lives – embodying more or less the same ideals they expect of Christian monks and nuns. There is a great need for a clearer understanding of the way of life that Buddhist monks and nuns in the West are trying to practice.

There is also a need for both ordained and lay Buddhists to explain their motivation in becoming Buddhists. Often their motivation is rooted in a profound dissatisfaction with living a senseless life. They sincerely want to make meaningful use of their precious human lifetime. They find Buddhist philosophy helpful and genuinely wish to implement it. It is especially helpful when young Buddhists come into direct contact with a Buddhist teacher and a group of spiritual friends who are all striving in the same direction. The relationship between these "newborn" Buddhists and their teachers is crucial to their ongoing involvement on the Buddhist path.

"Teachers" in the West include both fully qualified teachers trained in traditional Asian settings and also their Western disciples, who support them, translate for them, orient them to Western life, and organize Buddhist centers for them. This group of disciples has a very difficult task, especially if they chose to emulate their teacher by becoming a monk or nun. Let us take a typical scenario.

A male Buddhist teacher comes to the West on the invitation of a group of men and women who wish to receive Buddhist teachings from a qualified teacher. This teacher, sent by an organization or monastery in Asia, wishes to spread Buddhism to interested Westerners, and at the same time to help his own people materially and sometimes – as with the Tibetans, Vietnamese, and Cambodians – politically. Because they have in-depth knowledge of the political situation and sufferings of their people, they raise their students' awareness of the need for freedom in their countries. Their students, ingrained with a sense of social responsibility due to their own Judeo-Christian cultural backgrounds, naturally adopt these causes espoused by their teacher and begin organizing political support groups and raising donations for welfare activities to benefit "refugees" both in Asia and in the West.

Despite their mutual core interest in the Buddhist teachings, cultural differences and misunderstandings between teachers and students may arise along the way. These difficulties become especially obvious if the Asian teacher does not speak a Western language and is dependent upon certain members of the inner circle to interpret his (most are male) wishes and ideas. Without these interpreters, the teacher would be unable to fulfill his mission and might return to Asia, leaving a large group of followers alone and without guidance.

Westerners particularly admire teachers who teach through example, not merely with words. Fully qualified teachers – good role models held in high esteem – are rare. But becoming a Buddhist or being a Buddhist does not necessarily mean that we are saints. Human beings are constantly challenged by their shortcomings, and Buddhist groups are especially challenged to cope with the human tendencies to admire and overestimate, to indulge in wishful thinking, to expect ideal behavior, and to experience sexual attraction, particularly to teachers. Naive with expectations, students frequently overlook the weaknesses of human nature.

Dealing with Sexual Attraction

Sexual attraction is one of the deepest human instincts. It may be the most difficult to acknowledge and deal with. Under the power of sexual desire, we may deny it, disguise it, or postpone dealing with it until situations becomes dangerously out of control.

All human beings – men, women, laypeople, and monastics – are vulnerable to sexual desire. Therefore we cannot ignore the critical issue of sexual attraction in human relations. Whatever lifestyle we choose, harmful and ambiguous sexual relations will stand as obstacles in our path. Women, in particular, being vulnerable to assault, must be constantly mindful and aware. Under the influence of sexual desire, others cannot be trusted to have our best interests in mind. Relations with teachers are especially prone to ambiguity and the potential for exploitation.

Situations of sexual attraction with teachers are especially important occasions for awareness, whether it be attraction arising from the teacher's side or the student's. Teachers and practitioners alike need to develop mindfulness to recognize sexual desire, and clarity to deal with the situation honestly. Mindfulness, clarity, and honesty help us see how sexual desire makes us vulnerable to exploitation: sexual, financial, and psychological. We need confidence to make wise, forthright decisions, especially when our perceptions are clouded by desire.

Our emotional responses affect not only ourselves, but also the object of our desire. Monastics, particularly those with little sexual experience, are extremely vulnerable. Unaccustomed to the sudden rush of emotions, they may compromise their better judgment. If they are not careful, they may break the precepts before offering them back or refuse to accept responsibility for their actions. Such situations may lead to hypocrisy or worse. They rarely produce lasting happiness, and may lead to lifelong regrets.

An incident of sexual attraction may be ideal for observing the emotions, but this practice is also very dangerous. Because we are not yet capable of controlling our emotions, it is like honey on the edge of knife. Carelessness in matters of sexual attraction can lead to some very messy situations.

Secrecy and Sexual Practices in *Tantric* Buddhism

The requirements for *tantric* practice with a consort make it clear that both practitioners are required to have equal spiritual attainments, all the same empowerments, and many extraordinary qualifications. The accounts of women such as Machig Labdronma (*Ma gcig lab sgron ma*) give vivid descriptions of spiritual life in Tibet during the 11th and 12th centuries. Female consorts were often the teaching partners of lama practitioners. After the 13th century, however, we find few biographies of great female *tantric* masters. If *tantric* practitioners can only fulfill their objective through practice with partners of equal spiritual attainment, and qualified female *tantric* masters were lacking, we can assume that the practice declined over the past eight centuries as male practitioners secured the services of women without the required qualifications. Under the circumstances, many were forced to keep their special sexual relationships a lifelong secret under the threat of going to Vajra Hell. Not only were women compromised by these unequal relationships, but after the initial phases of the practice, they were not empowered to teach or share their experiences with others. As happened some centuries after the Buddha's passing, women were here again deprived of female spiritual role models.

Gelugpa teachers such as my own now emphasize the symbolic meaning of the sexual imagery. The sexual union between men and women (*yab-yum*, or "father-mother") shown in painting and sculpture represents the union of compassion and wisdom that is needed for achieving the goal of Buddhahood. Therefore June Campbell's book, *Travellers in Space*, was an eye-opener for me.[3] Similar claims of sexual involvement with well-known teachers followed in other women's accounts, causing disbelief and outrage among followers. I met with June Campbell personally to increase my understanding. Her main objective in sharing her experience with the public arose from a concern that these secret sexual practices, which grew out of the Tibetan cultural context and are understood in the West as a means of furthering one's spiritual development, would lead to intolerable situations when practiced by Western women drawn to Buddhism as a path of gender equality, especially when they involved secret pledges (*samaya*) and guru devotion to the teachers as sexual partners.[4] Campbell regards these practices as culturally formed behavior that is not part of the Buddha's teachings. Women need to be very clear about this and decide wisely whether they wish to take part in practices that are alien to our understanding of equality and openness between sexual partners. Misuse of power in this sphere can only be resolved through an open discussion of such practices, and when open discussion is construed as breaking *tantric* pledges and a breach of guru devotion, many misunderstandings can arise that may overshadow the deeper wholesome aspects of *tantric* Buddhist practice.

As Lori Pierce points out with reference to racism,[5] the question of sexism and sexual exploitation cannot be adequately addressed simply by considering the feelings and actions of individuals. The question must take into account the structural flaws in a system that allows sexism and sexual exploitation to continue, and may even perpetuate it. June Campbell asserts in her book that the system perpetuates unequal power relations. By privileging men over women in spiritual training and by maintaining male-dominated power structures, such as the *tulku* system, Buddhist institutions contribute to women's feelings of powerlessness, subordination, and inadequacy. In a system where nearly all gurus are male, where gurus are revered as enlightened beings, and where disciples are advised to please their teachers, women are clearly at risk.

Traditional societies have safeguards in place to protect women from exploitation, albeit frequently at the cost of women's independence. Without this cultural security system, sexual symbolism is likely to be misunderstood and misused. In such a situation women may feel privileged to participate in sexual relationships with gurus who are respected in near-mythic proportions – and who may also be extremely wealthy. Even so, these "brushes with greatness" often end tragically for both partners. Sexual relations are prohibited for monks and the monastic vows cannot be restored once broken. Even when both partners are aware of this, a temporary lapse of mindfulness has led to the disrobing of many a monk. There are many dangers for a monk living in a culture where people do not know what it means to be a monk. More disturbingly, since monks are usually trained only in religion and have few other means of earning a living, some continue to wear the robes of a monk even after they have relinquished their precepts, enjoying the privileges of being a monk without living by the precepts of a monk. This leads to confusion and misunderstandings in the community.

Many Buddhist women are still in the process of recognizing sexism in their temples and traditions and only beginning to ponder what to do about it. The process of Buddhist feminist awakening includes awareness of the way the feminine is glamorized, essentialized, and divorced from the immediate needs, both social and psychological, of flesh and blood women. How do women gain access to spiritual authority when males hold all the keys? The symbolism of the *ḍākinī* (woman as intuitive wisdom) is potentially liberating for women, but it fails to deliver in real terms when, like Holy Mary in the Catholic Church, it is defined, controlled, and manipulated by men. If this liberating ideal does not translate into real social freedom and spiritual benefit, it remains an empty symbol, useless for helping women realize their spiritual potential. By masking women's powerlessness in the system, the myth of women's spiritual equality merely perpetuates male domination. Women are left where they started, unable to actualize their spiritual potential.

It is a source of special concern among spiritual friends when women voluntarily allow themselves to be sexually exploited. Traditional Buddhist ethics teaches that individuals bear personal responsibility for their own moral conduct, and this does not explicitly extend to recognizing and preventing the sexual harassment and exploitation of others. Yet to shirk this responsibility may diminish the moral integrity of all parties and lead to disharmony in the practice community. Questionable sexual ethics among teachers creates competition, jealousy, and confusion in the Dharma community and may have far-reaching consequences beyond. Situations of cultural difference often make it more difficult to discern the boundaries of propriety, especially in relation to a dominant spiritual authority.

That is one reason traditional practices that pledge one to secrecy are coming into serious question. The question of women's spiritual identity in a system that teaches selflessness, examined by both Campbell and Anne Klein, has important implications for sexual ethics.[6] As Campbell discusses, surrendering the body and mind may lead to a diminishing of ego, but this sacrificial role that women have traditionally been expected to play is not without its dangers and costs. Public disclosures of promiscuous behavior by Buddhist teachers, sometimes distorted, are likely to reach the press, meaning that the public's first introduction to Buddhism may be some sexual scandal. For all these reasons, it is essential that methods of intervention, constructive dialogue, and reconciliation in line with Buddhist values and goals be devised to ensure healthy, functional individuals and Dharma communities.

Making Ethical Decisions

Among teachers and members of the "inner circle," or core group, there may also be temptations to misuse power. Because incidents of misconduct have already occurred in Buddhist circles, several centers have made pioneering efforts to formulate codes of ethics to guide interactions of Western Buddhists in these crucial formative stages. These codes are not meant to replace traditional Buddhist ethical guidelines, but to supplement them. The views of the San Francisco Zen Center, the Insight Meditation Center, and the Buddhist Peace Fellowship have been compiled by Alan Senauke in a book called *Safe Harbor: Guidelines, Process and Resources for Ethics and Right Conduct in Buddhist Communities.*[7]

Questions for Discussion

Useful and meaningful guidelines grow out of informed consideration of the dilemmas that can confront centers and practitioners in contemporary Western society. One way to begin that process is to reflect on some "what if?" scenarios. How would you handle situations like the ones outlined below?

1 Your beautiful 15-year old niece has developed an interest in Buddhism. She calls to let you know that she will be doing a seven-day retreat in the mountains with a Buddhist teacher. This teacher has been accused of sexually exploiting women in Dharma centers all over the country, and you have confirmed that the allegations are based in fact.
2 Your local Buddhist temple recently invited a young monk from Asia to become its resident teacher. You attend several teachings and then sign up for a language class being offered. When you arrive for the class, you find that you are the only student. Nobody else is at the temple.
3 Your mother or sister recently passed away. As a Buddhist, you want to have some special practice or ceremony performed for her. You also feel very sad about her death and need some spiritual counselling to help cope with your loss. You make an appointment to see the teacher at your local Buddhist center. During the interview the teacher, a handsome layman, takes your hand to console you.
4 Your closest friend has decided to become a Buddhist nun. She is very sincere and confides to you that she will become ordained with the monk in charge of a nearby Buddhist temple. You know that this monk does

not keep the precepts purely. Even though he is wearing robes, you know that he has had many girlfriends, has seduced nuns, and even forced one to have an abortion.

5 Your local Buddhist women's association is selecting a Board of Advisors. The executive committee enthusiastically decides to include a particular individual who wears monk's robes, claiming that he is a *bodhisattva* and has been a staunch supporter of nuns. You know that this individual has been living with a woman for many years, has had many other sexual liaisons, behaves totally inappropriately for a person in robes, and is notorious for this behavior. You do not feel that he is a suitable person to serve as an advisor to Buddhist women.
6 Your resident teacher has been raising money to build a school in his homeland. For several years you and other members of the center have been organizing special events, doing publicity for this project, raising money, and giving it to your teacher to send to the school. After five years, some of the students have an opportunity to visit the school. When you get there, the people tell you they have never received any money from your teacher.
7 As part of an international research project, monks at a particular monastery received a set of computers, an electrical power system, and earmarked financial support. When visiting this monastery you learn that this equipment is not available for the monks in the project, but is being used for other purposes by order of their abbot.

★ ★ ★

With this brief introduction to the topic, I invite readers to explore their own experiences, understanding, and views on the application of Buddhist ethics to practical situations. The exercise presented here can be approached reflectively, as an individual, or interactively in a group. To raise awareness, workshops on the topic of ethics can be organized in Buddhist centers or among friends. The questions suggested here focus on appropriate responses to situations of sexual conduct and appropriation of funds. Creative groups will certainly investigate other questions, too, leading to fruitful discussions.

Notes

1 See Gunapala Dharmasiri, *Fundamentals of Buddhist Ethics* (Antioch, Calif.: Golden Leaves, 1989); Thich Nhat Hahn, *For a Future to be Possible: Commentaries on the Five Wonderful Precepts* (Berkeley: Parallax, 1993); David Kalupahana, *Ethics in Early Buddhism*; Damien Keown's books, *Buddhism and Bioethics* (New York: St. Martin's Press, 1995) and *The Nature of Buddhist Ethics* (New York: St. Martin's Press, 1992); Dudjom Rinpoche, *Perfect Conduct: Ascertaining the Three Vows* (Boston: Wisdom Publications, 1996); and H. Saddhatissa, *Buddhist Ethics: Essence of Buddhism* (London: Allen & Unwin, 1970; Boston: Wisdom Publications, 1997).

2 Resources on this topic include Marie Fortune, *Is Nothing Sacred? When Sex Invades the Pastoral Relationship* (San Francisco: Harper and Row, 1989), and Peter Rutter, *Sex in the Forbidden Zone: When Men in Power – Therapists, Doctors, Clergy, Teachers and Others – Betray Women's Trust* (New York: Fawcett Crest, 1991).

3 June Campbell, *Travellers in Space. Female Identity in Tibetan Buddhism* (New York: George Braziller, 1996) and the revised German translation, *Göttinnen, Dakinis und ganz normale Frauen: Weibliche Identität im Tibetischen Tantra* (Berlin: Theseus Verlag, 1997).

4 Katja Sindemann, "Missbrauch von Macht [Misuse of Power]," an interview with June Campbell, *Ursache & Wirkung* [Cause and Effect] 28 (Spring 1999): 22–25.

5 See Lori Pierce, "Diversity as Practice: Thinking about Race and 'American' Buddhism," in this volume, pp. 277–84.

6 Anne Carolyn Klein, *Meeting the Great Bliss Queen: Buddhists, Feminists, and the Art of the Self* (Boston: Beacon Press, 1995).

7 Available from Buddhist Peace Fellowship, P.O. Box 4650, Berkeley, CA 94704. Articles on sexual ethics have appeared in *Turning Wheel*, BPF's newsletter, available from the same address.

CHAPTER TWENTY-FOUR

Daylighting the Feminine in American Buddhism

Mushim Ikeda-Nash

> *From ancient times, living female Buddhas have accomplished the Way. The spiritual attainment and practice of females have flowed in a continuous yet hidden stream to the present time.*[1]

I recently heard the term "daylighting" used by a kindergarten teacher at the Oakland public school my son attends. Urban environmentalists use this term, she explained, for the uncovering of small streams that run through Oakland beneath streets and sidewalks. Often the presence of these creeks and streams is unknown to the people who live near them. At a meeting where the volatile issue of institutionalized racism in the public school system was being discussed, the teacher suggested we think of our work as a process of daylighting the complex, deeply buried forces that make it difficult for many children of color and poor children to be successful.

Daylighting, I thought, would involve jack-hammering asphalt and cement, building bridges, landscaping, creek maintenance. Initially it would involve planning, noise, expense, and disruption of parts of neighborhoods. Often people are not interested in the work of uncovering something that has been successfully hidden since before their birth – revealing knowledge they are accustomed to living without. I have been thinking about this work of uncovering, discovering, recovering, reclaiming, and maintaining the well-springs of our ecological and human communities, and our individual lives.

Thus, in reading Nakao Sensei's "The Lineage of Women," the working draft quoted above, I am deeply struck by the sentence "The spiritual attainment and practice of females have flowed in a continuous yet hidden stream to the present time." These bold words encourage me as an American Buddhist woman, mother, Japanese American, and artist. They confirm and connect something deep within me that I, in my mid-40s, know needs to be daylighted in order for me to reach my potential.

I remember the excitement I felt as a young college student in 1973 when I read Adrienne Rich's new book of poems, *Diving into the Wreck*. The title poem ends with these lines:

We, I am, you are
by cowardice or courage
the one who find our way
back to this scene
carrying a knife, a camera
a book of myths
in which
our names do not appear.

The image of the woman poet descending into the ocean depths to acknowledge the ways in which "our names do not appear" and to recover women's submerged experiences, their varied stories and wisdom, was powerful. My growth as a feminist was directly related to my slowly emerging realization that the cultural conditioning I had received as a woman and as a *sansei* (third-generation Japanese American) to be silent and to conform needed to be cracked open in order to daylight my energy, creativity, and vision. This process has been a gradual unfolding over the past 30 years.

The revolutionary implications of researching and revealing women's history, building supportive environments for women artists and activists, addressing women's healthcare needs, creating alternatives for childcare and family structures – all these possibilities burst open like a great sun rising for many of us, women and men alike, who participated in the women's movement in the United States during the 1970s. As women, we were doing the hard and rewarding work of daylighting and affirming our bodies, our talents and skills, our identities. We were reconnecting to images of feminine authority, sexuality, nurturance, and self-acceptance.

Thus, when I came to Zen practice in the early 1980s, I did not doubt that the feminist work being done in other fields would at some point be applied to American Buddhism as well. The lineage of the matriarchs would some day, though perhaps not in my lifetime, stand alongside the lineage of the patriarchs. I want to emphasize the word "alongside" here; I did not think of the lineage of the matriarchs as supplanting the lineage of the Zen patriarchs. However, I kept all of these thoughts to myself. "Put aside your own opinions" and "Stop picking and choosing" were standard admonitions from the Asian-born Zen teacher and the North American senior students during my initial Zen training. The teacher often scolded us students as being over-educated and stuck in our intellectual minds, some of which was certainly true. As a matter of fact, it was the practice itself, experience rather than theory, that eventually connected me to the "continuous yet hidden stream" of the feminine principle in Buddhism.

I remember one morning, 15 years ago, before dawn, when I was on temple wake-up duty. The first task was to creep downstairs in the darkened temple, light the candles on the altar, and offer fresh water in the bronze bowl, making three prostrations before the figure of Śākyamuni Buddha. Then I would ring the handbell throughout the house, calling everyone to the meditation hall. On this particular morning, as I stood with my palms together, preparing to prostrate myself, I had a vivid impression that I was surrounded by all the Buddhist practitioners and Buddhas who had come before me, women and men together, and the words "nameless ones and healers" came to me. I was convinced at the time, as I have been since, that these "nameless ones," many of them women, were part of the "hidden stream" that sustained my spiritual life.

Some of Which is Hidden has Remained Secret

Many years after that pre-dawn moment, I read Egyoku Nakao Sensei's words:[2]

> So when I reflect upon the practice of women, I begin by affirming the obvious. The obvious is that for an immeasurable, hundreds, thousands, ten thousands, millions, trillions of *kalpas*, women have practiced, manifested, realized, and accomplished the Buddha Way. Who are all these women whose names have been forgotten or left unsaid?

Nakao Sensei had the resources, determination, and support to validate her spiritual conviction with research that revealed the names of some of these nuns and laywomen.[3] Other Buddhists have been doing the same work of recovery, and some Buddhist groups now chant the names or thank the nameless women in their regular services.[4] "The lineage of the Matriarchs is to be revered," Nakao Sensei says.[5]

In her search for the Buddhist matriarchs, however, Nakao Sensei also comments that "women too often seem to find it necessary to whisper this concern [lack of a female lineage].... Can we women trust ourselves to reveal the means that will illuminate this wisdom?"[6] Why have we been whispering? Is it still "necessary" to whisper? What means of illuminating women's wisdom are we now revealing? What does "trust ourselves" signify in a spiritual practice in which we begin by admitting our delusions: greed, hatred, and ignorance? I want to embrace these questions, not academically, but with compassionate attention.

During the year I lived at Green Gulch Zen Center in the early 1990s, my friend Wendy Johnson and I were both nursing babies between one and two years old. She was married and I was a single mother. I had done monastic-style Zen practice and extended retreat periods. Wendy was a seasoned Zen practitioner and teacher who later received Dharma transmission from Thich Nhat Hanh. Wendy nursed my son Joshua on occasion, and I breastfed her daughter Alisa; we supported one another through the rigors of staying up nights with ill or teething babies. During this intense time, I vividly recall Wendy saying, "I feel this is a wonderful secret practice I'm doing." I agreed. And this raised certain questions for me.

During my residency at Green Gulch, though I rarely appeared in the meditation hall, I felt my practice was more alive than ever, more deeply challenged, and more joyful. Other, very real considerations were that I was rundown, exhausted, and financially strapped. But most of the time I felt that the heart of my spiritual practice was secret – a subterranean stream that only Wendy, myself, and a few other Buddhist mothers and fathers in our community could hear.

What seemed obvious to me was that our American Zen practice, transplanted from Asian monastic roots, had not yet adapted in form or in spirit to the needs of laywomen practitioners with children. Changes would occur as women's voices were heard, and for those voices to be heard, we women needed to practice within the old forms while developing a vision of the new. And this vision would evolve organically, based on a deep understanding of our lives, our bodies, our families, and Buddhist history and theory.

I reflected on this during a one-day *tangaryō* sitting that I did to formally mark my desire to enter the Green Gulch Sōtō Zen community. Since Joshua had a babysitter for the day and was elsewhere, I ended up sitting in meditation as my breasts quickly became engorged, rock-hard, and painful. After lunch, I ran up to the trailer where I was living, jumped into a hot shower to induce the let-down reflex, and began trying to express the milk by hand. As I stood with the hot water pouring down my body, mixed with streams of rich milk, I began to laugh. I don't think this was an experience that any Asian Zen patriarch had ever had! As I dressed to return to the meditation hall, I felt refreshed, blessed by the outpouring of sweet milk that my body so miraculously produced for my son. I remembered what the Buddha had said:

> To be a mother is sweet,
> And a father.
> It is sweet to live arduously,
> And to master yourself. . . .
>
> And wisdom is sweet,
> And freedom.[7]

What other stories of women's lives and practice have we yet to hear?

Daylighting: The Work Ahead

Whether they breast- or bottle-feed their babies, aware mothers understand the significance of bonding and nurturing to be profound, spiritual dimensions of human experience – experiences that affect human beings at the very earliest stages of their lives. Psychologist Donald Winnicott has advanced the theory that art and religion, two defining aspects of human culture, are intimately related to our first experiences with exploring self and other within the mother-child (or mother figure-child) relationship.[8] It is important that we hear the testimony of Buddhist mothers' spiritual experience in order to complement presentations of the Dharma filtered through the male experience. For example, the well-known Japanese Zen teacher Kosho Uchiyama Rōshi has written:

> When people complain of being unhappy and of living a meaningless or empty life, I wonder if it is not because they have taken it for granted that the meaning of their life is to be found simply in some sort of emotional pleasure or joy. Normally we waste our whole lives playing with toys. As I described briefly in *Approach to Zen*, the first toy people clamor for when they are born is their mother's breast. Then, it is on to teddy bears and electric trains, and as we get older, bicycles, watches, cameras, and finally, jewelry, clothes, and the opposite sex.[9]

The book in which Uchiyama Rōshi's essay appears, *Refining Your Life*, holds an honored place on my bookshelf. The book in its entirety is encouraging and helpful for American Zen students. Nevertheless, the excerpt I have pointed out underlines a needed task. Women must offer each other Buddhist stories and images that affirm who we really are, in the midst of a patriarchal consumer culture that equates parts of our bodies with "bicycles, watches, [and] cameras." In forging an American Buddhism, we bring our national characteristics of energy and idealism, our values of equity and democracy, to Buddhist teachings and practices that have come to us from ancient Asian cultures. Many American women bring the questions and affirmations, the naming of the previously unnamed, from feminism and the women's movement, to their Buddhist practice. Women who have rejected those movements for not taking into account sufficiently the needs of women of color or working-class women likewise bring valuable questions. The work of daylighting the feminine in American Buddhist practice will not be a smooth process of integration and forward progress. Rather, it will be a spiraling – sometimes frustrating in that we will circle back again and again in order to uncover what is essential and seek to find what meaning and application our discoveries have in our fast-flowing world of cyberspace, cell phones, and movies where everything and everyone is shot, blown up, and burned. And there is the danger that, should we work too superficially, we will daylight only another chunk of our own dualism. In a recent issue of *Tricycle: The Buddhist Review*, Thinley Norbu Rinpoche, a Tibetan male teacher, says that he "can't understand the idea of American Buddhism at all. Sometimes it looks like communism, sometimes like democracy, sometimes like socialism, and sometimes like nothing, only circling between worldly systems, never cutting from them but only circling between negative phenomena."[10] I personally think that American Buddhism is a worthy experiment, but Thinley Norbu Rinpoche has a point: What is the relationship between women's liberation in terms of women's rights, and women's liberation in terms of spiritual resolution?

Spirals and Circles Bring Us Face to Face

When Thinley Norbu Rinpoche talks about "circling," he seems to refer to circling in *saṃsaric* and nihilistic activity. I find it illuminating to juxtapose what he says with a quotation from Egyoku Nakao Sensei. In the process of Dharma transmission from Rōshi Bernard Glassman, she reflects on realizing her own need to locate female Dharma ancestors. She writes, "As I began to explore my female Buddha ancestors, I sensed the lineage of women as a spiral, moving in wide, all-encompassing circles. I sensed, too, that in swallowing and promoting the male-dominated forms and milieu of my inherited tradition, I had concealed myself as a woman to myself and to other women."[11]

How, then, do we reveal ourselves to ourselves, and to one another? In creating American Buddhist forms that embody feminine as well as masculine principles, women are in the process of manifesting their Buddhist practice in ways that integrate, rather than avoid, their female bodies and experience. *Being Bodies: Buddhist Women on the Paradox of Embodiment*, edited by Lenore Friedman and Susan Moon, is a benchmark in this regard.[12] It explores territory only recently opening up, as expressions of women's Buddhist experience begin to cross cultural boundaries, creating spaces to say and hear what has previously been unspeakable or was never validated as significant.

The fact that the word "*saṅgha*" is now commonly used in the West to indicate any community of Buddhist practitioners, monastic or lay, reflects an increased validation of lay practice. In its original meaning, the term "*saṅgha*" referred to the community of ordained Buddhist monks and nuns. Along with the shift this represents comes the potential for women to bring to light the often hidden, unrecorded wisdom traditions and contemporary insights surrounding menstruation, conception, pregnancy, childbirth, mothering, and menopause to illuminate our spiritual paths. The *saṅgha* of women in the West is now commonly understood to include both nuns and laywomen. We are coming closer to one another.

Buddhist practice has traditionally held forth the values of intimacy and true spiritual completion in all relationships. Jiko Linda Cutts, an American Zen teacher, has compared the process of Dharma transmission and the teacher-student relationship to the process of bonding between mother and child. She writes:

> So in *menju*, "Face-to-Face Transmission," Dōgen strongly emphasizes the point that this is face to face, eye to eye. This is not like reading a book and feeling you understand what some teacher says. It has to be face to face, eye to eye. So this intimate practice together, face to face, is part of our lineage. Mahākāśyapa and Śākyamuni Buddha practiced together for a long time.
>
> The teacher cannot be a teacher unless there is a disciple or student; and a student cannot be a student unless there is a teacher. It is really one word: teacher-disciple. They come up together, each creates and conditions the other. . . . You need each other to complete the practice.
>
> This need is reflected in various works in Western psychology. The psychologist Heinz Kohut talks about the importance of childrens' having someone reflect back to them, mirror back to them, all their interest, their love and excitement about their various activities and states of mind. Someone there looking at the child eye to eye is pivotally important for developing a stable sense of self. In the gaze between mother and child, the eyes dilate and there's a great intensity, and this reflection back and forth between the parent actually develops certain capacities of the brain. . . . This mirroring, the "gleam in the mother's eye," is not dissimilar to the face to face reflecting back and forth between teacher and disciple. The same caring and intimacy is there.[13]

Walking Beside the Stream

After we have done the hard work of daylighting the hidden stream, uncovering and affirming the feminine principle in Buddhism, what will we do? Walk beside the stream and enjoy it: that's my plan.

American Buddhist women's contribution to Buddhism is finding multiple expressions: (1) continuing practice participation in American Buddhist communities; (2) being trained for and assuming leadership positions in both lay and monastic communities; (3) engaging in Buddhist feminist scholarship and research expressed through lectures and writing; (4) exploring non-patriarchal forms of Buddhist practice and Buddhist community structures; (5) exploring and expressing women's experience integrating practice with everyday life; (6) creating networks of friendship and support between Buddhist women with similar interests; and (7) expressing Buddhist women's spiritual experience and understanding through artistic media.

I have written from my own experience as an American Zen practitioner, a poet, and a mother. Whatever forms our lives take, I hope that we Buddhist women can support one another's choices. In addition to recognizing the leaders among us, I hope we can retain an appreciation for the invisible and common "women's" work that has traditionally left few traces, yet enriches life immeasurably: cooking, cleaning, sewing, settling disputes, nurturing. Whatever our choices, our talents, our circumstances, I know we can come face to face – mirroring one another, illuminating one another.

Notes

1 Sensei Wendy Egyoku Nakao, "The Lineage of Women," in *ZCLA [Zen Center of Los Angeles]/Buddha Essence Temple Sangha Letter* (July/August 1998): 2.

2 Sensei Wendy Egyoku Nakao, "Women Acquiring the Essence," Ibid., p. 1.

3 Nakao, "The Lineage of Women," p. 1.

4 See Susan Moon on changing forms and symbols at Berkeley Zen Center in, "My Big Self," *Turning Wheel* (Spring 1999): 27–28. Homage to female Zen ancestors has also been instituted in the California Diamond Sangha's chanting service. These two groups are personally known to me; there are many other American Buddhist groups now working to acknowledge their own "lineage of Matriarchs."

5 Nakao, "The Lineage of Women," p. 2.

6 Nakao, "Women Acquiring the Essence," p. 1.

7 *The Dhammapada: The Sayings of the Buddha*, trans. Thomas Byron (New York: Vintage Books, 1976), p. 125.

8 Donald Winnicott, "Transitional Objects and Transitional Phenomena: A Study of the First Not-Me Possession," *International Journal of Psycho-Analysis* 34 (1953): 1–25.

9 Kosho Uchiyama Roshi, "How to Cook Your Life," in Dōgen and Uchiyama, *Refining Your Life: From the Zen Kitchen to Enlightenment* (New York: Weatherhill, 1983), p. 93.

10 Thinley Norbu Rinpoche, "Words for the West, on Nihilism, Spiritual Surrender, and the Importance of Lineage and the Guru," *Tricycle* 8, no. 1 (Fall 1998): 48.

11 Nakao, "Women Acquiring the Essence," p. 1.

12 Lenore Friedman and Susan Moon, eds., *Being Bodies: Buddhist Women on the Paradox of Embodiment* (Boston: Shambhala, 1997).

13 Jiko Linda Cutts, "Face to Face: The Meaning Comes Alive," *Windbell* 31, no. 2 (Summer 1997): 23.

CHAPTER TWENTY-FIVE

Buddhism, Human Rights, Women's Rights, and Democracy[1]

Kassie Neou

In discussing the relationship between Buddhism and human rights, I would first like to explain the central place and resilient nature of Buddhism within Cambodian culture and history. This focus has remained true, despite the savage destruction of the Khmer Rouge years (1975–1979). When they seized power, the Khmer Rouge made every effort to eliminate Buddhism. All Buddhist temples were closed, some were destroyed, while still others served as prisons, torture chambers, and even pigsties. Statues of the Buddha were shattered. Of about 65,000 Buddhist monks in Cambodia before the war, only about 3,000 survived. The rest were executed, or died of starvation and disease aggravated by conditions in forced-labor camps.

But the Buddhist ideal never left the hearts of the people, especially country folk. Today we see a great revival of Buddhism in Cambodia. From the 3,000 monks who survived, we now have about 47,000. As one survivor of the Khmer Rouge years told an interviewer, "They could only destroy the outward signs of our religion, not our deeply held inner beliefs." Therefore, we must understand that Buddhism in Cambodia is deeply embedded in the culture and strikes a deep chord within people's hearts and minds.

Buddhist teachings provide us with rich indigenous lessons on human rights and non-violence that can be drawn upon when discussing these concepts. The Buddhist canon contains many references to what we now call human rights. Although the phrasing may be different from modern human rights terminology or political theory, the concepts remain the same. The Buddha taught kindness, compassion, and respect for human beings and other living things. He counseled nonviolence. He forbade killing, and instead called upon people to develop kind and compassionate social perspectives. He instructed people to abstain from stealing and cheating, and to respect the rights and property of others.

Buddhist scriptures outlined political rights.[2] Citizens had the right to participate in the political life of their state. In fact, citizens' participation was actively encouraged. The scriptures called for public assemblies and referenda in order to reach decisions within communities. In addition, monks and nuns participated in the governance of their communities by means of frequent assemblies. There are even references to the concept of elected leaders (*mahāsammata*), demonstrating that democracy and elections resonate within Buddhism. Buddhist doctrines embrace freedom of speech and assembly. During the Buddha's era many different competing schools of thought existed, and although the Buddha may have disagreed with what these schools espoused, he did not try to suppress them. Instead, the Buddha tolerated contending views and stated that tolerance was one of the most important duties of a king.

Buddhism emphasizes the equality of all people. The Buddha demonstrated his commitment to this principle by elevating Upāli, a former barber and slave, to a powerful position within the community of monks. In so doing, he showed his rejection of the caste system of the time. Buddhist doctrine also emphasizes justice and the rule of law. The Buddha clearly condemned any miscarriage of justice. We can see this in the Jātaka tale in which an evil king, wanting the wife of a merchant for himself, fabricated charges against the merchant, tried, and then executed him. Later, the king realized his sins and repented. The ten duties of kings related in this story prescribe honesty and integrity as core values.

The Buddha called for peaceful settlement of disputes. This is a valuable point in teaching nonviolent conflict resolution to people who respect the Buddha. The Buddha taught this by living a nonviolent life. One of the most famous instances of this is recounted in a *sutta* where the Buddha personally walked onto a battlefield to halt the killing. Compromise dominated his teaching on conflict resolution. He stressed that people must not insist on their own way, but instead show understanding and compassion toward the viewpoints of others.

We need only look at the life of the Buddha to see the respect with which he treated women. The Buddha launched the first women's liberation movement in the world. He stated that men and women held equal places both spiritually and intellectually. He demonstrated this belief by creating the order of nuns, just five years after the formation of the order of monks. Women, just like men, were regarded as capable of and encouraged to strive toward achieving the exalted spiritual state of *nibbāna*.

The Buddha called on husbands and wives to respect each other: A husband had a duty to honor, respect, love, and be faithful to his wife; a wife's primary duty was to love her husband. The Buddha also outlined the ideal virtues of a woman. Among other virtues, he advocated that a woman should be learned and knowledgeable, hard-working and mentally alert. This advocacy demonstrates that the Buddha understood that women and men possess equal intellectual abilities. He believed in equality for all, irrespective of color, class, ethnic group, or sex.

The Cambodian Institute of Human Rights has recognized the importance of placing concepts of human rights within the context of the Buddhist teachings. In teaching ordinary citizens our tactics, we draw upon the strength of the Buddhist faith. When we have a class, we may ask "How many of you are Christians?" Usually no hands are raised. "How many of you are Muslims?" Possibly one hand may be raised. "How many of you are Buddhists?" All the other hands then go up. "Then," we continue, "do you believe in the teachings of the Buddha?" They all agree that they do. This provides a point of departure for explaining the connection between Buddhism and human rights. We stress that the Buddhist approach to life, with its emphasis on kindness, compassion, nonviolence, and respect for people and all living things, captures the essence of human rights.

Placing human rights in the context of Cambodia's Buddhist culture is a powerful technique. Even tough, hardened military men have told us that they now understand and appreciate human rights when they are explained in terms of Buddhist principles. For human rights educators in Cambodia, the longstanding devotion of the majority of the people to Buddhism is undoubtedly our greatest resource.

Peace Education: What the Buddha Taught

Cambodia, my homeland, suffered the ravages of war in the 1970s that resulted in unparalleled suffering over the last 25 years. In the early 1970s, the war with the Khmer Rouge accelerated under the Lon Nol regime. Many Cambodians thought that peace had arrived when the Khmer Rouge took over the government in April 1975. What we did not foresee then was the nature of their regime and the future genocidal madness. During the Khmer Rouge period, 1975–1979, over a million Cambodians died of execution, disease, or hunger. Khmer Rouge rule ended only with the Vietnamese invasion and occupation in 1979. The new, Vietnamese-backed government then fought against armed resistance from the Khmer Rouge and non-Communist forces as well. The country, impoverished and exhausted, finally heard the promise of peace, and the Paris Peace Accords at last were signed by the warring factions in October 1991. The people participated in free elections in 1993. And yet Cambodia still does not enjoy a true or lasting peace. The underlying reason for this unrest is that Cambodians, both the leaders and common people, acquired a culture of war from the many years of fighting. Now it is our difficult task to replace this warring mentality with a culture of peace.

My own experience gives some hint as to how this might be done. Given my country's terrible recent history, I am very lucky to be here with you today. For the crime of speaking English, I was taken to a Khmer Rouge prison camp, chained, and tortured. I soon came to realize the camp was not just a prison camp. It was an extermination camp. To my knowledge, no prisoner left it alive, except me. By telling Aesop's fables and classic

Khmer children's stories about animals to my guards, who themselves were just children or teenagers, I was able to escape the executioner.

Ever since the time of my imprisonment, I have been haunted by the image of mere children, as young as 10 or 12, carrying weapons and torturing and killing thousands of people without hesitation. Their only experiences in life involved war and death. Too many adult Cambodians learned a similar lesson: to resolve their differences at the point of a gun. This mode of operation has seriously hindered the progress of my country even since the peace process supervised by the United Nations. Why, I wondered, couldn't the people instead be educated in the ways of peace, human rights, and democracy?

Teaching Peace, Human Rights and Democracy to the Children of Cambodia

In 1993, my colleague Ms. Meng Ho Leang and I formed the Cambodian Institute of Human Rights and, along with other organizations, embarked on a program of education for peace, human rights, and democracy. We aim to transform a culture of war into a culture of peace. Our efforts have resulted in some setbacks as well as some successes. In the long run, we hope we will be able to produce major changes. Our primary focus is on the children. A child's mind is an empty jar that can be filled with good things or evil. Our task is to fill it with good.

The Institute's largest program, "Human Rights Teaching Methodology," trains primary and secondary schoolteachers to teach the values of peace, democracy, and human rights. The subjects presented in this training are now an official part of the school curriculum for all grades, using teacher's manuals we developed in conjunction with the Ministry of Education. In fact, the government has asked us to train all the schoolteachers in Cambodia to use the curriculum. By March 31, 1999, we had taught 24,218 teachers. This is just over 30% of all Cambodian teachers, so we have about 50,000 to go! We have been very fortunate to receive generous funding from several donors, but not on the scale needed to achieve our target of reaching all teachers within three years. This represents an enormous task, but we cannot refuse to meet this need. Peace and human rights are mandatory for Cambodia's future.

Through these training programs, we hope to instill the values of nonviolence, human rights, and democracy in the schoolchildren, so that by the time this generation graduates they will be able to think in new and positive ways. Picking up a gun to solve problems will be a thing of the past. Instead, we hope they will have the skills to deal with difficult questions peacefully and democratically.

What Can We Do about the Adults?

In society today, war-based thinking is instigated by adults, not by children. Teaching peace to adults presents different problems because of adults' set ways of thinking. Changing an inflexible mindset is tremendously challenging. It is not possible to gather all the adults together in a classroom, but there are ways to reach them. The first effective method is through extensive use of the media. The Institute's regular television shows, radio programs, and newspaper articles provide cost-effective ways to promote messages of peace, democracy, and human rights for the general public.

We reserve more expensive training courses for key target audiences, such as officials in the countryside who wield great power over the population. For these officials, the Institute started one-week "good governance" training courses which instruct local leaders in how to adapt successfully to modern, democratic environments. We hope to reach all significant officials, from those in high positions down to the grassroots (commune) level in the rural provinces of Cambodia. It may be unrealistic to hope that officials' lifelong values and attitudes can be changed through a short instructional course. After all, people can learn about peace and democracy without becoming more peaceful or democratic. But so far, the results have been encouraging. In a typical poll, a majority of our trainees indicated they intended to apply what they learned in class to their daily lives and predicted that the training would make a difference in the attitudes and behavior of those who received it.

Women's Rights are Human Rights

Children are our main hope for the future, but the nation's largest resource today is its women. Women are valued as mothers and produce three-quarters of the nation's food, yet they are often neglected. Why do many of us ignore the Buddha's teachings on respect and equality for women?

The Cambodian Institute of Human Rights has adopted an "affirmative action" program to address this gender imbalance and it starts in our own organization. Ms. Meng Ho Leang, my co-director, is one of a small handful of women prominent in Cambodian public life. She is President of the Coalition for Free and Fair Elections, a nationwide organization of 68 NGOs (non-government organizations), and founder of the Cambodian Girl Guide movement. Ms. Meng Ho's example is an inspiration to women and girls, demonstrating that a confident woman can succeed in circles dominated by men.

Because women and girls are so under-represented in public life, our Human Rights Teaching Methodology project includes measures to ensure the fair involvement of girl students and women teachers. Special seminars for women help them acquire the same skills, knowledge, and opportunities as men. We encourage nuns to join our good governance training so that they can play more prominent roles in the affairs of their temples and local communities. The Institute's flagship national radio program, "Distant Learning for Rural Women," discusses human rights, family, and health issues. It was pivotal in encouraging women to exercise their right to vote in the 1998 elections, independently of their husbands. Women are usually in the majority at our "Culture of Peace" rallies and most active on the organizing committees. In these ways, the Institute endeavors to implement the Buddha's teachings on respect and equality for women.

How to Reach the Top Leaders

The very top governmental leaders, such as ministers and prime ministers, are not likely to sit still for "lessons" in peace and democracy or human rights. These are, after all, intelligent and able people who have made their way to the top of the political system. Probably they believe that they do not need to learn new things. Yet these are precisely the persons with the power to take a nation to war and to create or destroy a democratic society. They may have rigid attitudes based on past experiences, and may live and work in relative isolation. Advisors may be reluctant to advance new ideas, especially if they contradict their leaders' beliefs.

How, then, can these leaders be reached? One way is to enlighten their advisors, in hope that the leaders will consequently be affected by this new approach. Another is through discreet, private meetings directly with the leaders. In this way, leaders can be exposed to new ideas without risk of embarrassment. These must not, of course, be presented as "lessons" of superior wisdom that the leaders should accept without question. An approach respecting the dignity and position of the leader often yields more fruitful results.

Another way to reach leaders is through the people. If the people want democracy, leaders will feel pressured to respond positively. Educating grassroots communities in peace and democracy – creating a constituency – becomes an important task. In Cambodia, this means the involvement of NGOs, Buddhist monks (who are highly respected and influential in Cambodian society), women's groups, village communities, and others. These groups can, in effect, lobby the government at all levels.

Informal Sessions with World Leaders

An additional method to teach leaders involves informal sessions in which current world leaders can exchange views and learn from other *retired* leaders for a short period of time. The format could resemble a corporate "retreat." Leaders could discuss their problems in private, informal, and relaxed atmospheres, off the record. Former chiefs of state can be more effective as advisors in these situations, because they may have more time than current government heads, while at the same time having the stature and experience to communicate as equals with current leaders. Especially desirable participants would be former leaders who have themselves successfully guided their countries through the transition from a repressive form of government to democracy.

Some retired world leaders, such as former U.S. President Jimmy Carter, travel the globe to help in resolving crisis situations. Although these praiseworthy efforts often produce effective outcomes, it is even better to engage in crisis *prevention*, by communicating with leaders *before* disasters threaten. Establishing relations between former and existing leaders has the potential to offset potential problems through friendship, advice, and empathetic listening. An organization such as the Council of Freely-Elected Heads of Government could play a constructive role in such situations.

Objectives and Methodologies for Peace Education, Human Rights, and Democracy

Our objective at the Cambodian Institute of Human Rights is not simply to provide *information* about peace, democracy, or human rights. Instead, we aim to instill values, attitudes, and behaviors that encourage people to live peacefully, democratically, and with respect for the human rights of all. Democracy needs democrats, and a peaceful society needs peacemakers.

Changes in attitudes and cultural values are difficult to achieve. At the Institute, we have used several approaches, and are still expanding our methodologies. We try to relate the concepts of peace, democracy, and human rights to our students' personal experiences, practical interests, and to familiar elements of Cambodian culture. Despite Cambodia's tragic history of war and oppression, the roots of human rights, peace, and democracy do indeed exist in Cambodia's traditional culture. These roots need only be nurtured and highlighted in order to thrive.

The Buddha Shows the Way

In drawing on Cambodian culture, our greatest ally is Theravāda Buddhism. Nearly all Cambodians consider themselves to be Buddhists. Buddhist doctrine contains the values of human rights, peace, and democracy. The phrasing may be different from modern human rights instruments or political theory, but the concepts are the same. When we use familiar concepts to explain peace, human rights, or democracy, the chances that our words will be heeded increase considerably.

The basic Buddhist principle of nonviolence, or *ahimsa*, is not just a slogan, but a way of living. On a very practical level, it tells people how to start by building peace within themselves – inner peace – and extending it to their families, their communities, the nation, and the world. In addition, the Buddha's teachings and actions provide models for peaceful dispute resolution. Moreover, the Buddhist doctrines of tolerance and compassion powerfully support human rights and respect for others.

Although the political systems current in India 2,500 years ago were very different from today's, the Buddha's teachings nonetheless contain the essence of democracy. His admonition to run the community of monks democratically and his advocacy of citizen participation in government and opposition to tyranny underscore this concept. But we can also look beyond the specific teachings and see democracy in the very creation of the religion, for in Buddhism enlightenment or liberation is available to everyone. In this respect, everyone is equal, regardless of social class or caste. In Buddhism, sacred knowledge is not held in secret by a small priestly class dispensing favors but, rather, is open to all. We therefore can describe Buddhism as a democratic religion – one in which all can participate equally.

They Cry "Peace, Peace," but There Is No Peace

It is useless simply to tell people that peace is good for them and admonish them to behave more peacefully. The leap from the word "peace" to real action is huge. But Buddhist teachings provide a philosophical and moral basis for peace, in addition to practical ways to *achieve* peace, both for individuals or for nations. The Institute teaches concrete methods of peaceful conflict resolution, some based on the many examples found in the Buddhist scriptures and some based on contemporary techniques. We use familiar, traditional Cambodian methods of conflict resolution known as *somroh somruel*, whereby a dignitary such as a Buddhist abbot or local official helps mediate local disputes. The pursuit of inner peace in the heart of each individual is a traditional aspect of the Buddhist teachings and of Cambodian culture. The person who maintains serenity, even in adversity, attains respect in classical Cambodian society.

Successes and Failures

I have discussed some of the concepts and methods we are using to make peace education a real and meaningful presence in Cambodia. Yet we admit that peace, democracy, and human rights in my country have had a turbulent history and their future is still uncertain. To be sure, the situation is much better today than during the savagery of the Khmer Rouge era. The improvement is due to the enormous efforts of the international community to restore peace in Cambodia and to the determination of the Cambodian people to attain peace. In this respect, I think that the people are more advanced than their leaders. In concrete terms, we have made significant progress towards peace, human rights, and democracy since the 1991 Paris Peace Accords. There are many more democrats and peacemakers now, and peace education has played an important role in this achievement. The Cambodian government, to its credit, has supported the widest possible education in our core values. Our surveys regularly verify that the people we educate have an increased appreciation for and commitment to these ideals.

Yet there have also been painful setbacks and failures. Against a background of high expectations, progress has been far too slow. Political pluralism and freedom of the press both still rest on tenuous footing, and there have been too many incidents of violence. Intense factionalism has led to serious conflicts and we hope it will not lead us again to civil war. We and other NGOs and individuals are doing our utmost to prevent this.

The most disturbing recent incident was the battle of July 5–6, 1997, and the resulting ouster of the First Prime Minister of Cambodia. The sounds of rockets, artillery, and machine gun fire echoed through the streets of Phnom Penh, bringing back terrible memories of war to the population. Fortunately, the fighting was limited and relative peace has been restored since then, but these events were a stark warning that Cambodia's peace process is fragile and much progress remains to be made.

Recently I viewed a photograph of a training class I conducted in 1997, taken before the fighting of July 5 and 6. The class included the most senior members of the Cambodian armed forces, including the Co-Ministers of Defense. I was proud of these students, who asked good questions and demonstrated their understanding of democracy, human rights, and the role of the military in maintaining peace. As I looked at the row of faces in the photograph, I realized that some of these officers had been killed in the fighting and some of the others had probably issued the orders that resulted in their classmates' deaths. This incident reminded us, in the most graphic way, of how big a challenge we face, but we are more determined than ever to succeed. I had to remind myself over and over again in 1998 of the need to maintain this determination. I was instrumental in arguing for an independent body to oversee the National Assembly Elections scheduled for July 1998, so it was poetic justice that I was asked to join the National Election Committee as its vice-chair. I hoped and believed that Cambodia could organize free, fair, and credible elections, despite the events of July 1997, and we almost succeeded. However, almost as soon as we relaxed in the knowledge that millions of people had indeed exercised their vote in a peaceful atmosphere, the political factions argued over the results, which led to protests in the streets, violence, and deaths. Once again, we were plunged into the same old vicious circle. Our leaders had ignored not only the wishes of the majority of people, but also the teachings and values of the Buddha.

As we approached the end of 1998, the situation seemed hopeless. Then suddenly the two main political parties agreed to form a coalition government. They eventually accepted the people's verdict, expressed at the polls, that they must work together. As of this writing, Cambodia has experienced real peace for almost six months and the signs are very optimistic. We have been readmitted to the United Nations and world community, have joined ASEAN, and donors and investors are arriving to help Cambodia develop so that it will no longer languish as one of the poorest countries in the world.

Our institute is helping create peace by organizing "Culture of Peace" rallies. Recently one was held in the former jungle stronghold of the Khmer Rouge. How heartening it was to see thousands of people openly and loudly proclaiming peace, led by our spiritual leaders, the Buddhist monks and nuns. Even a few months ago, no one would have thought this possible. Our recent efforts target former Khmer Rouge teachers. They have told us about their former doctrinaire understanding of life and their opposition to Buddhism. Now nearly all express their appreciation at having developed a more enlightened view. Even the most hardened former stalwarts now appreciate tolerance, universal human rights, and the wisdom intrinsic to Cambodian culture based on the teachings of the Buddha.

Of course, we are conscious that this peace could prove to be fragile and short-lived. In the past we often wondered whether our work was futile. We have discovered that building a culture of peace out of a culture of war is a very difficult, uncertain, and slow process. Cambodia has come a long way since the days of Pol Pot's terror, yet we still have a long path to travel. We believe we can reach our goal by touching the hearts of each individual, just as the Buddha taught. We believe we have devised some methods and gained some wisdom to help make peace a permanent reality in Cambodia and elsewhere in the world.

Notes

1 I gratefully acknowledge the cooperation of Jeffrey C. Gallup (Associate Director), John Lowrie (Senior Advisor), and Aine Doody (Advisor) at the Cambodian Institute of Human Rights in the preparation of this manuscript.

2 Scholarly studies on Buddhist views on governance and kingship include John P. Ferguson, *Sangha and State in Burma* (Ithaca, NY: Cornell University Press, 1975); Stanley Tambiah's *World Conqueror and World Renouncer: A Study of Buddhism and Polity in Thailand* (Cambridge: Cambridge University Press, 1976); and three works edited by Bardwell L. Smith: *The Two Wheels of Dhamma* (Chambersburg, Pa.: American Academy of Religion, 1972); *Religion and Legitimation of Power in Sri Lanka* (Chambersburg, Pa.: Anima Books, 1978); and *Religion and Legitimation of Power in Thailand, Laos, and Burma* (Chambersburg, Pa.: Anima Books, 1978).

CHAPTER TWENTY-SIX

Engaged Buddhism

"Moving" and Recreating Women's Stories

Trina Nahm-Mijo

When I met her more than 18 years ago, Gloria was sitting on the porch of a local women's shelter, an old plantation-style house, somewhat rundown, but still grand in size. It was my first visit to the shelter and my initiation to being on its Board of Directors. Gloria, a middle-aged African American woman, was sitting in a wheelchair. Her husband had hit her with a sledge hammer and destroyed her kidneys. She was undergoing regular dialysis treatment. Gloria was soft-spoken, but something in her eyes left an indelible imprint on my psyche and a scar on my heart. Our brief conversation changed my life and became part of my cellular structure. It was disturbing, because I knew she was a part of me, and her reality a part of the world we all inhabit. I never saw Gloria again, but her story lived inside of me as if we had daily contact. Here on paper, Gloria's suffering and survival lives and breathes.

Around the same time that I met Gloria, in 1979, I began exploring movement with a group made up of two wheelchair performers – Eddie, a double-amputee Vietnam veteran, and Danny, a quadraplegic with muscular dystrophy – and two female able-bodied dancers, Wendy and me. The four of us created a piece called "Wheels," which explored our interdependence and the universal human handicap of limited perspective. I began to experience the fluid nature of categories – as distinctions such as disabled and able-bodied, art and therapy, performer and audience began to melt away. My direct experience began to tell me that as such categories dissolved, my compassion grew. I was no longer the "helper" but a participant in a wonderful "practice" which required that we be fully present at any moment, since we relied on each other for balance, support, and locomotion which was minutely timed. Without concentrated focus, one of us could get hurt. We became a part of each other, taking on dependent, initiatory, and interdependent roles at different points in the dance.

This embodied awareness cultivated in "Wheels" began to feel like a "moving meditation." It informed my study and practice of Buddhism, mainly Zen, to which I had been introduced several years earlier by Aitken Roshi at Koko-An Zendo in Honolulu. During graduate school at the University of California, Berkeley, I had integrated Zen Buddhist concepts into my doctoral dissertation on transformational psychology and the interconnectedness of mind-body.[1]

Buddhism, art, and social action all informed one another – like a three-tiered waterfall with a rotating source. Without intending to, I began to create dances that told a story of pain or loss. The retelling seems to unknit the scar tissue and offer up a story of courage and survival – the survival of the human spirit. The process of creating dances began to resemble what Joanna Macy has described as the process of "compassion:" "Breathe in that pain like a dark stream . . . Let it pass through your heart . . . Surrender it for now to the healing resources of life's vast web . . . We can let it strengthen our belonging in the larger web of being."[2]

The contemporary "engaged Buddhist" movement emphasizes that everything is interdependent and interconnected, thus fostering a sense of universal responsibility.[3] Cultural artists dealing with universal themes that confront our violence, war, and oppression toward one another – whether overt or subtle – offer themselves and their audiences the possibility of experiencing an empowered awareness which can awaken human dignity.

In 1984, I choreographed "Children of War" based on a story told to me by a Vietnam veteran who had fallen in love with his Viet Cong prisoner. This dance moved through their roles – beginning as enemies, to captive and captor, to lovers – expressing the elusive nature of our identity in categories and our attachment to these categories. "To Omoni" (1991) was inspired by a poem by Mi Ok Bruining, one of the first Korean adoptees to the United States. It tells her story as a young Korean orphan who survived the chilling emptiness of abandonment and who wonders about and longs for her birth mother (*omoni* in Korean). The dance is performed to an oral interpretation of the poem which in its closing lines speaks poignantly of the *karmic* cycle:

> the moment I will miss
> you the most will be
> when I give birth
> to my future *teal* (daughter).
>
> then the circle will be
> complete, and a gift of
> *ae-jeong* (love) will have entered
> into this mortal world
> for us, Omoni.[4]

As an artist who participates in the retelling of stories about the human condition, I attempt to engage myself and the audience in a kind of action meditation: "To be aware, to see the truth, frees us."[5] Chogyam Trungpa has called this "Dharma Art."[6]

In early 1992, I was invited to perform at the opening of a multimedia show, "Caught Between the Sheets," to be held in Los Angeles that July. The show would feature the work of Korean American women artists. I planned to do a piece about gender identity. In April, however, life intruded. I found myself at the bedside of my creative partner of 17 years, Earnest Morgan, an African American man dying of AIDS. Earnest was responsible for bringing contemporary dance to Hawai'i, a native son who had danced professionally with Paul Taylor's company in New York City and had come home to inspire a new generation of young people in the arts. With our company, Dance O' Hawai'i, we had performed in every gymnasium on the Big Island, and toured all the other islands giving lecture-demonstrations and performances.

April 1992 also saw the eruption of race riots in Los Angeles following the Rodney King beating verdict. The media focused on fanning racial tensions between the Korean American and African American communities where these communities intersected in Koreatown. As I labored over each remaining breath of the African American man who had taught me so much about the quality of life, art, humanity, and service, just 3,000 miles away, a 15-year-old African American girl, Latasha Harlins, was shot to death by a Korean shopkeeper.[7] My heart broke open.

Three months later, enroute to the opening of "Caught Between the Sheets," I drove past the burned-out shells of the shops remaining in Koreatown – looking more like a war zone than the bustling community it had once been. I had created a new piece for the show, "My Brother was Black, My Sister is Black," because Earnest had passed away in May and I felt that I, as well as the Korean community, needed healing. When I came to perform in L.A., I did not come with a lot of steps in mind. I wanted a healing for my loss, and especially for the pain and suffering of the Black and Korean American communities torn apart by racial and socio-economic strife.[8]

In 1993, a Korean woman minister who had attended that performance called me to commission a work to be presented at the California-Pacific Regional Methodist Conference to garner support for a resolution that would be presented to the U.N. World Conference on Human Rights. Reverend Katherine Koh was a member of a coalition of community, religious, and academic leaders who formed the Coalition Against Military Sexual Slavery by Japan to shed light on this historical event as a "crime against humanity." The dance she commissioned me to do, "Chungshin-dae" (a Korean term meaning "sex slave"), enacted the story of the 200,000 Asian women, 80 percent of them Korean, who were forced into sexual service by Japanese soldiers during World War II. The girls, most between 12 and 25 years old, were coerced, abducted, and forcefully taken from their villages to service between 40 and 60 soldiers a night in cold military barracks under the most barbaric living conditions. Many of these girls were virgins, and "suicide was a common alternative to death from venereal disease, beatings, widespread illness, or abortions."[9]

In the process of choreographing this work, I experienced a phenomenon unlike any that I had experienced before, but which again seemed to have the reciprocal effect of informing my Buddhist practice, while my practice informed my art expression. That is, when I began putting the story of the *chungshindae* into movement and imagery, I would break down into uncontrollable sobbing, as if the suffering of these women inhabited my body. Again, on the cellular level, I was "seeing reality," the reality of the *chungshindae* whose story wanted to be told 50 years later, a reality where past and present intersected. Perhaps this is what Chogyam Trungpa has termed the "iconography of the cosmos:"

> You are able to experience a sense of reality that does not depend on reinforcement. You don't have to ask your neighbor, "Am I seeing reality?" The experience is unconditional. Nobody has to confirm your experience – you can confirm it yourself.[10]

By bringing the story of the *chungshindae* to the California-Pacific Regional Methodist Conference, through the directly experienced vehicle of dance, Reverend Koh and I were able to engage the largely white, middle-class membership in an international issue of social consciousness. Our work allowed them to vicariously experience what Theo Van Boven, from the United Nations Commission on Human Rights, has called "one of the largest-scale and most blatantly organized examples in history of wartime sex crimes."[11] Ours was one example of the many collaborations between spiritual leaders, artists, academics, and community activists who finally made the rape of women during war an international war crime in 1994 at the Geneva Human Rights Convention. Retelling a story can reinvent society.

In working as a dance artist, I have been fortunate to have been inspired by other artists with a similar vision for world peace and a "nonaggressive" approach to art cultivated by Buddhist practice. These women, also residents of Hawai'i, participate in the retelling of stories in a way that informs our social consciousness and exemplifies engaged Buddhism. The following examples show that individuals can work in other artistic media, come to Buddhism in very different ways, and practice different Buddhist traditions, but also "swim against the stream," breaking molds and categories, and broadening our capacities to potentiate "sacred practice" in creative, evolving forms.

Fay Hovey is a businesswoman and writer who resides in Haiku, Maui. Fay and I have collaborated on poem/dance pieces for over 12 years. She wrote the poetic preface to "Chungshindae" after reading through accounts by the Korean sex slaves. Fay began practicing Nichiren Daishonin's

Buddhism in 1988 and since 1996 has written a series of short stories based on her study of the Daishonin's letters. These stories have been published in *Living Buddhism* magazine and tell how certain women disciples of Daishonin "read these letters with their lives" during the 13th century. In her own words, Fay describes the process of writing these stories:

> As I progress in my practice, there have been times when I have felt burdened by my karma, puzzled by my setbacks, frustrated at how the same problem would reoccur time and time again. While trying to deeply understand these things, often I would toss and turn in bed, and I began to see that my awakening at such times could be more constructively put to use by studying the Daishonin's letters.
>
> Soon, the "The Drum at the Gate of Thunder" became an old friend, and I returned to it to gain renewed confidence in my journey. His complete conviction that women could also become enlightened (without first being born a man), is a legacy that extends across the centuries and encourages us today. What seems obvious today, perhaps, was not accepted wisdom during Sennichi-ama's time. I began to reflect on how most of us, men and women, do not have a fundamental belief that enlightenment is our birthright and how that stands, like a giant boulder, in the way of stepping into that most ordinary and extraordinary state of life.
>
> A simple letter to a humble and devout follower, a woman who lived centuries ago, encouraged me to continue in hope, and I went back to sleep one night, reflecting that time doesn't really exist in the world of enlightenment. From that place, we access all things, all beings at any time in history and understand that the people that lived before us had hearts that quickened to the same joys, hearts that throbbed with the same sorrows. At the edges of awakening dawn, I became aware of an irresistible urge to write and sat down at the computer and a first-person account by Sennichi-ama began to pour forth. I entered a timeless realm ... I was in thirteenth century Japan on Sado Island walking with an old woman in her garden, sitting on a bench under a spreading tree and hearing her story.[12]

In the recreation of Sennichi-ama's story, Fay Hovey has told us something very old and something new. Since the practitioners of the past inform our own practice today, and the engaged Buddhist movement rests on this connection, this constitutes "interbeing" as described by Thich Nhat Hanh: "Being in touch with suchness is like digging a well and reaching the point where the water forces its way up. Once we can drink directly from the well of understanding, we are no longer caught by the signs of a self, a person, a living being, or a life span."[13]

Thich Nhat Hanh describes one of the most disturbing and powerful images of our times during the Vietnam War:

> Venerable Thich Quang Duc went to the crossroads of Phan Dinh Phung, sat in the lotus position, poured gasoline on himself, and transformed himself into a torch. By burning himself, Thich Quang Duc awakened the world to the suffering of the war and the persecution of the Buddhists. When someone stands up to violence in such a courageous way, a force for change is released. Every action for peace requires someone to exhibit the courage to challenge the violence and inspire love.[14]

Keiko Bonk was in the ninth grade when the image of a burning monk left a cellular scar on her heart and became part of her story as a Buddhist, artist, and social activist.[15] Raised in Naalehu, Hawai'i, in a Buddhist family, Keiko is another example of a woman whose multiple identity defies categories and allows her to swim upstream against the tide of religious and social convention. Her mother, Fumi Matsuoka, came from the Shin Buddhist tradition, which was brought over to the plantations of Hawai'i from feudal Japan. Fumi met Keiko's father, Bill Bonk, at a Buddhist temple in New York City during the 1940s. Bill, like a number of American men, was introduced to Asian religion and philosophy when he went overseas during World War II. Keiko was the first Green Party candidate to be elected to public office in the state of Hawai'i. In 1992, she won the County Council seat in her district and was re-elected to that seat in 1994 and served as Council Chair. In 1996, she lost a bid for Hawai'i County Mayor by a couple thousand votes, and she plans to run again for this office in the year 2000.

Before returning home and entering politics, Keiko was a visual artist and a rock musician in New York City for ten years. Keiko is an example of a woman who is moving and recreating women's stories – her own story – by her involvement in diverse yet interrelated arenas. She sees the interface between Buddhism, art, and social action as "seeking truth." Her music speaks of two sides of love – suffering and joy – as a Buddhist path beyond distinctions:

> The more woes and wrongs that manifest
> The more beauty and peace we need
> The more blind and greedy mankind gets
> The more I pray for us to see.
>
> We bust the earth and rape her
> Again and again
> Sometimes the dirt, the trees
> Are my only friends.
>
> Sometimes I wanna escape and do nothing at all
> But I'm in love, I can't help it
> I'm in love with the things
> There ain't too much of.[16]

This state of being in love is referred to as the "world as lover" in an essay by Joanna Macy.[17] The erotic and the visceral are returning to their place as part of the fabric of spiritual experience. In this body I dwell, and in dancing my stories, the stories of other women, and indeed the stories of all humankind, I see the universe expanding. In swimming upstream, one feels the rush of pushing against the flow, having to catch one's breath, and experiencing the effort of moving. If one stays stuck in concepts, this could be seen as non-flowing, fighting, or struggling. Trying to merge one's identity with any one concept like Buddhism, dance, or social action can be like that, but breathing these in as a lover would is pure Dance. In Japanese *tanka* form this can be expressed:

Landscapes of untold
Stories reshape the teller
In earnest telling ...
The far reaches of my soul
Revealed sharing the terrain.

Notes

1 Trina Nahm-Mijo, "Spiritual and Physical Movement: An Inquiry into Human Growth Potential," Ph.D. diss., University of California at Berkeley, 1979.
2 Joanna Macy, "Taking Heart," *The Path of Compassion: Writings on Socially Engaged Buddhism*, ed. Fred Eppsteiner (Berkeley: Parallax Press, 1988), p. 207.
3 Kenneth Kraft, "Engaged Buddhism," *Engaged Buddhist Reader*, ed. Arnold Kotler (Berkeley: Parallax Press, 1996), p. 65.
4 Mi Ok Bruining, "To Omoni, In Korea," *Making Face, Making Soul*, ed. Gloria Anzaldua (San Francisco: Aunt Lute Books, 1990), p. 153.
5 Jack Kornfield, "Spiritual Practice and Social Action," *Engaged Buddhist Reader*, p. 17.
6 Chogyam Trungpa, *Dharma Art* (Boston: Shambhala Publications, 1996), p. 6.
7 Holly Wagner, "Du, Harlins Families Settle Suit," *Korea Times*, English edition, July 13, 1992, p. 1.
8 Trina Nahm-Mijo, *Sho: L.A.'s Asian and Pacific Islander Arts and Entertainment Calendar* 1, no. 5 (Sept.–Nov. 1992).
9 Carol Chung, "Methodists to Consider Resolution on Comfort Women," *Korea Times*, English edition, June 16, 1993, p. 8.
10 Trungpa, *Dharma Art*, p. 95.
11 Chung, "Methodists to Consider Resolution on Comfort Women."
12 Fay Hovey, personal communication, November 6, 1998.
13 Thich Nhat Hanh, *The Diamond That Cuts Through Illusion* (Berkeley: Parallax Press, 1992), p. 113.
14 Hanh, "Love in Action," *Engaged Buddhist Reader*, p. 60.
15 Keiko Bonk, personal communication, November 8, 1998.
16 Keiko Bonk, "Save the World, Be My Girl," copyright Fragile Flower, Hawai'i, 1996.
17 Joanna Macy, "World As Lover, World As Self," *Engaged Buddhist Reader*, pp. 150–61.

CHAPTER TWENTY-SEVEN

Inner Transformation for World Peace

Tenzin Palmo

To create world peace, we must eradicate delusion, anger, and desire. That's it. What more is there to say?

The world we inhabit is the world we prepare for ourselves. The universe is held together by the collective karma of the beings who inhabit it. Therefore, the kind of world that we experience is the result of the seeds of all the actions (*karma*) of body, speech, and mind that we have created in the past. If we continually create violence through unskillful actions of body, speech, and mind, we cannot expect there to be peace. It is not enough to draft a proposal that says, "From now on, we are going to hold hands and be peaceful," because we have already created the causes for a very aggressive society.

Our society is based on greed and violence. Even our entertainment reflects this, so how can we hope to achieve peace simply by mouthing platitudes? Little children watch cartoons where the characters blow people up. Both boys and girls at two and three years of age imitate these cartoons, trying to blow each other up with whatever they find. Their idea of play is pretending to kill each other: "Bang, bang, bang!" We also take for granted the amount of meat we eat in the world. Animals are raised in intolerable conditions and then slaughtered. Millions of animals are killed everyday. We need to reflect on the results of the karma that comes from our greed.

As long as we have traces of these unwholesome actions in our minds, and these actions are encouraged by society, we cannot expect to enjoy universal world peace. We cannot enjoy peace if we are not creating the causes for peace. Even peace organizations are often plagued by aggression. In one interview, while advocating peace causes, John Lennon suddenly became very angry and aggressive. He was perpetuating war by juxtaposing "us" so neatly against "them," the enemy. That is what war is about: pitting "us" against "them." If peace organizations have this mentality, how will we achieve peace? This mentality is reflected in environmental programs for saving whales, for example. Concern escalates into anger, aggression, and hatred against whalers. Sometimes activist groups simply create more conflict in the world, instead of the peace, love, and good will they intend.

Buddhism is a creed based on nonviolence, with many teachings on love and compassion. We would hope that Buddhist countries could set an example for the world of peaceful, loving, religious communities. But when we look at Buddhist countries today, what do we find? When we look at current conflicts in Cambodia, Sri Lanka, and Burma, we must ask: Where is the Buddhism in all of this? In practically every Buddhist country today there is strife, either through civil war or surrender to the West's consumer ideology. I cannot think of one Buddhist country at the moment that we can hold up as an example to the world. The specter of civil war, with its brutality and savagery, among people who are supposedly good Buddhists, is quite terrifying. What happened to the Buddhist values their mothers taught them? How did they forget the Buddha's teachings and become like demons to their own people?

The profound way to generate world peace is through purifying our minds everyday of delusion, greed, and hatred. If we can do this, we can become exemplars of peace like Bhikkhu Mahaghosananda. But how many Mahaghosanandas do we see in the world today? Personally, I feel quite disappointed that the Buddhist countries have made such a poor showing. Of course, the people in Buddhist countries usually have nothing to do with the politics that create strife. Amidst the terrible sufferings of these countries, most people are innocent and many have been victims of terrible brutalities. But it was not just one politician who caused the strife: somebody had to carry out the orders. If everyone refused to cooperate, where would the politicians be? It is because people are willing to pick up weapons, shoot, and torture one another that strife continues.

To my mind, the Buddhist way is perfect and pure. If we can practice it with our heart, not just our head and our mouth, it is a transformative path. It is obviously not easy, because we see very few people completely transformed. Even in Buddhist countries, where people go to the temples and many take ordination, there are terrible problems of savagery and war.

The answer is to take the Buddhadharma to heart and completely purify our minds of these terrible stains. In Buddhist history, the way has been individuals transforming their hearts. For this to happen on a global scale, we need enlightened leaders, instead of leaders who are personifications of delusion, anger, and desire. Gandhi, for example, despite his shortcomings, was a selfless leader. Because he really believed in nonviolence, he was able to initiate a mass movement that remained nonviolent even under extreme provocation. So far there have been few Gandhis and more Pol Pots, yet we know the path of nonviolence is possible.

Buddhism aims at the happiness of self and others, and the two are closely interrelated. It is natural to desire happiness for ourselves and more difficult to desire happiness for others. Sometimes fear prevents us from bringing happiness to others – the fear that if we are open to others, we may get hurt. So we put up barriers and retreat behind them. Fear and anxiety prevent us from opening our hearts.

All possible love is inside our hearts, but it has been covered up. This love is like a very deep stream from an underground source that has been covered with soil, mud, and stones, and looks dry. We don't have to import water from outside. All we have to do is clear away the stones and earth and get to that source. As we clear away the stones and earth, little dribbles return. Gradually the soil gets moister and eventually, the water just gushes out, with sheer frenzy, unstoppable. Similarly, when we clear away the dross from our hearts, love gushes forth and there is no room for fear.

Recently I spoke with a Catholic nun who said, "In Christianity we are always told to love our neighbor and be compassionate, but we are not told how to do it." What she especially liked about Buddhism was that it does not just talk about love, it has many techniques for learning *how* to love. In the beginning these techniques may seem rather artificial and intellectual, but as we become accustomed to them, love slowly begins to trickle down from the head and percolate into the heart.

We have to check to see whether our meditation is producing results. When we sit on our meditation cushions, we become filled with so much love, but when we get up or somebody interrupts our practice, we may get angry and think, "Here I am meditating on love. Why are you making so much noise!" Still, if we meditate properly, we will notice a change. We will begin to remove the heavy stones, earth, and mud that have covered up the wellspring of our genuinely loving nature.

First we need to develop loving kindness (*maitrī*), the wish that all beings be happy. We begin by sitting with a calm mind and visualizing the person we love most. Traditionally, this is one's mother, but this very first lesson may be really difficult for Westerners. The Buddhist teachings say we must love all sentient beings like our kind mother, but many Westerners hate their mothers! We need to remember that our parents gave us life and we are here because of them. They might not have intended to have us, but here we are. When we were small, screaming, hungry, and demanding all their attention, they did not get tired of us or throw us out. They took care of us and loved us.

Ironically, none of us consciously remembers the time when we got the most love and attention – the time when everyone found us adorable. Later on, by the time we remember, they had changed their opinion. Still, our parents took care of us, fed us, and educated us. Except for really abusive parents, the kindness of the mother is beyond words. If we imagine our mother being tortured, in great pain or sorrow, we would want to release her. Therefore, unless we have complicated feelings, our mother or father is a good person to visualize in developing loving kindness. We generate the wish that this person be happy. Parents can also visualize loving kindness toward their child. Meditating like this, we develop a heart of loving kindness.

The Buddha compared loving kindness to a mother's love for her own child. Imagine the intensity of a mother's love for her child. We can visualize anyone toward whom we have strong positive feelings, but it may be difficult to visualize one's spouse or partner. It may be better to visualize someone a bit more neutral, because the feelings our partner arouses may be a bit complicated – we are trying to arouse loving kindness, not desire or attachment. Then we think, "May you be well and happy. May you be peaceful."

In another method, we first generate loving kindness toward ourselves. If we are full of self-contempt and self-loathing, we cannot give genuine love. His Holiness the Dalai Lama once remarked that whereas most Tibetans feel at ease with themselves, many Westerners have low self-esteem. Therefore, we sit and think, "May I be peaceful. May I be at ease. May I be happy." When we generate compassion toward all sentient beings, we must remember that we are also sentient beings deserving of love and compassion. So, we first generate genuine loving kindness toward ourselves, like a small child – forgiveness, understanding, and nurturing.

Naturally everybody has flaws. If we were perfect, we would all be Buddhas with shining auras. But we are still in *saṃsāra*, the realm of birth and death. Are we so proud that we imagine we must be perfect when nobody else is? If we can forgive others, why can't we forgive ourselves? In the West we tend to focus on our negative traits and inflate them until they totally overshadow the positive qualities. We end up feeling despondent and hating ourselves. Maybe this comes from our cultural background – the idea that we are born in sin, and the guilt that goes with that. In Buddhism, our essential Buddha nature, the potential for perfect enlightenment, is infinite wisdom, compassion, purity, and power. Our minds are like the sun obscured by clouds. We are all interconnected and united in having this Buddha nature. Like the sky, Buddha nature does not have divisions like "yours," "mine," "his," or "hers."

Meditation on loving kindness is like the sky – vast and inconceivable. We have faults, but we do not identify with them, cling to them, or get depressed about them. We need to recognize our positive qualities, too, and develop them further. A person may get upset easily, but also be very generous. Like a plant, if our good qualities are in the shade, they will wither and die for lack of acknowledgment. If we can strike a balance, our minds become light and joyful, instead of heavy and onerous.

As we meditate on loving kindness, we generate loving kindness toward ourselves, thinking, "May I be happy." We feel a sense of peace, well-being, warmth, and happiness in our hearts. Then we think of someone we love and wish happiness to that person, too, from the depths of our heart. We imagine light going out, transforming the person into happiness. Then we concentrate on a neutral person, someone toward whom we feel indifferent, and generate the wish for that person to be happy, too. "May she be happy! May she be peaceful!"

Then we think of someone we do not like, someone who is disagreeable and gives us problems. We try to generate exactly the same feelings of loving-kindness and compassion for that person. "May she be happy! May she be peaceful!" We watch how we feel as we do this. There may be some resistance at first, but we just notice it and let it go.

Gradually we extend these loving feelings out to include everyone in the country, everyone in the world – those who are sick, those we meet on the street, shop assistants, everyone – and generate a feeling of wanting them all to be happy. We can divide space into parts – north, south, east, west, above, and below – and wish all beings within it to be happy. We can think about people in certain circumstances, countries, or professions, and send them compassion. It helps to be specific. We think, "May they be happy! May they be peaceful!" Gradually our compassion becomes vast, until eventually it includes all beings and the heart opens up completely.

Sometimes people think that Dharma practice is something we only do while sitting on a meditation cushion. We may practice loving kindness meditation for some time, then waste the rest of the day with worldly thoughts. People sometimes feel they have no time for practice. I have even heard lamas say, "I am so busy, I have no time for practice." But consider the six perfections (*pāramitā*): generosity, ethical conduct, patience, diligence, meditation, and wisdom. Each one is needed for Buddhahood, but only one of them is meditation. Generosity means giving with an open heart and open hands. Ethical conduct means being careful not to harm anyone with one's body or speech. And the Buddha called patience the greatest perfection. Those who cause us the most trouble give us the greatest opportunity to develop this quality.

We sometimes think that family life, society, and work are obstacles to the practice, but actually they *are* the practice. When else are we going to practice? Sitting on the cushion is only one small part – every single encounter of our whole lives is an opportunity for Dharma practice. Life is like heavy dough, so we need some yeast. Understanding everyday situations as opportunities for practice is like yeast. When we add it, we get a light dough that makes delicious bread!

Every situation, every person we meet, is an opportunity for developing loving kindness, including our intimate family. Sometimes it is hardest to express loving kindness in the family circle. Notice the way partners speak with each other behind closed doors. Sometimes we say things we would not say to our worst enemy, and this is the person we say we love. When we sit and think, "May all sentient beings be happy. May all sentient beings be at their ease," it is very easy to imagine all the sentient beings out there on the horizon and feel full of love. But these sentient beings include, foremost, our family, partner, children, friends, co-workers, as well as people who annoy us, who are wonderful objects of practice. It is very easy to be loving to those who are kind to us and far more difficult to love those who are nasty. But the people who annoy us are the best objects for developing loving kindness and patience. The Tibetans say, "If one speaks sweet words and strokes us, while another curses and cuts us with a knife, we should feel equal love toward both."

Each person thinks she is the center of the universe. When we see a group photo, who is the first person we look for? No one wants others to be cruel or rude. Everyone alike wants others to be kind and polite. Every single person we encounter is the most precious being at that moment. Remembering that this person is just like us – vulnerable, just wanting to be happy, afraid of being hurt – we say, from our heart, "May you be well!" When we smile, it will be from our heart.

Many people have met His Holiness the Dalai Lama, or seen him on film. He has infinite qualities, but one special quality is being completely with the person who is right in front of him. He looks people straight in the eye with total love and acceptance, whether it is the pope, a president, a politician, journalist, politician, dignitary, or beggar. He is so genuine, he forces other people to be genuine, too.

The next quality to develop is compassion (*karuna*), the wish that all beings be free from suffering. Compassion literally means "to feel with," so it is a feeling of empathy with the sufferings of others and a wish to relieve their sufferings. In Mahāyāna Buddhism, wisdom and compassion together constitute the intrinsic nature of a Buddha.

Some people are afraid to open their hearts to the sufferings of others, fearing that they will become overwhelmed and unable to cope. In this case, it is good to reflect on beings who embody great compassion. We can think of someone like His Holiness the Dalai Lama, who is considered an embodiment of the Bodhisattva of Compassion, and genuinely exemplifies great compassion. He had to leave his country, and his people are so oppressed, and there are so many problems and sufferings everywhere he goes – Tibet, India, and Nepal, and the whole world situation. He has such a tender heart; when he sees these sufferings, he weeps. But along with his tender, open, infinitely loving compassionate heart, he has twinkling eyes and a big belly laugh, full of joy and optimism! Optimism and joy do not conflict with his vast compassion.

To become overwhelmed with the enormity of the sufferings in the world just makes us heavy, gloomy, and unable to help others or effect transformation. We must balance a genuine acknowledgment and concern for the sufferings of others with the ability to transform those sufferings.

In the Tibetan tradition, there is a meditation practice called *tong len*, "giving and taking." We visualize sending out light, ejecting all the darkness, gloom, and suffering from ourself, and breathing in all light, joy, and goodness. Then we visualize someone who is suffering from great sickness or sorrow. As we breath in, we imagine breathing in all the person's sadness, sickness, and grief in the form of a dark light. We absorb this into ourself and send the person a vast reservoir of goodness, joy, light, and peace.

The thought of wishing to exchange ourselves for others is exquisite. The object is not to get overwhelmed, but to open our hearts. If we feel overwhelmed, we reflect, "Why am I afraid of being hurt?" We sense a knot inside – the "me" that we cherish so strongly and always try to protect. We visualize the sufferings of others coming into ourselves, absorbing into this "I," and dissolving into emptiness. The dark, tight sense of "me" dissolves into spaciousness and light. We can also visualize our Buddha nature as a little bright and shiny crystal. Buddha mind is vast, brilliant, and indestructible. We visualize all sufferings absorbing into that. Like water hitting a very hot pan, the moment the sufferings reach our genuine Buddha nature, they transform into light.

Enlightenment is possible for everyone, female or male, for in the nature of the mind there is no male or female. The Buddha himself said that women were totally, indisputably capable of enlightenment. And throughout Buddhist history, there have been so many examples of enlightened women. In addition, one may be male in this lifetime and female in the next. Who knows? All males have been females, all females have been males. All sentient beings have the capacity to achieve perfect enlightenment.

Just like ourselves, everyone wants happiness and no one wants to suffer. When we realize that, we think, "May I help her be happy. May I help her be free from suffering." We tend to think of the spiritual path as something very high and unattainable, but kindness is really very simple. All we need to do is be kind in every word and deed.

EPILOGUE

Transforming Women's Position in Buddhism

Strategies

In the past two decades, perceptions of what is possible for Buddhist women have totally transformed. Feminist thinking is reaching Buddhist cultures, setting off small revolutions in its wake. Buddhist thinking is also reaching Western cultures, having a similar effect. Glass (and opaque) ceilings still exist for Buddhist women, but changes are in motion that bode well for the future. Changes are apparent not only in heightened awareness of women's potentialities, but also in women's achievements – in monasteries, hospitals, retreat centers, communications, creative arts, education, research, and publications. As if the tradition were awakening from a long sleep, women's accomplishments are winning the approval of governments, the public, and male power elites within Buddhist institutions.

Attention is being directed to Buddhist women's advancement in new and creative ways. Buddhist women themselves are mobilizing, realizing that as long as one is deprived, all are diminished. Institutionally, opposition to full ordination for women is gradually being dispelled. Many conservative monks are rethinking the issue and coming to the conclusion that, given women's talents and energy, the ordination of women is in the best interests of Buddhism and the world. As one Theravāda monk expressed it at the International Monastic Seminar in Toronto in October 1998, "We monks realize that full ordination for women will come about eventually. It is like a big wave that cannot be stopped. So it is best if we monks support the ordination, for if we do not, it will only make Buddhism look bad."

Ordination for women is also being recognized as a human rights issue. The world has become too small and too sophisticated to let gender barriers go unchallenged. If men have the right to full ordination, women should also have the right. Opponents to the full ordination of women will definitely go down in history as unenlightened and unjust.

The extent to which Buddhist thought can be extracted from Buddhist cultures is still an open question, but the future of Buddhist women clearly involves a coalition of women not only across cultures, but also across economic strata, lifestyles, and the artificial boundaries that separate scholarship, practice, and real life. An effective coalition must encompass the concerns of all Buddhist women – poor, rich, lay, ordained, neither-lay-nor-ordained, mothers, nuns, workers, artists, meditators, scholars – forging unity among diverse schools of Buddhist thought and practice.

An ecumenical grassroots initiative such as this requires patience and understanding. As became clear on an international scale at the Women's Conference in Beijing (1995), despite their biological resemblance, women's concerns are often worlds apart. While Western women struggle with issues of sexuality, environment, and sexual exploitation, Asian Buddhist women struggle for adequate food, shelter, and education. Psychologically, too, there may be enormous gaps. For instance, while Western Buddhists strive to enhance their self-esteem, Asian Buddhists strive to understand the illusory nature of the self. Western Buddhists tend to value lay practice, while Asian Buddhists value ordination. Due to their cultural backgrounds, practitioners East and West often understand Buddhism in very different ways.

Creating an alliance among women of vastly different attitudes and life experiences is a challenging task. It would be far easier to create a movement among people who think and act alike, but it would not be nearly as interesting. An initiative of women willing to step outside their own accustomed ways of doing things to appreciate the qualities and problems of others can accomplish many goals. Relinquishing petty allegiances, crossing cultural boundaries, pooling resources, and consolidating women's power are significant steps in the reenvisioning and restructuring of Buddhism.

Precisely because women presently have no power in Buddhist institutions, they have a chance to do things differently. New questions, arising out of distinctive cultural situations, are stimulating a reevaluation of many traditional Buddhist assumptions. Educated women in both East and West are questioning centuries of inequality: If Buddhist education and full ordination are valuable for men's achievement of enlightenment, are they not equally valuable for women?

Being a woman, which has for centuries been seen as a limitation in Buddhism, is being transformed into a strength and a new kind of freedom – to view things from new perspectives. As the lotus emerges pure and stainless from the mud, Buddhist women emerge from their perceived confines to new achievements and insights.

The most eye-opening element of Buddhism for women is its liberative psychology. Enlightened mind, being totally pure and perfected, is not limited by gender or anything else. Since liberating insight and purity of heart – the goals of Buddhist practice – have nothing to do with gender, why should access to teachings and practice be limited by gender? By teaching a liberative ideology, the Buddha initiated a momentous shift in human consciousness which invites free inquiry and calls into question the very notion of categories. If the teachings are psychologically liberative, they should be socially liberative as well. Women are free to question who constructs the categories, who controls them, and how to transform them. Women need only embrace the liberating opportunities that are intrinsically theirs.

Bibliography

Allione, Tsultrim. *Women of Wisdom.* London: Routledge & Kegan Paul, 1984.

Aoyama, Shundo. *Zen Seeds: Reflections of a Female Priest.* Tokyo: Kosei Publishing Co., 1990.

Arai, Paula. "Soto Zen Nuns in Modern Japan: Keeping and Creating Tradition." *Bulletin of the Nanzan Institute for Religion & Culture* 14 (Summer, 1990), 38–51.

—— *Women Living Zen: Japanese Soto Buddhist Nuns.* New York: Oxford University Press, 1999.

Atkinson, J. M., and S. Errington, eds. *Power and Difference: Gender in Island Southeast Asia.* Stanford: Stanford University Press, 1990.

Aziz, Barbara Nimri. "Ani Chodon: Portrait of a Buddhist Nun." *Loka 2, Journal of the Naropa Institute.* New York: Anchor/Doubleday, 1976, 43–46.

—— "Buddhist Nuns." *Natural History* 98:3 (1989), 41–48.

—— *Tibetan Frontier Families: Reflection of Three Generations from D'ing-ri.* New Delhi: Vikas Publishing House, 1978.

—— "Views From the Monastery Kitchen," *Kailash* 4:2 (1976), 155–67.

—— "Women in Tibetan Society and Tibetology." In Helga Uebach and Jampal Panglung, eds., *Tibetan Studies.* München: Kommission für Zentralasiatische Studien Bayerische Akademie der Wissenschaften, 1988, 25–34.

Barnes, Nancy Schuster. "The Bodhisattva Figure in the *Ugraparipṛcchā.*" In A. K. Warder, ed., *New Paths in Buddhist Research.* Durham, N.C.: Acorn Press.

—— "Buddhism." In Arvind Sharma, ed., *Women in World Religions.* Albany, N.Y.: State University of New York Press, 1987, 105–33.

—— "Buddhist Women and the Nuns' Order in Asia." In Christopher S. Queen and Sallie B. King, eds., *Engaged Buddhism: Buddhist Liberation Movements in Asia.* Albany, N.Y.: State University of New York Press, 1996.

—— "Changing the Female Body: Wise Women and the Bodhisattva Career in Some *Mahāratna-kūṭasūtras.*" *Journal of the International Association of Buddhist Studies* 4:1 (1981), 24–69.

—— "Striking a Balance: Women and Images of Women in Early Chinese Buddhism." In Yvonne Y. Haddad and Ellison B. Findly, eds., *Women, Religion, and Social Change.* Albany, N.Y.: State University of New York Press, 1985.

—— "Women in Buddhism." In Arvind Sharma, ed., *Today's Woman in World Religions.* Albany, N.Y.: State University of New York Press, 1994, 137–69.

Bartholomeusz, Tessa. "The Female Mendicant in Buddhist Sri Lanka." In José Ignacio Cabezón, ed., *Buddhism, Sexuality, and Gender.* Albany, N.Y.: State University of New York Press, 1992, 37–61.

—— *Women Under the Bō Tree: Buddhist Nuns in Sri Lanka.* Cambridge: Cambridge University Press, 1994.

Batchelor, Martine. *Walking on Lotus Flowers: Buddhist Women Living, Loving and Meditating*. London: Thorsons, 1996.

Beck, Charlotte Joko. *Everyday Zen: Love and Work*. San Francisco: Harper & Row, 1989.

Benard, Elisabeth. *Chinnamasta: The Aweful Buddhist and Hindu Tantric Goddess*. Delhi: Motilal Banarsidass, 1995.

Beyer, Stephan. *The Cult of Tara: Magic and Ritual in Tibet*. Berkeley: University of California Press, 1973.

Blackstone, Kathryn R. *Women in the Footsteps of the Buddha: Struggle for Liberation in the Therīgāthā*. Richmond, Surrey: Curzon Press, 1998.

Blakiston, Hilary. *But Little Dust*. Cambridge: Allborough Press, 1990.

Bloss, Lowell W. "The Female Renunciants of Sri Lanka: The *Dasasil mattawa*." *Journal of the International Association of Buddhist Studies* 10:1 (1987), 7–32.

—— "Attitudes toward Women and the Feminine in Early Buddhism." In José Ignacio Cabezón, ed., *Buddhism, Sexuality and Gender*. Albany, N.Y.: State University of New York Press, 1992.

—— "Theravada 'Nuns' of Sri Lanka: Themes of the Dasailmattawa Movement." Unpublished monograph, 1984.

Boucher, Sandy. *Opening the Lotus: A Woman's Guide to Buddhism*. New York: Ballantine Books, 1997.

—— *Turning the Wheel: American Women Creating the New Buddhism*. Boston: Beacon Press, 1993.

Buswell, Robert E. "Is Celibacy Anachronistic? Korean Debates over the Secularization of Buddhism during the Japanese Occupation Period." Unpublished monograph, 1990.

Byles, Marie B. *Journey into Burmese Silence*. London: George Allen & Unwin, 1962.

Cabezón, José Ignacio, ed. *Buddhism, Sexuality, and Gender*. Albany, N.Y.: State University of New York Press, 1992.

Campbell, June. *Traveller in Space: In Search of Female Identity in Tibetan Buddhism*. New York: George Braziller, 1996.

Chang, Pao. *Biographies of Buddhist Nuns*. Translated by Li Jung-hsi. Osaka: Tohokai, Inc., 1981.

Chodron, Thubten. *Blossoms of the Dharma: Living as a Buddhist Nun*, Berkeley: North Atlantic Books, 1999.

Chonam, Lama, and Sangye Khandro, trans. *The Lives and Liberation of Princess Mandarava: The Indian Consort of Padmasambhava*. Boston: Wisdom Publications, 1998.

Devendra, Kusuma. "The Dasasil Nun: A Study of Women's Buddhist Religious Movement in Sri Lanka." Ph.D. diss., Department of Pali and Buddhist Studies, Colombo, 1987.

Devine, Carol. *Determination: Tibetan Women and the Struggle for an Independent Tibet*. Toronto: Vauve Press, 1991.

Drolma, Delog Dawa. *Delog: Journey to Realms Beyond Death*. Junction City, Calif.: Padma Publishing, 1995.

Dowman, Keith. *Sky Dancer: The Secret Life and Songs of the Lady Yeshe Tsogyel*. London: Routledge & Kegan Paul, 1984.

Dresser, Marianne. *Buddhist Women on the Edge: Contemporary Perspectives from the Western Frontier*. Berkeley: North Atlantic Books, 1996.

Eberhardt, N., ed. *Gender, Power, and the Construction of the Moral Order: Studies from the Thai Periphery*. Madison, Wis.: Center for Southeast Asian Studies, University of Wisconsin, 1988.

Edou, Jerome. *Machig Labdron and the Foundations of Chod*. Ithaca: Snow Lion Publications, 1995.

Falk, Nancy. "The Case of the Vanishing Nuns: The Fruits of Ambivalence in Ancient Indian Buddhism." In Nancy Falk and Rita Gross, eds., *Unspoken Worlds: Women's Religious Lives in Non-Western Cultures*. San Francisco: Harper & Row, 1979, 207–24.

—— "An Image of Women in Old Buddhist Literature: The Daughters of Māra." In Judith Plaskow and June Arnold, eds., *Women and Religion.* Missoula: Scholars Press, 1974, 105–12.

Feldman, Christina. *The Quest of the Warrior Woman: Women as Mystics, Healers and Guides.* London & San Francisco: Aquarian, 1994.

Findly, Ellison, ed. *Women Changing Contemporary Buddhism.* Boston: Wisdom Books, 1999.

Friedman, Lenore. *Meetings with Remarkable Women: Buddhist Teachers in America.* Boston: Shambhala, 1987.

—— and Susan Moon. *Being Bodies: Buddhist Women on the Paradox of Embodiment.* Boston: Shambhala, 1997.

Fürer-Haimendorf, Christopher von. "A Nunnery in Nepal." *Kailash* 4:2 (1976), 121–54.

Goonatilake, Hema. "Buddhist Nuns' Protests, Struggle, and the Reinterpretation of Orthodoxy in Sri Lanka." In Judy Brink and Joan Mencher, eds., *Mixed Blessings: Gender and Religious Fundamentalism Cross Culturally.* New York: Routledge, 1997.

Grimshaw, Anna. "Celibacy, Religion and Economic Activity in a Monastic Community of Ladakh." In Detlef Kantowshy and Reinhard Sander, eds., *Recent Research on Ladakh: History, Culture, Sociology, Ecology.* München: Weltforum Verlag, 1983, 121–35.

—— *Servants of the Buddha: Winter in a Himalayan Convent.* Cleveland: Pilgrim Press, 1994.

Groner, Paul. "Vicissitudes in the Ordination of Japanese 'Nuns' During the Late Nara and Early Heian Periods." Unpublished monograph, 1990.

Gross, Rita M. *Buddhism After Patriarchy: A Feminist History, Analysis, and Reconstruction of Buddhism.* Albany, N.Y.: State University of New York Press, 1993.

—— "Buddhism and Feminism: Toward Their Mutual Transformation." *The Eastern Buddhist* 19:2, Autumn 1986, 62–74.

—— "Buddhist from the Perspective of Women's Bodies." *Buddhist-Christian Studies*, Vol. 1 (1981), 72–82.

—— *Soaring and Settling: Buddhist Perspectives on Contemporary Social and Religious Issues*, New York: Continuum, 1998.

—— "Yeshe Tsogyel: Enlightened Consort, Great Teacher, Female Role Model." *Tibet Journal* 12:4, 1–18.

Gunawardena, R. A. L. H. "Subtile Silks of Ferreous Firmness: Buddhist Nuns in Ancient and Early Medieval Sri Lanka and Their Role in the Propagation of Buddhism." *The Sri Lankan Journal of the Humanities* 14, No. 1 and 2, 1988, 1–59.

Gutschow, Kim. "An Economy of Merit: Women and Buddhist Monasticism in Zangskar, Northwest India." Ph.D. diss., Department of Anthropology, Harvard University, 1999.

—— "Unfocussed Merit Making In Zangskar: A Socio-Economic Account of Karsha Nunnery." *Tibet Journal* 22:2, 1998, 30–58.

—— "A Novice Ordination in Tibet: The Rhetoric and Reality of Female Monasticism in Zangskar, Northwest India." In *Women Changing Contemporary Buddhism*, Ellison Findly, ed. Boston: Wisdom Books, 1999.

Hantrakul, S. "Prostitution in Thailand." In G. Chandler, N. Sullivan, and J. Branson, eds., *Development and Displacement: Women in Southeast Asia.* Centre of Southeast Asian Studies, Monash University, Australia, 1988.

Havnevik, Hanna. *Tibetan Buddhist Nuns.* Oslo: Norwegian University Press, 1990.

—— "On Pilgimage for 40 Years in the Himalayas: The Female Lama Jetsun Lochen Rinpoche's (1865–1951) Quest for Sacred Sites." In Alex McKay, ed., *Pilgrimage in Tibet.* London: Curzon Press, 1998, 85–107.

Heikkila-Horn, Marja-Leena. *Buddhism with Open Eyes: Belief and Practice of Santi Asoke.* Bangkok: Fah Apai Co., 1997.

Hirakawa, Akira. "History of Nuns in Japan," *Buddhist Christian Studies*, Vol. 12, 1992, 143–58.

—— *Monastic Discipline for the Buddhist Nuns: An English Translation of the Chinese Text of the Mahāsāṃghika-Bhikṣuṇī-Vinaya.* Patna: K. P. Jayaswal Research Institute, 1982.

Horner, I. B. *The Book of Discipline*, Vol. I-VI. London: Routledge & Kegan Paul, 1982.
—— *Women Under Primitive Buddhism: Laywomen and Almswomen*. Delhi: Motilal Banarsidass, 1975.
Huang, Chien-yu Julia, and Robert P. Wellnew. "Merit and Mothering: Women and Social Welfare in Taiwanese Buddhist," *Journal of Asian Studies* 57:2 (May 1998), 379–96.
Ingram, Paul O. "Reflections on Buddhist-Christian Dialogue and the Liberation of Women," *Buddhist Christian Studies*, Vol. 17, 1997, 49–60.
Kabilsingh, Chatsumarn. *The Bhikkhunī Pātimokkha of the Six Schools*. Bangkok: Thammasat University Press, 1991.
—— *A Comparative Study of Bhikkhunī Pātimokkha*. Varanasi: Chaukhambha Orientalia, 1984.
—— "The Future of the Bhikkhunī Saṅgha in Thailand." In Diana Eck and Devaki Jain, eds., *Speaking of Faith: Global Perspectives on Women, Religion, and Social Change*. Philadelphia: New Society Publishers, 1987.
—— *Thai Women in Buddhism*. Berkeley: Parallax Press, 1991.
Kajiyama, Yuichi. "Women in Buddhism." *Eastern Buddhist* (New Series) 15:2 (1982), 53–70.
Kalff, Martin M. "Ḍākinīs in the Cakrasaṃvara Tradition." In Per Kvaerne and Martin Brauen, eds., *Tibetan Studies*. Zürich: Völkerkundemuseum der Universität, 1978, 149–62.
Kamens, E., trans. *The Buddhist Poetry of the Great Kamo Priestess: Daisaiin Senshi and Hosshin Wakashū*. Ann Arbor: University of Michigan Center for Japanese Studies, 1990.
Karim, W. J. *"Male" and "Female" in Developing Southeast Asia*. Washington, D.C. and Oxford: Berg Publishers, 1995.
Kawanami, Hiroko. "The Religious Standing of Burmese Buddhist Nuns (thila-shin): The Ten Precepts and Religious Respect Words." *Journal of the International Association of Buddhist Studies*, 13:1 (1990), 19.
Keyes, Charles F. "Mother or Mistress but Never a Monk: Buddhist Notions of Female Gender in Rural Thailand." *American Ethnologist*, 11:2, May 1984, 223–41.
Khiang, Mi Mi. *The World of Burmese Women*. London: Zed Books, 1984.
Khin, T. *Providence and Prostitution: Image and Reality for Women in Buddhist Thailand*. Change International Reports (Women and Society), 1980.
King, Ursula, ed. *Religion and Gender*. Oxford: Blackwell, 1995.
Kikuchi, Shigeo. *Memoirs of a Buddhist Woman Missionary in Hawaii*. Honolulu: Buddhist Study Center Press, 1991.
King, Sallie B. "Egalitarian Philosophies in Sexist Institutions: The Life of Satomi-san, Shinto Miko and Zen Buddhist Nun." *Journal of Feminist Studies in Religion*, 4:1, Spring 1988.
—— *Passionate Journey: The Spiritual Autobiography of Satomi Myodo*. Boston: Shambhala, 1978.
Kirsch, A. Thomas. "Buddhism, Sex Roles, and the Thai Economy." In Penny Van Esterik, ed., *Women of Southeast Asia*. DeKalb, Ill.: Northern Illinois University, Center for Southeast Asian Studies, 1982, 13–32.
—— "Text and Context: Buddhist Sex Roles: Culture of Gender Revisited." *American Ethnologist* 12:2, 1985, 302–20.
Klein, Anne C. "The Birthless Birthgivers; Reflections on the Liturgy of Yeshe Tsogyel, the Great Bliss Queen." *Tibet Journal* 12:4 (1987) 19–37.
—— "Finding a Self: Buddhist and Feminist Perspectives." In Clarissa W. Atkinson, et al., eds., *Sharing New Vision: Gender and Values in American Culture*. Ann Arbor: UMI Research Press, 1987, 191–218.
—— *Meeting the Great Bliss Queen: Buddhists, Feminists, and the Art of the Self*. Boston: Beacon Press, 1994.
—— "Presence with a Difference: Buddhists and Feminists on Subjectivity." *Hypatia*, 9:4, Fall 1994.
—— "Nondualism and the Great Bliss Queen: A Study in Tibetan Buddhist Ontology and Symbolism." *Journal of Feminist Studies in Religion* 1:1 (1985) 73–98.

—— "Primordial Purity and Everyday Life: Exalted Female Symbols and the Women of Tibet." In Clarissa W. Atkinson et al., *Immaculate and Powerful: The Female in Sacred Image and Social Reality*. Boston: Beacon Press, 1985, 111–38.

Komatsu, Chikō. *The Way to Peace: The Life and Teachings of the Buddha*. Kyoto: Hōzōkan Publishing Company, 1989.

Ku Cheng-Mei. "The Mahāyānic View of Women: A Doctrinal Study. Ph.D. diss., University of Wisconsin-Madison, 1983.

Kunsang, Erik Pema. *Dakini Teachings: Padmasambhava's Oral Instruction to Lady Tsogyal*. Boston: Shambhala, 1990.

Law, Bimala Churn. *Women in Buddhist Literature*. Varanasi: Indological Book House, 1981.

Levering, Miriam. "Contemporary Discussion of the Eight Gurudharmas, with Some Observations Concerning their Observance and Effects Among Bhiksunis in Taiwan." Unpublished monograph, 1990.

—— "Lin-chi Rinzai Ch'an and Gender," in Jose Ignacio Cabezon, ed. *Buddhism, Sexuality, and Gender*. Albany, N.Y.: State University of New York Press, 1992.

—— "The Dragon Girl and the Abbess of Mo-Shan: Gender and Status in Ch'an Buddhist Tradition." *Journal of the International Association of Buddhist Studies*, 5:1, 19–35.

Li, Jung-hsi, trans. *Biographies of Buddhist Nuns*. Osaka: Tohokan, Inc., 1981.

Mackenzie, Vicki. *Cave in the Snow: A Western Woman's Quest for Enlightenment*. London and New York: Bloomsbury Publishers, 1998.

March, Kathryn. "The Intermediacy of Women: Female Gender Symbolism and the Social Position of Women among Tamangs and Sherpas of Highland Nepal." Doctoral diss., Department of Anthropology, Cornell University, 1979.

Miller, Beatrice D. "Views of Women's Roles in Buddhist Tibet." In A. K. Narain, ed., *Studies in History of Buddhism*. New Delhi: B. R. Publishing Co., 1980, 155–66.

Mills, M. B. "Attack of the Widow Ghosts: Gender, Death, and Modernity in Northeast Thailand." In A. Ong and M. Peletz, eds., *Gender and Body Politics in Southeast Asia*. Berkeley: University of Chicago Press, 1995.

Minamoto, Junko. "Buddhism and the Historical Construction of Sexuality in Japan," *U.S.-Japan Women's Journal*, Vol. 5, 1993.

Murcott, Susan. *The First Buddhist Women: Translations and Commentaries on the Therigatha*. Berkeley: Parallax Press, 1991.

Ngaosyvathn, M. "Buddhism, Merit Making and Gender: The Competition for Salvation in Laos." In W. J. Karim, ed., *"Male" and "Female" in Developing Southeast Asia*. Washington, D.C.: Berg Publishers, 1995.

Norman, K. R., trans. *The Elders' Verses II: Therīgāthā*. London: Luzac and Co. Ltd., 1966.

O'Halloran, Maura. *Pure Heart, Enlightened Mind: The Zen Journal and Letters of Maura "Soshin" O'Halloran*. Boston: Charles E. Tuttle, 1994.

Ong, A., and M. Peletz, eds. "Bewitching Women, Pious Men." In A. Ong and M. Peletz, eds., *Gender and Body Politics in Southeast Asia*. Berkeley: University of Chicago Press, 1995.

Ortner, Sherry B. "The Founding of the First Sherpa Nunnery and the Problem of 'Women' as an Analytic Category." In Vivian Patraka and Louise Tilly, eds., *Feminist Re-Visions: What Has Been and What Might Be*. Ann Arbor, Mich.: University of Michigan Press, 1983.

—— "Is Female to Male as Nature Is to Culture?" In Michelle Z. Rosaldo and Louise Lamphere, eds., *Women, Culture, and Society*. Stanford: Stanford University Press, 1978, 263–85.

—— and H. Whitehead, eds. *Sexual Meanings: The Cultural Construction of Gender and Sexuality*. Cambridge and New York: Cambridge University Press, 1981.

Palmer, Martin, and Jay Ramsay with Man-Ho Kwok. *Kuan Yin: Myths and Prophecies of the Chinese Goddess of Compassion*. London & San Francisco: Thorsons/HarperCollins Publishers, 1995.

Paul, Diana. "Buddhist Attitudes Toward Women's Bodies." *Buddhist-Christian Studies* 1 (1981), 63–71.

—— *The Buddhist Feminine Ideal: Queen Śrīmālā and the Tathāgatagarbha.* Missoula, MT: Scholars Press, 1980.

—— "Empress Wu and the Historians: A Tyrant annd Saint of Classical China." In Nancy Falk and Rita Gross, eds., *Unspoken Worlds: Women's Religious Lives in Non-Western Cultures.* San Francisco: Harper & Row, 1979, 191–206.

—— *Women in Buddhism: Images of the Feminine in Mahāyāna Tradition.* Berkeley: Asian Humanities Press, 1979. Reprinted Berkeley: University of California Press, 1985.

Phongpaichit, P. "Rural Women in Thailand: From Peasant Girls to Bangkok Maseuses." In Sulak Sivaraksa, ed., *A Buddhist Vision For Renewing Society.* Bangkok: Thai Inter-Religious Commission For Development, 1980.

Phuong, Cao Ngog. "Days and Months." In Fred Eppsteiner, ed., *The Path of Compassion: Writings on Socially Engaged Buddhism.* Berkeley: Parallax, 1988, 155–69.

Ray, Reginald. "Accomplished Women in Tantric Buddhism of Medieval India and Tibet." In Nancy Falk and Rita Gross, eds., *Unspoken Worlds: Women's Religious Lives in Non-Western Cultures.* San Francisco: Harper & Row, 1979, 227–42.

Reis, Ria. "Reproduction or Retreat: The Position of Buddhist Women in Ladakh." In Detlef Kantowshy and Reinhard Sander, eds., *Recent Research on Ladakh: History, Culture, Sociology, Ecology.* München: Weltforum Verlag, 1983, 217–29.

Rhys-Davids, Caroline, trans. *Psalms of the Sisters.* London: Oxford University Press Warehouse, 1909. Reprinted as *Poems of Early Buddhist Nuns (Therīgāthā)*, C.A.F. Rhys-Davids and K. R. Norman, eds. Oxford: Pali Text Society, 1989.

Sakya, Jamyang, and Julie Emery. *Princess in the Land of Snows: The Life of Jamyang Sakya in Tibet.* Boston: Shambhala, 1988.

Savvas, Carol D. "A Study of the Profound Path of gCod: The Mahāyāna Buddhist Meditation Tradition of Tibet's Great Woman Saint Machig Labdron." Ph.D. diss., University of Wisconsin, 1990.

Shaw, Miranda. *Passionate Enlightenment: Women in Tantric Buddhism.* Princeton: Princeton University Press, 1994.

Shin, Nan. *Diary of a Zen Nun: Every Day Living.* New York: E. P. Dutton, 1988.

Sidor, Ellen S. *A Gathering of Spirit: Women Treaching in American Buddhism.* Cumberland, R.I.: Primary Point Press, 1987.

Sīlmāthā, Pānadure Vijirā. *The Enlightened Nuns of the Buddha Era.* Colombo: National Book Development Council of Sri Lanka, 1994.

Sunim, Samu. "Eunyeong Sunim and the Founding of Pomun-Jong, the First Independent Bhikshuni Order." *Women & Buddhism.* Toronto: Zen Lotus Society, 1986.

Tanabe, S. "Spirits, Power and the Discourse of Female Gender: The Phi Meng Cult of Northern Thailand." In Manas Chitkasem and Andrew Turton, eds., *Thai Constructions of Knowledge.* London: School of Oriental and African Studies, 1991.

Talim, T. V. "Buddhist Nuns and Disciplinary Rules." *Journal of the University of Bombay,* 34:2 (1965), 98–137.

Tantiwiramanond, D., and S. R. Pandey. *By Women, for Women: A Study of Women's Organizations in Thailand.* Singapore: Institute of Southeast Asian Studies, 1991.

Taring, Rinchen Dolma. *Daughter of Tibet.* New Delhi: Allied Publishers, 1970.

Thorbek, S. *Voices from the City: Women of Bangkok.* London: Zed Books, Ltd., 1987.

Tollifson, Joan. *Bare Bones Meditation: Waking Up from the Story of My Life.* New York: Bell Tower, 1996.

Tsai, Kathryn A. "Biographies of Buddhist Nuns." *Cahiers d'Extreme-Asie* (Revue de l'Ecole Francaise d'Extreme-Orient), 1985.

—— "The Chinese Buddhist Monastic Order for Women: The First Two Centuries." *Historical Reflections/Réflexions Historiques* 8:3 (Fall 1981), 1–20.

—— *Lives of the Nuns: Biographies of Chinese Buddhist Nuns from the Fourth to Sixth Centuries*. Honolulu: University of Hawaii Press, 1994.

Tsomo, Karma Lekshe, ed. *Buddhism Through American Women's Eyes*. Ithaca, N.Y.: Snow Lion Publications, 1995.

—— *Buddhist Women Across Cultures: Realizations*. Albany, N.Y.: State University of New York Press, 1999.

—— *Sakyadhita: Daughters of the Buddha*. Ithaca, N.Y.: Snow Lion Publications, 1988.

—— *Sisters in Solitude: Two Traditions of Buddhist Monastic Ethics for Women, A Comparative Analysis of the Dharmagupta and Mūlasarvāstivāda Bhikṣuṇī Prātimokṣa Sūtras*. Albany, N.Y.: State University of New York Press, 1996.

—— "Tibetan Nuns and Nunneries." In Janice D. Willis, ed., *Feminine Ground: Essays on Women and Tibet*. Ithaca, N.Y.: Snow Lion Publications, 1989, 118–34.

Tulku, Tarthang. *Mother of Knowledge: The Enlightenment of Ye-shes mTsho-rgyal*. Edited by Jane Wilhelms. Berkeley: Dharma Publishing, 1983.

Uchino, Kumiko. "The Status Elevation Process of Soto Sect Nuns in Modern Japan." In Diana Eck and Devaki Jain, eds., *Speaking of Faith: Global Perspectives on Women, Religion and Social Change*. New Society Publishers, Philadelphia, 1987, 159–73.

Van Ede, Yolanda. *House of Birds: A Historical Ethnography of a Tibetan Buddhist Nunnery in Nepal*. Ph.D. diss., University of Amsterdam, 1999.

Van Esterik, John. "Women Meditation Teachers in Thailand." In Van Esterik, Penny, ed., *Women of Southeast Asia*. DeKalb, Il.: Northern Illinois University, Center for Southeast Asian Studies, 1982, 33–41.

Van Esterik, Penny. "Laywomen in Theravāda Buddhism." In Penny Van Esterik, ed., *Women of Southeast Asia*. DeKalb, Il.: Northern Illinois University, Center for Southeast Asian Studies, 1982, 55–78.

—— "Rewriting Gender and Development Anthropology in Southeast Asia." In W. J. Karim, ed., *"Male" and "Female" in Developing Southeast Asia*. Oxford: Berg Publishers, 1995.

Watkins, Joanne C. *Spirited Women: Gender, Religion, and Cultural Identity in the Nepal Himalaya*. New York: Columbia University Press, 1996.

Wawrytko, Sandra A. "Sexism in the Early Sangha: Its Social Basis and Philosophical Dissolution." In Charles Wei-hsun Fu and Sandra A. Wawrytko, eds., *Buddhist Behavioral Codes and the Modern World*. Westport, Conn.: Greenwood Press, 1994, 277–96.

Wayman, Alex and Hideko. *The Lion's Roar of Queen Srīmālā: A Buddhist Scripture on the Tathāgatagarbha Theory*. New York: Colombia University Press, 1974.

Willis, Janice D. *Feminine Ground: Essays on Women and Tibet*. Ithaca: Snow Lion Publications, 1989.

—— "Nuns and Benefactresses: The Role of Women in the Development of Buddhism." In Yvonne Haddad and Ellison Findly, eds., *Women, Religion and Social Change*. Albany, N.Y.: State University of New York Press, 1985, 59–85.

Willson, Martin. *In Praise of Tara: Songs to the Saviouress*. London: Wisdom Publications, 1986.

Wilson, Liz. *Charming Cadavers: Horrific Figurations of the Feminine in Indian Buddhist Hagiographic Literature*. Chicago: University Press, 1996.

Young, Serinity, ed. *An Anthology of Sacred Texts By and About Women*. New York: Crossroad Publishing Co., 1993.

Index

Abhidharma 51, 271
Aburkhil 52–53
ācariya see *ācārya*
ācārya (Pāli: *ācariya*)
  bhikṣu 172–74
  bhikṣuṇī 174
  dharma-ācārya 172–74
  instructing 172–74
  Ong 89
  Theravāda 172
agnigṛiha 86
Agrasara
  Girl's College 47, 51
  Orphanage 47
ahimsa 308
Aichi Senmon Nisōdō 125
Aidaotang Nunnery 131–32
aina 243
Aitken, Roshi Robert 313
ajari xxiii, 249, 253–54, 256, 261
alcohol 76, 102
ali'i 246
All Ceylon Buddhist Congress 266
alms 81
Ambedkar, B. R. 177
anāgāmī (Pāli: *anāgāmin*) 10
anagārikā 16, 22, 24
Anan Kōshiki xxi, 123–29
Ānanda xxi, 7, 9, 123–29
Anantan ritual 127–28
ānāpānasati 26, 47
anatta 267
ancestors
  in Bangladesh 52
  in Japan 128
  in Korea 143
Angkor Thom 84, 86
Angmo 213
ani xxvi, 201–11
Anti-Asiatic League 239
Anulā 9
Anuttarayoga Tantra 133, 141
Aoyama, Shundo 127–28
Apuma 49
arahant see *arhat*
Arakan 44
ārāma 44, 87
arhat (Pāli: *arahant*) 10, 28, 124
arts, the xxv, 312–18, 326
ārya 45
asceticism 32, 61–62, 76, 152
Asgiriya 37, 41
Aśoka, Emperor 9, 36, 61, 85
Association of Nuns and Laywomen of Cambodia (ANLWC) 91, 93–95
asura 256
authority xxii, 252
  claims 159
  ecclesiastic 189, 192
  feminine 295
  positions of 160
  structures xxiv
Avalokiteśvara 84, 135, 146, 259
Avīci 257

BBC World Service 265, 270
Babuillarma 52
Bandarban 49, 51
Bangladesh xx, 42–57
  Buddhist Women's Association 42–43, 52
  cultural identity 42, 54–55
  education 43, 46–48, 51, 54, 57
  meditation 49–50

monks 43–44, 47–56
nuns 42, 47–51, 53, 55–56
tribal peoples 42–43
bare chuyegu 19
Barua 42–44, 45, 47, 51, 56
Ananya 47–48
Mira 48–49
Priti Kana 52
beggars 40, 74, 92–93, 266
Bekung Gonpa 201–11
Bengal 42, 44
bhajans 19
bhante 14, 81
Bhante, Uchala 50–51
Bharateswari Homes 46–47
bhāvanā 272
bhikkhu see *bhikṣu*
bhikkhunī see *bhikṣuṇī*
bhikṣu (Pāli: *bhikkhu*)
in Bangladesh 47–56
in Nepal 14, 20, 23
ordination by 6, 192
ordination of 170–71, 181
in Nepal 18
in Thailand 73–75
in Thailand 63
in Tibet 133, 136, 187–89
bhikṣuṇī (Pāli: *bhikkhunī*) xxvi, 5, 92
lineage 13, 168, 192
in Bangladesh 51
in China 183, 186–87, 194
Dharmagupta 13, 131, 136, 190–91
in Korea 194
Mūlasarvāstivāda 13, 136, 190–91, 196
to Sri Lanka 183
in Taiwan 186–87
Theravāda 13, 16, 172, 179, 191
in Tibet 179, 191
in Vietnam 194
order
in Bangladesh 48, 53
in China 168–98
founding of xix, 5–7, 10
in Sri Lanka xx, 10, 92
in Taiwan 168–98
ordination 5–12
by *bhikṣus* 6–7, 196
in Bodhgaya xxii, 168–98
in China 186–87
controversy xix, 181–83
in Hong Kong 179
in India 5–9
in Los Angeles 13, 33, 184
Mahāprajāpatī's 6–8, 11
in Nepal xx, 13–16, 22
ritual 35
in Sārnāth 5, 33, 39, 41, 173, 179, 196, 266
in Sri Lanka 9, 16, 30–40
in Taiwan 190
in Thailand 70
in Theravāda 94
in Vietnam 107
Prātimokṣa Sūtra 170, 191
Vinaya 190
Bhīṣma 85
Bhutan xxiii, 229–30
Blavatsy, Helena Petrovna 236–38, 245, 248
Blumenback, Johan Friedrich 278
Bodhgaya 18, 49, 206
bhikṣuṇī ordination xxii, 14, 43, 168–98
bodhi tree 244
bodhicitta 119, 217, 325
Bodhidharma 156–60
Bodhiraksa 72, 75, 78, 80
bodhisattva 146, 208, 251
Avalokiteśvara (Kuan Yin) 84, 244, 248
ideal 28, 85, 107, 171
Jizō (Kṣitigarbha) xxiii, 124, 249–52, 255–58, 261
precepts 108, 114, 215
Böll, Heinrich xxv, 91–95
bonbai 125
Bonk, Keiko 317
bowing 257
in Bangladesh 53
to *bhikṣus* 6–8, 71
to laywomen 8
at Santi Asoke 81, 83
brahmacāra (Pāli: *brahmacariya*) 5
brahmin 17, 85, 257, 268
Bruining, Mi Ok 313
Buddha 143–46, 149–50, 244, 251, 322
Maitreya 145, 216
Śākyamuni 6, 13, 124, 127, 188, 257, 275
bhikṣuṇī ordination 5–12, 179–80
lineage 155–66, 190
ordination of Mahāprajāpatī 5–12

teachings 110, 124, 311
transmission 155–66, 300
on women's potential xvii, 303
statue 48, 88, 130, 132, 296
Yakushi 258
Buddha nature 325
Buddhadharma 138, 320
Buddhaghosa 9–10, 88, 271
Buddhahood 193
Buddhist Churches of America (BCA) 280–81, 284
Buddhist Peace Fellowship 291
Burma 5, 16, 84, 94, 186, 190, 320
bhikṣuṇīs 180
Candramaṇi 18, 22–23
Dharmācārya certificate 24
education 25–26, 51
Gunavati 24
meditation in 14, 49–50
monks 22
nuns 23–24, 177
ordination 50

Calcutta 18
Dhammarajika Vihar 242
Cambodia 5, 190, 195, 273–74, 320
bhikṣuṇīs 172, 180, 194
children 103, 305
education 86, 97
families 99, 102
Institute of Human Rights xxv, 303–11
Khmer Rouge xxv, 96, 98–100, 102, 302, 304, 311
monks 92, 98, 101–2, 302, 311
Mahaghosananda, Bhikkhu 102, 320
nuns (*don chee*) xxi, xxvi, 91–95
Pot Pol xxi, 92, 311
Śākyadhitā conference xviii, xxv, 91, 211, 265
women xx-xxi, 84–90, 96–103
Dong, Queen Ang 88–89
Eng, Queen 88
Hay, Somaly 97–99, 103
Keo-Keng-Ya, Queen 86, 90
Kuoch, Theanvy 99–103
Campbell, June 289–90
Canavarro, Marie de Souza 241
Candramaṇi 18, 22–23
caste (*jāti*) 35–36, 62, 303, 309
in Bangladesh
in Nepal 17, 19, 21, 29
Catholicism 142, 271, 281, 290, 321
celibacy 5, 20, 31, 43, 62, 76–77, 286
Central Institute of Higher Buddhist Studies 229–31
Chakma 43, 45, 50
Champa 84–86
Chan/Zen 131, 155–67
chanting
in China 130, 137
in Japan 126–28, 256–57
in Korea 150
in Thailand 68
in Tibetan 130
Chih-an 162–63
childbirth 21, 299
in Thailand 63
children 296–98
in Bangadesh 57
in Nepal 24
in Thailand 63–64
in Vietnam 109, 112–13
China xxi-xxii, 13–14, 104, 241
bhikṣuṇī lineage 182–98
Buddhist texts 114, 120, 261
Chan/Zen 131, 154–67
Confucianism 104–5, 164
laborers 237, 245
monasteries
Aidaotang 131–32
Jincisi 131
Tiexiangsi xxi-xxii, 130–41
Yonghegong 130, 133
ordination 170
People's Republic 168–69
Republic of (Taiwan) 186
Taoism 104
in Tibet 205
Tiexiangsi xxi-xxii, 130–41
in Vietnam 104
Chinese Buddhist Association (R.O.C) 190
Chittagong 43, 45, 51–52
Cho-dang-chip 160
Chöden, Dawa 201–3
Chodron, Bhikṣuṇī 174
Chogye order 174
Ch'ông, Shim 142–53
Chosôn Dynasty 142
Christianity xxiii, 279, 282, 304, 314
in Bangladesh 57
Catholicism 142, 271, 281, 321
in Hawai'i 236–37, 240–41, 244–48, 247

in Korea 142–43
monastic orders 14, 286
in Vietnam 104
chungshindae 314–15
Claremont, Śākyadhitā conference xviii, xxv
Coḷa invasions 16, 168
Communism 118, 207, 304
compassion xviii, 86, 103, 120, 216, 302, 322–25
in action 102, 106, 111–12, 275, 313
Confucianism
in China 104–5, 164
in Korea 142–43
consort practice 288–90
consumerism 265, 275, 298
in Bangladesh 44
Cu Da Temple 105
Cullavagga 5–10
Cultural Revolution 132, 186
Cutts, Jiko Linda 299

Daishi, Dengyō (Saichō) 252–53, 258–61
ḍākinī 290
Dalai Lama 13, 130, 169, 187, 213, 218, 266, 322, 324
Dambulla 33, 37, 39, 41, 173
dāna (generosity) 16, 216
in Bangladesh 47, 51–53, 56–57
in Cambodia 85, 89, 92
Foster, Mary 241–44, 247
in Nepal 20, 27
in Sri Lanka 30, 32, 34–35, 37
in Thailand 65, 69, 73–75
in Vietnam 108–16
in Zangskar 220–21
dance 97, 312–15
dasasilmātā ("ten-precept mother") xx, xxvi, 30–41, 92, 94, 192
dayaka 242
death 20, 143, 145–46, 150, 206, 223, 256
defilements (*kleśa*) 28, 77, 116, 267, 271–73, 275
democracy 302–11
Deskyid 213
deva 256
Dhammarajika Vihar
Bangladesh 43, 46, 51, 57
Calcutta 242
Dhammavati, Bhikkhunī xx, 13, 22–28
Dhammavihari, Professor 272
dhammayietra 93, 274
Dhammayietra Centre for Peace and Non-violence 274
Dharamsala 206, 211
dharma 258
Dharma 11, 99, 138, 320
decline of 9–11
studies 68
teaching 75
dharma-ācārya 24, 29, 172–74
Dharmacarī 21
dharmadhātu 141
Dharmagupta 13, 131, 136, 190–91
Dharmakirti Vihar 24–28
Dharmapāla, Anagārika xxiii, 18, 235–36, 239, 241–42, 244, 247
Dharmapāla, Raja 33–34, 38–39
Dharmasiri, Gunapala 273
Dharmavijaya Vihāra 244
dhyāna 136–37
Dingjing, Bhikṣuṇī 131
discipline
lax 20
mānatta 6
monastic 5–12, 13, 15, 50
rules (*śikṣā*) 8–9, 12
breaking 73
discrimination
ethnic 54–55
gender 24
racial xxiv, xxv, 277–84
disrobing 289–90
in Bangladesh 50
in Cultural Revolution 132
in Nepal 19–20, 205–6
at Santi Asoke 72–73, 82
divorce 55, 205
Dōgen 158–66, 300
Dōkai, Fuyō 162
don chee xxi, xxvi, 91–95
movement xxi
Dong, Queen Ang 88–89
Dong Do Buddhist order 105
Drepung Monastery 133
Dronma, Karma Chopel 195
dual ordination 71, 131, 139, 181, 192
Duangchan, Yupin 65
Duc, Thich Quang 316–17
Duc Vien Temple 111–19
dukhang 204–5
dukkaṭa 8

dukkha 21, 23, 28, 103, 108–9
Dung, Thich Tri 118
Duoc Su Temple 106

Ebrey, Pat 164
economic
  self-sufficiency 198
  support 204, 221–25, 228, 255
  survival 54
education 177, 195
  in Bangladesh 43, 46–48, 51, 55
  in Bhutan 229–30
  in Burma 23–25, 51
  in Cambodia 86, 97, 100
  in India 65, 129–31
  in Nepal 24–27, 206
  in Sri Lanka 25, 30, 35–37
  in Taiwan 193, 198
  in Thailand 25–26, 61–71
  in Vietnam 105–7, 111–16
  Western 176
Emerson, Ralph Waldo 236
empowerment xxiv, 123–25, 128, 154
emptiness 258
Eng, Queen 88
engaged Buddhism xxv, 36, 38, 312–18
Enryaku Temple 252
entertainment 77–78
equality
  gender xvii-viii, 62, 91, 191–93
    in Japan xxi, 124
  social 168, 303
ethics (*śīla*) 120, 323
  in Cambodia xxi, 93
  sexual 285–93
  in Thailand 68
ethnic
  Buddhism xxiv
  discrimination 54–55
  diversity xvii-xviii, 201, 277, 282–83
  identity 42–43, 185
  minorities 278–80
    in Bangladesh 42–57
  tensions 45

Fah-Ngum 86–87
faith 114, 144, 257
Falguni Purnima 52, 56
family 25, 27, 55, 230, 303
  background 195
  in Cambodia 99
  monastic 164, 185, 191
  in Thailand 63–64, 71
fasting 205, 228
Fazun 134
feminine, the xxiv, 144, 295
feminism xxii, 295
  folklore 143
  perspectives xviii, 154, 158, 179, 191, 326
  scholarship xviii, 143–44, 300
festivals
  in Bangladesh 52, 56
  in China
    Ullambana 135
  in Korea
    Kangnûng Tano 145
  in Tibet
    Great Prayer Festival 213–14, 221
    Losar 214
Fields, Rick 238
filial piety 145–51, 153
Foguangshan (Fo Kuang Shan) 13–14, 169, 174–77, 180, 184, 188–90
folklore xxii, 142–53
Foster, Mary xxiii, 235–48
Foster, Thomas R. 240
Fo-t'ung 162–63
Friedman, Lenore 299
Fujinkai 243

Ganden Choling Center 224
Ganden Monastery 214
Gandhi, Mahatma 46, 320
garudhamma see *gurudharma*
Gates, Henry Louis 278
gātha 126–27, 140
Gelugpa 205
  nunneries
    in China xxi-xxii, 130–41
    in Zangskar 212–28
gender
  in Bangladesh 55
  in Buddhism 154–55
  discrimination 24
  equality xvii-viii, 62, 91, 191–93
  inclusive language 35
  in Korea 144
  politics 186–87
  in Taiwan xxii
  transformation of Buddhism xviii
generosity (*dāna*) 16, 216, 323
  in Bangladesh 47, 51–53, 56–57
  in Cambodia 87

in Nepal 20, 27
in Sri Lanka 30, 32, 34–35, 37
in Thailand 65, 69, 73–75
in Zangskar 220
Genshin 124
geshe 207, 219–20
gihi (ten lay precepts) 32
Glassman, Bernard 299
globalization 201, 210–11
Goenka, U. S. N. 26–27
Golan 19
gonpa 202–210
Goonatilake, Hema 94
Gorkhas 17, 22
Gotamī, Mahāprajāpatī 6–8, 11
government support
in Thailand 67
gratitude 123–29
Green Gulch Farm 159, 296
Gross, Rita 155
gtong len 216
Gunavarman 183
Gunavati 24
guru 136
devotion 141, 289
lineage 164
Guru Pūja 137, 213
gurudharma (Pāli: *garudhamma*) 6–10, 12, 16, 36
gurumā 13
guruparampara 157
Gyanyi, Vinaya Master 131

Haba, Bishop 252, 255, 260
Hanh, Thich Nhat 38, 113–14, 116, 119, 296, 316
haole 239, 245
Harlins, Latasha 314
Hawai'i
Foster, Mary xxiii, 235–48
Honpa Hongwanji 239
Koganji 249–62
Lili'uokalani, Queen xxiii, 236, 239, 242, 245, 247
Hay, Somaly 97–99, 103
health 73, 256
examination 174
Khmer Health Advocates 100
problems 96
reproductive xix
Heart of Wisdom Sūtra 252
Heian 124
Hengjing (Heng-ching), Bhikṣuṇī 191, 193
Hiei, Mt. 252–53
hierarchy xxii
ecclesiastic 189
at Santi Asoke 80
in Tibet 218
Himalayas
meditation in xxv, 217, 225
nuns
in Nepal xxii, 201–11
in Zangskar xxiii, 212–28
Himi, Inamaluwe Sumangala 33–34, 37–39, 49, 173, 195
hindrances, five 125, 129, 160
Hindu 18, 26, 46, 157, 206
caste 19
devotionalism 15
monasticism 17
practice in Nepal 16–17
Hiraoka Zenmyō-ji 124
history
of Buddhist nuns 120, 168, 182
of Buddhist women xvii-xix, 5–12
in Cambodia 84–90
in Vietnam 104–5
hondo 249
Hong Kong 179, 194, 248, 267
Honolulu xxiii, 235–44, 249, 252
Honpa Hongwanji 239, 243, 246–48
Ho'omana Na'auao 236–37, 246
Hovey, Fay 315
Hsi-lai (Xilai) 13, 33, 177, 179
Hsien, Fa 124
Hui-kuang 162–63
Hui-k'o 160
Huimin, Bhikṣu 191
Hui-neng 155–59, 161
human rights 315, 326
in Cambodia xxv, 302–11

identity xviii
cultural
in Bangladesh xx, 42–43
in Tibet 186
Mahāyāna 171
monastic 108, 178
religious xix, 111, 175, 210
sectarian 191
Im, Luang Pho 65
image, Buddha 48, 88, 130, 132
Imamura, Bishop Yemyo 242, 280

independence 23
  nuns 64, 69–70, 76
  political 104
  Santi Asoke 73
India
  Ambedkar, B. R. 177
  Aśoka, Emperor 9
  bhikṣuṇī ordination 5–9
  Bhikṣuṇī Saṅgha 16, 183
  education in 65, 129–31
  Hindu devotionalism 15
  lineage 155–56, 164
  monks 22
  nuns 5–12, 124, 177–78
  Theosophy 237–38
Indradevī 84–85, 90
inheritance 28
ino 127
Insight Meditation Center 291
Islam 18, 304
  in Bangladesh 44, 46, 52, 54
  in India 102

Jamitjuri Meditation Center 52
Japan xxiii, 241, 316
  meditation 253
  laborers 237, 245
  nuns xxi, 123–29
  ritual xxi, 123–29
jasmine (*vassika*) 6
jātakas 22, 85, 90, 108, 303
  Mahādhammapāla Jātaka 11
Jayarājadevī 84–86, 90
Jayavarman 84–86
Jefferson, Thomas 279
jhānas 10
Jincisi 131
jinfanyu 182
Jingjian 183
Jizō (Kṣitigarbha) xxiii, 124, 249–52, 255–58, 261
Jizō Bodhisattva Sūtra 257
Jōdo Shinshū 242–43, 280, 317
Jōdo-shū 280
Johnson, Wendy 296–97
jomo xxvi
Jōrin, Mizuno 124
Ju-ching 161, 163
justice 303, 310
  gender xxi

Kabilsingh, Chatsumarn 273–74
Kachen, Meme 220
Kagyu, Drukpa 204, 212
Kagyu Samye Ling 173
Kalachakra 219
Kalākaua, King 240
kalpa 296
Kamakura 124
kami 260
Kammu, Emperor 258
Kanduboda Meditation Center 34
Kangyur 207
Kankō-ni 124
Kapilavastu 11
karma 108, 145, 153, 155, 160, 208, 313, 316, 319
Karma Drubgyu Targye Ling 179
Karsha 212–28
karuna 324
Kassapa 268
Kassapa Sihanāda Sūtra 268–69, 272
Kathmandu Valley 206
  nuns in xix-xx, 13–29
kaṭhina
  Kaṭhina Chibar Dāna 52
  in Thailand 74
Kaufman, H. K. 73
Kemarama Nunnery 23
Keo-Keng-Ya, Queen 86, 90
kesaloma 26
Khaṇḍaka, *Bhikkhunī* 35
khenpo (abbot) 202–3, 205, 207–9, 231
Khmer
  don chee xxi, xxvi, 91–95
  poems 89
  women xx-xxi, 84–90, 96–103
    Dong, Queen Ang 88–89
    Eng, Queen 88
    Hay, Somaly 97–99, 103
    Keo-Keng-Ya, Queen 86, 90
    Kuoch, Theanvy 99–103
Khmer Health Advocates 100
Khmer Rouge xxv, 96, 98–100, 102, 302, 309
Khong, Sister Chan 116
khun mae 71
kilesa see *kleśa*
killing 77, 302
killing fields 98, 103
Kimdol 21
Klein, Anne 290
kleśa (Pāli: *kilesa*) 28, 77, 116, 267, 271–73, 275

koan 277, 282
Koganji xxiii, 249–62
Kohut, Heinz 300
Koko-An Zendo 313
Korea 195
  bhikṣuṇī lineage 13, 182, 194
  bhikṣuṇī ordination in Sārnāth 39
  folklore xxii 142–53
  history 142
  p'ansori xxii, 144–53
  ritual 142
  Three Kingdoms period 142
Kōsen 124
kōshiki 123–29
  Anan Kōshiki xxi, 123–29
  Shiza Kōshiki 124
Kozan-ji 124
krak 79
Kṣitigarbha (Jizō) xxiii, 124, 249–52, 255–58
Kuan Yin 244, 248
Kuoch, Theanvy 99–103
kuṭi 34, 81
Kusuma, Bhikkhunī xix, 196
kuyō 124
Kwak-ssi 145–46
Kwan-orn, Prathin 64–66

Labdronma, Machig 288
Ladakh xxiii, 220
Lam Ty Ni Orphanage 106, 108
lama 204, 288
lamrim 137–38, 140, 216, 219
Lamrim Chenmo 133
language
  difficulties 96, 177, 287
  inclusive 35
  terms of address xxvi-xxvii, 117
  translation 175–76
  Vietnamese 111–12, 114
Laos 5, 86, 90, 190
laymen 5
  in Nepal 14
  in Thailand 73
laypeople
  in China 132
  foreign 16
  in Nepal 14, 19, 24
  relations with 68
  in San Franciso 156
  in Sri Lanka 30, 37
  in Thailand 68–69
  in Vietnam 119
laywomen 5
  in Bangladesh 42–56
  in Nepal 14
  in Thailand 62, 64, 73
leadership 307–8
  bhikṣuṇī 42, 193
  effective 20
  men's 144
  opportunities for xvii
  political 303, 307, 310
  women's
    in Bangladesh 56
    in Cambodia 306–7
    in Nepal 24
    in United States 300
Leang, Meng Ho 305–6
Leng, Kim 274
Lennon, John 319
Lhasa xxiii, 213–14
Lianzong Nunnery 134
Liao-jan, Mo-shan 161, 166
liberation (*nirvāna*) 5, 13, 15, 22, 29, 128, 148, 259, 272, 303, 327–28
Lien, Bhikṣu To 105
Lili'uokalani, Queen xxiii, 236, 239, 242, 245, 247
Lin-chi 167
lineage 181
  bhikṣuṇī 13, 168, 192
    in Bangladesh 51
    in China 183, 186–87, 194–96
    Dharmagupta 13, 131, 136, 190–91
    in Hong Kong 178–79, 194–95
    in Korea 194
    Mūlasarvāstivāda 13, 136, 190–91, 196
    to Sri Lanka 183, 195–97
    in Taiwan 178–79, 186–87, 194–97
    Theravāda 13, 16, 172, 179, 191
    in Tibet 179, 191, 197
    in United States 179
    in Vietnam 194
  Chan/Zen 154–67, 295–301
  Dharma xxii
  Vinaya 188
    Dharmagupta 13, 131, 136, 190–91
    Mūlasarvāstivāda 13, 136, 190–91, 196
  of women 159, 165, 294–96, 301

literacy 14
  in Bangladesh 55
  in Nepal 21
  in Vietnam 107
Little Buddha 266
liturgy, vernacular 114, 119
lobön 205, 207
lokiya 69
lokottara 69
Longlian, Bhikṣuṇī 131, 134, 141, 196
lotus (*uppula*) 6, 150
Lotus (Saddharmapuṇḍarika) Sūtra 249, 253, 257–60
loving kindness 321–25
Lumbini xxvii, 206
Luu, Bhikṣuṇī Dam 104–20

Macy, Joanna 313, 318
mae śila 50
mae nen 82
mae chi xxvi, 61–71
  education of xx, 63–71
  status of 69, 81, 192
Magadha 44–45
magic 77, 150
Maha Bodhi Society 18, 39, 242, 247
Mahābodhi Stupa 170
Mahaghosananda, Bhikkhu 102, 320
Mahākāśyapa 156–57, 300
Mahānāyakas 38
Mahāprajāpatī (Pāli: Mahāpajāpati)
  founding the order of nuns xix, 191
  gātha by 127
  ordination of 6–8, 11, 182–83
mahāsammata 303
mahātherī 50–56
Mahāthero
  Ashvaghosh 173
  Dhammānanda 172
  Inamaluwe Sumangala 33–34, 37–38, 49, 173, 195
  Nyaneinda 173
  Rastrapala 173
  Wipulasara 172
mahātma 46
Mahāvaṃsa 9
Mahāyāna 13, 141, 155, 324
  in Bangladesh 44
  in Cambodia 84
  in China 171, 190, 259
  in Nepal 17
  in Vietnam 114
Mahinda, Bhikṣu 9
maitrī 321
Man, Minh 107–8
mānatta 6, 71
maṇḍala 136–37, 141, 215, 218, 253
Mäniyan, Sudharmachari 36
Mañjuśri 133, 135, 137, 141, 257
Manshō-ji 124
mantra 137–38
māras 116, 129
Marma 43, 45, 47, 49–51, 56
  Paisanu 47–48
Marques, Auguste 236, 239, 241
marriage 14, 20, 25, 28
  in Thailand 63
  in Vietnam 105
media xxiv, 265–76
meditation 272, 312
  ānāpānasati 26, 47
  in Bangladesh 47, 49–50, 56
  in Burma 26, 50
  centers
    Insight Meditation Center 291
    Jamitjuri 52
    Kanduboda 34
    Koko-An Zendo 313
    San Francisco Zen Center 156, 158, 166, 291
  in China 136–37
  forest xviii
  in Himalayas xxv, 217, 225
  on impermanence 107
  jhānas 10
  kesaloma 26
  mindfulness 26, 47, 76
  in Nepal 14–15, 26–28, 206
  perfection of 116, 323
  in Sri Lanka 31, 34, 36
  in Thailand 61, 65, 68
  vipassanā
    in Bangladesh 49
    in Burma 114
    in Nepal 14–15, 19, 26–27
    in Vietnam 110
  in Zangskar 217–18, 225
menju 300
merit (*punya*)
  Ānanda 127
  in Bangladesh 52
  in Nepal 16, 22, 26, 28
  in Thailand 68–69, 72–76, 82
micchela 50–51

Ming Dynasty 135, 142
minorities 278–80
  in Bangladesh xx, 42–57
missionaries
  Christian 236–37, 239
  Theravāda 18, 20, 25
mochi 249
monasteries
  in Bangladesh 43
  in China 130–41
    Gelugpa 130–41
    Jincisi 131
    Tiexiangsi xxi-xxii, 130–41
    Yonghegong 130, 133
  in Japan 123–29
  in Nepal 16
    Bekung Gonpa 201–11
  in Tibet
    Drepung 133
    Ganden 214
    Sera 205
    Tashilhunpo 213
monastic
  discipline 5–12
  regulations 169
  relation with laity 68
monasticism
  for men
    in Nepal 19–20
  for women xix-xx
    in Bangladesh 48, 53
    in China 168–98
    founding of xix, 5–7, 10
    in Japan xxi, 123–29
    in Nepal 13–29
    in Sri Lanka xx, 10, 92
    in Taiwan 168–98
    in Thailand 61–71
    in Zangskar xxiii, 212–28
money 210
  handling 97
monks
  Bangladeshi 43–44, 47–56
  Cambodian 92, 98, 101–2
  cooking for 65–66, 92
  Korean 147–49
  Ladakhi 218–20
  Thai 69
  Vietnamese xxi, 119
    Dung, Thich Tri 118
    Lien, Bhikṣu To 105
    Tu, Thich Thanh 117
Morgan, Earnest 314
mother xxiv, 31, 299–300, 313, 321
  of Buddha 6–8, 11, 127
  ten-precept (*dasasilmātā*) 30–41
  Queen, of the West 146
  of Viśuddhānanda 51
motivation 64
Moulmein 23
Mūlagandhakuṭi Vihāra 235
Mūlasarvāstivāda 13, 136, 190–91, 196
Murong 50
Mutsoody, Prativa 46–48

Nāgārjuna 259
Nagendratunga 86
Nakami-Kaiko 124
Nakao, Egyoku 294, 296, 299
Narendrāśrama 86
Narith, Phich 94
narrative
  Korean xxii, 142–53
  personal 231, 245, 312–18
Nenghai, Bhikṣu 130–35, 141
Nepal
  Bhikṣu Saṅgha 20
  bhikṣuṇī ordination xx, 13–16, 187
  education
    for children 24
    religious 25
    secular 26
  nuns 13–29, 177, 201–11
  Tibetan nuns in xxii, 13–29
Newar
  bhikṣus, first 18
  Buddhists 17–20
  nuns xix-xx, 15–16, 29
nibbāna see *nirvāna*
Nichiren 280, 315–16
nikāyas 37
  Siam 37
nirvāna (Pāli: *nibbāna*) 5, 13, 15, 22, 29, 128, 148, 259, 272, 303
nisei 249
Noble Eightfold Path 285
nonviolence xxv, 302–11, 320
Norodom, King 88
novices 215
  in Bodhgaya 177
  in China 133
  in Nepal 15, 19
  in Sri Lanka 32, 34
  in Thailand (*samaneen*) 64, 72

in Tibet (*dge tshul ma*) 213–14
in Zangskar 212–28
nunneries 23
in Burma
Kemarama Nunnery 23
in China
Aidaotang Nunnery 131
Lianzong Nunnery 134
Tiexiangsi xxi-xxii, 130–41
in India
Karma Drubgyu Targye Ling 179
in Nepal
Bekung Gonpa 201–11
Dharmakirti Vihar 24–25
in Thailand
independent 64, 69–70
Thammacarini 61–71
nuns
in Bangladesh 42, 47–51, 53, 55–56
Apuma 49
Ma Chan Daw Wadi 49
in Cambodia 97
in China
Dingjing, Bhikṣuṇī 131
Longlian 131, 134, 141, 196
in Japan xxi, 123–29
Kaiko 124
Kankō-ni 124
Mother Theresa 52
in Nepal
Dhammavati xx, 13, 22–28
Santi 21
Subha 27
Sushila 21
Newari xix-xx
Sōtō 123–29
in Sri Lanka 30–31
in Thailand xx, 61–71, 72–83
Western 174, 176, 185
in Zangskar 212–28
Zen 123–29
Nuon, Princess 89
Nyingma 202
nyungne 205, 228

obstacles, five 125, 129, 160
Ōhara Tendai 125
Olcott, Henry Steel 236–39
Ong 89
ordination 326–27
benefits of 38–39
bhikṣu 181
in Nepal 18
in Thailand 73–75
bhikṣuṇī
by *bhikṣus* 6–7, 196
in Bodhgaya xxii, 168–98
in China 187
controversy xix, 181–83
in Hong Kong 179
in India 5–9
International Ordination Ceremony xxii
in Los Angeles 184
in Sārnāth 5, 33, 39, 41, 173, 179
in Sri Lanka 9, 37–38
in Vietnam 107
dual 71, 131, 139, 181, 192
Hanh, Thich Nhat 116
in Japan 128, 254
lifetime 72
Mahāprajāpatī's 6–8, 11
opportunities for xvii, 326
self 32
sikkhamat 74
śikṣamāṇā) 6, 9, 71, 131, 171, 181
śrāmaṇera 181
in Bangladesh 48
in Bodhgaya 171
in Thailand (*samaneen*) 64
in Vietnam 105
śrāmaṇerikā 181
in Bodhgaya 171
in Sārnāth 173
in Sri Lanka 34–39
in Tibet 213–14
in Zangskar 32, 213–14, 219
temporary 25, 50
in Thailand 63
at Santi Asoke 73, 79–80
ornaments 78
orphanages
in Japan 250
in South Asia 241–42
in Vietnam 106, 108
orphans
in Bangladesh 47–48, 57
in Korea 313
in Nepal 26, 28, 205

pa 79
pabbajjā see *pravrajyā*
pagoda 101

Pāli
  canon 5
  education 51, 65–66
  teaching 48
  texts xix, 25, 268–70
Panchen Lama 130, 218
Pandita, U 27
pañña see *prajñā*
p'ansori xxii, 144–53
Paramāthakemarāja 86
Parbatiyas 20
Parliament of World Religions 235, 281
Pasman, Mahā 86–87
Patan 16, 22
pāṭimokkha see *prātimokṣa*
paṭivedha 10
patriarchy 55, 155, 295, 300
patriline 159–65
pavāraṇā 6, 71
peace
  education 304–11
  inner 319–25
  Paris Peace Accords 304, 310
  world xxv, 319–20
pecha 202, 205, 208, 210
penalty 8–9
Penh, Lady 87–88
perfections, six 116, 120, 323
phapha 65
Phnom Penh xxvii-xviii, xxv, 43, 88, 91, 100, 211, 265
Pierce, Lori 289
Pieris, Aloysius 272
pilgrimage 18
  to India 25, 206
  to Tibet 212–14, 221
pilgrims
  Chinese 44, 170, 177
  Zangskari 215, 218
Pimeanakas 84
pirit 35–36
Plum Village 113–14, 116, 119
Pot Pol xxi, 92, 311, 320
pracīna examinations 34
praise 116
  to Ānanda 128
prajñā (Pāli: *pañña*) 28, 120, 137
Prajñāparamitā 127
prātimokṣa (Pāli: *pāṭimokkha*) 5, 139
  Bhikṣuṇī Prātimokṣa Sūtra 170, 191
  lessons on 170
  recitation of 135
pravrajyā (Pāli: *pabbajjā*) 15–16
prayer 34, 99, 143, 149, 151, 253
  beads 48, 147
  Great Prayer Festival 213–14, 221
precept masters 171–74, 182–83, 188
precepts 289–90
  bodhisattva 108, 114, 215
  eight
    in Bangladesh 46, 50, 56
    in Cambodia 92
    Mahāyāna 220
    in Thailand 62, 64, 66, 70, 74–75
  eight special (*gurudharmas*) 6–9, 12, 15–16, 36, 71
  five 285
    in Cambodia 92
    in Sri Lanka 32
    in Thailand 70, 74–75, 83,
    in Zangskar 213, 219
  gihi (ten lay) 32
  laxity in 75
  in Nepal 28
  pävidi (ten monastic) 32
  prātimokṣa 5
  śikṣā 8–9
  six 71
  śrāmaṇera 32
  śrāmaṇerikā 32, 213–14, 219
  ten
    in Bangladesh 56, 62
    in Cambodia 89
    in Thailand 70
  ten-precept nuns (*dasasilmātā*) 30–41
  in Theravāda 26, 62, 64
  in Tibet 213–14
  upāsaka (layman) 14
  upāsikā (laywoman) 14, 62, 64
prediction 10
preliminary practices 214–15
preta 256
Prever, Rebecca 240
probationary nun (*śikṣamāṇā*) 6, 9, 71, 131, 171, 181, 194
prostrations 80–81, 208, 215, 218
protest 118–19
pūja 205, 209
pūjāri 17
punishment 8, 149
punya (Pāli: *puñña*)
  in Nepal 16, 22, 26, 28
Pure Land 114–15, 247, 256

Quan Su Temple 105
queens
  in Cambodia
    Dong, Queen Ang 88–89
    Eng, Queen 88
    Keo-Keng-Ya, Queen 86, 90
  in Hawai'i
    Lili'uokalani, Queen xxiii, 236, 239, 242, 245, 247
  Vaidehī, Queen 127

race 277–284, 314
racism xxiv, xxv, 277–80, 289
Rahula 56
rains retreat (*vassa*) 6, 71
  in Bangladesh 52
  in China 135
rakan 12
Rakkhaine 50
Rana regime 17, 18, 21, 202
Rangiri Dambulla Rāja Mahā Vihāra 33
Rangiri Dambulla Arāṇya Senāsanaya 33, 37
Rebato, Bhikkhu 48
rebirth 14, 82, 127, 143, 182, 217, 223, 325
Record of the Universal Flame 161
Red Cross 109–10
refuge 14, 118, 136, 141, 215, 238, 285–86
refugees 287
  Cambodian 96–103
  in India 185
  in Nepal 185
  Vietnamese 104–20
relics 119–20
renunciants, female xxvi
  in China 130–41
  in India 5–12, 124, 177–78
  in Japan 123–29
  in Nepal 13–29
  in Sri Lanka 30–41
  in Thailand 61–71
  in Zangskar 212–28
renunciation xvii, 15–16, 32, 272–73
respect 6–8, 210
  in Bangladesh 53
  in Cambodia 101
  in Thailand 70, 81–82
Rich, Adrienne 294–95
rights
  human xvii, 277–78, 326
    in Cambodia xxv, 302–11
  inheritance 28
  women's xxi, 306–7, 326
Rinpoche
  Drukpa 204–5
  Kangsa 133, 136
  Thinley Norbu 298–99
  Yeshe Losal 173–74, 195
Rinzai 167
ritual
  Anantan 127–28
  bhikṣuṇī upasampadā 6, 35, 180–84
  boundary (*sīmā*) 37
  fasting 205, 228
  in Japan xxi, 123–29
  in Korea 142
  in Nepal 17, 20, 25
  in Zangskar xxiii, 216–28
robes 292
  in Cambodia 92
  in Japan 126, 254
  in Thailand 63, 74
    at Santi Asoke 80
  in Tibet 214
  yellow 56
Robinson, James 236, 240
Rose, Bishop Jikyu xxiii, 249–62
rules
  eight special (*gurudharmas*) 6–9, 12, 15–16, 36, 128
  prātimokṣa 5
  Sōtō 124
  for *thammacarini* 67
  in Theravāda 26
  Vinaya 118, 137
    eight precepts 46
    five precepts 32
    śikṣā 8–9
    ten precepts 32
    violation of 73, 113

sacrifice 145, 149–51
saddharma 10
Saddharmapuṇḍarika Sūtra 258
Saichō (Dengyō Daishi) 252–53, 258–61
saimon 124, 126
sakadāgāmī (Pāli: *sakadāgāmin*) 10
sakavadi 89
Sakkamuni see Śākyamuni
śākya/śākyabhikṣus (temple priest) 17, 22

Śākya clan 29
women, ordination of 6–7, 11
Śākya, Ganesh Kumār 22–23
Śākyadhitā 181, 184
conferences
Bangkok xxvii
Bodhgaya xxvii, 43
Claremont xviii, xxv, xxvii
Colombo xxvii
Ladakh xviii
Lumbini xxvii, 206
Phnom Penh xvii-xviii, xxv, 43, 91, 211, 265
Santa Barbara xxvii
Sri Lanka 92
trainings for nuns 30
Śākyamuni (Pāli: Sakkamuni) 6, 13, 124, 127, 188, 257, 275
bhikṣuṇī ordination 5–12, 179–80
lineage 155–66, 190
ordination of Mahāprajāpatī 5–12
teachings 110, 124, 311
transmission 155–66, 300
on women's potential xvii, 303
samādhi 120
samaṇera see *śrāmaṇera*
samaṇerī see *śrāmaṇerikā*
Samantapāsādikā 6
Samanthabhadra 216
Samastha Lanka Silmātā Jātika Maṇḍalaya (SMJM) 33, 36
saṃsāra 16, 323
Samuel, Geoffrey 203
San Francisco Zen Center 156, 158, 166, 291
Saṅgha 277
admission of women to xix, 5–7, 10
in Bangladesh 47–56
Bhikṣu
in Thailand 63
Bhikṣuṇī 5–12, 183
in Nepal 24
family 164
four-fold 165
offerings to 51–52
in Taiwan 193
in Thailand 72
in the West 299
saṅghadāna
in Bangladesh 51–53
in Bodhgaya 170–71
Saṅghamitra 9, 61–62
Saṅghanāyaka 94
Saṅgharāja 94
Sangharakshita 266–67
sansei 249, 295
Sanskrit
chanting 126
meters 85
Santi 21
Santi Asoke xx, 72–83
ordination 79–80
vegetarianism 72, 74–75, 77–79, 82
Santikaro, Bhikkhu 273
Sarasvatī 86
śarīra 120
Sārnāth
Maha Bodhi Society 247
Mūlagandhakuṭi Vihāra 235
bhikṣuṇī ordination 5, 33, 39, 41, 173, 196, 266
Sarvodaya 30
sāsana 9–10, 34, 36, 38, 181–82
bhikṣuṇī 36
sayādaw 50
Sayadaw, Mahasi 26–27
Sayadaw, U Kumara 56
sectarianism 119
seiza 253
Senāsanaya, Rangiri Dambulla Arāṇya 33, 37
Senauke, Alan 291
Sennichi-ama 316
sentient being 321–25
Sera Monastery 205
Seth, Sou 89
Seven Years in Tibet 266
sex 250
illicit 77
industry xx, 63, 71
media, in the xxiv, 78
sexism 154
sexual
characteristics 38
conduct xxiv, 285–93
desire 77, 287–88
misconduct xxiv, 266–67
slavery xxv, 314–15
sexuality 15, 152–53, 295
shakujo 127
shamanism 145
Sherpas 208
Shim, Blindman 145–51

Shingon 280
Shinran 242
Shintō 245, 260
shishiki 126
Shiza Kōshiki 124
Shōnin, Myōe 124
Sichuan Buddhist Higher Institute for Bhikṣuṇīs 132, 134, 136
Siddhārtha, Prince 89
Sihinouk, Norodom 89, 97
sikkhamat xx, xxvi, 72–83
  ordination 74
  status of 78
sikkhamānā see *śikṣamāṇā*
śikṣā (Pāli: *sikkhā*) 8–9
śikṣamāṇā (Pāli: *sikkhamānā*) 6, 9, 71, 131, 171, 181, 194
śīla (Pāli: *sīla*) 120
śīla-upādhya 171, 174
silmātā see *dasasilmātā*
sīmā 37, 180
śivamārgi 16
skandha 259
Soan, Bhikṣuṇī Dam 105–6
Sobunvy, Chan 94
sotāpanna see *sotāpatti*
sotāpatti (Pāli: *sotāpanna*) 10
Sōtō Zen xxi, 123–29, 280, 297
  lineage 160, 162
spirits (*phi*) 77, 88, 149
spirituality, Hawaiian 244
śrāmaṇera (Pāli: *samaṇera*)
  in Bangladesh 48
  ordination 181
    in Bodhgaya 171
  in Thailand (*samaneen*) 64
  in Vietnam 105
śrāmaṇerikā (Pāli: *samaṇerī*)
  in Sri Lanka 34–39
  ordination 181
    in Bodhgaya 171
    in Sārnāth 173
    in Tibet 213–14
    in Zangskar 32, 213–14, 219
śravaka 114
Sri Lanka 94, 190, 273, 320
  Bhikṣuṇī Saṅgha 9, 61–62, 189–90, 194–97
  bhikkhunīs xx, 5, 12, 168, 180–82
  Buddhist scholarship xix
  Coḷa invasions 16
  dasasilmātā xx, 95
  Dharmapāla, Anagārikā xxiii, 18, 235–36, 241–42, 244, 247
  media 265–66
  monks in Cambodia 87
  Nepali monks in 22
  nuns xix-xx, 30–41
    ordination in Sārnāth 5, 33, 39, 41, 173, 196, 266
Sri Lanka Bhikkhunī Re-Awakening Organization (SLBRO) 34, 39
Śrījñana, Atiśa Dīpaṅkara 44
statue, Buddha 48, 88, 130, 132
status xx, 38
  bhikṣuṇī 192
  of *mae chi* 69
  of monks 41
  of nuns 55, 169
  of Saṅgha 50
  at Santi Asoke 78, 81
  of *sikkhamats* 78, 81
  of women 67
storytelling 142–53, 217
stūpa (Pāli: *thūpa*) 16, 17, 24
  Mahābodhi 170
Subha 27
suffering 21, 23, 28, 103, 108–9, 124, 275, 312, 324–25
Sukhothai 61–62
Sumangala, Inamaluwe 33–34, 37–38, 49, 173, 195
Sumon, Khun mae 64–65
Sung Dynasty 156–57, 160–61, 164
sūtra (Pāli: *sutta*) 5, 35, 99, 267, 303
  Bhikṣuṇī Prātimokṣa 170, 191
  Heart of Wisdom 252
  Jizō Bodhisattva 257
  Kassapa Sihanāda 268–69, 272
  Majjhima Nikāya 268
  path 203, 210
  Prajñāparamitā 127
  recitation 47, 50, 52, 123
  Saddharmapuṇḍarika (Lotus) 249, 253, 257–60
  Sūtra of Eternal Life 256
  Suvarṇaprabhāsa 120
  Vāseṭṭha Sutta 35
  Visuddhimagga 236
sutta see *sūtra*
Suzuki, Shunryu 156, 166

Tabrah, Ruth 239
Taiwan (Republic of China)

bhikṣus 39
bhikṣunī ordination 168–98
bhikṣuṇīs xxii, 39, 55, 176–78, 190–94
Chinese Buddhist Association 190
monastic life 177
Vinaya 190
Tamalinda 84
Tambiah, Stanley 74
tangaryō 297
T'ang 127, 140
tantra 130, 133, 136, 139–41, 203, 210, 217, 288–91
Taoism
in Hawai'i 245, 248
in Korea 142
Tao-shen 163, 165
Tashilhunpo Monastery 213
Tathāgata 11, 126, 257
temples
in Cambodia 302
in China
Tiexiangsi xxi-xxii, 130–41
Yonghegong 130, 133
in Hawai'i
Honpa Hongwanji 239
Koganji xxiii, 249–62
in Japan
Enryaku 252
Hiraoka Zenmyōii 124
Kozan-ji 124
Manshō-ji 124
in Taiwan
Foguangshan 13–14, 169, 174–77
in United States
Xilai 13, 33, 177, 179
in Vietnam
Cu Da 105
Duc Vien 111–19
Duoc Su 106
Quan Su 105
Tendai xxiii, 126
in Hawai'i 249–62, 280
Ōhara 125
Tenzin, Lama 207–8
texts 302
Kangyur 207
Mahādhammapāla Jātaka 11
Mahāyāna 114
memorizing 212
Pāli xix, 25, 268
pecha 202, 205
sūtra (Pāli: *sutta*) 5, 35, 99
Bhikṣuṇī Prātimokṣa 170, 191
Cullavagga 5–10
Heart of Wisdom 252
Jizō Bodhisattva 257
Kassapa Sihanāda 268–69, 272
Majjhima Nikāya 268
Prajñāparamitā 127
recitation 47, 50, 52, 123
Saddharmapuṇḍarika (*Lotus*) 249, 253, 257–60
Samantapāsādikā 6
Sūtra of Eternal Life 256
Suvarṇaprabhāsa 120
Vāseṭṭha Sutta 35
Visuddhimagga 236
Theravāda 25
Vajrayoginī Tantra 217
Thai Nuns Institute 61–63
Thailand 5, 16, 48, 94, 190
bhikṣuṇīs 172, 180
education
for girls xx
for *mae chi* xx
meditation in 61, 65
nuns 61–71, 72–83, 195
ordination (*nak boat*) 64
lifetime 72
sex industry xx, 63, 71
thammacarini 67
Theosophy 236–39, 241, 245–46
Theravāda 94, 171–72, 238, 271
in Bangladesh 44–45, 48, 55
bhikṣuṇī ordination xxii, 139, 168, 180, 184, 186–87
Bhikṣuṇī Saṅgha
in Nepal xx, 13–16
in Sri Lanka 9, 30, 32, 61–62
bhikkhunīs xx, 5, 11
in Cambodia 308
in China 135
dasasilmātās xx
laypeople in 73
meditation 26–27, 47
missionaries 18, 20, 25
monks 18–19
nuns xix-xx
in Nepal 13–29
in Sri Lanka 30–41
in Thailand 61–71
Theresa, Mother 52
Therīgāthā xxvii, 159, 162

Thero, U Paa Jotha 50
Thoreau, Henry David 236
three trainings 137
thūpa see *stūpa*
Tiantai 258
Tibet xxii, 164, 204, 238, 266, 287
  Atiśa Dīpaṅkara Śrījñana 44
  Dalai Lama 13, 130, 169, 187, 213, 218, 266, 322, 324
  education 129–31
  Ganden Throne Holder 212–3
  Government-in-Exile 186–87
  Great Prayer Festival 213–14, 221
  monasteries
    Drepung 133
    Ganden 214
    Sera 205
    Tashilhunpo 213
  nuns 178–79, 201
  oppression in xxv
  ordination
    bhikṣuṇī xxii, 139, 168–81, 184–90, 193, 197
    śrāmaṇerikā 213–14
  Panchen Lama 130, 218
Tiexiangsi xxi-xxii, 130–41
tila shin xxvi, 50
Tilokottara 86
Tisdale, Sallie Jiko 154–55, 159, 162, 166
tong len 324–25
tonsure 171, 185
Training Institute for Nuns (Dharmsala) 91
Tran, Nghai 115
transmission
  bhikṣuṇī 183
  Chan 155–67
  Dharma xxii
  face-to-face 300
  mind-to-mind 159–60
  oral 16, 267
  Sōtō 125, 160
  tantric 133
  Zen 155–67, 155–56, 295–301
Tripiṭaka 24, 86, 88
Triple Gem 14, 80–81, 137, 164, 209, 257, 285
Triple Platform Ordination 171, 182
Tsering, Tashi 169–70, 187, 191, 197
tsog offering 135
Tsomo, Karma Lekshe 174
Tsongkhapa 130, 133, 135, 137, 140, 212–14, 216
Tsum Gonpa 207
Ts'ung-chih 160
Tu, Thich Thanh 117
tulku 289

Uchiyama, Kosho 298
Udong 88–89
Ukhiya 48
Ullambana 135
United Nations 305, 311
United States
  African Americans 282
  Buddhism in 154–59, 162, 165–66, 280–81, 294–301
  Cambodians in 96–103
  Native Americans 282
  Vietnamese in 104–120
  women's movement 295
United Vietnamese Buddhist Church 106
Universal Declaration of Human Rights xvii
Upāli 303
Upamai, Srisalab 65–66
upasampadā, bhikṣuṇī 6
  in Bodhgaya 168–98
  in Los Angeles 13, 33
  Mahāprajāpatī's 6–8, 11
  in Nepal xx, 13–16, 22
  ritual 35
  in Sārnāth 5, 33, 39
  in Sri Lanka 16, 30–40
  ordination 5–12
  ritual 180–84
  in Thailand 70
  in Theravāda 94
  in Vietnam
uposatha 6
uppula (lotus) 6
upāsaka 14
upāsikā 14, 62, 64

Vacchagotta 268
Vajra Hell 288
Vajrabhairava 133
vajrācārya 17
Vajrasattva 208
Vajrayāna 155, 231
  in China 133, 136–38
  in Nepal 17–19, 21, 25, 28
Vajrayoginī 217, 219

Vaidehī, Queen 127
Vaṃsāvalī 17
Vārāṇasi 5, 206, 229–30
vassa (rains retreat) 6
vassika (jasmine) 6
vegetarianism 319
  in Bangladesh 46, 53
  in China 135
  in Santi Asoke 72, 74–75, 77–79, 82
  in Vietnam 108–9
Vietnam 92, 287, 312
  bhikṣuṇī lineage 13, 182, 194
  in Cambodia 100, 304
  education 105–7, 111–16
  monks xxi
    Dung, Thich Tri 118
    Hanh, Thich Nhat 38, 113–14, 116, 119, 296, 316
    Lien, Bhikṣu To 105
    Tu, Thich Thanh 117
  nuns xxi
    Luu, Bhikṣuṇī Dam xxi, 104–120
    Nguyen, Bhikṣuṇī Nhu 118
    Soan, Bhikṣuṇī Dam 105
  war 104, 313
vihāra 24, 87–88
  Dharmakirti 24–28
  Dhammarajika
    in Bangladesh 43, 46, 51, 57
    in Calcutta 242
  Dharmavijaya 244
  Mūlagandhakuṭi 235
  Rangiri Dambulla Rāja Mahā 33
Vinaya 268–69, 271–72
  Bhikṣuṇī 5–12, 35
  in China 131, 134
  Dharmagupta 13, 131, 136, 190–91
  Mahāsaṅghika 196
  Mūlasarvāstivāda 13, 136, 190–91, 196
  ordination procedures 6–12, 37
  precepts 118
    eight 46
    five 32
    śikṣā 8–9
    ten 32
    violation of 73, 113
  in Sri Lanka 37–38
  teachings 115
violence 319
  in Cambodia 302, 310
  domestic 55
  racial 314
vipassanā
  in Bangladesh 49
  in Burma 114
  in Nepal 14–15, 19, 26–27
Visakha 242
visualization 137, 217
Viśuddhānanda 51
Visuddhimagga 236
Vivekananda, Bhikṣu 43, 48
Vong, Bhikṣu Tep 172
Vy (Somaly Hay) 97–99, 103

Wadi, Ma Chan Daw 49
wai 81
wan phra 63, 67–68
Wang Enyang 134
Ward, Victoria 240, 243
wat 61, 92
Wat Batumvatai 90
Wat Keo 87, 90
Wat Onnalom 89
Wat Paknam Bhasicharoen 65–66
Wat Phnom 88
Wat Somanas 65
Wat Thann 89
Wenger, Michael 158
Western Buddhist Order 269
Western Buddhists xxii, xxiv, 155, 178, 201, 203, 207–11, 280–81, 285–301, 327
Whitman, Walt 236
Wichiencharoen, Khunying Kanitha 61, 274
widows 21, 28, 55, 124, 205
Wisalo, Paisan 273
wisdom xviii, 5, 14, 28, 112, 120, 256, 297, 323
wives 31, 303
Woo, Bhikṣuṇī Kuang 174
Wuming, Bhikṣu 179
Wuqian, Bhikṣu 172, 194
Wutai, Mt. 137
Wuyin, Bhikṣuṇī 190

Xiangguangsi (Luminary Buddhist Society) 190
Xiaoyun (Shig Hiu Wan), Bhikṣuṇī 193–94
Xilai (Hsi-lai) Temple 13, 33, 177, 179, 184
Xinding, Bhikṣu 174
Xingyun (Hsing-yun), Bhikṣu 172–73, 180, 184, 190

yab-yum 289
yakudoshi 260
Yama 256
Yamada, Etai 255, 260
Yeshe, Chomo xxiii, 212–25
yidam 133, 135, 137
yogatantra 137
yogi 28
yoginī 28
Yonghegong 130, 133
Yongxing, Bhikṣu 172, 194

Zangskar xxiii, 212–228
  meditation in xxv, 217, 225
  nuns 212–28
  pilgrims 212–15, 218, 221
  precepts
    five 213, 219
    śrāmaṇerikā 32, 213–14, 219
  ritual xxiii, 216–28
Zen
  in Japan 123–29
  lineage 155–67, 295
  practitioner xxiv
  ritual xxi, 123–29
  in United States 294–301, 313
    Koko-An Zendo 313
    San Francisco Zen Center 156, 158, 166, 291
  in Vietnam 105
Zhang, Kecheng 133
Zhaohui, Bhikṣuṇī 183, 191, 193
Zhengyan (Chengyen), Bhikṣuṇī 193
Ziji (Tzu-chi) Foundation 193
Zhiyi (Chih-i) 259
Zodpa, Geshe Lobzang 219–20
Zoku Sōtōshū Zensho 123